ReFocus: The Films of Agnieszka Holland

ReFocus: The International Directors Series

Series Editors: Robert Singer, Gary D. Rhodes and Stefanie Van de Peer

Board of advisors:
Lizelle Bisschoff (Glasgow University)
Stephanie Hemelryck Donald (University of Lincoln)
Anna Misiak (Falmouth University)
Des O'Rawe (Queen's University Belfast)

ReFocus is a series of contemporary methodological and theoretical approaches to the interdisciplinary analyses and interpretations of international film directors, from the celebrated to the ignored, in direct relationship to their respective culture – its myths, values and historical precepts – and the broader parameters of international film history and theory.

Titles in the series include:

ReFocus: The Films of Susanne Bier Edited by Missy Molloy, Mimi Nielsen and Meryl Shriver-Rice
ReFocus: The Films of Francis Veber Keith Corson
ReFocus: The Films of Xavier Dolan Edited by Andrée Lafontaine
ReFocus: The Films of Pedro Costa: Producing and Consuming Contemporary Art Cinema Nuno Barradas Jorge
ReFocus: The Films of Sohrab Shahid Saless: Exile, Displacement and the Stateless Moving Image Edited by Azadeh Fatehrad
ReFocus: The Films of Pablo Larraín Edited by Laura Hatry
ReFocus: The Films of Michel Gondry Edited by Marcelline Block and Jennifer Kirby
ReFocus: The Films of Rachid Bouchareb Edited by Michael Gott and Leslie Kealhofer-Kemp
ReFocus: The Films of Andrei Tarkovsky Edited by Sergey Toymentsev
ReFocus: The Films of Paul Leni Edited by Erica Tortolani and Martin F. Norden
ReFocus: The Films of Rakhshan Banietemad Edited by Maryam Ghorbankarimi
ReFocus: The Films of Jocelyn Saab: Films, Artworks and Cultural Events for the Arab World Edited by Mathilde Rouxel and Stefanie Van de Peer
ReFocus: The Films of François Ozon Edited by Loïc Bourdeau
ReFocus: The Films of Teuvo Tulio Henry Bacon, Kimmo Laine and Jaakko Seppälä
ReFocus: The Films of João Pedro Rodrigues and João Rui Guerra da Mata Edited by José Duarte and Filipa Rosário
ReFocus: The Films of Lucrecia Martel Edited by Natalia Christofoletti Barrenha, Julia Kratje and Paul Merchant
ReFocus: The Films of Shyam Benegal Edited by Sneha Kar Chaudhuri and Ramit Samaddar
ReFocus: The Films of Denis Villeneuve Edited by Jeri English and Marie Pascal
ReFocus: The Films of Antoinetta Angelidi Edited by Penny Bouska and Sotiris Petridis
ReFocus: The Films of Ken Russell Edited by Matthew Melia
ReFocus: The Films of Kim Ki-young Edited by Chung-kang Kim
ReFocus: The Films of Jane Campion Edited by Alexia L. Bowler and Adele Jones
ReFocus: The Films of Alejandro Jodorowsky Edited by Michael Newell Witte
ReFocus: The Films of Nuri Bilge Ceylan Edited by Gönül Dönmez-Colin
ReFocus: The Films of Claire Denis Edited by Peter Sloane
ReFocus: The Films of Steve McQueen Edited by Thomas Austin
ReFocus: The Films of Yim Soon-rye Edited by Molly Kim
ReFocus: The Films of Annemarie Jacir Iqra Shagufta Cheema with Stefanie Van de Peer
ReFocus: The Films of Joachim Trier Anne Gjelsvik
ReFocus: The Films of Larisa Shepitko Edited by Lida Oukaderova
ReFocus: The Films of Agnieszka Holland Elżbieta Ostrowska

edinburghuniversitypress.com/series/refocint

ReFocus:
The Films of Agnieszka Holland

Elżbieta Ostrowska

EDINBURGH
University Press

Edinburgh University Press is one of the leading university presses in the UK. We publish academic books and journals in our selected subject areas across the humanities and social sciences, combining cutting-edge scholarship with high editorial and production values to produce academic works of lasting importance. For more information visit our website: edinburghuniversitypress.com

We are committed to making research available to a wide audience and are pleased to be publishing an Open Access ebook edition of this title.

© Elżbieta Ostrowska, 2024, under a Creative Commons Attribution licence

Grateful acknowledgement is made to the sources listed in the List of Illustrations for permission to reproduce material previously published elsewhere. Every effort has been made to trace the copyright holders, but if any have been inadvertently overlooked, the publisher will be pleased to make the necessary arrangements at the first opportunity.

Edinburgh University Press Ltd
13 Infirmary Street
Edinburgh EH1 1LT

Typeset in 11/13 Ehrhardt MT by
IDSUK (DataConnection) Ltd, and
printed and bound in Great Britain

A CIP record for this book is available from the British Library

ISBN 978 1 3995 1467 5 (hardback)
ISBN 978 1 3995 1469 9 (webready PDF)
ISBN 978 1 3995 1470 5 (epub)

The right of Elżbieta Ostrowska to be identified as the author of this work has been asserted in accordance with the Copyright, Designs and Patents Act 1988, and the Copyright and Related Rights Regulations 2003 (SI No. 2498).

Contents

List of Figures	vi
Acknowledgements	viii
Preface	x
Introduction: authorship, women's cinema and transnational screen cultures	1
1 Early years: pains and joys	25
2 Art, politics and gender: Holland's participation in socialist Poland's screen cultures	44
3 European exilic cinema	81
4 Transatlantic journey/adventure, or the re-phase	116
5 From cinematic *metteur en scène* to television *auteur*?	157
6 'Back home' or 'There's no such place as home': post-communist political cinema revisited	191
7 Performing authorship: from celebrity director to celebrity activist	226
Conclusion	263
Filmography	269
References	274
Index	291

Figures

1.1	Agnieszka Holland with her parents (Agnieszka Holland's family archive)	29
1.2	Agnieszka Holland on the set of her student film at FAMU (Agnieszka Holland's family archive)	35
1.3	*Jesus Christ's Sin* (1969)	39
1.4	*Jesus Christ's Sin* (1969)	39
2.1	*Sunday Children* (1976)	53
2.2	*Screen Tests* (1976)	57
2.3	*Screen Tests* (1976), Agnieszka Holland and Andrzej Wajda	58
2.4	*Provincial Actors* (1978)	65
2.5	*Fever* (1980)	70
2.6	*A Woman Alone* (1981)	72
3.1	Agnieszka Holland and Artur Brauner on the set of *Angry Harvest* (*Bittere Ernte*) © CCC Filmkunst GmbH	87
3.2	*Angry Harvest* (1985)	89
3.3	*To Kill a Priest* (1988)	95
3.4	*Europa, Europa* (1990)	100
3.5	*Olivier, Olivier* (1992)	105
4.1	*The Secret Garden* (1995)	123
4.2	*Washington Square* (1997)	129
4.3	*Total Eclipse* (1995)	131
4.4	*Total Eclipse* (1995)	133
4.5	*Copying Beethoven* (2006)	137
4.6	*The Third Miracle* (1999)	140
4.7	*Julie Walking Home* (2002)	143
5.1	*Red Wind* (1995)	160

5.2	*Shot in the Heart* (2001)	163
5.3	*A Girl Like Me: The Gwen Araujo Story* (2006)	165
5.4	*Treme*, episode 1, 'Do You Know What It Means' (2010)	174
5.5	*Rosemary's Baby* (2014)	176
5.6	*Burning Bush* (2013)	183
5.7	*Burning Bush* (2013)	185
6.1	*Janosik – A True Story* (2009)	199
6.2	*In Darkness* (2011)	202
6.3	*Janosik – A True Story* (2009)	203
6.4	*Janosik – A True Story* (2009)	204
6.5	*Charlatan* (2019)	205
6.6	*In Darkness* (2011)	207
6.7	*Spoor* (2017)	210
6.8	*Charlatan* (2019)	214
6.9	*Janosik – A True Story* (2009)	217
6.10	*Mr Jones* (2019)	219
7.1	Agnieszka Holland with her daughter, Kasia Adamik, Warsaw 1972; photo by Pista Adamik, from Agnieszka Holland's family archive	230
7.2	*Screen Tests* (1976)	232
7.3	Agnieszka Holland in *Interrogation* (Ryszard Bugajski, 1982/1989)	232
7.4	Andrzej Żuławski, Andrzej Wajda, Agnieszka Holland, Roman Polanski, Ryszard Bugajski, Krzysztof Kieślowski at the 43rd Cannes Film Festival. Photo by Micheline Pelletier © Getty Images	236
7.5	Agnieszka Holland at the ceremony of implanting a star with her name on the main street of Łódź. Photo by Tomasz Komorowski © Tomasz Komorowski for the Museum of Cinematography in Łódź	242
7.6	Agnieszka Holland receives honorary degree from FAMU in Prague. Photo by Petr Jan Juračka, © Archiv Akademie múzických umění v Praze, Udělení titulu 23.3	243
7.7	Agnieszka Holland comments on current political situation in TVN news on 7 September 2022. Screenshot	246
7.8	Agnieszka Holland at the rally against Russian aggression on Ukraine, 6 March 2022. Photo by Tomasz Molina. CC	247
7.9	Agnieszka Holland on the cover of the Polish LGBTQIA magazine.	250
7.10	Agnieszka Holland with her daughter, Kasia Adamik. Photo by Weronika Ławniczak/Papaya Films for *Zwierciadło*, © Weronika Ławniczak	252
7.11	The cover of Agnieszka Holland's biography by Karolina Pasternak	257

Acknowledgements

Although I have been exploring Agnieszka Holland's work for some time, it was the POLS grant financed by the Norwegian Financial Mechanism 2014–2021 (2020/37/K/HS2/02327) that I received in 2021 which was instrumental in writing the book. While working on it, I have been surrounded by many wonderful people who generously aided me in various ways. First and foremost, I thank Agnieszka Holland, who patiently answered my questions and allowed me to visit the set of *The Green Border* at the time when the whole production was still clandestine. I am also grateful for permission to use the photos from her private archive. My special thanks go to Helena Goscilo, who has assisted me on this work since its conception, for her encouragement, inspiration and readiness to give me a helping hand any time I needed it. The enthusiasm and genuine care I have been receiving from her for more than twenty years go far beyond scholarly collaboration. I would also like to express genuine gratitude to Brigid Haines, who has provided me not only with expert editorial assistance but also many beneficial comments that I cannot overvalue. With her critical and inquisitive eye, she would spot weak points or gratuitous rants. While appreciating her generous help, I take responsibility for any imperfections, weaknesses or errors in the book. My thanks also go to my colleagues and friends who have read various parts of the book as the work was progressing. I am especially indebted to Sebastian Jagielski, who has read several chapters, providing me always with insightful and appropriate comments. During our conversations, he would display an ongoing enthusiasm for the project, instilling me with energy when this was sometimes waning. Ewa Mazierska and Kamila Żyto have also read some parts of the book and shared with me their critical thoughts. My research assistant Jarosław Grzechowiak helped me with collecting archival sources, while Adam Wyżyński from the National Film

Archive Library has been providing me with generous assistance in identifying and locating relevant materials. Dominika Bodziony and Mateusz Matysiak have made my research in Andrzej Wajda's Archive exceptionally productive and pleasant. Marek Čermák has generously helped me with obtaining some sources and translations from Czech to English. Isabelle Louise Bastian, Uschi Rühle and Jens Kaufmann from Deutsches Filminstitut & Filmmuseum have provided me with professional assistance in acquiring the archival materials concerning Holland's collaboration with Artur Brauner. I have also received help from Marcin Adamczak, Roman Gutek, Anna Michalska, Felix Plawski and Paolo Villa. Finally, for obtaining the photos and permission to use them in the book, I thank Weronika Ławniczak, Michaela Grün, the Museum of Cinematography in Łódź, Tosca Schönberg and Viola Trinh. I would also like to express my gratitude to Dean of the Faculty of Philology at the University of Łódź, Joanna Jabłkowska, and Chair of the Institute of Contemporary Culture, Piotr Sitarski, who responded to the project enthusiastically and has supported it throughout its implementation. Wioleta Hencz, Joanna Korczyńska and Renata Rudnicka have provided administrative aid and friendly advice. I am grateful to Gillian Leslie, Sam Johnson and Kelly O'Brien at Edinburgh University Press for their professionalism and assistance, as well as Robert Singer, Gary D. Rhodes and Stefanie Van de Peer, the editors of the ReFocus series, for their encouragement and support. Last but not least, I would like to thank my family for unshaken faith in my creativity, expertise and productivity, and all my friends for their companionship and the laughs we have had throughout the years.

Preface

Agnieszka Holland, born in 1948 in Poland, is the most internationally recognised Polish filmmaker; she has been active in screen cultures for more than fifty years. Nominated three times for an Oscar and the recipient of many film festival prizes, she was elected President of the European Film Academy in 2021. Her versatile output ranges from Holocaust dramas such as *Europa, Europa* (1990) to episodes of the HBO series *The Wire*. She started her professional trajectory in socialist Poland, then lived in political exile in Paris, from where, in the early 1990s, she moved to Hollywood. In the mid-1980s she settled down in Brittany, France, while still working overseas and in her native Poland. Her visibility in contemporary culture is due not only to her works but also to her activity in the media and her publicly expressed political radicalism. Despite her artistic achievements and popularity with world-wide audiences, her work and her persona remain under-researched. This volume compensates for that neglect, while also reflecting my long-lasting interest in Holland's work – an interest that has evolved through the years.

Approximately a decade ago, I had a conversation with one of my Western academic colleagues about Agnieszka Holland's authorship. During our exchange, in my eagerness to avoid the trap of a dated *auteurist* approach, I located her work within the paradigm of nomadic cinema, with its semantic and stylistic de-centeredness. My colleague was sceptical about both frameworks, claiming that Holland was just a skilful professional filmmaker working in global Hollywood. While I was critically interrogating the concept of the auteur as customarily applied to Holland's oeuvre by Polish film scholars and critics, he was implying that she was 'only' a *metteur en scène*, as some in the West tend to see her. While I was thinking about *A Woman Alone* (*Kobieta samotna* 1981/1987), one of the most compelling cinematic portrayals of the socialist female subaltern, he was most likely thinking about one of her Hollywood films, such as *The Secret Garden* (1993) or *Washington Square* (1997), which are not stamped with a vivid 'authorial signature'.

Several years later, when I had an opportunity to observe Holland at work, I once again realised that no single critical or theoretical framework is sufficient to embrace her oeuvre. On 1 April 2023, I visited the filmset at a Warsaw hospital where she was shooting her new film, *The Green Border* (*Zielona granica*), an international co-production about the migratory crisis on the Polish-Belorussian border that had started in 2021. The script was written by Holland, Maciej Pisuk and Gabriela Łazarkiewicz-Sieczko. On that day, the crew was shooting a sequence about the character of a female Afghan teacher of English – played by the Iranian actress Behi Djanati Atai – also including Polish border guards, medical personnel and activists. The scene was coordinated through the use of both Polish and English. From a distance, I observed Holland moving energetically across the set to discuss details of the scene with her collaborators. She would confer with the Czech assistant director, Pavel Svaton, proffer advice to the actors and talk over the scene with the director of photography, Tomasz Naumiuk, to decide the camera movement and the lens to be used. Along with her daughter and long-term collaborator, Kasia Adamik, she silently observed each retake on the monitor screen, with only her facial expressions subtly betraying her responses to what she was observing. After each retake, she would walk swiftly to the actors, Naumiuk and Svaton to discuss the details that she considered necessary to adjust or change. Then she would return to the monitor, ready to call 'camera action' and 'cut' as needed. During the short breaks, Kasia would hand her a cup of tea from a thermos, while Holland herself would offer to those around her a piece of dark chocolate.

The film itself and Holland's actions and demeanour on the set eloquently demonstrated her approach to filmmaking – or cultural production in general, for that matter – which combines the collaborative with the authoritative. Furthermore, *The Green Border* examines the urgent issue of migration, and as such, it belongs to socially and politically engaged cinema, which Holland's work has always favoured. It is also situated in transnational cinema in both its narrative content and mode of production, while also representing collaborative authorship. On that day I witnessed how Holland simultaneously displayed both professional authority and a highly effective collaborative method of working.

The Green Border may also be seen as a continuation and extension of Holland's public activities – specifically, her energetic opposition to the Polish right-wing government's politics of migration. In working on this project, she fulfils two roles: that of filmmaker and of political activist, thereby shifting the concept of authorship from the field of textuality to the sphere of cultural production under specific geopolitical circumstances. Holland's involvement in politics became even more manifest when, two weeks after my visit to the film set, the government-controlled media informed the public about the film or, more precisely, attacked it, predicting that it would present a false image of the situation at the Polish-Belorussian border. The cover of the right-wing magazine *Sieci* asked, 'Agnieszka Holland is working on a film about bad Poles in uniforms and good migrants. Will this hybrid attack harm Poland?'[1] The official discourse thus subjected her work to political scrutiny even before its completion. Piotr Gliński, the Polish minister of culture, assured Poles that the project had not received any subsidy or funding from the government.[2] As happened almost a half-century ago under the Poland of late socialism, today Holland is once again considered an enemy of the state. This imposed status was prompted by her publicly expressed disapproval of human rights violations and her reputation in the transnational film industry, which enabled her to make *The Green Border* without any financial backing from Polish state institutions. In other words, her strong, indisputable authorial agency emerges not only from the solid textual corpus of her work, but also from a complex flux of public activities and various auxiliary discourses developed around both her films and her persona.

This book aims to explore Holland's versatile work and trace her constantly evolving authorship. I approach both from an interstitial position: a native Pole, I completed my academic education in Poland and worked there for some time before relocating to North America, first as a recipient of the Kościuszko Foundation Fellowship at the University of Pittsburgh, and then moving to Canada, where I taught cinema at the University of Alberta for almost twenty years. In 2021, I returned to Poland, to my *alma mater*, the University of Łódź, where I embarked on a research project titled 'The Transnational Cinema of Agnieszka Holland', funded by the Norwegian Financial Mechanism 2014–2021 (2020/37/K/ HS2/02327). That research forms the basis of this book. *The Films of Agnieszka Holland* brings to fruition my long-lasting scholarly interest in Holland's diverse output, which I have always viewed as contending with oppositional forces within political, cultural and affective structures in terms of the politics of representation. To address these tensions, I adopt sundry approaches so as not to reduce Holland's robustness and complexity to a constrictive uniformity. Her professional trajectory from Polish communist cinema to global screen cultures illuminates some key geopolitical and cultural transformations in post-Cold War cultural, social and political history.[3] Since her professional activity shows no sign of abating, my monograph remains open to, and invites, other scholars' responses to her cinema and my perspective on it.

P.S.

The Green Border premiered on 5 September 2023, at the Film Festival in Venice. By then the manuscript of this book was with the publisher. While at this stage it is not feasible to proceed with a detailed examination of the film and the ancillary discourses that emerged around it, a few relevant facts need to be provided here. On 4 September, a day before the festival screening of the film, the Polish minister of justice, Zbigniew Ziobro, made the following comment on the social platform X (previously Twitter): 'In the Third Reich, the Germans produced propaganda films showing Poles as bandits and murderers. Today, they have Agnieszka Holland for that.'[4] The film was well received by the festival audience and was awarded the Special Jury Prize. Critical response has also been very positive so far; for example, Peter Bradshaw wrote in *The Guardian*: 'Agnieszka Holland's brutal and timely drama shines a dark spotlight on the horrors faced by refugees in the exclusion zone between Poland and Belarus'[5]; in her review published in *The Hollywood Reporter*, Leslie Felperin called *The Green Border* a 'profoundly moving, flawlessly executed multi-strand drama'.[6] Holland demanded an apology from Ziobro, and after he failed to respond appropriately, she decided to sue him for defamation. Quite unwittingly, Ziobro has helped to advertise the film by condemning it sight unseen.

7 September 2023

NOTES

1. *Sieci*, no. 16, 2023.
2. P. Gliński: nowy film Agnieszki Holland nie jest finansowany ze środków MKIDN i PISF, PAP, 16 April 2023, https://www.portalsamorzadowy.pl/finanse/p-glinski-nowy-film-agnieszki-holland-nie-jest-finansowany-ze-srodkow-mkidn-i-pisf,455159.html
3. Throughout my study I rely on three different terms to identify Poland's location within Europe: Central Europe, Eastern Europe and East Central Europe. Given the history of that area, none of these terms is devoid of political overtones. While nowadays specialists in Polish history and culture customarily call Poland part of Central Europe, and such is my preference, until the collapse of the Soviet Union the unanimous geographical designation was Eastern Europe, partly owing to the existence of the politically based Eastern Bloc, of which Poland was an official member (1947–90). That choice conveniently identified Poland and other countries under the thumb of the USSR as the antipode to the West. Since many of the sources I cite in the monograph still use that term, so as to avoid verbal schizophrenia I follow their example in passages that engage their ideas. East Central Europe is a label on which fewer scholars rely and therefore occurs infrequently in my text, where I follow the same principle of adhering to their usage, and do so for the same reason.
4. Vanessa Gera, 'Polish Director Demands Apology from Justice Minister for Comparing Her Film to Nazi Propaganda', ABC News, 7 September 2023, https://abcnews.go.com/Entertainment/wireStory/polish-director-demands-apology-justice-minister-comparing-film-102991775
5. Peter Bradshaw, 'Green Border Review – Gripping Story of Refugees' Fight for Survival in the Forest', *The Guardian*, 5 September 2023, https://www.theguardian.com/film/2023/sep/05/green-border-review-refugees-venice-film-festival-

agnieszka-holland#:~:text=The%20result%20is%20a%20sombre,frantic%20 survival%2Dstruggle%20experienced%20by
6. Leslie Felperin, '"Green Border" Review: Agnieszka Holland's Knockout Drama Follows Refugees Stuck in Limbo', *The Hollywood Reporter*, 5 September 2023, https://www.hollywoodreporter.com/movies/movie-reviews/green-border-review-agnieszka-holland-1235582893/

Introduction: authorship, women's cinema and transnational screen cultures

Agnieszka Holland started directing films in her native Poland in the 1970s; later she worked on various film and television projects in Europe and North America, which she continues to do to this day. Her prolific oeuvre embraces art, national, European, Hollywood, transnational, popular, women's and queer cinemas, as well as projects for global television networks. She has worked as an assistant director, screenwriter, director, producer and actress. She has also been active in other sectors of cultural production: she translated Milan Kundera's Czech novel *The Unbearable Lightness of Being* (*Nesnesitelná lehkost bytí*) into Polish and has delivered occasional lectures and workshops in various educational institutions. Finally, she is indefatigable in giving countless interviews and commenting on current (especially Polish) social and political affairs on radio, television and the internet. Over time she has developed a chameleon-like authorship that has adjusted to sundry production conditions and socio-ideological contexts – a flexibility that does not necessarily entail subordination. In socialist Poland she had to struggle with censorship; during her European exile she had to adjust to the artisanal mode of production required by independent producers; in Hollywood she was subjected to generic conventions of popular cinema and producers' control; and while working for global streaming platforms she had to adapt to the overall stylistic conventions of the TV series. Finally, in more recent transnational European productions, she has had to accommodate various regulations of the funding bodies. Accordingly, my study explores precisely the multifaceted nature of Holland's authorship and, additionally, situates her work in the context of transnational women's cinema, inasmuch as her significant contribution to that capacious category has not received adequate attention.[1] Arguably, Holland's oeuvre reflects all the uncertainties of the contemporary concept of authorship in film and media, and by the same token it may indicate problematic aspects of studies in screen culture. In what follows, I map out the most relevant approaches to authorship, which I subsequently contextualise within the fields of women's and transnational cinemas. While not comprehensive, the presented theoretical considerations indicate the tools and strategies pertinent to my analysis of Holland's oeuvre in the book's later chapters.

AUTHORSHIP: COLLABORATION AND CROSS-POLLINATION

In his 2008 essay on authorship in cinema, John Caughie wrote:

> Returning to auteurism and authorship after a decent interval, I am struck by two contradictory perceptions: first, that the auteur seems to have disappeared from the centre of theoretical debate in Film Studies; second, that this disappearance may in fact be an illusion and that the grave to which we consigned him – and, by implication, her – is, in fact, empty. (Caughie 2008, 408)[2]

Holland is a perfect example of such an author, who cyclically disappears, only to return soon in a changed form with a different agenda.[3] As will be discussed throughout the book, her disappearances and reappearances as a film *auteur* depend on her physical location at any one time, on changing geopolitics around her, and on the developments in authorship theory. Whereas in her native Poland, her status as film *auteur* has always been relatively firm from the very beginning of her cinematic career, abroad she has gradually developed a reputation as a skilful and reliable filmmaker-for-hire. The difference results partly from the subordination of her authorial agency to diverse forms of control: in socialist Poland it was mostly political censorship; in Europe it was financial constraints imposed by independent producers; and in Hollywood it was the relevant studio's supervision over the aesthetic and narrative content of the films. Her authorship disappears and re-appears owing not only to the textualities of her work but also to the various distribution and critical strategies that are mobilised around it. Holland's case demonstrates what is conceptualised in more recent film theory: namely, film *auteurs* are fabricated rather than emerging intrinsically from their oeuvre.

Holland debuted in the late 1970s, several years after Roland Barthes' proclamation of 'the death of the author'.[4] Despite this announcement of symbolic 'authorcide', the concept of *auteur*, as proposed by the French critics in the 1950s[5] and later modified by Andrew Sarris,[6] persisted, and maintained its cultural currency. Operative within the realm of art cinema,[7] it regulated aesthetic hierarchies regardless of poststructuralist efforts to dispense with the figure of the Romantic genius as a solitary source of meaning and aesthetic uniqueness.[8] In European cinema of the 1970s, as noted by Steven Neale, the category of authorship was crucial in stabilising art cinema as an institution within the film industry (Neale 1981). In socialist Poland – and other countries of the Eastern Bloc, for that matter – the figure of the author acquired special significance (see Imre 2017). First and foremost, the idea of a solitary genius working against the system had subversive potential and resisted the official doctrine of communism which proselytised unity and uniformity. The idea of the Romantic artist at odds with the oppressive regime was appealing to both film audiences and critics. While such filmmakers' struggles for artistic freedom were conceived as acts of political defiance, making popular films was often deemed opportunistic, supporting official values. To most of the Polish film critics, only *auteurs* made 'true' national cinema.[9] Notwithstanding the necessity to reconsider this critical discourse on Polish cinema, operating as it does within facile binary oppositions,[10] its very existence indicates that the concepts of art cinema and *auteur* always operate within specific geopolitical contexts that determine their cultural and political significance. Accordingly, the artistic and political currency of the concept of *auteur* cinema can be increased, diminished or sometimes ignored as obsolete. In Polish cinema under state socialism the concept of the film *auteur* thrived, as demonstrated by such (male) directors as Andrzej Wajda, Andrzej Munk, Krzysztof Zanussi and Wojciech Has, its vitality fortified by auxiliary discourses of distribution, exhibition and criticism, which I shall discuss in due course.

Authors of the three Polish monographs devoted to Holland[11] approach her work from various critical perspectives but seem to agree on one point: that she is an *auteur*, a fact which by itself guarantees the artistic and cultural significance of her oeuvre.[12] Scholarly interest in Holland's work in her native Poland exemplifies the double structure of desire mobilised by *auteur* theory as identified by Dana Polan:

> On the one hand, in auteur theory, there is a drive to outline the desire of the director, his or her (but usually his) recourse to filmmaking as a way to express personal vision. The concern in auteur studies to pinpoint the primary obsessions and thematic preoccupations of this or that creator is thus an attempt to outline the director's desire. On the other hand, there is also desire for the director – the obsession of the cinephile or the film scholar to understand films as having an originary instance in the person who signs them. (Polan 2001a)

Such a double desire mobilises Polish critical discourse to identify Holland as an *auteur*, while the structure is practically absent in Western writing on her work.[13] Polish film scholars tirelessly search for her film and television projects' semantic centre, narrative patterns and stylistic consistency 'authorizing' – as Justin Wyatt called it – Holland's work, which is a process that relies on various discourses that use, or constitute, the director's name as a unifying factor for her/his films (Wyatt 1996). According to this approach, there are many sundry agencies that establish authorship, but these do not operate exclusively during the process of creation/production, for they are also active in distribution, exhibition and critical reception. Polan proposes to see this composite nature of cinematic authorship as a Foucauldian 'space of dispersion' (Polan 2001b, 12). As he notes,

> [t]he place of the director is a divided one – divided, for instance, internally by the complexities of the psyche (against authorship as conscious intention, psychoanalysis reminds us of all that is unconscious and even conflictual in expressions of will, intention, desire, deliberative agency), but also divided by social forces, which means that the director's voice is only one among many (the many others who work on the film, but also the many who distribute and promote the film, and the many who consume it, all according to their own social agencies and agendas). (Polan 2001b, 8)

A similar approach to authorship is offered by Deb Verhoeven in her monograph on Jane Campion. She takes inspiration from Wyatt's essay, stating: 'filmmakers, studios, distribution companies, funding agencies, media, critics and academics are all engaged in a process of authorising (or actively de-authorising) film directors' (Verhoeven 2009, 27). Mark Gallagher further develops the concept of the extratextual constituents of authorship. In his book on Steven Soderbergh, he argues that 'authorship is a site of, and can be constituted through, various discourses. These include discourses emerging from criticism, industrial practice, reception, textual systems, genres, and cinephilic and other taste cultures' (Gallagher 2013, 86). He underscores the need to look at 'the work *of* authorship' and how film criticism certifies filmmakers as *auteurs*, thereby affecting the process of signification (Gallagher 2013, 5, 6). Contemporary research on film and media authorship proposes that it is not the immanency of the work itself but, rather, various auxiliary social and cultural practices that establish it.

Throughout her professional career, Holland has participated in many different systems of cultural production, and each has established and employed its own strategies of 'authorizing' or 'de-authorizing' her work. In Poland under state socialism, Holland contributed to the Cinema of Moral Concern, a movement that epitomised the model of Eastern European politically engaged cinema.[14] When Holland's feature debut, *Provincial Actors* (*Aktorzy prowincjonalni*, 1978), won the FIPRESCI Critics' Prize at the 1980 Cannes

Film Festival, her status as a film *auteur* acquired ultimate confirmation.[15] It strengthened her position within Polish national cinema and established her cultural capital,[16] which was so useful in her later career in transnational cinema and media. Her departure from Poland in 1981 and new alignment with transnational and then global Hollywood cinema resulted in a readjustment of her authorial agency according to the production and distribution circumstances of her new professional identity. The relatively solid authorship Holland established in her native Poland in the last decade of state socialism gradually transformed into a less manifest form during her professional journeys abroad. However, its diminished visibility does not equal its disappearance. Frequently, Holland's 'authorial signatures' remain hidden in her international works and, therefore, she can be addressed as a 'self-effacing auteur' to borrow from William Brown, who applied the concept to Michael Winterbottom's work. According to Brown, the British director's oeuvre does not represent generic, thematic or stylistic consistencies, yet is perpetually responsive to contemporary challenges, whether of a political or aesthetic nature (Brown 2016). Similarly, Holland's international work does not offer a strong authorial trademark in terms of style and narrative motifs, yet constantly and passionately interrogates hegemonic ideologies of both the past and the present.

Working within many different production systems has resulted in the development of Holland's authorship as 'a space of dispersion' between various authorial agencies represented by the director herself, her producers working within specific systems of film productions, and regular collaborators.[17] Her work is a manifest example of collaborative authorship as conceived by Robert L. Carringer. He distinguishes his reflection from 'multiple-authorship studies, which characteristically (in spite of themselves) devalue text and authors because of the sharing of agency, and from that of collective-authorship studies, which tend to regard the dispersal of agency as the given to be contemplated' (Carringer 2001, 377–8). He postulated a two-step analysis of collaborative authorship: 'The first entails the temporary suspension of single-author primacy [. . .] to appraise constituent claims to a text's authorship. In the second phase primary author is reinscribed within what is now established as an institutional context of authorship' (Carringer 2001, 377). The act of critical suspension facilitates the re-emergence of the single author as the main collaborator who controls the whole process of creation/production and as such deserves to be given credits for the final outcome (Carringer 2001, 378).[18] While Holland's textual authorship establishes a space of dispersion, she exercises her controlling agency in selecting the scripts, production companies and creative personnel. Thereby her case exemplifies how, instead of the concept of Romantic inspiration traditionally ascribed to the figure of a film artist, nowadays control is a key feature attributed to authorship in film and media. As Thomas Elsaesser noted, control 'can be exercised in many different ways:

organizational, financial, political, artistic, and intellectual, and many of these types of control are indeed involved in the making, marketing, distributing, and "owning" of a film' (Elsaesser 2016, 23). Consequently, Holland's composite authorship, which is subject to various distribution, exhibition and critical practices, needs to be located within the framework of 'post-auteurism' that, as Verhoeven claims,

> shifts the emphasis from the single image of the individual author, a driven artist struggling to overcome a variety of institutional obstacles in order to find an outlet for their expressions, to a composite picture that emphasizes instead the director's collaborative relationship, their industrial context and their artistic ascriptions. (Verhoeven 2009, 23)

Verhoeven uses the framework of 'post-auteurism' to examine the work of Campion, which cannot be embraced within the singular concept of *auteur* due to her mobility across various modes of cinema and production cultures.[19] Accordingly, she proposes to approach her as an 'endemic auteur' and the 'dispersible auteur' – terms that refer respectively to her functioning within (national) New Zealand and Australian cinemas and global (transnational) cinemas (Verhoeven 2009, 88). The distinction applies to Holland's work as well in that it is categorised as *auteur* cinema by Polish film scholars and critics, while Western critics locate her work mostly within global genre cinema. The former category establishes her as an (endemic) *auteur*, while Western critics mostly approach her as a professional filmmaker-for-hire, or, less frequently, a global *auteur*.

Holland's work for global Hollywood and international streaming platforms has resulted in her authorship being gradually transformed into a 'brand name' that, as Timothy Corrigan explains, refers to the commercial value of an *auteur* and significantly determines the critical reception of her or his work (Corrigan 2011, 420).[20] Building on this argument, Yannis Tzioumakis discusses authorship as not established textually but rather as an industrial category that is manufactured by promotional and distribution strategies. As he argues, '"industrial auteurism" could potentially reveal "a different author," an author whose presence is assigned institutionally, which often makes sense only in light of distributors' attempts to market a specific product to a particular audience' (Tzioumakis 2006, 60).[21]

In a similar vein, Verhoeven pointed out how the contemporary film industry 'contains' the *auteur*. Regulated by the rules and principles of neoliberalism, with its basic assumption that everything possesses monetary value, the industry exploits the commercial potential of authorship. The *auteur* is a crucial component in a film's financing, contracting of key personnel (crew, stars) and marketing (Verhoeven 2009, 15). In other words, authorship functions as a regulatory mechanism for production, distribution and exhibition practices. No longer perceived as an inspired artist,

> [t]he auteur is now a critical concept indispensable for distribution and marketing purposes, i.e. social interactions in a political economy beyond textual interpretation. Hollywood auteurs are strategic commercial agents endorsed by mass audience, like 'brand names' that guide and stimulate their consumption. Rather than being rooted in the notion of fixed identity or autonomous authority, today's auteur takes a multifaceted, modulable 'agency' for organizing various modes of communication with its audience in the global market of film culture. (Jeong and Szaniawski 2016, 4)[22]

Importantly, throughout her career, Holland has personally constructed or attempted to control this 'modulable agency' and, thus, developed her own 'authorizing' discourse around her work and contribution to various sectors of screen culture. Her consistent efforts to control her public persona may be approached as Foucauldian 'technologies of the self' (Foucault 1988, 18) that she uses to 'self-fashion' herself into a film *auteur*.

In this book, I approach Holland's authorship as established by both her works and the ancillary discourses of film production, distribution, exhibition and criticism, conceived as 'authorising' strategies that remain markedly different in her native Poland and the rest of the world. Instead of looking for semantic and aesthetic unity as conceptualised by the classical concept of *auteur* or Foucauldian author-function, I see it 'a cross-platform phenomenon' (Gallagher 2013, 13) of various systems of film and media production and circulation in specific geopolitical circumstances. Throughout the book, I argue that over the course of Holland's long professional career stretching back five decades, her textual authorship has developed into 'a space of dispersion', while simultaneously she has been strengthening her subjective agency within the fields of media production and screen cultures.

WOMEN'S CINEMA: IN AND OUT

One of the paradoxical developments within authorship theory is that the poststructuralist turn coincided with the emancipatory impulses of various marginalised groups. As Caughie noted, Barthes announced 'the death of the author' 'just at the point at which previously "un-authorized" constituencies began to speak with authority' (Caughie 2008, 408). In a similar vein, Alison Butler noted that the author disappeared from the field 'just as feminists began to demand equal access to the means of cultural production' (Butler 2008, 399). Early film feminism adhered to poststructuralist reconsiderations of authorship and predominantly conceptualised it as disembodied agency,[23] while mostly disregarding the specific cultural and political locations within which the actual female filmmaker worked.[24] Alongside the early development of feminist film theory, a feminist film practice emerged, soon forming 'a feminist canon in the 1970s and 1980s that was dominated by cinematic counterparts of the theory in the work of formalist filmmakers such as Chantal Akerman, Marguerite Duras, Bette Gordon, Sally Potter, Yvonne Rainer and Helke Sander' (Butler 2008, 393). Just as the publications of feminist theorists defined certain fundamental principles that by the end of the twentieth century had become classic feminist statements, so these directors established the canon of women's cinema, the category that subsequently has been debated and constantly redefined, as attested by the later publications in the field.[25] Female filmmakers working in other than avant-garde or art cinema sectors of cultural production were not included in the canon and Holland was one of these overlooked directors.

To overcome the limitations of a theoretical approach to female authorship, Kathleen McHugh located women's cinema within geopolitical developments in the women's movement and screen technologies. She directed her attention towards the 'transnational generation' of female filmmakers who were born between 1945 and 1960[26] – including Holland in that cohort – when global mass media rapidly developed and participated in a redefinition of the concept of womanhood. She considered their work

> a counterbalance to text-based feminism, national film history, and Hollywood's own theorization of feminism – all of which shift attention away from women as producers. It also provides an alternative to second- and third-wave feminism as periodizing rubrics that actually account for concurrent activities in film production in the postwar era. (McHugh 2009, 119)

McHugh noted that these women made their films in various modes of cinema, from experimental film to documentaries, while witnessing and participating in the postwar upsurge of national cinemas that were built on the ruins of erstwhile empires and consequently were part of the emergence of postcolonial geopolitical formations. Their films frequently tackled the themes of transnational identities as related to feminism. At the time of these female filmmakers' activity, the concept of a film *auteur* was gaining currency and many of them were identified as such, mostly owing to their visibility at international film festivals. As McHugh argues, 'These women grew up and came to maturity in the context of postwar transnational feminisms that had diverse discursive, material, and cultural effects' (McHugh 2009, 121). She does not limit the impact of feminism on the films' narrative content and formal strategies but also recognises its effect on the production cultures in terms of working out various mechanisms facilitating female filmmaking.

While McHugh includes Holland in the cohort of the 'transnational generation', her case does not exemplify the general issues treated in the article, for she did not operate within 'the networks [...] inflected by or overtly connected to feminist purpose or infrastructure' (McHugh 2009, 122). Unlike such filmmakers as, for example, the Costa Rican-born, Jewish Mexican filmmaker Guita Schyfter, whose cinematic career has been tied to feminism (McHugh 2009, 123), Holland's affinity with the movement and its cinematic expression has not been evident for most of her cinematic career. Likewise, her mobility was not motivated by gender politics, as was the case of other filmmakers discussed by McHugh, but was initially forced by political circumstances – specifically, the introduction of martial law in Poland in 1981. Furthermore, in her native Poland during the period of state socialism, there was no institutional or financial support for increasing women's activity in the media and film production, unlike in Germany and Australia as mentioned in the article. Despite these differences between Holland and women directors from other parts of the world, there are some similarities in terms of their declared relationship with feminism. For example, Jane Campion, as McHugh remarks, was initially reluctant to identify with the feminist agenda:

> Especially early in her career, [...] [she] depoliticized her engagement with women's issues and female protagonists, framing her interest as a creative rather than an ideological identification, something natural and self-evident, a characterization of a piece with her self-fashioning as an art cinema auteur. (McHugh 2009, 138)[27]

Holland in the first part of her career likewise baulked at being identified with women's cinema. Her situation, however, differed radically from Campion's, for in Poland, unlike in Australia, there were no 'feminist structures of opportunity' (McHugh 2009, 129) that would have facilitated her professional career. Nor did such opportunities arise for Holland during her life in exile in Europe. The only possibility for her to stay active in the film industry was to adapt to hegemonic structures, while negotiating their artistic and ideological scripts.

Owing to her participation in various hegemonic screen cultures in Poland and the West, Holland's position within women's cinema is as ambiguous as that of many other female filmmakers such as Alice Guy (1873–1968) in the past and Katherine Bigelow in the present (see Paszkiewicz 2018, 100–33). Kimberly Tomadjoglou's essay on the former may provide useful inspiration for an examination of Holland's work. As the author admits, it is difficult to examine the pioneering French director Guy's persona within a single critical framework. Apart from her career being fractured between two continents, she was 'a multidimensional figure and throughout her life played a range of roles: secretary, director, screenwriter, producer, distributor, manager, and art director, not to mention mother'. A transnational framework on the other hand, as Tomadjoglou argues, makes it possible to embrace Guy's multidirectional film career and her authorship (Tomadjoglou 2015, 97). Furthermore, the author advocates using 'the term *metteur-en-scène*[28] rather than *auteur*' in relation to Guy, while simultaneously recognising her agency, demonstrated in her non-directorial activities performed in both France and the US. Working within two different systems of cultural productions resulted in Guy's problematic position within the category of national cinema and consequently in her being 'largely misjudged or underrecognized by both French and American film historians' (Tomadjoglou 2015, 100–2).

Similar factors have prevented Holland's work from being subjected to comprehensive analysis. She achieved a strong position within Polish screen industries in the 1970s, yet this drastically changed when she lived in exile in Paris as a single mother who had to accept available projects in order to support herself and her child. Throughout her long and convoluted professional career, Holland has managed to stay active within various systems of production cultures,[29] which testifies to her agency as a female filmmaker, while her works have resisted the customary label of women's cinema usually connected with a (Western) feminist agenda. In this, Holland is similar to Guy, who, as Tomadjoglou suggests, 'prefigured the modern-day celebrity and cultural spokesperson. In this sense, Alice Guy can be a feminist when she has social power and has control of her female identity' (Tomadjoglou 2015, 103). Holland's strong position within contemporary screen cultures as testified, for example, by her role of president of the European Film Academy, demonstrates her (feminist) agenda. Like Guy, Holland and many other female filmmakers attest to Christine Gledhill and Julia Knight's call for more inclusive and nuanced historical analysis of the works of female filmmakers:

> women's film history has to perform a delicate balancing act between establishing the roles women *did* play in film history and recognition of practices that, arising from women's gender positioning, are outwith both feminist politics and traditional concepts of historical significance. (Gledhill and Knight 2015, 9)

During the period of state socialism in Eastern Europe, Holland – like most Polish women at that time – expressed anti-feminist attitudes and sentiments that originated mostly from the manifest disparity between the official 'gender equality' doctrine and its problematic implementation in socio-political reality. As Anikó Imre noted, 'state feminism itself was an ambivalent force. While it generally associated feminism with a demonized capitalist West beholden to consumerism, it also afforded generous social provisions to women and adapted to shifts in socialist ideology with remarkable flexibility' (Imre 2017, 89). The prolonged enmity towards communist genealogies of Polish feminism resulted from the traditional opposition between the national and the communist/socialist (mostly associated with Soviet oppression).[30] The former functioned as the primary identification framework for Eastern European societies, containing and subordinating all other subjectivities based on gender, sexual orientation or race. Polish feminism, which developed at the intersection of state feminism and Western-style feminism(s), had its own dynamics and agendas. The leading Polish feminist scholar Agnieszka Graff claims that Eastern European societies 'skipped the radical 1960s and got a double dose of the conservative 1980s' (Graff 2007, 147). She elaborates, 'Polish gender politics do not fit the Anglo-American chronology [. . .] our chronology is different', for Polish feminism emerged 'between the waves' – that is, between second- and third-wave feminism (Graff 2007, 142). As she further explains, 'despite not having had much of a second wave feminism, we Polish women did experience a backlash. In fact, many of us internalized its message before discovering feminism' (Graff 2007, 144). The disturbed chronology explains the ambivalent attitude of many Polish and Eastern European women to feminism.

Likewise Eastern European intellectuals and artists often expressed distrust of Western feminism and refused to embrace it. Many female filmmakers from the region whose work frequently focused on gender issues habitually rejected any overt links with feminism. As Dina Iordanova reported: 'leading female directors from the region have distanced themselves from "feminism," a situation that leaves us facing the curious phenomenon of clearly committed feminist film-makers who are nonetheless reluctant to be seen as such' (Iordanova 2003, 123). Holland's work and her public statements substantiate this paradoxical relationship with feminism. In the 1970s, Holland unambiguously represented this ambiguous, if not hostile, attitude to feminism and the category of women's cinema,[31] while simultaneously subverting patriarchal structures of power inherent in the national film industry (see Chapter Two).

This ambivalent attitude to gender as a constituent of screen cultures has manifested in Holland's activities since the beginning of her career. Apart from her sceptical opinion about feminism expressed in the early stage of her career, Holland has been moderately active in women's cinema culture. As Monika Talarczyk-Gubała reported, in 1976 Holland participated in the seminar 'Woman – Filmmaker' organised by the cine-club in Szczytno, Poland, while also contributing to a special issue of the periodical *Film in the World* (*Film na świecie*) devoted to 'women's cinema' with a translation from Czech to Polish of an article on Hungarian female filmmakers (Talarczyk-Gubała 2013, 32).[32] Furthermore, as I shall explain in due course, although her Polish films cannot be identified with the tenets of Western second-wave feminism, they still advocate for female subjectivity in a way relevant to the emancipatory impulses emerging in socialist Poland. While not fitting the model of feminist counter-cinema, insofar as they do not deconstruct the hegemonic codes of the dominant model of cinema, they nonetheless do not reproduce the patriarchal system of signifying practices. For example, in her early television works, Holland explored issues of pregnancy and motherhood that were traditionally marginalised in mainstream film production. The films revealed how female experiences are embedded within larger social and cultural discourses on the level of cultural production and its consumption. Notwithstanding a transparent style and a chronological narrative typical of hegemonic modes of cinema, the films employed visual devices such as tight framing, cluttered mise-en-scène and an imperfect illumination of space and characters to reflect on the situation of entrapment experienced by many Polish women at that time. This aesthetic and ideological in-betweenness indicates that Holland is, indeed, one of 'the few isolated Eastern European and Soviet women directors [who] present a problem to, rather than a transnational extension of, a gendered inquiry' (Imre 2017, 88).

In addressing the problem of Holland's intricate position within women's cinema, Alison Butler's concept of 'women's cinema' as 'minor cinema' (inspired by Deleuze and Guattari's concept of 'minor literature', see Deleuze and Guattari 1986) proves operative. As she explains, 'the plurality of forms, concerns and constituencies in contemporary women's cinema now exceeds even the most flexible definition of counter-cinema. Women's cinema now seems "minor" rather than oppositional' (Butler 2002, 20). And as such it is at odds with any model of cinema, borrowing, reworking or subverting all of them. Since female filmmakers work within various geopolitical localities and engage different identity projects, they defy an essentialist conceptualisation of gender, which renders impossible a single and exclusive definition of women's cinema. Moving across liminal areas of cultural formations, they are permanently moving 'in' and 'out', as if refusing to occupy a stable position within one of them (Butler 2002, 22). Butler deliberately opens up the space of women's cinema to a plurality of gender identities and subjectivities, indicating also the necessity of overcoming a rigid adherence to (Western) second-wave feminism.

Most importantly, though Western feminism accommodated the postcolonial perspective that proved the most fruitful and expansive strand of transnational feminism,[33] it has gradually marginalised impulses coming from other than post-Third-World localities, including the Second World, understood as the countries of the former Soviet Bloc. As Imre noted in 2007, Eastern European feminism was 'forced to choose between first and third-world identifications'.[34] Those film and television projects that Holland made in various geopolitical localities – communist Poland, Western countries and global Hollywood – destabilise the First/post-Third world binarism that has formed a conceptual framework for transnational feminism and transnational cinema.

FROM EXILIC TO TRANSNATIONAL CINEMA AND SCREEN CULTURES

Along with many other transnational filmmakers, Holland participates in re-mapping world cinema and toppling traditional aesthetic hierarchies, which has not been adequately recognised in the field literature.[35] In his pioneering book, *Accented Cinema: Exilic and Diasporic Filmmaking* (2001),[36] Hamid Naficy only mentions Holland in passing, as her work does not provide a strong case for his key concept of 'accented cinema', which he defines according to the following criteria: artisanal mode of production; international cast and personnel; heteroglossia; and international circulation facilitated by film festivals as well as a preoccupation with the issue of territoriality (Naficy 2001, 25). Holland's first phase of her professional career abroad could be identified with exilic cinema, but the succeeding stages, especially in the aftermath of the collapse of communism in Poland (1989), escape this classification. Nor is Holland a diasporic filmmaker, as recently she has been relatively active in her native Poland. Furthermore, only a few of her films belong to an artisanal mode of production, whereas others benefitted from a moderately large budget. Her films rarely examine the larger subject matter of migration[37] or diaspora (cf. Naficy 2001, 222–87) and most of her transnational productions are not accented stylistically inasmuch as they tend to be formally transparent.

In addressing Holland's ambivalent position within transnational cinema, Mette Hjort's distinction between cosmopolitan versus *auteurist* and 'unmarked' versus 'marked' transnational cinemas proves useful. Decisive in the cosmopolitan type is the director's ability to control the process of filmmaking in diverse circumstances and production contexts while relying on an unobtrusive style and dominant codes of visual representation (Hjort 2010, 20). In other words, cosmopolitan cinema is usually 'unmarked' inasmuch as it does not foreground its transnationality by means of various formal and narrative devices. By contrast, *auteurist* and 'marked' transnational cinema focuses on various types of hybrid identities, while employing distinct formal devices that may be seen as an 'authorial signature' (Hjort 2010, 13–14). As Hjort notes, cosmopolitan and *auteurist* transnationality frequently intersect, and indeed they do in Holland's work.[38] For example, *Europa, Europa* (1990) represents *auteurist* and marked transnationality; Holland managed to involve international producers in the project, recruited an international crew and cast, and forced through multilingual dialogues in German, Russian and Polish; finally, the film concerns the uncertainties of ethnic and racial identities. In contrast, films such as *Olivier, Olivier* (1991), *Washington Square* (1997) or *Copying Beethoven* (2006) employ mostly transparent cinematic codes (cf. Stalnaker 2003) and do not focus on hybrid identities. Thus, they represent unmarked and cosmopolitan transnationalism, which constitutes a large segment of film production addressed as global cinema.

Holland's work problematises any dichotomous concept of transnational cinema, as proposed, for example, by Elizabeth Ezra and Terry Rowden in their introduction to the collective volume *Transnational Cinema: The Film Reader* (2006). As they write, 'The transnational comprises both globalization – in cinematic terms, Hollywood's domination of world film markets – and the counterhegemonic responses of filmmakers from former colonial and Third World countries' (2006, 1). As in the case of transnational feminism, the concept of transnational cinema suggested here is embraced within the binary opposition of the West and the postcolonial East, while leaving aside the former Eastern Bloc and its cultural production. Moreover, Ezra and Rowden's conceptualisation of transnational cinema perpetuates the customary division into popular and art cinema, while repositioning these into adjusted geopolitical localities.

While constantly moving across the division between global/cosmopolitan/unmarked and accented/*auteurist*/marked cinema, Holland practices 'sojourner cinema' adopted by 'traveling filmmakers, whose work (in the sense of labor and product) poses a challenge to nation-based narration both diegetically and [. . .] extradiegetically' (Lopez 2000).[39] The strategy is frequently used by other Eastern European filmmakers such as István Szabó, Goran Paskaljević and Emir Kusturica, who, as noted by Iordanova,

> Since 1989 [. . .] have worked predominantly outside their home countries and could, therefore, easily qualify as 'migrant'. Yet we do not think of them in this way, perhaps because they switch countries all the time and have access to financial resources quite different from those available to more traditional migrant and diasporic film-makers, or, most significantly, because their films are not primarily concerned with issues of identity and bridging cultures. (Iordanova 2010b, 66)

Their work has been mostly omitted from all major publications in the field of transnational cinema and media because it cannot be contained within its dominant paradigm, which opposes global Hollywood with post-Third World cultural production. Holland represents the relatively large body of Eastern European filmmakers who, after the collapse of communism, 'are not permanently based in one country, but rather make films transnationally, with *ad hoc* arrangements of financing and other elements on a "'per project" basis' (Iordanova 2010a, 65). As Iordanova explained, they are not concerned with issues of migration, for they can move freely across borders. They benefit from newly emerging European film funds and thus they can easily go over the limits of national cinemas. In result, they 'benefit from a supranational status that supplies them with a unique immunity'. As she further observes, they move freely in search of the best options for making movies and thus they cannot be identified as migrant or exilic filmmakers, but instead as supra-national 'transnationally mobile filmmakers' (Iordanova 2010a, 65).

The movement from national to transnational/supra-national cinema parallels the evolution of the traditional model of authorial agency – which implies control of the aesthetic and semantic aspects of individual creative projects – into a post-auteurism, where the emphasis falls on various collaborative networks, including industrial factors as well as artistic scripts.[40] Global 'travelling filmmakers' often negotiate their authorship by using the status of *auteur* established elsewhere as their cultural capital when entering the Hollywood system of production, while their 'brand name'[41] acquired in Hollywood serves as an asset for non-Hollywood (art) film projects.[42] Holland's successful European arthouse films such as *Angry Harvest* (*Bittere Ernte*, 1985) and *Europa, Europa* (1990) facilitated her Hollywood career, while her reputation achieved in the field of global media production has helped her to obtain funding for more ambitious projects aimed at the film festival circuit.

The case of travelling filmmakers demonstrates how the category of authorship nowadays is indeed becoming a 'space of dispersion', as conceptualised by Polan, of which Holland's work is a manifest example. As Iordanova pertinently commented, 'her work [is] becoming more versatile but less recognisable' (Iordanova 2003, n. 197; see also Quart 1993). However, though the textualities of her work are not forming a consistent *auteurist* oeuvre in terms of thematic preferences and stylistic choices, her extratextual authorial agency has been solidified over decades and thus the concept of authorship provides the most productive framework for its analysis. Throughout the book, I approach Holland's transnational female authorship as established both textually in her works and extratextually by various authorising discourses that encompass production networks, distribution and exhibition strategies, as well as critical reception. Rather than consecrating Holland to the position of a female transnational film *auteur*, the book aims to interrogate the authorising and de-authorising discourses established around her work. The following analyses of her work may also shed some light on the historical evolution of the critical concepts of authorship, women's cinema and transnational cinema, and their geopolitical diversification. Her work is too versatile to be safely and conveniently sheltered under the umbrella of any of these concepts yet researching it is instrumental in illuminating the interstitial areas within both cultural production and critical discourses. Finally, her professional trajectory, which started in the Eastern Bloc, continued in Western Europe and North America, and returned to a unified Europe that offered new schemes for media production, epitomises the transformations of post-Cold War cultural production.

THE STRUCTURE OF THE BOOK

The structure of the book follows the chronological order of Holland's professional career and traces the evolution of her authorship as she moved between various modes of production cultures. I divide her professional trajectory into different stages, with necessary overlaps as these were emerging from the various systems of screen media production within which she worked.

Chapter One examines Holland's early biography as an important constituent of her authorship, which – as I argue throughout the book – has been manifested in the textualities of her work and her activities in various media. I locate this information within two theoretical frameworks: firstly, authorship, conceived as personal agency determined by individual and collective histories, and secondly, Gilles Deleuze's concept of three lifelines that address the paradoxical nexus of continuity and discontinuity from which an individual emerges (Deleuze and Parnet 2007, 124). While outlining the earliest parts of Holland's biography, I focus on the experiences she would later present as nodal points affecting her personal and professional life trajectory. I also examine her film education and her political activity during the period she spent in Prague. While not aiming at a complete presentation of Holland's early biography, I foreground those parts that contextualise her work within the specific historical experiences of Eastern European communities. Finally, the chapter presents a close reading of her student diploma film, *Jesus Christ's Sin* (*Hřích boha*, 1969), as it foreshadows certain properties of her work that subsequently crystallise. The main aim of this chapter is to bring to light the complex nexus of Holland's individual life experience, politics and cultural production.

In Chapter Two, I examine Holland's professional career in Poland between 1972 and 1981, with a special focus on gender, in terms of both her struggles in the film industry and the politics of representation in her works. First, I discuss Holland's position within the institutional and informal networks of the Polish film industry in the 1970s. Her participation in the collective film and television projects is analysed within the framework of collective authorship, while her individually directed films contributing to the Cinema of Moral Concern are discussed as representing national cinema. Throughout the chapter, I demonstrate how Holland's increasingly strong position in the Polish screen industries subverted their patriarchal structures, while in her subsequent films the female characters gradually lose their subjective agency. In my analysis of these contradictory forces affecting Holland's work in Poland under late state socialism, I interrogate how the socialist emancipatory gender discourses – significantly different from their Western counterparts – that were reflected in Holland's early works were eventually subordinated to the hegemonic national discourse developed in the Cinema of Moral Concern.

Chapter Three discusses Holland's professional activity from 1981 to 1992 during her exilic stay in Europe. It examines that output in chronological order to show her progressive distantiation from Polish national culture, with a simultaneous shift towards sub-national identities. Discussion of her participation in Polish émigré culture in Paris is followed by analyses of *Angry Harvest* (*Bittere Ernte*, 1985), *To Kill a Priest* (1988), *Europa, Europa* (1990), and *Olivier, Olivier* (1991). While discussing the films, I demonstrate how Holland's transition from socialist to Western modes of film production resulted in a thematic and stylistic versatility in her exilic work compared to her Polish oeuvre from the 1970s, which treated contemporary subject matters in realistic form. Holland's gradual adjustment to independent production modes as established by Artur Brauner in Germany and Margaret Ménégoz in France facilitated her entry into European transnational cinema, but also limited her thematic and generic choices. Her move away from the Polish national discourse was especially conspicuous in the two Holocaust movies *Angry Harvest* and *Europa, Europa*, which significantly departed from the then hegemonic narratives that equated Jewish and Polish victimhood while erasing anti-Semitic acts. Instead, as I argue, these two films acknowledged some Poles' position as 'implicated subjects' (Rothberg 2019). Ultimately, Holland's exilic European output showed a gradual dispersion of her authorship, which was paralleled by the narratives of the films featuring protagonists who frequently questioned or resisted any singular subject position.

Chapter Four, devoted to Holland's North American films, demonstrates how these adapted the European tradition of art cinema within the constraints of the Hollywood model of popular cinema. Accordingly, it traces how Holland's position gradually evolved from that of an *auteur* working in (trans) national cinema into a filmmaker-for-hire active in global Hollywood. As four of the six films made in North America are costume dramas or adaptations of classical literature, I locate them within the framework of heritage cinema, largely identified with European cultural production. In these sub-genre films, multidirectional transfers between European and American cinematic traditions occurred, which resulted in an aesthetic merging of popular and art cinema. A similar ambiguity characterises the gender and ethnic politics of these films, for they neither condone nor subvert Western hegemonic discourses. Some of them, such as *Washington Square* (1997) and *Copying Beethoven* (2006), include feminist emancipatory impulses, which, however, are embedded within conservative ideologies. Consequently, the North American period in Holland's career demonstrates both her further engagement with issues of identity politics and a dispersion of her authorship, which results from working within the mode of 'sojourn cinema'. In the chapter's final part, I examine how American film criticism developed a discourse that diminished her authorial agency, whereas Polish cultural workers, especially film distributors and critics, saw it as consolidated and argued for her American films' affinity with European art cinema.

Chapter Five addresses Holland's television work as an integral part of her oeuvre that reveals her authorial agency, albeit often in a dormant form. First, I discuss *Red Wind* (1995), an episode of the TV series *Fallen Angels* (1993–6, Showtime), and two feature films made for American television stations: *Shot in the Heart* (HBO, 2001) and *A Girl Like Me: The Gwen Araujo Story* (Lifetime Movie Network, 2006). These three television projects concern sensitive sociopolitical issues pertinent to American society of the time, and as such they contrast with Holland's feature films made during this period, which were either costume or metaphysical dramas. I then discuss Holland's selected works made for global streaming platforms (episodes of *Cold Case*, *The Wire* and *Treme*), demonstrating how these developed her storytelling skills, while also continuing certain themes of her earlier work. Finally, I present Holland's collaboration with Polish postcommunist private television and Eastern European divisions of global streaming platforms. These projects, I suggest, may be seen as her symbolic return home, while also belonging to national/regional as well as transnational cultural production in terms of financing, the participation of international creative personnel and intertextual embedding within global genres.

Chapter Six turns to Holland's films made in the new millennium. I look at them in the context of the changes in European film industries resulting from the new geopolitical order after the accession to the European Union (EU) of several countries of the previous Eastern Bloc and their consequent enlargement. The films *Janosik – A True Story* (2009), *In Darkness* (*W ciemności*, 2011), *Spoor* (*Pokot*, 2017), *Mr. Jones* (2019) and *Charlatan* (*Šarlatán*, 2020) are all European co-productions that examine historical or political issues relevant to the region of Eastern Europe. Except for *Spoor*, these films depict the lives of real people, and as such they can be seen as a continuation of Holland's exploration of the genre of biopic in her American feature and television works. Simultaneously, they mark a further shift towards sub-national identities such as ethnicity (*In Darkness*), gender (*Spoor*) and sexuality (*Charlatan*). As I argue, with the vital subject matters and moderate departures from the conventions of mainstream cinema, Holland's European transnational film productions represent socially engaged cinema designed for the specific sector of the film festivals circuit and exhibition in other than cineplexes movie theatres. While discussing these films, I take inspiration from Thomas Elsaesser's discussion of European 'festival films', especially his concept of 'double occupancy' (2019, 34), which refers to the different expectations of both national and transnational audiences. Finally, I comment on how during her European re-phase, Holland has increased her visibility in European screen cultures and strengthened her reputation as a politically engaged filmmaker.

The last chapter, Chapter Seven, examines how Holland's public persona has evolved from politically engaged director working within socialist cinema, through celebrity director embedded within the system of neoliberal democracy, to activist celebrity director advocating for human rights. While discussing this development, I indicate how this transformation of her public persona exemplifies the evolution of film authorship from the Romantic notion of the artist, through the idea of authorial agency conceived as a brand name, to a cultural worker who uses her symbolic capital to call for changes in global and local politics. Throughout her career, Holland has employed various methods and strategies to shape and control her public persona, which I propose to see as Foucauldian 'technologies of the self' (Foucault 1988, 18). Through self-fashioning, the filmmaker is establishing herself as an *auteur*, which is either acknowledged and reinforced, or diminished and erased by other participants in the authorial discourse. In self-fashioning her persona in the early years of her career, Holland consistently gendered it to various degrees, while refusing to be linked with women's cinema or feminism. In the last two decades or so, she has finally embraced feminist agendas and has also evolved from celebrity director into activist celebrity director. To examine how Holland uses various 'technologies of the self', I look at her interviews, appearances in various media, journalistic portrayals of her persona and instances of official recognition she was given throughout her long career to reconstruct her 'as a discursive figure who continually mediates and is mediated by her film, her publicity, and her own public articulations' (Lane 2000, 47). From these mediations the *auteur*-celebrity nexus emerges, with Holland making every possible effort to regulate it.

The final section recapitulates the ways in which Holland has negotiated her authorship in various geopolitical circumstances and versatile sectors of cultural production. While participating in global screen cultures, she has worked with a close circle of friends and relatives, as if trying to counterbalance her status of a travelling filmmaker. During her decades-long career, Holland has established an effective collaborative authorship that can be seen as effectively questioning the masculinist concept of individual *auteur* and the corresponding model of art cinema.

NOTES

1. Holland's work is recognised in companion-type publications that offer a general survey of women's cinema or female filmmakers: *The Women's Companion to International Film* (Kuhn and Radstone 1994); *Women Directors: The Emergence of New Cinema* (Quart 1988); *Women Filmmakers: Refocusing* (Levitin, Plessis and Raoul 2003). *A Lonely Woman* is included in Jane Sloan's *Reel Women: An International Directory of Contemporary Feature Films about Women* (2007). However, her films are rarely subjected to more substantial feminist analysis. To give a few examples of recent publications on women's cinema: in

her book *Women's Cinema, World Cinema*, Patricia White only mentions Holland along with Márta Mészarós as two female filmmakers from socialist countries who made it to the cosmopolitan cohort invited to the Cannes Film Festival (White 2015, 37). Importantly and rather surprisingly, Holland's work is not included in Mark Cousins' cinematic portrayal of female filmmakers, *Women Make Film* (2018).
2. Scholars frequently, and with a kind of delight, use the metaphor of the author as being prematurely 'buried'; for example, in the introduction to the volume *The Global Auteur: The Politics of Authorship in 21st Century Cinema*, Seung-hoon Jeong and Jeremi Szaniawski write: 'The auteur. It has evolved through the decades, has been put to rest by some schools, only to staunchly re-emerge time and again' (Jeong and Szaniawski 2016, 1).
3. The issue of film authorship has been widely examined within film studies, with the first selection of critical writing on it offered in Caughie 1981. For further discussions and reconsiderations, see, for example: Gerstner and Steiger (2003); Wexman (2003); Grant (2008); Jeong and Szaniawski (2016); Elsaesser (2016); Hodsdon (2017).
4. The essay, originally published in 1968, was published in English translation in 1977 in *Image-Music-Text* and reprinted in Caughie 1981. As Caughie explains in his 2008 essay, Barthes 'was reacting against an interpretative criticism, which seeks in the personality of the author the truth of the fiction and the guarantee of the interpretation' (Caughie 2008, 415). For an explanation of the 'anti-auteurist' turn in film studies, see Elsaesser 2016, 21–2.
5. The selection of writings published in *Cahiers du cinéma* is included in Caughie 1981, 38–47.
6. Extracts from Sarris's writings are reprinted in Caughie 1981, 62–7.
7. For discussion of the term 'art cinema' and its ambivalence, see Galt and Schoonover 2010.
8. A useful and concise survey of the evolution of the concept of authorship is provided by Jeong Seung-hoon and Jeremi Szaniawski 2016, 1–20.
9. In their book *The Modern Cinema of Poland*, Bolesław Michałek and Frank Turaj include several chapters presenting the most important cinematic movements in history of Polish cinema and devote four chapters to Polish film *auteurs*: Andrzej Munk, Jerzy Kawalerowicz, Andrzej Wajda and Krzysztof Zanussi (Michałek and Turaj 1988). Likewise, in their pioneering book *The Most Important Art: Soviet and Eastern European Film after 1945*, Mira Liehm and Antonín Liehm structure the section on the Polish Film School around *auteurs* and their films (Liehm and Liehm 1977, 174–198).
10. Already initiated, such revisions have resulted in frequently fascinating reinterpretations of Polish cinema. The collection of essays titled *Popular Cinemas in East Central Europe: Film Cultures and Histories* offers the most comprehensive and systematic revisions of popular Eastern European cinema (Dorota Ostrowska, Pitassio and Varga 2017); for Polish revisions of popular cinema see *Polskie kino popularne* (Zwierzchowski and Mazur 2011).
11. Mariola Jankun-Dopartowa (2000), Sławomir Bobowski (2001) and Katarzyna Mąka-Malatyńska (2009). In addition, a collection of essays on Holland's works has been published in 2012 (Majmurek 2012).
12. The most radical in her judgement is Mariola Jankun-Dopartowa, who claims, 'Both a film scholar and a fan of this [Holland's] cinema is somehow fated to discover that Agnieszka Holland's output is a constantly developing whole [. . .] that gradually reveals an artistic consistency almost impossible to describe' (Jankun-Dopartowa 2000, 13). The author of another monograph, Sławomir Bobowski, claims that all of Holland's films encourage us to search for '[a]uthentic life, based on a search for truth about the world and ourselves' (Bobowski 2001, 6), which he identifies as the main message of her work. Katarzyna Mąka-Malatyńska, author of the most recent monograph about the filmmaker, asserts

that her work develops along two lines: 'Holland's work is sometimes elitist art addressed and accessible to a narrow group of viewers; on the other hand, many of her films address average viewers and are often box-office successes' (Mąka-Malatyńska 2009, 7).
13. International film criticism rarely if ever locates Holland's work within the framework of *auteur* cinema; it mostly addresses her individual films. For example, *Angry Harvest* (1985) and *Europa, Europa* are examined as Holocaust films (see Insdorf 2003); Paul Coates analyses *To Kill a Priest* and *The Third Miracle* (1999) in his book on religion and film (Coates 2003); Emma Wilson offers an astute close reading of *Olivier, Olivier* (1992) in her psychoanalytical discussion of the cultural significance of the motif of missing children in contemporary films (2003); Katarzyna Marciniak examines *A Woman Alone* as contributing to transnational feminism (2005); and finally, *Washington Place* (1997) is an object of consideration in essays and books on filmic adaptations of Henry James's work (see, for example, Griffin 2002; Raw 2006; Rowe 2006, 2023).
14. Not all films identified with the Cinema of Moral Concern represent the model of art cinema, yet they all criticised, more or less explicitly, the socio-political reality of late socialism, and as such were distinguished from popular cinema, which some critics and viewers at that time regarded as political opportunism.
15. As Thomas Elsaesser noted, 'many, if not all, of the directors whom we now regard as auteurs of both national and world cinema [. . .] owe their auteur status, at least initially, to a European film festival' (Elsaesser 2019, 31).
16. I use the term as conceptualised by Pierre Bourdieu (1986).
17. For general discussion of collaboration in creative industries see Graham and Gandini 2017.
18. Carringer's concept of collaborative authorship is employed by Aaron Hunter in his monograph on Hal Ashby (Hunter 2016, 1–12).
19. Kathryn Bigelow's authorship is equally problematic. Carl Sweeney proposes viewing her as the neo-star *auteur* (Sweeney 2021).
20. In her discussion of the evolution of authorship in cinema, Catherine Grant usefully comments on how an author functions as a 'brand name' in mainstream and non-mainstream cinema. Specifically, she uses the example of Third Cinema director Patricio Guzmán (b. 1941) and his 'participation on the "fringes" of *auteurist* commerce, as an "individual" director engaging in many press interviews and in numerous personal appearances at international commercial as well as non-commercial screenings'. These activities, she argues, 'undoubtedly enhanced his continuing ability to make films and to have "his existing films broadcast to television audiences around the world"' (Grant 2000, 104).
21. For a detailed discussion of authorship used in promotional discourse, see Hadas 2020.
22. Caughie made a similar observation: 'Meanwhile, slowly vanishing from academic debate, the auteur appears everywhere else – in publicity, in journalistic reviews, in television programmes, in film retrospectives, in the marketing of cinema. Sometimes around the point at which Film Studies began to be embarrassed by its affiliation to the author, the film industry and its subsidiaries began to discover with renewed enthusiasm the value of authorial branding for both marketing and reputation' (Caughie 2008, 409).
23. In her foundational essay 'Women's Cinema as Counter Cinema', Claire Johnston did not echo the poststructuralist dismissal of the concept of *auteur* but appropriated it for the purposes of a feminist-oriented analysis of cinema. She combined two contradictory concepts of authorship: one that is regulated by unconscious and, therefore, uncontrollable forces, whereas another that stems from the subjective and volitional agency of female filmmakers, which subverts hegemonic codes of patriarchy. Notwithstanding the contradictions of her proposed model of authorship, it proved indispensable for addressing

female subjectivity in cinema (Johnston [1973] 1985). Kaja Silverman likewise insisted on the importance of female authorship, but embraced Barthes' poststructuralist theory, reconceiving it as subjectivity manifested exclusively in the film text (Silverman 1988). Finally, in *The Woman at the Keyhole: Feminism and Women's Cinema*, Judith Mayne openly equated women's cinema with feminist epistemology as manifested through the cinematic form of authorial address (Mayne 1990).

24. As the editors of *The Routledge Companion to Cinema and Gender* note, current research in the field is still significantly influenced by classical film theory (Hole et al. 2017, 2).
25. The most recent research on women's cinema works towards expanding the concept, while simultaneously pondering its currency and legitimacy. Patricia White asked whether women's cinema should be defined according to the criteria of authorship (films made by women) or content (films about women): 'Is it defined by that feminist "essence" (the cinema that reflects women's sensibilities), feminist activism (the cinema women make by and for themselves), or postfeminist consumption (the market for chick flicks)?' (White 2015, 8–9). Similarly, Ivone Margulies and Jeremi Szaniawski, editors of the 2019 collection of essays on female filmmakers, ask a provocative question: 'Does it even make sense, in our current global context, to gather a series of films under the label "women's films"? Is there specific valence to an assessment of a work defined by the gender of its author?' (2019, 1). Despite these uncertainties, the content of the volume *On Women's Films: Across Worlds and Generations* provides an affirmative answer to these questions, as demonstrated by the selection of the 'filmmakers associated with a personal idiosyncratic cinema over distinct film generations and discursive moments' (Margulies and Szaniawski 2019, 2). Acknowledgement of the ambivalence of the concept of women's cinema frequently goes along with its firm association with personal art cinema. Likewise, Sue Thornham proposes to use the inclusive category of 'women's cinema' in relation 'to films made – directed, and with a visible signature – *by* women', while implicitly linking it with art cinema (Thornham 2019, 1). However, current research in the field goes beyond textual analysis as it 'must be supplemented by consideration and theorization of institutional questions – of production, distribution, exhibition, and reception' (White 2015, 13). For example, Lucy Bolton noted the limitations of using women as a theoretical category and proposed that instead of sexual difference, which was a key notion for early feminist film theory, individual texts should be positioned 'within the contexts of their social, economic, cultural and national production, as a theoretical analysis of intra-textual mechanics' (Bolton 2011, 20). Finally, White's research on women's cinema operating within transnational/global cinema recognised women's cinema's problematic relationship with feminisms. Specifically, she acknowledged that, in the era of post-feminism, women's cinema was most frequently linked with popular Western chick-flick movies, whereas films advocating for female agencies were usually located within postcolonial cinemas and cultures (White 2015, 4).
26. Her list includes: Chantal Akerman, Maryse Alberti, Gillian Armstrong, Beth B., Rakhshan Bani-Etemad, Kathryn Bigelow, Antonia Bird, Jane Campion, Gurinder Chadha, Martha Coolidge, Busi Cortés, Julie Dash, Claire Denis, Doris Dörrie, Su Friedrich, Bette Gordon, Marleen Gorris, Leslie Harris, Mona Hartoum, Amy Heckerling, Agnieszka Holland, Ann Hui, Barbara Kopple, Diane Kurys, Clara Law, Deepa Mehta, Márta Mészáros, Trinh T. Minh-ha, Tracey Moffatt, Mira Nair, Maria Novaro, Ulrike Ottinger, Euzhan Palcy, Pratibha Parmar, Lourdes Portillo, Sally Potter, Dana Rotberg, Patricia Rozema, Valeria Sarmiento, Guita Schyfter, Marisa Sistach, Moufida Tlatli, Monika Treut, Margarethe von Trotta and Tizuka Yamasaki (McHugh 2009, 120–1).
27. Female filmmakers of a younger generation are also sceptical about being identified with the category of 'women's cinema'. Kate Ince noted 'Hansen-Løve's own ambivalence

towards the significance of her gender as a factor in her filmmaking: this is an issue on which she has sometimes commented, but in a distinctly non-committal fashion' (Ince 2021, 9).
28. In her analysis of *The Other Lamb* (2019) by Polish filmmaker Małgorzata Szumowska, Aga Skrodzka emphasises the importance of the *metteur en scène* persona: 'In World Cinema, the *metteur en scène* role of the director is essential, and arguably often exceeds the *auteur* function, as the film must project a comprehensive, lasting, and immersive place that resonates an autonomy' (Skrodzka 2021, 181). Furthermore, she proposes 'theoretical connections between the female director, the *metteuse en scène*, and the feminist as the de-monstrator' (182).
29. I borrow the terms from John Caldwell, who examines film and media production not only in terms of economic strategies but also as a set of practices involving various social rituals and cultural practices (Caldwell 2008).
30. The communist genealogy of post-Second World War Polish feminism has remained unrecognised for a long time if not altogether suppressed. Only recently have female researchers of the younger generation undertaken the task of recovering this part of Polish women's history (Fidelis 2010; Mrozik 2022), thereby making an important intervention in the field. As Skrodzka claims, communist female agency 'threatens not only to deconstruct the consecrated national myths but also to circumvent the claims of Western style feminism [. . .], identity politics, and liberal democratic ideas of gender equality' (Skrodzka 2020, 673).
31. Holland expressed this attitude many times; for example, in the interview given to the *Kurier Polski*: 'I've never made women's cinema in terms of expressing a female point of view' (Agnieszka Holland, 'Na zamówienie: Agnieszka Holland', interview by Kazimierz Sobolewski, *Kurier Polski* 1989, no. 127, 2). However, she acknowledged the difficulties a female filmmaker needed to overcome that were mostly connected with her female duties: 'All women need to reconcile their professional career with their destiny to be a wife and a mother' (Agnieszka Holland, 'Emancypacja? Coś jest nie tak', interview by Jerzy Pawlas, *Echo Dnia* 1978, no. 141, 4).
32. 'Świat widziany oczami węgierskich reżyserek', trans. Agnieszka Holland, *Film na świecie* 1976, no. 7, 89–92; the original article was published in *Film a Doba* 1976, no. 2.
33. Inderpal Grewal and Caren Kaplan in their seminal essay originally published in 1994 advocated relating issues of feminism to 'scattered hegemonies such as global economic structures, patriarchal nationalisms, "authentic" forms of tradition, local structures of domination and legal-juridical oppression on multiple levels' (2003, 17). Ella Shohat proposed to replace the concept of post-colonial with the term post-Third-Worldism. She identified: 'post-Third-Worldist film culture as a critique simultaneously of Third-Worldist anticolonial nationalism and of First-World Eurocentric feminism. Challenging white feminist film theory and practice that emerged in a major way in the 1970s in First-World metropolises, post-Third-Worldist feminist works have refused a Eurocentric universalizing of "womanhood", and even of "feminism"' (Shohat 1997, 184). Bolton commented on how postcolonial intervention affected analytical strategies: 'Post-colonial theory has given prominence to black women in film and as spectators. [. . .] The approach to film-production and consumption has therefore evolved [. . .] and become as much a question of situating individual texts within the contexts of their social, economic, cultural, and national production, as a theoretical analysis of intra-textual mechanics' (Bolton 2011, 20).
34. One of the first calls to include the Second World in transnational feminism was made by Marciniak in her article on Holland's film *A Woman Alone*. She recalls the graduate seminar 'Transnational Feminist Practice' that she designed and taught at Ohio University in 2003.

As she reports, while assigning readings for the course, she could find no theoretical texts discussing Second World women's feminist practice. Not one even mentioned Second World women. Marciniak saw the absence as a sign of the urgent need to 'expand the scope of transnational feminist studies, to stretch its parameters, so that the voices and perspectives from the Second World may find their way into the field that many consider a radical and indispensable direction for feminist studies' (Marciniak 2005, 4). As she noted later, transnational feminism had not yet covered the areas of media and film (Marciniak, Imre and O'Healy 2007, 10). Although the collection of essays titled *Transnational Feminism in Film and Media* is a significant milestone in the field, the task of amplifying transnational feminism adequately in relation to Eastern Europe remains.

35. For example, the books *Transnational Cinema: The Film Reader* (edited by Elizabeth Ezra and Terry Rowden, Routledge, 2006) and *World Cinemas: Transnational Perspectives* (edited by Nataša Ďurovičová and Kathleen Newman, Routledge, 2010) ignore Holland's oeuvre, whereas Hamid Naficy's *An Accented Cinema: Exilic and Diasporic Filmmaking* (2001) mentions it, but only briefly. I used the framework of transnational cinema as it is discussed here to examine Holland's cinema (Ostrowska 2014).

36. Naficy's concept of 'accented cinema' served as a point of departure for many scholars who explored the cultural production occurring beyond the framework of national cinemas (Shohat and Stam 2003; Berghahn and Sternberg 2010; Ballestros 2015), while embedding it mostly in a postcolonial context.

37. *The Green Border* (*Zielona granica*, 2023) is Holland's first film that focuses on the issue of migration.

38. Gordana Crnković identifies Holland's works as cosmopolitan, but her understanding of the concept fits Hjort's 'marked' and *auteurist* transnationality (Crnković 2004).

39. The category of 'sojourner cinema' is analogous to Hjort's concept of cosmopolitan and unmarked transnationality.

40. In their work, travelling filmmakers mobilise the constant flow of exchanges between cultural and economic capital. For example, as Catherine Grant points out, some Latin American filmmakers whose films made their names recognisable outside of the region worked with producers and distributors 'who have ceaselessly capitalized on those names. They have collaborated fully with contemporary commercial-auteurist practices, fronting the marketing of their movies, allowing themselves repeatedly to be interviewed and profiled in the international media, and thus securing coproduction and other international funding tied to television and video distribution deals, in addition to any available state patronage' (Grant 2000, 105).

41. For a useful discussion of how the Romantic concept of authorship has been appropriated by the film industry and transformed into a 'brand name', see Grant 2001, 114.

42. Gallagher's monograph on Soderbergh makes a similar observation: 'Filmmakers from around the world repeatedly use reputations acquired in the international art cinema as calling cards for transit to Hollywood studio filmmaking' (Gallagher 2013, 92).

CHAPTER I

Early years: pains and joys

'I think it's certainly good for my work to have some extreme life experiences', Holland said in an interview (Crnković and Holland 1998–9, 5). She saw a link between her biography and her work, something for which she would surely be reprimanded by Roland Barthes, who, in 1968, with his fellow poststructuralists, proclaimed 'the death of the author'.[1] Since the poststructuralist turn, scholars have pointedly ignored artists' biographies or approached them as a discursive construct.[2] David Bordwell's concept of the 'biographical legend' exemplifies this ambivalent perspective on the issue. He argued that: '[t]he biographical individual is indispensable to the history of the cinema', while also emphasising that '[t]he artist's relation to the work is always socially mediated' (Bordwell 1988, 5). In his monograph on Yasujiro Ozu, he adopted Boris Tomashevsky's concept of the 'biographical legend' as potentially an important factor regulating the textual and formal strategies of cinematic works (Bordwell 1988, 5–6). However, as he claimed, not all filmmakers should be subjected to 'biographical' analysis as some of them, for example Ingmar Bergman, have biographies, while others don't (5). This figurative statement refers to the fact that not every filmmaker's life story has the potential to make them a 'biographical legend' (6). In today's world of social media and the proliferation of various digital platforms of communication, the means of constructing 'biographical legends' are greater than before. As will be analysed here, Holland voluntarily contributes to her 'biographical legend', while simultaneously controlling her public persona by careful selection of the information to be publicised. At various stages of her professional career, she has emphasised specific moments in her biography in order to authenticate, contextualise or personalise her then current projects. Arguably, in some of her films a 'fictional-biographical overlap' (Erhart 2019, 68) can be noticed in both the narratives and imagery.[3]

Bordwell's efforts to incorporate (some) filmmakers' biographies in his analyses of cinematic production were followed in the twenty-first century by further attempts to examine the relationship between real-life directors and their work. This change was facilitated by the turn towards cultural studies and identity politics in film and media studies. Thus, after a poststructuralist hibernation, the author has resurfaced, while critics have acknowledged that 'media products are not only produced by discourses and ideologies, but also by individuals of flesh and blood' (Grodal, Larsen and Laursen 2005, 7). Sarah Kozloff was the most radical in her claim to include filmmakers' biographies in the study of authorship. She advocated for examining of 'how the filmmakers' biographies, intentions and agency combine with [. . .] larger social structures that influence the text' (Kozloff 2014). Feminist critics acknowledged the importance of female filmmakers' biographies much earlier; as Catherine Grant noted:

> women's agency [. . .] after decades of embarrassed deconstruction, [is] finally to be subjected to analysis in the form of its textual, bio-*graphical* traces, alongside more conventionally 'legitimate' activities for feminist cultural theorists, such as applying theories to 'primary' literary and film texts in formal 'readings'. (Grant 2001, 123)[4]

Throughout this book, I will use Holland's biography (or her 'biographical legend') as an important context of her authorship as it manifests in the textualities of her work and her activities in the system of cultural production. Her professional career trajectory that has crossed over various screen cultures has been determined by her personal history and the collective histories of communities she has belonged to. I argue that the generic and aesthetic versatility of her work – that has sometimes been viewed as inconsistency and has been used to prevent her from being admitted to the traditional elitist *auteurist* club – can better be viewed as resulting from her life journey which has followed anything but a linear and progressive line. To theorise these biographical diversions, I will adopt Gilles Deleuze's concept of lifelines. He introduced this in a conversation with the French journalist Claire Parnet: 'Whether we are individuals or groups, we are made up of lines and these lines are very varied in nature' (Deleuze and Parnet 2007, 124). As he further explains, the first line divides itself into separate segments that are distinguishable by clear oppositions, such as: family life versus professional life, work time versus vacation time, being a child versus being an adult. This line – that he later called a 'molar line' or 'break line' (Deleuze and Guattari 2019, 234) – cannot be seen as a linear sequence of stages because the movements of these segments occur 'in all kinds of directions' (Deleuze and Parnet 2007, 124). The molar line develops in a chronological progression, yet it is not linear as it involves binary oppositions through which it manoeuvres. Deleuze calls them 'binary machines' (128) and claims they operate diachronically, which means that if one is neither A nor B, then it is C which mobilises another 'binary machine' (128). Thus, the molar line conveys a primary form, or desire, for the organisation of a life trajectory into clearly discernible segments that can be assembled into an orderly configuration.

The 'molecular line', as Deleuze explains, marks segments of a differing nature as they are not clearly discernible and emerge as 'blocs of becoming' and 'combinations of fluxes' (130). They are constantly changing and mutating over some thresholds that are crossed. As Deleuze explains, 'the molecular lines make fluxes of deterritorialization shoot between the segments, fluxes which no longer belong to one or to the other' (131). He connects these lines with complex yet often imperceptible processes of becoming that are not necessarily marked by the segmentation of the 'molar line'. They indicate changes where these are not expected to be found. He compares the molecular line to a plate that cracks; often these cracks are imperceptible, yet they are there leading up to it being broken up. These cracks are

> secret, imperceptible, marking a threshold of lowered resistance, or the rise of a threshold of exigency: you can no longer stand what you put up with before, even yesterday; the distribution of desires has changed in us, our relationships of speed and slowness have been modified, a new type of anxiety comes upon us, but also a new serenity. (Deleuze and Parnet 2007, 126)

Importantly, these cracks are not conceived as necessarily negative changes as 'things go better for you when everything cracks on the other line, producing immense relief' (126). Thus, the crack line may lead to destruction but also progression. It rather involves the constant 'movements of deterritorialization and the processes of reterritorialization' (134).

Finally, there is 'the line of flight' that Deleuze sees 'as if something carried us away, across our segments, but also across our thresholds, towards a destination which is unknown, not foreseeable, not pre-existent' (Deleuze and Parnet 2007, 125). The 'line of flight' emerges in a vivid form, but not in every person's life, as its mobilisation occurs only through an act of detachment from the molecular and molar lines. According to Deleuze, these three lines co-exist in the same temporality and 'the line of flight' conditions all changes to emerge. While concluding his reflections on the lifelines, Deleuze describes '[t]hree lines, one of which would be like the nomadic line, another migrant and the third sedentary (the migrant is not at all the same as the nomadic)' (Deleuze and Parnet 2007, 136).

However problematic it may be to apply Deleuze's theories to the recording of actual individual lives, I argue that these are useful in conceptualising life narratives that resist linearity. Specifically, they help to map out the complexity of the long-lasting and complex trajectory of Holland's personal and professional life, with its breaks, returns and detours that challenge any single categorisation of her work as transnational, migrant or nomadic cinema. The first years of her life until leaving for Czechoslovakia to study at FAMU (The Film and TV School of the Academy of Performing Arts in Prague) can be seen as constituting the 'molar line', yet as I will soon explain, certain events and circumstances of her childhood and youth can be seen as mobilising the 'crack line' that eventually converged with the 'line of flight' towards new subjectivities and sociopolitical territories.

In what follows I discuss Holland's early biography, her childhood and youth, focusing on the moments or experiences she would later present as nodal points determining her personal and professional life trajectory. Given Holland's closeness to her mother, I will briefly describe the background of gender politics in post-Second World War socialist Poland. I will also address two potentially traumatic events in Holland's childhood and youth as these affected her future life, albeit indirectly. Special attention will be given to her youthful cinephilia, which will be discussed in the context of socialist film culture and her later decision to study film in Czechoslovakia at FAMU. The final sections of the chapter examine her film education and her political activity during the time she spent in Prague. Her personal story will be cast against larger historical processes, specifically the events of the 1968 Polish political crisis, known in Poland as March '68, and the Prague Spring, as these affected many of her future professional decisions. Thus, while not aiming at a complete presentation of Holland's early biography, I zoom in on the experiences that contextualise her work within the histories of Eastern European countries and movements. Finally, I present a close reading of her student diploma film, *Jesus Christ's Sin* (*Hřích boha*, 1969), as it marks her first foray into the realm of transnational (Eastern European) screen cultures. The main aim of the chapter is to bring to light the complex nexus of Holland's individual life experiences, politics and cultural production.

IN THE SHADOW OF THE (ABSENT) FATHER

Agnieszka Holland was born on 28 November 1948 in Warsaw to a Polish mother, Irena Rybczyńska-Holland, and a Jewish Polish father, Henryk Holland, both of whom were journalists, and for some time members of the Communist Party.[5] As atheists, they brought up Agnieszka[6] and her younger sister, Magdalena,[7] outside of any religion and the attendant rituals. Yet the siblings participated in the traditional Polish Catholic celebrations such as Christmas and Easter at their maternal grandmother's house. Their grandmother also took care of their religious education. In her early childhood, Agnieszka was unaware of her mixed ethnic identity until – to her astonishment – one of her friends stopped playing with her, explaining that she did not

Figure 1.1 Agnieszka Holland with her parents (Agnieszka Holland's family archive)

want to deal with an unbaptised person. Although her mother did not provide Agnieszka with a detailed knowledge of the history of her Jewish family from her father's side, she insisted her daughter be proud of her origins (Pasternak 2022, 321). Agnieszka did not learn about her Jewish family from her father either. He divorced her mother when she was only nine years old, and soon died in mysterious circumstances. Years later, Agnieszka found out that his family had perished in the Holocaust. His sister and he were the only survivors (Preizner 2012, 366; see also Persak 2006, 135).[8]

After 1945, Henryk Holland vehemently supported the Polish Communist Party, and harshly criticised its opponents. After the October Thaw in 1956, he joined the revisionist circles in the Party, while also befriending many foreign journalists from the Western European countries to which he occasionally travelled. In November 1961, he received unofficial information concerning Nikita Khrushchev's 'Secret Speech' denouncing Stalin's political persecutions.[9] Holland passed on the news in a phone conversation to *Le Monde* journalist Jean Wetz, who published an article on the subject. The conversation was surveilled and recorded by the communist secret service which soon identified Holland's voice and arrested him on 21 December 1961. During the search of his apartment, he jumped out of the window. At the time of her father's death, Agnieszka was at a youth camp and learned about it by accident from her friend, who read about it in a newspaper. For years his death was an object of speculation; some believed that the functionaries murdered him, while others claimed it was a fatal accident. His funeral at the Powązki Cemetery in Warsaw was attended by many significant figures representing intellectual elites, such as Zygmunt Bauman, Leszek Kołakowski and Oskar Lange.[10] The communist authorities considered participation in the funeral as a political demonstration of discontent with the system. Agnieszka did not take part in the funeral, and for many years she did not know whether her father's death was suicide, a political murder or an accident. Finally, on the basis of the archival sources (the recorded conversations at Henryk Holland's apartment during its search), the historian Krzysztof Persak proved it was suicide (2006). Nevertheless, Agnieszka would never have learned about her father's motives for this desperate gesture.

Initially, especially in her 1970s interviews, Holland held back from mentioning her father, however, she was implicated in the kind of legend that was established around his mysterious death. As Henryk Holland's daughter, she was a recognisable figure for both the representatives of the regime, for whom she became a 'usual suspect', and for their opponents, for whom she was seen as a victim of the situation. Arguably, her father's mysterious death stigmatised her, while also affecting her professional career in both negative and positive way as, on the one hand, it obstructed it, but, on the other hand, it located her within the dissident circles.[11] On the more personal level, her absence from her father's funeral may have disturbed the process of mourning and possibly postponed its completion. Likewise, her belated recognition of her Jewish origins and the death of her relatives in the Holocaust may have resulted in a 'biographical displacement'. Recently, Holland made another amendment to her publicly known life story. The newly published biography reports her being sexually abused in her youth by a family friend over many years until she left to study in Prague (Pasternak 2022, 155–67).[12] Admittedly, Holland's early personal history consists of non-reported (her mother not speaking of the death of her father and her not reporting her sexual abuse) and non-memorised events (the perishing of her father's family in the Holocaust), that can be seen as establishing Deleuzian 'micro-cracks, as in a dish [. . .] subtle and supple [. . .] [that] *occur when things are going well on the other side*' (Deleuze and Guattari 2019, 233; emphasis in the original). And things were going well for Holland 'on the other side'.

FAMILY LIFE AND ADOLESCENT FASCINATION: SOCIALISM (DE)ACTIVATED

As difficult as it was to cope with her parents' divorce and the mysterious death of her father, Agnieszka – as she reported on various occasions years later – was enjoying a happy life with her mother and her mother's second husband, also a journalist, Stanisław Brodzki, a graduate of the University of Geneva, who started his professional career during the Second World War. As Agnieszka recollected, her family home was frequented by communist-oriented intellectuals, journalists and artists who engaged in endless political debates on the situation in Poland and the rest of the world. Years later, Agnieszka would describe it as a Chekhovian home.[13] In her memories of childhood and youth, her mother, Irena Rybczyńska-Holland, occupies centre stage.[14] Continuing her family tradition of strong and independent women, she fought in the Warsaw Uprising as a member of the anti-communist Home Army. After the Second World War, she began her studies in the Journalism Department at the University of Warsaw, while becoming a supporter of the new political doctrine. Then she pursued a robust journalistic career, being appointed, among others, as a chief editor of the communist periodical *New Village* (*Nowa Wieś*), the aim of which was to educate the inhabitants of the Polish countryside to transform them from peasants into members of the modern working class. In 1968, she did not support the anti-Semitic campaign and consequently she lost her erstwhile high position. From 1970 she worked for the women's magazine *You and Me* (*Ty i Ja*)[15] that was exceptional in the socialist press market in that it mostly published non-ideologically charged material devoted to fashion, cooking, art and interior design.[16] It addressed the non-fulfilled consumerist aspirations of a Polish society living under socialism. Leaving aside the ideological agendas of the magazines Rybczyńska-Holland worked for, she was a successful, professionally active woman who was able to have a fulfilling family life (which admittedly was rather turbulent initially due to her divorce and her first husband's death). This thriving professional and family life might not have been possible without the help she was receiving from a live-in housekeeper who babysat the girls and performed various domestic chores.[17] The support she was receiving from her employee (who was treated as a member of the family rather than a domestic worker) did not interfere with Irena Rybczyńska-Holland's image of a modern woman. Admittedly, she was not a helpless victim of patriarchy or socialist authoritarianism. While her privileged situation was rather exceptional compared to the majority of Polish women who lacked a similar cultural, economic and social capital, for both her daughters, Rybczyńska-Holland represented the model of femininity that was associated with emancipation rather than oppression. She has retained a strong position in her family, as noted by her grand-daughter, Gabrysia Łazarkiewicz-Sieczko: 'Strong women are the foundation of our family and Granny Renia [Irena] is a queen of this clan' (Pasternak 2022, 43).[18]

Due to her parents' robust professional and social life, Agnieszka spent much of her time entertaining herself, mostly by reading. With the chronic illness she suffered as a child, it was the only available form of entertainment. In a relatively short time, she became acquainted with many of the world literary classics. Her cultural education was also extended by her father, with whom she occasionally attended opening nights in Warsaw theatres, art exhibitions and film screenings. Her parents facilitated her sound and wide-ranging cultural education which she later continued in a more liberal fashion. Despite her atheist upbringing (or perhaps because of it), the teenage Agnieszka experienced a strong fascination with Catholicism. She secretly participated in holy masses and religious lessons and was eventually baptised by a friend, as the priest refused to. Learning from another female friend about her mystical experiences after receiving Holy Communion, she decided to take it as well. When her friend saw this, she called it a blasphemous act that would be punished with death. Terrified, Agnieszka spat it out (Holland and Kornatowska 2012, 73). This was her last attempt to join organised religion, yet this youthful fascination with religion can be seen echoed in the films she made in the 1990s and 2000s.

Another example of Agnieszka's youthful independence was her decision to transfer from a girls' high school to a co-educational one. This may be seen as a desire to experience a less restrictive model of education. During the years she spent in the high school, Agnieszka was an avid cinema buff. As she recalled, she occasionally played truant to attend screenings in cine-clubs. Sometimes she watched four films daily. During that time, she discovered the films of the Czechoslovak New Wave, which she appreciated for their realism and irony. Simultaneously, she admired Robert Bresson and films by Ingmar Bergman, Federico Fellini, Akira Kurosawa and Andrei Tarkovsky. Holland's juvenile cinephilia, whose object was foreign rather than vernacular cinema, can be seen as forming another Deleuzian 'crack line' in her biography as it slowly yet consistently saw her progress from the national to the transnational film culture emerging in the 1960s in Europe.

In Poland in the late 1960s, the cine-clubs that Holland frequented played a more complex role than they did in Western Europe, for example, in France. At that time Polish cinema was subjected to tight control under authorities that requested filmic affirmation of the achievements of state socialism. The cultural production of the decade was called 'small stabilization' after the title of Tadeusz Różewicz's play *Witnesses, or Our Small Stabilization* (*Świadkowie albo nasza mała stabilizacja*, 1964). Polish filmmakers responded in various ways to this cultural policy; some made 'safe' but also often escapist adaptations of Polish classical literature,[19] whereas others obediently followed the political guidance and started making films glorifying Polish war heroism and the achievements of the 'new' Poland. Finally, there were a few who searched for the possibilities of making films abroad.[20] Because of the general mediocrity of Polish film production, Polish audiences preferred imported entertainment to vernacular films with their propagandistic messages. As Marek Haltof writes, 'the most popular fare among Polish audiences remained commercially oriented productions, for example, *Vinnetou* (1964–65, Harald Reinl), released in 1968 (4.7 million viewers), and *Cleopatra* (1963, Joseph L. Mankiewicz), which premiered in 1970 (5.7 million viewers)' (Haltof 2002, 111). It is difficult to imagine a bigger contrast between this cinematic universe populated by ancient beauties, Indian heroes and home-grown knights and the realistically depicted world with a flair of surrealism of Czechoslovakia that was celebrated with tenderness by the New Wave filmmakers whom Holland was fascinated with.

Unlike the Polish films of 'small stabilization' and the imported entertainment exhibited in regular cinemas, the Czechoslovak and other European New Wave films were distributed through the nationwide network of cine-clubs (DKF). The cine-clubs received state subsidies, yet they functioned as relatively independent and mostly democratically managed institutions. A special network of cinemas whose repertoire consisted exclusively of arthouse production (*kina studyjne*)[21] complemented cine-clubs as an alternative channel of film distribution and exhibition. The official state distribution agency, the Repertoire Council [Rada Repertuarowa], made special purchases of films to be distributed in these cinemas only (Koniczek 1994, 488).[22] This 'limited distribution' concerned not only art cinema but also films that were 'suspicious' for political reasons (Koniczek 1994, 488). As Ryszard Koniczek noted, this 'limited distribution' restricted the possibility for many people to see these films, while maintaining the illusion of a liberal cultural policy (448).[23] Cinephilia flourished in this alternative cultural space, extending the limits of the socialist cultural politics.

As the case of alternative networks of film distribution and exhibition demonstrates, the geopolitical division of Cold War Europe was negotiated on the level of cultural production and consumption.[24] The numerous Polish cine-clubs that presented a wide selection of Western European art cinema functioned as a symbolic bridge over the Berlin Wall. Cinephilia linked Holland with the tradition of European art cinema,[25] while her subsequent decision to study abroad implicitly connected her with female travelling filmmakers who also started their artistic peregrinations around that time[26]: in 1967, Agnès Varda left France for New York, while in 1971, Chantal Akerman left Brussels for the same destination. Ultimately, through her juvenile cinephilia, Holland symbolically distanced herself from vernacular cinema. Thomas Elsaesser noted the de-territorialising aspects of cinephilia which he described as 'always already caught in several kinds of deferral: a detour in place and space, a shift in register and a delay in time' (Elsaesser 2005, 30). Holland's cinephilia initiated her journey across transnational screen cultures.

AT FAMU: ALIENATION, INTEGRATION AND LOVE

Cinephilia, especially Holland's fascination with the Czechoslovak New Wave, was one of the reasons why she decided to study at FAMU. Unlike her older and prominent colleagues such as Wojciech Has, Andrzej Wajda and Krzysztof Zanussi who initially did not want to be filmmakers, she was certain about her future profession: 'I knew then that I did not want to study anything else but film' (Zawiśliński 1995, 18; Czerkawski 2019, 156).[27] However, at that time, one of the requirements for admission to the directing department of the Łódź Film School was a degree obtained from another faculty, but she did not want to waste her time studying something that would not be interesting to her. Moreover, when her mother used her informal social networks to make enquiries about her daughter's chances of being admitted to the film school, she learned that, due to the suspicions surrounding her father's death, she would not be welcomed there. Thus, to a certain extent, Agnieszka was forced to take an alternative route to pursue her film education. Her decision to study in Czechoslovakia can be seen as both her first 'informal' exile and the beginning of her nomadic life.

Holland began her study at FAMU on 15 September 1966. Among the admitted students, there was one Slovak, Laco Adamik – her future husband – and two Czech students; the rest were mostly from other Eastern European countries. She started her film education in truly international company. Among her teachers were Milan Kundera, Elmar Klos and Otakar Vávra. Notwithstanding the symbolic importance of Holland's decision to study in Prague, the film training provided by FAMU was not that different from what was offered in the Łódź Film School.[28] In both the Polish film school and FAMU, 'the curriculum combined the study of literature and art with theory and practice' (Hames 2013, 217). As Duncan Petrie notes, 'these film schools enshrined a vibrant environment in which the intellectual dimension of a filmmaker's education continued to be stressed in conjunction with the acquisition of practical skills' (Petrie 2010, 36). Both schools represented 'the European conservatory model' as opposed to the technical training model of education dominating in the US (Petrie 2010, 40).[29] In the 1960s, the most prosperous decade in history of FAMU, 'the school openly cultivated the cinéma d'auteur' (Dvořáková 2021, 521).[30] Some film *auteurs* such as Vittorio de Sica and Vsevelod Pudovkin occasionally delivered guest lectures. The works of other *auteurs* – including those whose films were not purchased for regular distribution, such as Antonioni, Fellini, Godard, Malle, Buñuel, Dovzhenko and Eisenstein – were screened to the students who thus had an opportunity to get acquainted with the international history of cinema. As mentioned, the school was well attended by many students from abroad; it was especially popular with the aspiring filmmakers from the former Yugoslavia: Aleksandar Petrović, Rajko Grlić, Srdjan Karanović, Emir Kusturica, Goran Marković, Goran Paskaljević and Lordan Zafranović (Hames 2013, 217). However, only three women – compared to thirty-eight men – graduated from FAMU in the 1960s: Věra Chytilová, Angelika Hanauerová – who did not pursue her professional career due to political reasons – and Agnieszka Holland (Dvořáková 2021, 518).

Figure 1.2 Agnieszka Holland on the set of her student film at FAMU (Agnieszka Holland's family archive)

Upon her arrival in Prague, Holland felt estranged: 'It is a bit like in prison here. Or simply like abroad. One needs to learn how to live here. One needs to learn how to be independent. And how to be lonely', she wrote in her letter to her aunt Hanna Bielawska-Adamik, dated November 1966, which was shortly after she had arrived in Prague (Pasternak 2022, 17). In 1968, she decided to marry Slovak Laco Adamik, her fellow student. Her mother could not attend the ceremony, and Holland reports that the wedding was celebrated by their friends only. After years of co-habitation in various places, they finally settled down in a small apartment. It is worth noting that she did not take her husband's name but stayed with the 'politically suspicious' name of her father, a small detail, yet important when seen in the context of her future biography.

Although Holland's leaving Poland for Prague can be seen as a new segment on the Deleuzian 'molar line', it initiated a 'crack line' in that it smoothly yet persistently 'ungrounded' her from the structures of vernacular culture. First and foremost, she did not participate in the political events of March '68 in Poland that represented a generational experience. To explain it briefly, in the late 1960s, a political fraction led by General Mieczysław Moczar aggressively promoted the nationalist variant of socialism aimed at 'cleansing' Poland from 'alien' elements. According to Norman Davies, '[the] campaign [. . .] had covertly anti-Soviet as well as overtly anti-Semitic overtones' (Davies 2001, 325).

The Polish intelligentsia and students vehemently protested this eruption of xenophobia and populist nationalism. The students' revolt was set off by the censor's ban on the performance of Adam Mickiewicz's romantic drama *Forefathers' Eve* (*Dziady* 1968, Teatr Polski, Warsaw, directed by Kazimierz Dejmek) on the grounds of its anti-Russian, and therefore also anti-Soviet, message. Without workers' support, though, the protest was doomed to failure. Nevertheless, Moczar's aspirations to seize power failed, and in April 1968, General Wojciech Jaruzelski was appointed as a new pro-Soviet head of the military forces. Soon, Poland joined the Warsaw Pact forces in suppressing the Prague Spring. Holland neither participated in nor witnessed the events of 1968 in Poland. Although she marched together with her Polish fellow students to the Polish Embassy in Prague to deliver a protest letter addressed to the PZPR (Polish United Workers Party) against the anti-Semitic campaign, she did not have direct experience of the generation-defining events of March '68 in Poland. As the historian Marcin Zaremba explains:

> It created a distinct generational community with March '68 as its formative experience. This shared March experience translated into political and aesthetic choices and contributed to the creation of a network of strong ties. [. . .] For many in the Polish intelligentsia, the Solidarity revolution was a continuation of March '68, and the Solidarity strikes of 1980 were a culmination of the student strikes of 1968. To this day, people of the March generation continue to play an important role as public intellectuals. (Zaremba 2018, 772)

In 1968, Holland participated – reluctantly at first – in the Prague Spring. As she admits, initially she was rather indifferent to the political unrest in Czechoslovakia, yet she was captivated by the aesthetic ferment that accompanied it, especially the revival of theatre life and the flourishing of avant-garde art (see Czerkawski 2019, 147). If her Polish fellows were exposed to the negative social effects of hatred towards Jews and mutual distrust between the intelligentsia and the workers, Holland experienced, or rather observed, national unity among the Czechoslovak citizens in their massive call for political change. As Kristina Andělová argues, although the Czechoslovak generation of 1968 was polarised,[31] its participation in the Prague Spring was a common formative experience: 'many of the key political figures who formulated liberal non-communist critiques in 1968 later – that is, 20 years later, in 1989 – became prominent exponents of the Velvet Revolution, most importantly the "two Václavs": Václav Havel and Václav Klaus' (Andělová 2019, 896). Holland joined her Czechoslovak fellows in the students' strike, yet she never engaged in political activity outside of academic circles.

During the Prague Spring and its aftermath, Holland, along with her fellow Polish students at FAMU, was subjected to the surveillance of the Polish secret service. The secret agent working under the operative name 'Paweł Kański' reported that the students established contacts with the Western media and that they were participating in anti-Polish protests; there was also a note that they all were of Jewish origins (Pasternak 2022, 38). When, in December 1968, the students went to Poland for Christmas, the Polish border officers confiscated their travel documents, which made their return to Prague impossible. After three months, during which their parents and relatives used their social networks to solve the problem, the travel documents were returned to them. Back in Prague, Holland and her Polish friends were still subjected to surveillance by the Polish and Czechoslovak security services, though Holland was not aware of this. Thus, when, in May 1969, Maria Tworkowska and Maciej Kozłowski, two couriers of the Parisian *Culture* (*Kultura*) – the most important centre of Polish émigré life – came to Prague to ask her for help to make some copies of samizdat publications to be smuggled to Poland, she agreed without much hesitation. Unfortunately, the couriers were caught at the Polish border, and at their subsequent trial, they denounced Holland as their helper in Prague. Consequently, she was arrested and spent a month in the Prague prison. As she recollected, she talked to the investigative officer about Simone Weil, while on her daily walks she sang revolutionary songs (Holland and Kornatowska 2012, 116). Although she was released from the prison after four weeks, the trial in Prague lasted until 1971. The Polish secret services surveilled her until the end of the 1980s.

Despite her political engagement, Holland's direct participation in the Polish and Czechoslovak formative generational experiences was, so to say, lacking. She remained outside the larger collective bodies of both Polish and Czechoslovak communities, and from this outsider's position she came to a pessimistic conclusion concerning collective political subjectivity. As she has frequently admitted, after the military intervention of the Warsaw Pact forces, including Polish troops, in Prague and the subsequent period of 'normalisation', she lost her faith in the possibility of genuine revolution and social change (Holland and Kornatowska 2012, 172). Disappointed with the passivity and opportunism of Czechoslovak society during the period of 'normalisation', in 1971, Holland and her husband, Laco Adamik, decided to leave Prague for Poland. However, as it soon transpired, for her it was only a temporary stop on the nomadic journeys she had already begun.

JESUS CHRIST'S SIN (*HRÍCH BOHA*): START OF AN INTERNATIONAL JOURNEY

Before returning to Poland, Holland completed her third-year film assignment *Jesus Christ's Sin* (*Hrích boha*) in 1969. It was accepted as her diploma film and secured her earlier graduation in case she was sentenced to longer imprisonment in the political trial. The film was an adaptation of a short story by Isaac Babel, a Soviet writer of Jewish origins, who initially was a vehement supporter of the Soviet Revolution, yet eventually became a critic of it and was ultimately executed by the communist authorities.[32] Thus, Holland chose for adaptation a literary work that did not originate from either Polish or Czechoslovak culture. The film tells a story of a young woman, Arina (Jaroslava Pokorná[33]), who has an insatiable sexual drive, while also being abused by various men. When her lover, who is also the father of her twins, is conscripted to the army, she appeals to God and complains about the prospect of her solitude. To help her, the Almighty gives her an angel for companionship. Holland's film presents the protagonist and the narrative in a highly stylised form. Years later, she described it as a 'naïve-formalist approach, something between Paradjanov and Pasolini'.[34]

Jesus Christ's Sin starts with a long frontal shot of an embracing couple against the backdrop of a building with a sign above the entrance reading 'Hotel'. An extra-diegetic narrator introduces the character of Arina and her lover, who are consecutively shown in close-up inserts. The frontal static camera placement and the characters' look into the camera produce the effect of spectatorial estrangement. The next scene contains dialogue, yet the camera remains static and there are long pauses in Arina and her boyfriend's conversation, which foregrounds the cinematic form. The film does not employ the method of continuity editing either. For it presents a sequence of tableau-like images which illustrate a narrative that is consequently transformed into a kind of parable. In terms of gender politics, the film breaks with several cultural taboos imposed on female sexuality, while also undermining conventional imagery in its representation. First and foremost, the film presents a pregnant woman who experiences sexual drive, which detaches female sexuality from its reproductive function. Second, the male angel that is given to Arina enters the scene naked, and for a brief moment his genitals are visible on screen (see Fig. 1.3). The woman looks at him and touches his body with a visible delight. When they feast and he devours huge portions of meat on the bone, she fills up his glass with vodka until he is too drunk to get into bed on his own. So she carries him to the bed and then starts dancing to express her joy at having the angel at her disposal (see Fig. 1.4). When she ultimately gets to bed and lies on top of him, she suffocates him to death. Being alone again, Arina starts sleeping around with men and, disappointed with the situation, she goes to God again and states that her promiscuity is his rather than her sin because she is his creation. He admits his sin and asks for absolution, yet she refuses it and leaves. The absurd fairytale-like story presents the divine creature as unable to help the woman. In Holland's diploma film, the sublime merges with the trivial, while God resides, not in heaven but in her attic; yet, despite this proximity to humans, he is unable to ease their lot. The God in Holland's film is neither benevolent nor ruthless; instead, he is indolent and helpless. The human being is left on its own.

EARLY YEARS: PAINS AND JOYS 39

Figure 1.3 *Jesus Christ's Sin* (1969)

Figure 1.4 *Jesus Christ's Sin* (1969)

With the absurd narrative and stylised form, *Jesus Christ's Sin* is like the films of the Czechoslovak New Wave which focused on the tragicomic nature of human existence.[35] This approach will return in a more complex expression in many of Holland's later films, with *Europa, Europa* being the most conspicuous example. Its representation of female sexuality resists a simple inscription into a single ideological system. Arina is provided with agency, and she exercises it with determination and strength, yet it does not protect her from sexual exploitation. The short film features, albeit only implicitly present, the motif of a clash between individual desires and social norms that will resurface in Holland's later work. Finally, the diploma film marks her entrance into the transnational screen cultures of Eastern Europe: it was based on a Russian short story, made in Czechoslovakia, delivered in the Czech language, and directed by a Polish female student. *Jesus Christ's Sin* marks Holland's detachment from the system of national cinema and culture.

To conclude, Holland's study at FAMU was for her a 'topsy-turvy', so to say, formative experience in that it ungrounded her from vernacular culture and political life, while not assimilating her with the host culture. Her decision to leave Poland for Czechoslovakia prompted a series of 'crack lines' that imperceptibly yet slowly mobilised the 'line of flight' unlocking the possibilities of becoming the other, a transnational filmmaker. When, in 1971, Holland was leaving Prague for Warsaw, she already was a nomad, who, as Deleuze and Guattari claim, 'goes from one point to another', however, 'every point is a relay and exists only as a relay [. . .] The life of the nomad is the intermezzo' (Deleuze and Guattari 2019, 443). Arguably, the years she spent in Prague were not merely a preparation time for her nomadic cinematic career but were the actual initiation into it, where she learned how to unground herself in cinema from any singular aesthetic and ideological system. Or to paraphrase Holland's letter to her aunt, one can say that, in Prague she learned how to be independent in world cinema and accept that it would also mean loneliness or estrangement in it.

NOTES

1. In his famous 1968 essay 'The Death of the Author', Barthes noted that 'The *explanation* [emphasis in the original] of a work is always sought in the man or woman who produced it, as if it were always in the end, through the more or less transparent allegory of the fiction, the voice of a single person, the *author* "confiding" in us', when, in fact, 'It is language which speaks, not the author.' The 'proclaimed death of the author' was in defence of the reader's agency and interpretative freedom (Barthes [1968] 1981, 209).
2. Arguably, the change of approach to the issue can be connected with the 'biographical turn' in the 1980s that resulted in the gradual acceptance of biographical analysis as a valid research method (Renders, de Haan and Harmsma 2017, 3). Proponents of the biographical turn maintained that '[t]he study of individual lives explores the divergent

roles taken and made throughout a life, laying bare the correspondences, overlaps, oppositions and conflicts among them' (5). Filmmakers perform various roles, while their public personas emerge at the intersection of many different and often contradictory discourses.
3. Julia Erhart employs the concept 'fictional-biographical overlap' in her analysis of critical discourses around the public persona of Jane Campion (Erhart 2019). Torben Grodal's analysis of Lars von Trier's works reveals a 'fictional-biographical overlap' in that his films concern universal issues, while certain themes 'have their background in very personal problems'. Although Grodal admits that von Trier's biography cannot 'provide an absolute key to understanding his films', it 'may contribute to an understanding of the strength' of certain features of his films (Grodal 2005, 131).
4. 'Biographical methodology' has only occasionally been practised in feminist studies on authorship in film and media. Judith Mayne's *Directed by Dorothy Arzner* (1994) is a notable example of it, for it explores the complex and frequently latent relationship between Arzner's work and her public persona as disseminated by various media. Catherine Grant recognises the importance of Mayne's pioneering study as 'enabling the earlier text/author impasses to be broken down' (Grant 2001, 122). In her article, Grant refers to Susan Martin-Márquez's analysis of authorship of the Spanish filmmaker Pilar Miró, which proposes an even more radical approach as it examines not only Miró's work and biography, but also various critical discourses created around them (Grant 2001, 124).
5. In relating Holland's biography, I draw on her interviews, especially the two book-length ones (Zawiśliński 1995; Holland and Kornatowska 2012), and the recently published biography (Pasternak 2022).
6. In this chapter, I refer to Holland by her first rather than her last name in order to distinguish her from her relatives of the same name.
7. Magdalena Łazarkiewicz is six years younger than her sister and is also a filmmaker.
8. Holland started talking about her Jewish origins in the 1980s when she was living abroad, while earlier being rather somewhat discreet about it (see, for example, Zawiśliński 1995, 22).
9. Henryk Holland received the information from Stanisław Brodzki, the second husband of Agnieszka Holland's mother.
10. As Krzysztof Persak reports, the funeral was a kind of political demonstration protesting the violation of human rights by the security apparatus (see Persak 2006, 272–4).
11. Admittedly, for many, Henryk Holland's political conversion and his revisionist approach to communism do not locate him in the 'dissident circles' as he was not rejecting the ideology. However, I will not follow the precepts of the dominant historical discourse developed by the radical right-wing politicians and historians who see communism and the dissident as mutually exclusive.
12. Karolina Pasternak presents this account in Holland's biography in the form of a conversation with Holland, presumably to bring out the personal aspects. I examine this part of the book in a more detailed way in Chapter Seven.
13. While recollecting her family home, Holland frequently compared its atmosphere to Chekhov's plays (see Zawiśliński 1995, 21).
14. Irena Rybczyńska-Holland reflected on her experience of motherhood in a fictionalised personal narrative presented in a book *How to Love a Daughter?* (*Jak kochać córkę?*). The book includes Agnieszka Holland's afterword (Rybczyńska 1995).
15. It was published during 1960–1973 and then the censors requested that it be replaced with *Family Magazine* (*Magazyn rodzinny*), for which Irena Rybczyńska-Holland also worked until 1980.
16. For an insightful cultural analysis of the magazine, see Kurz 2013.

17. Having a live-in housekeeper was not exceptional in the aftermath of the Second World War, though it was limited to these households that could afford it; often, it was practised in the families where both husband and wife were professionally active, usually in the sector of state administration and cultural production. Holland recollects her babysitter as a simple yet very wise woman (Holland and Kornatowska 2012, 72–4). In her autobiographical novel, Janina Bauman remembers how her mother-in-law, Zygmunt Bauman's mother, employed many live-in housekeepers. Once they started working for her family, she began looking for a real job for them and she was always successful in these endeavours (see Janina Bauman 1988, 66). Holland also mentions various country girls living with them, while attending schools; most likely they also helped with domestic chores (Holland and Kornatowska 2012, 71).
18. Małgorzata Fidelis astutely explains the postwar changes in gender discourse in Poland: 'The reconfiguration of gender roles during the war, the increasing number of working women, and communist efforts to implement equality of the sexes all created unprecedented conditions for social change. This mix opened an opportunity for a profound break from the essentialist notion of gender difference, in which women were inevitably linked to motherhood and the family, and men to the public realm of economic and political activity. Yet postwar ideas and policies on equal rights did not completely reject the Western-liberal division of society into male producers and female reproducers ingrained in the nineteenth-century tradition. Rather, this longstanding gender dichotomy was reshaped and reinterpreted in postwar Poland' (Fidelis 2010, 24). For a detailed analysis of the specificity of the Polish postwar feminist discourse, see Mrozik 2022.
19. For example, in 1968, Jerzy Hoffman's *Colonel Wolodyjowski*, an adaptation of very popular historical novel by Henryk Sienkiewicz.
20. In the 1960s, Roman Polanski and Jerzy Skolimowski emigrated from Poland, while Andrzej Wajda made some films abroad, for example *Siberian Lady Macbeth* (Poland, Yugoslavia, 1961) and *Gates of Paradise* (UK, Yugoslavia, 1962).
21. In 1968, there were eighteen such movie theatres, whereas in 1972 their number increased to twenty-seven. Additionally, some of the regular movie theatres introduced so-called 'arthouse cinema days' (*dni studyjne*) (Koniczek 1994, 488).
22. As Ryszard Koniczek reports, in 1968 the following films were shown, among others: *Black Peter* (*Černý Petr*, Miloš Forman, Czechoslovakia, 1963), *Diamonds of the Night* (*Démanty noci*, Czechoslovakia, Jan Němec, 1964), *Four in the Morning* (Anthony Simmons, UK, 1965), *On the Bowery* (Lionel Rogosin, US, 1956) *The Red and the White* (*Csillagosok, katonák*, Miklós Jancsó, Hungary, 1967), *The First Teacher* (*Pervyy uchitel*, Andrei Konchalovsky, USSR, 1965), *Repulsion* (Roman Polanski, UK, 1965), and *Last Year at Marienbad* (*L'Année dernière à Marienbad*, Alain Resnais, 1961) (Koniczek 1994, 488).
23. The screenings in the cine-clubs were always introduced with a brief lecture and followed by discussion. The clubs had access to the collection of the National Film Archive (Filmoteka Narodowa). They would also organise preview screenings of films purchased for general distribution. Once a year the clubs organised a seminar with a film programme accompanied by lectures delivered by prominent film critics and scholars.
24. Most of the research on cinephilia replicates the logic of the Cold War and examines its forms only in the Western localities; see, for example, Keathley 2006.
25. As Rosanna Maule notes, 'a common characteristic of the European film author is an affiliation to a cinéphile culture promoted at cine-clubs, film archives, art house film theatres, and film festivals during the 1950s and 1960s, and documented by a young generation of film critics and the foundation of new film magazines' (Maule 2008, 14). Likewise, Marijke de Valck and Malte Hagener in the introductory essay to the collective

volume on cinephilia indicate its close connection to the concept of *auteur* cinema (de Valck and Hagener 2005, 11–24).
26. Kathleen McHugh discusses the postwar generation of female travelling filmmakers (2009); I present the main argument in the Introduction.
27. In this respect, she is like Roman Polanski, who also often emphasised the passion for cinema he had developed as a small child and nurtured even during the Second World War.
28. After the Second World War, film education was relatively well developed in Eastern Europe, as exemplified by the fact that the International Association of Film and TV Schools (CILECT) 'was founded in Cannes in 1955 with the intention of stimulating a dialogue among film schools in the deeply divided world of those times'. As Hjort further explains: 'Its membership was drawn from eight countries: Czechoslovakia (presently the Czech Republic), France, Great Britain, Italy, Poland, Spain, the USA and the USSR (presently Russia). By the year 2012, CILECT had grown to include 159 institutions from 60 countries on five continents' (Hjort 2013, 5). Thus, initially three out of eight film schools were based in the Eastern Bloc.
29. In his memoirs, Miloš Forman claims that the model of education in FAMU was rather old-fashioned as it did not include any camera training or work with actors, see Forman 1993, 72.
30. The Czechoslovak New Wave was mostly created by the FAMU graduates and many of them can easily be identified as film *auteurs*, for example, Věra Chytilová, Jan Němec, Karel Vachek, Juraj Jakubisko, Evald Schorm, Jiří Menzel and Miloš Forman, see Hames 2005, 28.
31. As Kristina Andělová explains, the Czechoslovak generation of 1968 was divided into two groups: the first opted for the programme of 'socialism with human face', whereas the second group, including the students and young intellectuals, 'never fully identified with it nor believed Marxism to be a necessary ideological basis for formulating critiques of Czechoslovak society' (Andělová 2019, 882). Instead of reforms, they 'brought about the emancipation of non-Marxist political thinking in public discourse, which at that time represented a deep revolt against – rather than a careful revision of – Marxism' (Andělová 2019, 896).
32. It is easy to draw a parallel between Isaac Babel and Holland's father, who also underwent a radical political transformation and died tragically.
33. Many years later, Holland cast the actress in the TV mini-series *Burning Bush* (*Hořící keř*, HBO, 2013).
34. Agnieszka Holland, 'Potrzeba intensywności wyrazu', interview by Marek Pawlukiewicz, *Kultura* 1979, no. 50, 11.
35. For more detailed presentation of the Czechoslovak New Wave see Hames 2005; Owen 2011.

CHAPTER 2

Art, politics and gender: Holland's participation in socialist Poland's screen cultures

Thirty years after the premiere of *A Woman Alone* (*Kobieta samotna*, 1981/1987),[1] freelance critic Ela Bittencourt wrote:

> If communist Poland ever had a feminist film manifesto, it was Holland's *A Woman Alone* (1987), in which the protagonist, burdened by misery and hostility, robs money from the post office where she is employed. She elopes with her invalid hubby, is chased by the police, and dies a tragicomic death. In a way, Holland staged her own sarcastic, Eastern European version of *Bonnie and Clyde* (1967) – hapless and lacking in glamour. (Bittencourt 2018)

Compared with Holland's own indifference towards feminism at the time she made the film, Bittencourt's statement may serve as a useful point of departure for discussing the director's Polish works from the 1970s and early 1980s in their relation to women's cinema and feminism. While the label 'feminist manifesto' may seem inappropriate for *A Woman Alone*, Holland's scepticism towards feminism was not as radical as she herself declared either. Polish film historian Katarzyna Mąka-Malatyńska noted the ambivalence, claiming that, while Holland's work cannot be called women's cinema, nevertheless it does explore some feminist issues (Mąka-Malatyńska 2009, 90). To address these contradictions, this chapter outlines Holland's professional career in Poland between 1972 and 1981, with a special focus on gender, in terms of both her struggles in the film industry and the politics of representation in her works. First, it discusses Holland's position within the institutional and informal networks of the Polish film industry in the 1970s. Her participation in the collective film and television projects is examined within the framework of collective authorship, while her individually directed films contributing to the Cinema of Moral Concern are approached as representing national cinema. I will discuss how Holland's increasingly strong position in the Polish screen industries subverted its patriarchal structures, while, on the textual level of her works, the opposite happened, in that the female characters in her films increasingly lost the subjective agency they once had. In my analysis of these contradictory forces affecting Holland's work in the Poland of late socialism, I will demonstrate how the emancipatory discourses of socialism – which significantly differed from their Western counterparts – that informed early Holland's works were eventually subordinated to the hegemonic national discourse.

ENTRY INTO POLISH SOCIALIST SCREEN INDUSTRIES

After returning from Czechoslovakia to her native Poland in 1971, Holland found life there uninspiring. She noticed an overwhelming stagnation and indifference towards politics.[2] She also felt alienated from the film circles, and it took some time to reintegrate into them. She remembered an informal gathering of young filmmakers that Stanisław Latałło organised for her as especially important:

> I met there Krzysiek [diminutive form of Krzysztof] Kieślowski. They were very interested in my Czech experiences, whereas I was interested in what was happening in Poland in the aftermath of the December 1970 events.[3] Kieślowski, Tomek Zygadło, Jacek Petrycki were making a documentary about the Gdańsk shipyard workers *Workers '71: Nothing about Us without Us* [*Robotnicy '71: nic o nas bez nas*, 1972]. I liked them very much. They had a certain seriousness and personal strength that was most likely imposed by Krzysiek. My Prague friends that were quickly suppressed [during the normalisation period] have diminished in my mind. Suddenly, in Poland I saw a chance to create a group that could do something important.[4]

The meeting, which was followed by many others, imbued the young graduate of FAMU with a spirit of collectivity that she fostered in her work for the next several years. Despite various forms of ideological control and financial shortcomings, the organisational structure of the Polish film industry in the Poland of late socialism provided space for various collective film projects that often facilitated individual careers. However, women rarely benefitted from these initiatives. The industry was a hierarchical, patriarchal structure that relegated female professionals to the supportive positions subordinated to the male *auteurs*. Notwithstanding the large number of women employed in the Polish film industry, its organisation and gender politics prevented the emergence of women's film collectives. There were two options for female directors: either to accept and adapt to the masculinist mode of filmmaking, or to take a marginal position in it. Holland chose the first option, which provided her with considerable agency within the film industry structures.

From 1955 on, the Polish film industry was organised around film units that were 'semi-autonomous teams of film practitioners, funded by the state, and operating within the state-owned and state-run film industry' (D. Ostrowska 2012, 453). They served as an intermediary between the communist authorities and the filmmakers. The National Film Board (Naczelny Zarząd Kinematografii) represented the state that 'controlled and fostered' the cultural production (D. Ostrowska 2012, 454). As the result of the 1972 reform of the film industry, the film units were granted more control over the whole process of film production, whereas before it was limited to the scripts. As Marcin Adamczak explains: 'Each film unit was headed by an artistic director, selected from a number of renowned film directors, a literary director, usually a writer or literary critic, and finally, a chief production manager recruited from a group of production managers' (Adamczak 2012, 235–6). In this organisational structure, the film school graduates were obliged to do some apprenticeship in the film units under the guidance of more experienced and recognised filmmakers. Most frequently, the artistic directors fulfilled this role.

For Holland, it was first Krzysztof Zanussi and then Andrzej Wajda. The former was the artistic director of the film unit 'Tor', the latter of the unit 'X'. These two units were the most important players in Polish cinema of the 1970s, while their artistic heads enjoyed an international reputation. Although of comparable rank, these two creative teams represented different approaches to cinema that was reflected in their nicknames: the 'Tor' cohort were called 'calligraphers', whereas the 'X' team were addressed as 'journalists'; the former were more concerned with cinematic form and style, whereas the latter were preoccupied with the narrative content and its political message (Socha 2018, 136). Holland's collaboration with Zanussi and the 'Tor' unit was very brief, whereas her membership in Wajda's 'X' proved a decisive factor in determining her professional career in socialist Poland.

Holland's first professional appointment was an assistantship at Zanussi's *Illumination* (*Iluminacja*, 1973), an existential essay-like drama in which Stanisław Latałło, Holland's friend, played the protagonist who struggles to combine his academic career and family life, while also experiencing existential dilemmas. It was not easy for Holland to obtain the position. Unknown, as mentioned, in film circles and stigmatised by her father's politically suspicious death as well as her imprisonment in Prague, she approached Zanussi with a request to be appointed as his assistant. As he recollects, she approached him soon after her return from Prague with a request: 'You make moral and ethical films and, since I am a person who's been wronged, you should help me get a job' (quoted in Stalnaker 2003, 80). Once Zanussi appointed her as his assistant, he was summoned by the authorities, who requested cancellation of the work contract with Holland.

Famous for his diplomatic skills, he accepted the decision, yet requested an official document confirming the order. The document was never issued, and Holland completed her assistantship,[5] while also appearing in a cameo episode that was to be followed by many more in the future.

Holland's behaviour on the set of *Illumination* – that is now a well-known part of her 'biographical legend' – was aggravating, in that she was swearing, smoking and drinking excessively. Arguably, it was her first attempt at adopting a masculine masquerade in order to be accepted and respected by the masculinised film personnel. Years later, Zanussi claimed 'Agnieszka's presence in our group was for me the most normal thing under the sun [. . .] Professionally active woman were nothing unusual to me. My mother was a very strong woman who decided overnight to take over the management of the family factory from her father' (quoted in Pasternak 2022, 128). The director, known for his conservative attitudes, implies here the gender equality in Polish society (or at least in some social sectors of it), while locating its origins in the pre-socialist era of Polish emancipatory movements. Implicitly, he rejects postwar socialist gender equality politics as obsolete in a society that has been implementing equality for a long time already. Zanussi's normalising opinion on Holland's presence in his film unit contradicts the actual underrepresentation of women in the Polish postwar film industry. In the world of cinema Holland entered, the existence of gender inequality was denied or downplayed. From the onset, she struggled against the male-dominated system of Polish production cultures.

Right after her brief collaboration with Zanussi, in 1972, Holland joined the film unit 'X'. As she reported, it was Tadeusz Konwicki, a respected writer and filmmaker, and her friend, Stanisław Latałło who suggested that she should join Wajda's group (in Pasternak 2022, 106; Holland and Kornatowska 2012, 20; see also Mąka-Malatyńska 2009, 16).[6] These intermediaries are worth mentioning as they shed light on the networks operating within the Polish film industry. On the one hand, it was organised and controlled by the state authorities, on the other hand, it was also functioning as a community of friends, colleagues and acquaintances that established alternative alliances and collaborative schemes. This complex and multilayered network of institutions and collaborators can be located in the framework of Bruno Latour's theory of network-actors that he conceived as a constantly fluctuating system with a shifting centre of power (Latour 2005, 24, 217–18). In the case of the Polish film industry, the state that was financing film production and, thus, possessed an unlimited, in theory, control over it, can be identified as occupying the central position of power. It operated through the institution of the National Film Board that initially controlled the whole of the process of production, yet gradually, especially after the reform implemented in 1972, it shared its prerogatives with the film units. The latter can be conceived as local or mini-network-actors with their own hierarchies and dynamic. The heads of the unit – in the case of 'X' it was

Wajda – can be seen as local super-actors[7] who were sharing their authority with the literary and production directors; in the 'X' unit these were Bolesław Michałek and Barbara Pec-Ślesicka respectively. Their control spanned over the directors, cinematographers and other personnel. Within the units, specific hierarchies were formed with the emerging roles of leaders and subordinates. Although the actors in the social networks of the unit 'X' were predominantly male, there were two actresses whose power exceeded that of many men: Pec-Ślesicka, the only female Polish film producer at that time, and Holland, one of the most prominent members of the creative team. Within this multilevelled network of film production, the collective authorship emerged not only in the collective projects but also in individual works made by the young directors as these were supervised by Wajda and peer-reviewed by their colleagues (see Holland and Hendrykowski 1998, 252). In her monograph on the film unit 'X', Anna Szczepańska suggests it can be seen as a collective author (Szczepańska 2017, 133) of the films made by its members.

Thus, after experiencing for a brief time a certain alienation from Polish film culture, soon Holland integrated with it through participating in institutional collectives and informal networks. Her decision to join the unit 'X' was of paramount importance for her professional career in that it defined her production frameworks and affected her stylistic and thematic preferences. Many years later, Holland called Wajda a 'man of providence'[8] who had helped her to start her professional career.

SOCIALIST TELEVISION: COINCIDENCES, COLLABORATIONS AND CONTROL

In their efforts to find professional opportunities for young filmmakers, Wajda, Pec-Ślesicka and Michałek came up with an idea of collaborative projects made for television.[9] Polish television, as in other Eastern Bloc countries, '[r]ather than an instrument of propaganda, [. . .] was a profoundly ambivalent medium in the hands of party authorities' (Imre 2016, 7).[10] As Anikó Imre explains, socialist television muddled 'the entrenched idea of the binary opposition between official party-led cultures and dissident intellectual cultures' (Imre 2016, 10–1; see also Imre 2020). Many Polish film and theatre directors who can be termed 'dissident intellectuals' collaborated with television, especially with the so-called Television Theatre. This was a hybrid model of theatrical projects that were made exclusively for television broadcasting and thereby designed for the small screen.[11] Its first live production was broadcast in 1953. These television performances were usually directed by two people: a *metteur en scène*, and a coordinator of the screen presentation. The programmes were aired every Monday primetime, at 8.00 p.m., right after the main edition of the news. Some of these performances were produced by local television stations in such cities as Kraków, Gdańsk, Łódź and Poznań, which provided the local theatre actors with an opportunity to perform for the nationwide audience. As until 1970 there had only been one television channel in Poland, the viewers were somehow forced to watch these television plays, and it is safe to say that for many of them these were the only theatrical experience they had. Among the directors who collaborated with the Television Theatre were many renowned filmmakers such as Andrzej Wajda, Kazimierz Kutz and Krzysztof Kieślowski. Its repertoire included plays from the world canon (for example William Shakespeare, Pedro Calderon de la Barca and Anton Chekhov), as well as Polish classics (for example Adam Mickiewicz, Juliusz Słowacki and Witkacy).[12] It also presented works by contemporary playwrights such as Tadeusz Różewicz and Sławomir Mrożek, and, finally, by Soviet authors to fulfil the requirements of the politically decreed Polish–Soviet collaboration. One of these works was *The Debtors* (*Dłużnicy*), by the Soviet-Ukrainian writer Leonid Zhukhovitsky, which Holland directed as her first authorial work in 1974, in the Łódź branch of the Television Theatre.

As Holland reported,[13] the offer to direct the play for the Television Theatre came from Witold Zatorski, who, in the 1970s, worked as an actor and artistic director of the Nowy Theatre in Łódź; he also collaborated with the Łódź branch of the Television Theatre. As a member of Holland's mother's social circle, he decided to help Agnieszka and her then husband, Laco Adamik. After returning to Poland, Holland was subjected to tight censorship scrutiny and all her scripts were rejected.[14] Directing the Soviet play in a provincial branch of socialist television was a perfect camouflage for her troublesome name.[15] *The Debtors* was broadcast on 5 July 1974. Holland authored the script and directed it. The play was a realistic drama that featured several young and middle-aged characters gathered together for a birthday party. Its main theme was the difficulty of combining professional and marriage/family life, which she examined in many of her later works. The play was performed in a small television studio which required a careful planning of stage movement. These spatial limitations were compensated with rhythmical use of shot-reverse-shot sequences for dialogues. The production was reviewed by Irena Bołtuć, a recognised theatre critic, in *Friendship* (*Przyjaźń*), an official magazine of the Polish–Soviet Friendship Society. The review discussed the content of the play as an adequate representation of the problems of contemporary society, while not even mentioning the name of the director (which was included in the attached credits only).[16] Today, it is difficult to assess whether this was a result of the reviewer's choice or of obedience to the censor. Regardless of the omission, *The Debtors* was an important work in Holland's professional career for several reasons: first, it was her first work in the Polish cultural industry; second, it was her first collaboration with television which she then continued for her whole professional career, albeit in different models and formats; third, it was her first encounter with Witold Zatorski, with whom she later authored the script for her full feature debut *Provincial Actors* (*Aktorzy prowincjonalni*, 1978), and with the actors whom she later cast in her next (mostly television) projects (Zofia Grąziewicz and Zbigniew Nawrocki). Furthermore, the contexts of the assignment reveal how the socialist cultural production was embedded in various official and informal networks. Within such a nexus, the state-owned and state-controlled television became a laboratory for would-be dissident filmmakers such as Holland herself, Krzysztof Kieślowski, Feliks Falk and Janusz Kijowski.[17]

Polish filmmakers had worked in television since the 1960s, when the Radio and Television Committee established a special unit for film production. On 10 January 1964, an agreement was signed between the Ministry of Culture, the National Film Board and the Radio and Television Committee that decreed collaboration between the film industry and television. This cooperation was unusual compared to the competition between the two media in the West. As Dorota Ostrowska and Małgorzata Radkiewicz note:

> In the 1960s across Europe and the United States the production of large-scale, spectacular and costly historical blockbusters was seen as an expression of the battle between silver and small screen in which cinema was trying to attract the spectators with the spectacle they would not be able to see on their television screens. Cinema was to overwhelm and to become a true assault at the senses. In the socialist bloc countries such as Poland the same period was marked by quite a different development; instead of competition there was a deep synergy between the two media regarding production and exhibition of lavish adaptations of the classics of national literature. (Ostrowska and Radkiewicz 2007, 107)

Not all adaptations of national literary classics were lavish productions as some of them were low-budget projects that provided the filmmakers with opportunities to make movies outside of the mainstream structures of the film industry that were subordinated to the tightest control of censorship. Wajda, who himself made a short film for public television (*Roly Poly/Przekładaniec*, 1968), suggested to Holland, as well as to other young members of the 'X' unit, that they should use this option to gain professional experience.[18] After she completed two productions for the Television Theatre, he encouraged her to submit a project for a television film. In 1975, Holland had the chance to make her first independent film project for television, *An Evening at Abdon* (*Wieczór u Abdona*), based on a short novel by the respected Polish writer, Jarosław Iwaszkiewicz.

An Evening at Abdon was produced by the film unit 'X' for Polish television. Its action takes place in Maliny, a small Polish-Jewish city at the Eastern periphery of Poland, before the Second World War.[19] Abdon (Marek Bargiełowski), the protagonist, is a philosopher who lives a solitary life while observing his neighbours from afar.[20] He is fascinated with a local pharmacist's wife, Herminia (Beata Tyszkiewicz), who openly fulfils her sexual desire with a young boy, Michaś (Michał Bajor). Abdon, who also desires Herminia, responds violently to the situation and slashes the young boy's throat, nearly resulting in his death. In the film's ending, Abdon is shown in a high-angle long shot looking like an insect unaware of the fruitlessness of its efforts to escape across an endless terrain (see Bobowski 2001, 34). In contrast to Abdon's frenzied leave taking, those who stay in the town slowly return to the previous, well-established routine. The film focuses on an individual character who is unwilling, or unable for that matter, to establish any relationship with another person or community.[21] The film ends with a song entitled 'Not Loved', which serves as a lyrical but also somehow ironic comment on the narrative resolution.[22] *An Evening at Abdon* was harshly criticised by Holland's colleagues except for Piotr Szulkin – a Polish filmmaker whose work stands on its own and cannot be incorporated into any cinematic movement or style – who claimed it was her best film ever (see Mąka-Malatyńska 2009, 28; Czerkawski 2019, 150–1). Holland herself downplayed its importance in her oeuvre as a kind of counterproductive 'juvenile formalist experiment'.[23] Thus, soon she joined her colleagues who then opted for cinema that engaged with socio-political reality rather than abstract issues of libidinal desire and existential solitude. The collective film and television projects she and Wajda's other young protégés made examined exclusively contemporary themes and issues.

Pictures from Life (*Obrazki z życia*, 1975) was the first collaborative project produced by the unit 'X' for Polish television in which Holland participated (the other directors were Jerzy Domaradzki, Feliks Falk, Andrzej Kotkowski, Jerzy Obłamski, Krzysztof Gradowski and Barbara Sass).[24] It consisted of seven short novellas, the scripts of which were based on Jerzy Urban's columns in a liberal weekly *Politics* (*Polityka*) published under the penname Jerzy Kibic. They all presented aspects of Polish contemporary reality, whether in comedic, ironic or serious mode. Although not a big cinematic achievement,[25] the project was important in its retreat from historical themes that were frequently featured in the films by older (male) filmmakers, while turning towards contemporary issues not sufficiently reflected in Polish cinema of that time, or cultural production for that matter.[26] The project also provided the young directors with an opportunity to fulfil the official requirement to make two short films before being considered eligible to make a feature film debut (Szczepańska 2017, 128–9).[27] The film's collective authorship is indicated in the opening credits which include the names of all the directors, while not mentioning that it consists of seven independent novels. Szczepańska claims that *Pictures from Life* represents multiple authorship in several ways: there were seven directors of seven novels; the unit 'X' authored the project as its producer, and, finally, the author of the script, Jerzy Urban, adapted the work of his literary alter ego, Jerzy Kibic (Szczepańska 2017, 130). *Pictures from Life* can also be classified as an 'omnibus film' that probes the possibilities of 'transauthorial' cinema (see Diffrient 2014); however, as Szczepańska claims, the project was not so much aimed at exploring the possibilities of collective art in television but rather had the pragmatic purpose of accelerating and facilitating the young filmmakers' careers (Szczepańska 2017, 137). The participating filmmakers did not intend to continue their collaboration with television either; instead, they treated it as a trampoline for further career development, or a first step on the path leading to a full-length feature debut (Szczepańska 2017, 144).

Holland's novella *Girl and 'Aquarius'* (*Dziewczyna i 'Aquarius'*) tells the story of a teenage girl who abandons her family and school to follow a rock band she is fascinated with. While manifesting her disobedience, she is exceptionally passive and behaves as if hypnotised by the musicians and compelled by a mysterious force to travel with them. Her decision to leave her school life and shadow the band may suggests the character's emancipatory potential, yet this avenue is not further explored. In a sense, the girl foreshadows other female characters in Holland's films made in the unit 'X' in that they are provided with subjective agency yet never fully use it, or sometimes deliberately surrender it out of necessity or their own choice.

As Holland knew the collective television projects were for her the only chance to be professionally active, she approached Wajda on behalf of her colleagues with a proposal for another joint television project, the cycle titled *Family Situation* (*Sytuacje rodzinne*, 1976–9).[28] It consisted of seven approximately hour-long films, each directed by a different filmmaker, examining the broad theme of contemporary family life. Holland made two films in the cycle: *Sunday Children* (*Niedzielne dzieci*, 1976), and *Something for Something* (*Coś za coś*, 1977). In their realisation these projects encountered many obstacles, while involving many prominent figures from the film industry of the 1970s. Initially, the scripts were rejected by the Central Script Committee. To compensate for this, but also out of an appreciation of her artistic and intellectual capabilities, Wajda offered Holland the position of his assistant on the production of *Man of Marble* (*Człowiek z marmuru*). She started working on the film, coordinating, among other things, screen tests for Jerzy Radziwiłowicz, who played the protagonist, Mateusz Birkut; these materials were later incorporated in the final cut of the film (in the scenes of Birkut's job interview the questions are asked by Holland, who filmed it).[29] Regrettably, however, the Ministry of Culture did not approve Holland's employment on that film and threatened Wajda with cancellation of the project if she participated in it. In response, the whole team of the unit 'X' protested, and other respected filmmakers such as Krzysztof Zanussi and Jerzy Kawalerowicz also expressed their objections.[30] Despite the protests, the authorities did not overturn their decision. Yet Wajda managed to bargain for Holland's assistantship on *Man of Marble* in return for approval of one of her scripts submitted to the Script Committee. Thus, she eventually had the chance to make two films: *Sunday Children* (for Polish television, 1976) and *Screen Tests* (*Zdjęcia próbne*, a collaborative project co-directed with Jerzy Domaradzki and Paweł Kędzierski, 1976).[31]

Sunday Children explored the theme of (un)wanted pregnancy and adoption.[32] The protagonists, the married childless couple (played by Zofia Grąziewicz and Ryszard Kotys), who are perfect examples of postwar socio-economic advancement, live a monotonous, yet safe life within the limits of the socialist system. To complete their dream of a happy family, they initiate an adoption procedure, yet they are discouraged by its length and complexity and by the impossibility of selecting a child according to their preferences. Thus, they decide to 'buy' a pregnancy from a young girl, Jolanta (Krystyna Wachelko-Zaleska[33]) who was cheated on by her lover and rejected by her conservative peasant parents. She represents a large group of young women who benefitted from the socialist emancipation project, while being victims of insufficient access to birth control education and means (see Fig. 2.1). They often experienced a kind of moral dilemma as, on the one hand, they rejected traditional morality, yet on the other hand, they were unable to detach from it and accepted the condemnation of the out-of-wedlock pregnancy.

Figure 2.1 *Sunday Children* (1976)

The main theme of *Sunday Children* is presented against the background of everyday life in late-socialist Poland. The film focuses on moral aspects of the socialist variant of consumerism promoted by Edward Gierek, the leader of the Communist Party at the time. The ease with which the couple decide to 'buy' an unborn baby and the pregnant girl 'sells' it denounces the failure of the two competing ideological systems, represented by the Polish Catholic Church and the Communist Party, which were united in advocating for the traditional model of the (patriarchal) family. The consumerist attitude becomes especially manifest when the wife becomes pregnant with their own child and the couple unscrupulously withdraw from the transaction. After giving birth, the young mother equally unscrupulously abandons the now 'worthless' baby boy. The ending of the film that shows her reluctantly holding the baby is inconclusive: it may be the moment of awakening of her maternal instinct or simply a momentary expression of short-lived emotions (see Jankun-Dopartowa 2000, 94). Although the film directly addresses the oppressive ideological aspect of motherhood as developed within patriarchal culture, eventually it shifts its main criticism towards the rampant consumerism of late state socialism which led to the commodification of pregnancy and motherhood. Ultimately, the 'trade' of pregnancy serves in the film as a sign of the moral decay of Polish society.

Sunday Children shared with the other films in the cycle a realistic mode of representation and a preoccupation with contemporary social issues. The cinematic form was subordinated to the important social content which was also typical of the then current television film production. The documentary style is achieved mainly by means of camerawork (hand-held camera, random framing, and minimal camera movement motivated exclusively by action) and editing (used for the purpose of segmentation of the action, while subordinating its rhythm to dialogues), but also by the narrative structure. Although the film has a typical goal-driven narrative, Holland interlaces it with several subsidiary episodes, which are unnecessary for the development of the main plot. A clear example of such a narratively gratuitous episode is the scene in which a group of working girls go to a restaurant dance party. Its similarity to a dance scene in Miloš Forman's *Loves of a Blonde* (*Lásky jedné plavovlásky*, 1965) is striking.[34] The camera directs the viewers' gaze at the faces of the young people who try to hide their lack of confidence with exaggerated gestures of unconstrained boldness. The harsh lighting reveals imperfections in their complexion, overdone make-up and the poor quality of their clothes. The episode begins and ends abruptly without anchoring it in the main story. Rather unexpectedly, it cuts to the production line at which the pregnant girl stands, visibly tired. The function of the dance episode is not to propel the narrative forward but rather to provide a micro-observation of the mundane reality of Polish working-class youth in the 1970s that is far from the propagandistic socialist slogans, while also reflecting on the changes of gender discourse in postwar Poland. It is safe to assume that girls such as these portrayed by Holland frequented such parties not only because of their love for dance but also because they expected to exercise their newly acquired sexual freedom outside of the traditional institution of the family.[35] The leading character of the pregnant girl who accompanies her friends to the party is an example of these demographic and cultural changes. However, the film also testifies to the imperfections of these state-imposed emancipatory projects, specifically the lack of institutional support for young women for whom sexual freedom often brought unwanted pregnancy or single motherhood.

Despite its focus on female issues, *Sunday Children* was approached by Polish critics as a film representing the Cinema of Moral Concern,[36] a cinematic movement aimed at a realistic portrayal of the Poland of late socialism, as well as a typical television production. For example, one Polish critic claimed the film criticises the commodification of children who often functioned as an ultimate proof of family well-being.[37] In turn, the author of the review published in *Variety* located the film within the larger body of Eastern European cinema; specifically, she noted its similarity to the Czechoslovak New Wave: '*Sunday Children* gives ample evidence of the Forman-Passer-Papousek style of comic improvisation, that "slice of life" Czech humor of a decade ago'.[38] Both the Polish and foreign critics did not position the film within a feminist framework or 'women's cinema'. In an interview, Holland defended herself from being compartmentalised within such categories. She claimed that the main theme of the film was the dehumanisation and commodification of social relationships with a simultaneous criticism of the bureaucracy and infectivity of the Polish social services. When asked by the journalist about working in a profession that is considered typically male, Holland acknowledged some gender prejudices, while also claiming that her decisiveness and precision on the film set dismantled these biases.[39] However, in another interview she admitted that women's position in the film industry, as in many other professions, was more difficult than men's due to the asymmetric labour divisions within households.[40] Thus, while in the early years of her career, Holland protested her films being labelled 'women's cinema', she was simultaneously one of very few active and successful female filmmakers. Only years later, after achieving an international reputation, did she admit that the thematisation of pregnancy and motherhood in her script for *Sunday Children* was related to her own personal experiences at that time (Holland and Hendrykowski 1998, 243).[41] These postponed acknowledgements of female experience and feminine subjectivity inscribed in her work demonstrate the evolution of her perspective on women's cinema and feminism that will be discussed throughout the book.

Holland's next film in the cycle, *Something for Something*,[42] also interrogates the issue of (unwanted) motherhood[43] and the attendant hegemonic socio-cultural discourses. Like *Sunday Children*, it also merges progressive and regressive gender politics. Its female protagonist Anna (Barbara Wrzesińska) is an academic who decides, together with her husband, also a researcher, not to have children as these would interfere with their professional careers. Initially, she appears to be liberated from patriarchal constraints and able to pursue her own aims, while also experiencing sexual pleasure outside of the institution of marriage.[44] However, an accidental encounter with a young woman (Iwona Biernacka), who pretended to be pregnant in order to keep her married lover, unsettles her attitude to life. Although the film offers an open ending, some critics claimed Anna was eventually transformed 'from an academic into a woman'.[45] Leaving aside the gender bias expressed in many of the reviews of the film,[46] I would argue that Anna's character ultimately represents gender uncertainty rather than confidence and fulfilment with the chosen model of life as Talarczyk-Gubała suggests (2013, 229). The protagonist of Holland's film can be seen as either a liberated woman who controls her sexuality and reproductive potential, or a victim of the male-centred academic world where motherhood cannot be accommodated. Ultimately, she has two choices: either to accept the patriarchal rules and perform the male roles or to leave the male-dominated world. The film does not even allude to the possibility of or the need for a transformation of the system and its adjustment to female needs.

Notwithstanding the critical reception of the film, *Something for Something*, along with other films of the cycle *Family Situation*, evinces that Polish public television did not only serve as a propagandistic tool for socialist authoritarianism but also provided young filmmakers with opportunities to practise their skills before embarking on larger projects, while also allowing them to explore subject matters that were relevant for Polish society living in the era of late socialism. Holland explored issues of pregnancy and motherhood that were traditionally marginalised in Polish mainstream film production. Her television films revealed how female personal and individual experiences were embedded within larger social and cultural discourses on the level of cultural production and its consumption. Furthermore, they were probing the conflict between motherhood and professional career she was experiencing at that time. The situation of entrapment experienced by many Polish women at that time is evoked also by means of visual devices such as tight framing, cluttered mise-en-scène and the imperfect illumination of space and characters. The thematic and stylistic consistency of *Sunday Children* and *Something for Something* marks the emergence of Holland's female authorship and signals that they belong to women's cinema despite her own reluctance to use the term. For the films reflect on specifically female experience presented as entangled within many varied and often oppressive discourses, while also employing stylistic devices adequate to the explored issues.

SCREEN TESTS: TOWARDS LEADERSHIP

Holland's next collective project *Screen Tests* (*Zdjęcia próbne*, 1976) (co-directed with Paweł Kędzierski and Jerzy Domaradzki) was a full feature film produced by the 'X' unit. As with the previous collaborations, it also tackled contemporary subject matter and employed a realistic style that, as some of the reviewers claimed, made it similar to the Czechoslovak New Wave, especially Miloš Forman's *Talent Competition* (*Konkurs*, 1964) and *Loves of a Blonde* (1965).[47] The affinity with the Czechoslovak New Wave lies also in the young protagonists for whom sexual initiation brings about disillusionment rather than fulfilment.[48] *Screen Tests* consists of three parts that are linked to one another through the protagonists. The first part, directed by Holland, is devoted to Anka (Daria Trafankowska), who dreams about a better life than her working-class parents have. She decides to lose her virginity to a boy who, right after this, is ready to 'share' her with his friend (see Fig. 2.2). Bitterly disappointed, she travels to Warsaw to take part in an audition for which she has been shortlisted. The second part, directed by Kędzierski, tells the story of Paweł (Andrzej Pieczyński), a boy from an orphanage, who begins his independent adult life with an affair

Figure 2.2 *Screen Tests* (1976)

with his boss's wife. Like Anka, he is accepted for the audition in Warsaw, where they both meet; the meeting is presented in the third part of the film, directed by Domaradzki. Both disappointed with their initiation into adult life, they feel close to each other and get intimate. The next day, during the screen test, Anka recreates their amorous encounter. Paweł considers it a betrayal and frantically leaves the sound stage. The scene interrogates the ethical dimension of representing personal, intimate experiences on the cinema screen, something which has been explored by many film *auteurs* such as Federico Fellini (*8 ½*, 1963) and Jean-Luc Godard (*Le Mépris*, 1963). Not accidentally, some of the reviewers alluded to Wajda's *Everything for Sale* (*Wszystko na sprzedaż*, 1969),[49] one of the most manifest instances of self-reflexivity in Polish cinema.

In *Screen Tests*, self-reflexivity takes up an ostentatious form in cameo appearances by Agnieszka Holland, Andrzej Wajda, Daniel Olbrychski (at that time the most famous star of Polish cinema) and Maciej Karpiński, a well-known young writer and literary critic (see Fig. 2.3). This collective cameo follows the tradition of the French New Wave filmmakers who were stamping their films with their physical presence, while also evoking the collectivity of the members of the unit 'X' (see Kornatowska 1990, 82).[50] In her review, Dorothea Holloway noted that the 'Pic is a cut above average due to appearance of

Figure 2.3 *Screen Tests* (1976), Agnieszka Holland and Andrzej Wajda

vet helmer Andrzej Wajda to discuss the tests with the collective directorial team, as well as for insights into Polish society as a whole'.[51] The collective body that was self-reflexively represented in *Screen Tests* extended beyond cinematic circles, as testified by the cameo appearances of Janusz Głowacki and Jacek Kleyff,[52] who were well-known dissident artists at that time. Therefore, self-reflexivity in *Screen Tests* did not produce a Brechtian alienation effect provoking a critical reconsideration of the cinematic medium and its limitations but rather testified to the existence of a creative collective whose artistic and ideological credo was at odds with the official cultural politics.

Not surprisingly, a documentary about the unit 'X' made in 2011 by Michał Bielawski was entitled *Family Situations of the Unit 'X'* (*Sytuacje rodzinne Zespołu 'X'*), a title that on the one hand alluded to one of their collective television projects and on the other hand suggested the family-like bonds between its members. Admittedly, the relationship between Holland and Wajda was frequently compared to a father–daughter relationship, while it would be easy to see Barbara Pec-Ślesicka as a symbolic mother whose task was to distribute accessible sources among the family members. Finally, Bolesław Michałek perfectly performed the role of a helpful and supportive uncle who used his extensive social networks to facilitate 'the kids' entering the adult (professional) life. Given the traditional role of the Polish family being simultaneously the locus of political resistance in the national struggle and oppressive patriarchal structures (see E. Ostrowska 1998), addressing the unit 'X' through the family metaphor discloses its hierarchical aspect that Holland was eager to question. Yet she was also ready to follow Wajda's idea of cinema conceived as an important part of national culture.[53]

During the making of *Screen Tests*, Holland relied on the authority of Wajda and Pec-Ślesicka, but at the same time she managed to strengthen her status as the informal leader in the film unit 'X' (see Szczepańska 2017, 134), which was contested by some of her colleagues; for example, Jerzy Domaradzki stated: 'Wajda's authority was unquestionable and evident, thus if somebody could not accept it, s/he could go away, however the emergence of the, so to say, pseudo-leaders was dangerous' (quoted in Socha 2018, 140).[54] During the making of *Screen Tests*, Holland solidified her strong position in the collective. In the conflict between the young directors and the executive producer Zbigniew Tołłoczko, she denounced his unprofessional performance in a long letter addressed to Pec-Ślesicka and Wajda. She complained about Tołłoczko's negative attitude to the project, indolence, indifference and inability to organise a professional and reliable crew. She requested interventions from the production and artistic directors of the unit 'X', considering these necessary in order to complete the project (Wajda's Archive; see also Szczepańska 2017, 134). Although the position of executive film producer was not as strong as it was in Hollywood, it nevertheless provided significant power that Holland was strong enough to criticise and oppose. Ultimately, her action granted her the position of unprecedented power compared to other Polish female filmmakers at that time.

However, as was often emphasised by Holland's colleagues, she acquired this powerful position due to her perfect appropriation of stereotypical masculinist patterns of behaviour, while developing a close relationship with the men in her film circle. There was a popular saying that 'Holland is the only man in the unit "X"',[55] whereas one of the film critics entitled an article about her 'Zanussi in a Skirt'.[56] These figurative descriptions of her persona indicate her successful masculinist masquerade which was the only way to achieve a strong position within the film industry. Years later, Paweł Pawlikowski also commented on these performances, 'She had to be like a stereotypical image of a man: hard, secretive, hidden behind a story' (in Pasternak 2022, 131). In her professional career in Poland in the 1970s, Holland experimented with various gender scripts, yet she was adopting protective mechanisms rather than trying out alternate identities.[57] She developed efficient strategies to function in the masculinised environment of the film industry in the Poland of late socialism and the dissident cultural circles that voiced their discontent with the Polish political reality of the 1970s in the Cinema of Moral Concern.

THE CINEMA OF MORAL CONCERN: NATIONAL CINEMA AND POLITICAL ENGAGEMENT

The term Cinema of Moral Concern[58] refers to the group of films produced between 1976 and 1981, the action of which takes place in then contemporary Poland. Their protagonists struggle with ethical dilemmas experienced by the Polish society living in the period of late state socialism. The films employed a realistic style that enabled an unobtrusive presentation of urgent social and political subject matters. Two film units produced most of the works belonging to the movement: the 'Tor' and the 'X', with the latter making ten out of nineteen films that are identified as the core of the movement. Although the artistic heads of these units significantly contributed to the Cinema of Moral Concern, Zanussi with his *Camouflage* (*Barwy ochronne*, 1977) and Wajda with *Man of Marble* (*Człowiek z marmuru*, 1977) and *Without Anesthesia* (*Bez znieczulenia*, 1978),[59] it was mostly a generational movement. As Holland admits:

> this was the formation created thanks to a certain generational experience – the meeting of people sharing a similar sensibility and a strong need to receive feedback from the audience. This was not the film criticism that invented 'moral concern'. [. . .] This phenomenon was not artificial; it truly existed on the basis of 'social request'. It was created by the viewers. (quoted in Haltof 2002, 147)

In her monograph on the Cinema of Moral Concern, the Polish film historian Dobrochna Dabert identified the events of March '68 and the invasion of the Warsaw Pact military forces on Czechoslovakia as generational experiences shared by the young filmmakers in the movement (Dabert 2003, 16). Holland expressed her firm identification with the generation. While claiming the movement was 'created by the viewers', she implied successful communication between the audience and filmmakers. The latter responded to the expectations of the former, and thus, cinema provided an important arena for various social, political and cultural exchanges from which a kind of filmic Andersonian 'imagined community' (Anderson 2006) emerged that differed significantly from the one envisioned in the socialist project. In the late 1970s, the conflict between society and the state had become more pronounced than ever culminating in the emergence of the Solidarity movement. Paradoxically, the Cinema of Moral Concern expressed the former's discontent in the films that were financed by the latter. The bonds between the filmmakers and the national audience tightened further during the Solidarity period. Notwithstanding the national appeal of the films made by the young filmmakers, it needs to be emphasised that their works did not leave much space for other forms of spectatorial identification based on gender, ethnicity or social class. Their films featured male protagonists from the intelligentsia who were facing and struggling against maladies of the corrupted socialist system. Holland's films belonging to the movement by contrast negotiated between hegemonic (national) and alternative discourses on collective and individual identity.

In the late 1970s, Holland also negotiated between cinematic and television form. At that time, together with her then husband, Laco Adamik, she prepared two Television Theatre productions: Alfred de Musset's *Lorenzaccio* (1978) and Franz Kafka's *The Trial* (1980).[60] Polish critics located the television productions within the framework of the Cinema of Moral Concern despite these being adaptations of literary classics. Both featured male protagonists whose dramatic situation tacitly commented on the contemporary political situation. As *Lorenzaccio* takes up the theme of a futile attempt at overthrowing authoritarian rule, it was easy to interpret it as a symbolic representation of the political situation of late state socialism and its specific variant of authoritarianism.[61] The reviewers also noted that Adamik and Holland employed devices that were filmic rather than theatrical in that they made extensive use of close-ups and editing to produce a narrative flow instead of aiming for spectacle.[62] The link with cinema was also due to casting: the two main male roles were played by Jerzy Stuhr and Jerzy Radziwiłowicz, who appeared in two flagship films of the Cinema of Moral Concern, respectively *Top Dog* (*Wodzirej*, Feliks Falk, 1978) and *Man of Marble* by Wajda. Due to this casting decision, *Lorenzaccio* was located within a framework that encouraged political interpretation. Ultimately, the television project, produced by the Kraków local station, was approached by critics and most likely by the viewers as a hybrid of cinema, theatre and television, while being also placed within national high culture production. Likewise, Holland and Adamik's television adaptation of Kafka's *The Trial* was appreciated for its artistic qualities, while being also read as an open commentary on the then current political situation in Poland.

For Holland, participation in the Cinema of Moral Concern was an opportunity to (re)integrate into the national film culture she was separated from during her years spent at FAMU in Prague. The evolution of her cinematic and television works from the 1970s demonstrates her transition from her transnational experience of her study time in Prague to Polish national cinema. There are significant gaps between the ironic distance and visual stylisation of her diploma film *Jesus Christ's Sin* as well as her first Polish production *An Evening at Abdon*, and her realistic exploration of women's issues in the collective projects produced by the film unit 'X' and her last films made in Poland: *Provincial Actors*, *Fever* and *A Woman Alone*. Holland's diploma film and her Polish debut *An Evening at Abdon* displayed her individualism and ability to subvert cultural clichés and norms of Polish national culture, whereas her later works were collective projects in terms of the mode of production, their format or their relation to national culture. Although she performed the role of leader in the collective of the young filmmakers, while managing to change her relationship with Wajda from being his protégée to a trusted collaborator, in her work created back in Poland, she privileged the (national) collective over the individual. In this sense, she exemplifies the phenomenon succinctly analysed and identified by Sebastian Jagielski in his book *Przerwane emancypacje* (*Interrupted Emancipations*, 2021) where he argues that the emancipation projects initiated in Polish cinema in the late 1960s and early 1970s were interrupted and eventually annihilated by the Cinema of Moral Concern. As he convincingly argues, these films show how the earlier emancipatory gender discourses, even if articulated only at the margins of the dominant model of cinema, were replaced by the conservative representational gender politics developed within the hegemonic national culture. Holland's films reluctantly participated in this shift.

THE CINEMA OF GENDER (UN)CONCERN

The female protagonists in Holland's Polish films are frequently at odds with the system of patriarchal values and norms, however, they eventually abandon the potentially emancipatory life trajectories and accede to the conservative model of society with family at its centre. For example, in the novella *Girl and 'Aquarius'* the girl returns home and is subjected to examination by the male psychologist. *Sunday Children* reveals the oppressive patriarchal norm of 'true' femininity, equated with motherhood, however the film represents the commodification of pregnancy as a symptom of the moral crisis of Polish society rather than using it to critique oppressive patriarchal norms. The protagonist of *Something for Something* epitomises liberated femininity, yet at some point her emancipation appears to be a façade that hides fears and uncertainties fuelled by patriarchal ideology. Anka, the female protagonist of *Screen Tests*, initially exercises non-normative sexual behaviours, as demonstrated in the masturbation episode[63] and her decision to become sexually active with a partner of her choice, who, to her disappointment, cynically exploits her. As if to compensate for this, she later exploits and objectifies Paweł. In her relationship with him, she refuses to accept the position of passivity designated for women in the patriarchal script, but at the same time she detaches herself from her emotions that are considered a (female) weakness in the male-oriented world. She accepts the patriarchal rules as this is the only way to be successful in the professional world of filmmaking. Importantly, it is Holland herself who, as a fictional director, encourages Anka and Paweł to use their personal experiences in the improvised scene, yet this is not to help them express themselves but rather to produce an effect of intense emotionality. One may ponder whether Holland is smuggling into this episode another part of her female experience in the world of Polish cinema?[64]

In Holland's full feature debut *Provincial Actors* (*Aktorzy prowincjonalni*, 1978), one of the flagship films of the Cinema of Moral Concern, the emancipatory gender project is also terminated prematurely. Holland authored the script for the film with her friend Witold Zatorski, who, as mentioned, helped her and Laco Adamik to get Television Theatre appointments. In her interview given to John Tibbetts, she introduces the film as a very personal project, while also admitting its intended metaphorical message:

> Just before I did this movie I was directing the play in a provincial theatre,[65] so a lot of it was taken from my experiences and observations. [. . .] I wanted it to be realistic, to be seen in communist Poland as a metaphor for the country itself and not just a provincial theatre. (Tibbetts and Holland 2008, 134)

The narrative is also double: the preparation of the classical Polish play *Liberation* (*Wyzwolenie* by Stanisław Wyspiański) by the provincial theatre company is mirrored by the marital crisis of the lead actor, Krzysztof (Tadeusz Huk), and his wife, Anka (Halina Łabonarska). An actor in a puppet theatre for children, Anka is frustrated with her job, which seems to be below her artistic aspirations and capabilities. Allegedly, she was expelled from the acting department of the theatre school for having the 'wrong mental attitude', yet most likely it was due to her participation in the events of the March '68.[66] Her husband works in a 'proper' dramatic theatre, yet this is permeated with stagnation and apathy. Holland presents it as a highly hierarchical structure regulated by patriarchal rules, as demonstrated by the actresses' desperate attempts to hold on to their attractiveness, whatever it takes.

Anka, who is a puppeteer, is not subjected to such pressure, however, she occupies a lowly position in the local theatre community, something for which she is mocked by her husband. Her inferior status can be compared to the low prestige of Polish female filmmakers who made films for children.[67] Despite the low cultural capital of her profession, Anka derives satisfaction and pleasure from it, as shown in a few episodes which take place in the puppet theatre. Most importantly, the children in the audience are presented as experiencing a joyful and spontaneous pleasure which contrasts with the scant audience in her husband's theatre who hastily leave once the curtain goes down. No wonder that participation in the prestigious national theatre project brings only frustration and suffering for her husband. When a respected director comes from the capital, Warsaw, to direct the classic play and selects him to play a lead role, Krzysztof hopes to participate in a politically engaged theatrical enterprise. However, the cynical director opportunistically cuts out all sensitive parts from the play in order to avoid any issues with censorship. In despair, he exaggeratedly performs the role of oppressed artist, while expecting Anka to play the role of a supportive wife. Polish film critic Maria Kornatowska called him 'hysterical, egocentric, and infantile' in contrast to Anka, who was mature and thoughtful (Kornatowska 1990, 217). Initially, the female protagonist refuses to play the role he designated for her in his national-patriarchal script, yet her resistance seems to be of limited scope.[68]

Initially, Anka makes an effort to fix their marriage through rejuvenating their erotic life, and to this aim she wears a sexy nightgown. Her husband hardly notices her and falls asleep (Fig. 2.4). She moves to the kitchen to sleep on the folding bed, yet before she sleeps, she masturbates, as Anka did in *Screen Tests*. Her performance of sexually active femininity to attract him back fails because her husband's libidinal energy is entirely displaced into national art (see Bobowski 2001, 94). Their childlessness may be a hint of his impotence, especially when linked with his derogatory advice for her to 'make a baby instead of crying over a dead cat'. While heterosexual desire is practically absent in Anka and Krzysztof's relationship, as in all others in the film, homosexual desire is tacitly present through the character of Krzysztof's best friend, Andrzej, who is gay. Confused by their relationship, at one point Krzysztof asks him whether he is his friend or a 'gay in love with him', as if these two were exclusive. This exchange occurs in the scene when Krzysztof gets changed in his dressing room while his friend looks at his naked body. When the long shot cuts to Krzysztof's close-up, the viewer's gaze identifies with Andrzej's, with its potential homoerotic desire. Contrarily, throughout the film, Anka is

Figure 2.4 *Provincial Actors* (1978)

not presented as the object of anybody's gaze and it is rather she who looks at other people. Although the narrative presents many examples of misogynist behaviour, the film's politics of gaze thus resists the patriarchal logic.

At one point in the narrative, Anka realises there is no alternative gender project for her to pursue. She becomes conscious of this identity limbo during her guest theatre performances in Warsaw. By accident, she meets her schoolmate there, a successful architect and divorcee, who embodies an independent and successful womanhood. When Anka visits her spacious and modern apartment, they chat while her friend's younger lover is cooking a meal for them. Uncomfortable in this modern surrounding, Anka soon leaves. She feels estranged from both her husband playing the role of national artist and from her female friend incarnating liberated femininity.[69] It could thus be said that she feels alienated from both the national and the Western feminist discourses. Such an alienation was a typical experience of many Polish women in the late 1970s and 1980s. Elżbieta Kaczyńska's observation indirectly echoes this: 'We tend to talk about our [Polish] feminism as what it's not – it's not like what the communists meant by gender equality or what it's like in the West – but we seldom state positively what Polish feminism is, or could be about' (quoted in Bystydzienski 2001, 508). Throughout the film, Anka experiences a similar confusion concerning her femininity. Ultimately, and somehow unexpectedly, in the film's ending she accepts the role of a supportive wife who behaves like a mother protecting her helpless and vulnerable offspring. Their initial emotional and sexual alienation from each other ceases to be an issue when juxtaposed with the crisis of national art and the crisis of masculinity.

Jagielski notes, 'Although Holland attacks patriarchy, in the film's ending she emphasizes that the wife's place is at her (idealistic) husband's side in the state of crisis' (Jagielski 2021, 247).[70] According to the Polish film historian, Holland, along with other filmmakers representing the Cinema of Moral Concern, looks for the origins of male hysteria[71] in the destructive and degrading political system, whereas from the contemporary perspective it is evident that the crisis of masculinity was first and foremost a response to women's strong position achieved due to the post-Second World War emancipation project (see Fidelis 2010). However, within the filmic narratives these emancipatory impulses are put on hold and eventually the female characters undergo patriarchal adjustment. Jagielski concludes: 'although the Cinema of Moral Concern presented emancipated women, it did not challenge the patriarchy but instead supported it in that it offered a spectatorial identification with men who fought the system while at the same time humiliating women' (Jagielski 2021, 247). Contrarily, Brunilda Amarsllss Lugo de Fabritz claims that *Provincial Actors* develops 'a dual narrative' (Lugo de Fabritz 2003); the position of spectatorial identification is thereby split, and, it could be argued, it privileges the female protagonist. Anka's lack of agency is interrogated rather than corroborated.[72]

While Jagielski's claim that the Cinema of Moral Concern blocked emancipatory gender discourses due to the hegemony of patriarchy is valid, there were other factors contributing to this regressive politics. As Anikó Imre noted, socialist Eastern European cinemas developed two main ideological discourses, socialism and nationalism, and '[t]hese two powerful ideological blocks have acted as filters that reduced gender politics to the anti-Soviet politics of the national auteur, who might occasionally and incidentally be a woman' (Imre 2017, 88–9). Consequently, as she argued, the cinemas of the region established a uniquely stable and effective 'script of male universalist nationalism', while 'leaving little room for subnational identifications' (Imre 2017, 90, 91). Both Western and Eastern European critical discourses solidified the 'nationalisation' of the cinemas of the region, impeding the emergence of women's cinema or any critical recognition of the existing film practices as such. For example, the Polish female film historian Małgorzata Hendrykowska noted that the Cinema of Moral Concern eagerly appealed to patriotic sentiments, while *Provincial Actors*, along with the last film made in Poland by Holland, *A Woman Alone*, are 'universal stories about people' (Hendrykowska 2000, 191, 192). In a similar vein, Lugo de Fabritz, in her essay 'Agnieszka Holland: Continuity, the Self, and Artistic Vision', published in the seminal volume *Women Filmmakers:*

Refocusing, claims that, in *Provincial Actors*, 'Holland develops an allegory of the state of Polish society through her depiction of the way the different characters' identities are constructed and deconstructed by the communist system' (Lugo de Fabritz 2003, 99). This critical framework of dissident national cinema is still in use and Holland's Polish films are critically embedded in the national narratives. In her recently published biography of Holland, Pasternak uses a feminist perspective while presenting the director's life, whereas in her comments on the films, especially those made in the Poland of state socialism, she evidently places their narratives within the national scripts. She writes: 'I think about women from early films by Agnieszka and it strikes me how deeply tragic figures they are. Not because they lost [as women] as everyone lost there [in socialist Poland]' (Pasternak 2022, 111; see also Szczawińska 2012, 138, 143).[73] She implies their nationality and geopolitical positioning in the Eastern Bloc, rather than their gender, was the source of their oppression. Her claim that *Provincial Actors* is 'a metaphor of Poland' ultimately confirms Pasternak's entanglement into the national discourse (Pasternak 2022, 112). Thus, the author regurgitates the collective national discourse that she intended to question in her biography of Holland. Although she later claims that Holland's early Polish films were made from a feminine perspective in that they were taking up the themes of sexism and motherhood, and she calls *A Woman Alone* as 'thoroughly feminist' (Pasternak 2022, 123), she does not address the tension between the national and gender discourses that is a crucial issue in all Holland's Polish works.

Pasternak, along with most of the critics, also overlooks the economic factors determining women's emancipation as represented in *Provincial Actors* and other films made by Holland in the Poland of late socialism. Anka's schoolmate earns good money, as does Anna from *Something for Something*, and they both enjoy agency and (sexual) freedom. They both have younger sexual partners whom they manifestly dominate. Originating from a working-class background, Anka from *Screen Tests* aspires to be a sexually liberated young woman, yet she does not have access to the contraceptive pill as Anna from *Something for Something* does. Moreover, her partner mistakes her sexual emancipation for promiscuity, which reveals his deep attachment to the normative concept of femininity, with chastity being its pinnacle. The young pregnant girl from *Sunday Children* most likely also believed in her sexual freedom, yet she was not provided with sufficient knowledge of or the means to access birth control. Furthermore, living in the workers' hostel and sharing the room with her female friends, she would not be able to bring her baby up on her own even if she wanted to. Holland's films tacitly indicate that in socialist Poland, emancipation is a luxury not all women can afford. Gender and economic oppression are the main theme of Holland's last film made in Poland, *A Woman Alone*, which I will discuss shortly.

Compared to her previous works such as *Sunday Children*, *Something for Something* and *Screen Tests*, *Provincial Actors* – Holland's full feature debut and a flagship of the Cinema of Moral Concern – demonstrates her gradually increasing engagement with political and national matters at the expense of the women's issues explored in the earlier works. The shift from gender to nation converges with transferring from the television production framework to regular film production and standard distribution in movie theatres. Thus, rather unexpectedly, socialist television provided space for sub-national identifications that had been rarely explored in Polish (national) cinema. Admittedly, there is a visible evolution of the female characters in Holland's early films made in Poland: in her early works such as *Jesus Christ's Sin* and *An Evening at Abdon* they were mostly preoccupied with fulfilling their (libidinal) desires, then in her early television works they were confronting social forces that were at odds with their sexual needs, and finally, in her late films belonging to the Cinema of Moral Concern, they abandon or subordinate their emancipatory aspirations to the collective demands of their own families or the national community.[74]

NATIONAL (DISSIDENT) CINEMA AND GENDER UNCERTAINTIES

When the jury at the 1979 Polish Film Festival awarded *Provincial Actors* the prize for the Best Debut, there was political pressure to revisit the decision, and the prize was awarded to Filip Bajon and Janusz Kijowski. Only the cinematographer Sławomir Idziak dissented from the jury's decision (Wojtczak 2009, 230).[75] The political manipulation around Holland's film was harmful to her career, but at the same time it contributed to her status as dissident artist harassed by the oppressive political system.[76] This position was strengthened with her next two films, *Fever* (*Gorączka*, 1980) and *A Woman Alone* (*Kobieta samotna*, 1981, prem. 1987), that were also identified as belonging to the Cinema of Moral Concern,[77] especially since the latter one was shelved, which means it was not officially released until 1987.

Fever is an important film in Holland's output because it marks what I will call 'an unfulfilled desire for change'. It was based on Andrzej Strug's novel *History of One Bullet* (*Dzieje jednego pocisku*, 1910), the action of which takes place during the 1905 revolution in Russian Poland.[78] The historical theme, episodic narrative, sophisticated camera work, contrapuntal sound and dynamic editing mark the film's aesthetic distance from the realistic depictions of Polish then contemporary life offered by the core films of the Cinema of Moral Concern. However, this aesthetic distance does not equate with ideological detachment from the national 'imagined community'. The film reinforces it in that it emphasises the national aspect of the revolution that was aimed against tsarist Russia.[79] As the 1905 revolution expressed both social and national emancipatory impulses it was frequently compared with the Solidarity movement that was also challenging the economic oppression of the workers as well as Poland's dependence on the Soviet power.[80] Eventually, both protests became embedded within the national discourse. *Fever* presents the lost revolution as another national uprising rather than a failed social revolt. Frederic Jameson noted the absence of masses in the film: 'The patriotic young fanatics of *Fever* are anarchists and "infantile leftists" of the purest stamp: the framework of some larger underground socialist mass party is invoked but never represented; and the film explicitly makes the point that its terrorist initiatives are radically disjoined from any such mass political movement' (Jameson 1986, 322). As the film does not acknowledge the 1905 revolution's genuine emancipatory impulses its message converges with the public discourse constructed around the Solidarity movement[81] that eventually also downplayed its social programme while foregrounding national matters.[82]

Fever leaves very little space for identities other than national ones, which is especially evident in the female character of Kama (Barbara Grabowska). She is introduced as a revolutionary whose 'peculiar longing for martyrdom' (Jameson 1986, 322–3) makes her a perfect executor of the task of carrying out a terrorist attack. However, when the plan goes awry, she suffers an attack of hysteria and eventually ends up in an asylum (Fig. 2.5). Even before this symbolic act of 'sentencing' her to hysteria – a female psychic illness per se as designated by psychoanalysis – her reason for participating in the revolutionary activities is very unclear and there is a tacit suggestion that it might be because of her unrequited love for Leon (Olgierd Łukaszewicz), the leader of the revolutionary team. The scene of their sexual intercourse epitomises his objectification of the woman in that he performs the sexual act in an excessively mechanical fashion, avoiding both verbal and eye contact, while she gratefully accepts it, as shown by her kissing his hand afterwards. Jameson sees the scene as suggesting phantasmatic nature of her revolutionary involvement: 'her own ecstasy stands as sufficient comment on the fantasmatic nature of her passion for a figure who, [. . .] is little more than an absence driven and possessed' (Jameson 1986, 323). Her initial political agency is terminated, first by her sexual subservience, and then with her mental deficiency as culturally coded as hysteria. By contrast, her male companions' failure is marked either by death or imprisonment. In her feminist-oriented essay on *Fever* published almost twenty years after the film's release, Ewa Toniak suggested that for female viewers, watching the film can be compared to an act of self-aggression (Toniak 2007, 278).

With its historical theme, epic narrative perspective and sophisticated visual devices, *Fever* marked Holland's departure from the dominant aesthetic

Figure 2.5 *Fever* (1980)

of the Cinema of Moral Concern. According to Toniak, especially important is her abandonment of the claustrophobic spaces of tiny and crowded apartments that are traditionally ascribed to women and symbolise their domestication, while replacing these with the open public spaces that are frequently conceived as the male domain of public affairs. However, as Toniak notes, the open exteriors are closed off with tunnel-like alleys and narrow streets, taking away any promise of freedom for both male and female characters whose movement, and agency for that matter, is limited. Toniak calls the spatial pattern a visual expression of the castrating forces emanating from Polish public spaces (Toniak 2007, 281). Some critics interpreted *Fever* as a political allegory, or even a prophetic vision of the Solidarity movement that eventually proved to be disconcertingly similar to the 1905 revolution in that both were suppressed with the implementation of martial law. I would argue for another similarity that has not been acknowledged concerning the positioning of women. The film's narrative logic, specifically the expulsion of the female character of Kama from the narrative revolving around the (national) revolutionary struggles can be seen as foreshadowing the erasure of women's contribution to the Solidarity movement as described years later by the American female historian Shana Penn in the book *Solidarity's Secret: The Women Who*

Defeated Communism in Poland (2005). Seen from such a broad perspective, *Fever* is not only about impossible revolution as Holland maintained, but also about the impossibility of integrating women into collective (national) history. The film portrays attempts to integrate various social classes (aristocracy, peasantry, working class and petit bourgeoisie), as well as different ideological options (socialism and anarchism) in the revolutionary project, yet it leaves no space for gender equality.

Holland's next film, *A Woman Alone*, made for Polish television in 1981, the action of which takes place during the Solidarity period, foregrounds the marginalisation of the female subject in the national space. Its protagonist, Irena (Maria Chwalibóg), a single mother who works as a postwoman, is visibly excluded from the local community, whether this is constructed around the local Party committee, the Solidarity units or the Catholic parish. Katarzyna Marciniak calls her a social abject (2005, 7). Although suffering from poverty and social ostracism, Irena does not accept the role of a passive victim as codified by the national discourse in the mythical figure of the Polish Mother (see E. Ostrowska 1998). When she meets a young, disabled man, Jacek (Bogusław Linda), she reluctantly gets intimate with him. Eventually, she realises that the only option to break out of the vicious circle of oppression and humiliation is to break the law. She steals public money, abandons her son and then escapes with her lover whom she lets believe she inherited the money from her deceased auntie. Alas, due to a fatal crash, the escape plan goes awry, and he suffocates Irena to death, seeing this murder as a merciful act (see Fig. 2.6).

The protagonist of *A Woman Alone* transgresses the normative pattern of femininity as codified within the national culture on multiple levels: she is a single mother, she gets intimate with a younger partner, while also initiating the sexual relationship with him. Consequently, she is excluded from the 'imagined community' in both literal and figurative fashion. Her most radical divergence from the culturally prescribed model of femininity occurs when she decides to abandon her child in the orphanage. She can be seen as a symbolic older sister of the girl from *Sunday Children* who also transgressed the supposed eternal laws of maternity. Due to their inferior social and economic position they could not provide adequately for themselves or their children in either caring or financial terms. They could not afford to have children. As the action of the film takes place after the victory of the Solidarity movement, the film may suggest that women hardly benefitted from it, particularly if they did not strongly identify with the national 'imagined community' which was the case with Irena, who displayed ignorance about the important events in Polish history. Holland's film denounces women's subjugation to oppressive social and political forces, whether they originate from communist or nationalist ideologies, because both are embedded in patriarchal structures. The character of Irena also destabilises the normative model of femininity, yet her eventual

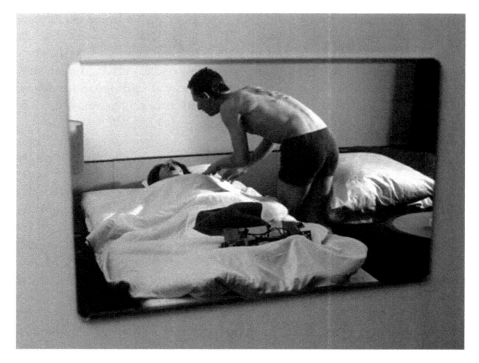

Figure 2.6 *A Woman Alone* (1981)

death at the hands of her lover can be seen as a symbolic punishment of her act of transgression. It is as if the position of victim were the only one available for women in the Polish national scenario.

A Woman Alone – as if mirroring the fate of its protagonist – was silenced through its ban from the official film distribution. After the introduction of martial law in Poland in December 1981, the censor shelved the film for seven years, and its premiere took place only in 1987. In the meantime, the film was distributed illegally on VHS released by NOWA, the first underground publishing house in Poland established in 1977. In 1988, the film was presented at the Polish Film Festival in Gdynia, where it was awarded the Special Jury Prize for its director, who was then living in exile. Critics and film historians approached the film as either one of the last films of the Cinema of Moral Concern (see Dabert 2003, 24), or as Holland's *auteurist* work (see Jankun-Dopartowa 2000; Bobowski 2001), while downplaying, or ignoring, its gender theme. Jankun-Dopartowa and Dabert claimed that the film was a modern variant of classical tragedy where death was inevitable and caused by fate rather than specific socio-political circumstances (Jankun-Dopartowa 2000, 180–1; Dabert 2003, 162). In my own essay on Agnieszka Holland published in 2006, I claimed that the character of Irena subverted the national myth of femininity embodied in the myth of the Polish Mother, while arguing that the film did not fit a feminist framework (Mazierska and Ostrowska 2006, 203). Now, years later, I would argue that Holland's film did not fit the Western second-wave feminist framework. In changing my previous perspective, I took inspiration from Katarzyna Marciniak's reflections on *A Woman Alone*. She examined its ideological ambivalence in relation to the film's politics of the gaze in that it did not objectify the female protagonist, while not providing her with subjectivity either: 'the spectatorial gaze is dislocated in its customary ocular comfort and bound to the visual and emotive experiences of abjection' that eventually leads to 'suffocation by the diegesis' (Marciniak 2005, 13, 15). Recognising the oppressiveness of diegesis, containing many various forces, Marciniak implicitly called for an analysis of Eastern European female experience beyond a gender-only feminist framework. Ultimately, the case of Holland's film prompted her to argue for the urgent need to expand the realm of transnational feminism and revise its theoretical and methodological apparatus to include female experience from the region in its specificity.

The genealogy of gender discourse in postwar Poland originates from the specific nexus of ideological, social and cultural factors. Arising from pre-war national emancipatory and communist movements, it merged with the postwar gender equality doctrine that was embedded within patriarchal Stalinist totalitarianism. As demonstrated by extensive research into genealogies of contemporary Polish feminism (Fidelis 2010), Polish women were provided after the Second World War with considerable possibilities of mobility in terms of both physical and social movements. The former referred to the massive postwar migrations from countryside to the cities, whereas the latter concerned social and economic advancement in that they were provided with possibilities to gain education and paid jobs. While earning less than men's salaries, nevertheless, they were gaining economic agency on an unprecedented scale. However, they were still subordinated to patriarchal social structures that were embedded within both communist and national discourses.

The female protagonist of *A Woman Alone* can be seen as a symbolic representation of women's oppression in the Poland of late socialism that resulted from the ineffectiveness of the officially proclaimed state feminism and the underdevelopment of the civil feminism movement that was suppressed by the national discourse. Intensification of the social and national protests in the late 1970s has either supressed women's emancipatory aspirations or subordinated them to the collective liberatory struggles. Hence the resistance or perhaps unwillingness to acknowledge gender oppression in Polish cinema, including in Holland's films. As mentioned, most of the women in Holland's films were provided with significant subjectivity, yet they eventually retreated from the emancipatory path and submitted to the core values of the national (patriarchal) culture. As such, they embodied the multifaceted oppression of Polish women, while attesting that gender-only feminism was an inadequate ideological project with which to examine the vernacular gender discourse and its cinematic representations.[83] I argue that the concept of 'restrained mobility' proves useful in investigating Polish women's movements across various political, social and cultural spaces that were developing rhizomatic trajectories of progress and regression with unexpected stops and pauses. These irregular and dynamic movements were expanding the available social and cultural territories, yet within strict limits of national and communist patriarchal systems.

Holland's own professional trajectory in Poland reflects the paradoxes of women's emancipation in Poland, or Eastern European 'restrained mobility'. Although her decision to study abroad was out of necessity, it allowed her to move across various cultural territories and thereby distance herself from the hegemonic socio-cultural discourses. After graduating from Prague, she (re) entered the system of Polish film culture from outside, yet soon she achieved a position of informal leadership in the film unit 'X' that required adjusting to the masculine norms regulating the film industry. Admittedly, she was successful because she effectively performed a gender masquerade. Her reluctant attitude to feminism originated from an unwillingness to acknowledge gender oppression or from confusing it with political oppression. As Holland recently admitted, 'Communism was the main enemy in Poland [. . .] we did not consider struggles for gender equality an urgent matter' (in Pasternak 2022, 126). Her statement echoes Maria Janion's observation made in 1996:

> the dominating way of thinking of the opposition in the 1970s and 1980s was that the struggle for independence was serious, the struggle for women's right was not [. . .] I remember when, during a feminist discussion in an international gathering in West Berlin at the end of the 1980s, I maintained that Solidarity, first, had to win independence and democracy for all of society and only then would it be able to deal with women's questions and improvement of women's situation. (Janion 1996, 326)

Several years later, Janion realised that post-1989 democracy meant for Polish women restrictions on abortion law and subjugating them to their family roles. At that time Holland was already abroad developing her transnational career that eventually transpired to be another 'restrained mobility'.

NOTES

1. The film is also known as *A Lonely Woman*.
2. In particular, she was disappointed with the indifference shown by Polish society towards the political dissidents who were at that time released from prisons after serving their sentences for participating in the events of March '68 (see Czerkawski 2019, 151).

3. She refers here to the workers' strikes in the Gdańsk Shipyard in December 1970s, during which several people were killed by militia.
4. Agnieszka Holland, 'Nasz kolega Jan Palach', interview by Tadeusz Sobolewski, *Gazeta Wyborcza*, no. 52, 2013, 34.
5. During her first professional appointment, Holland met Ryszard Bugajski (who worked as a second assistant) and was also a member of the film unit 'X' where he made the infamous *Interrogation* (*Przesłuchanie*, 1982), in which Holland acted a single-episode role of a communist, alongside Anna Biedrzycka, a costume designer, who many years later worked with Holland on *To Kill a Priest* (1986) and *Washington Square* (1997).
6. Wajda reports that Konwicki asked him to watch Holland's diploma film *Jesus Christ's Sin* (Wajda 2000, 209).
7. Wajda's close collaboration with young filmmakers meant also a significant amount of control over their projects; aside from various consultations during the processes of pre-production and production, he would frequently participate in the editing of their films (see Socha 2018, 133).
8. Agnieszka Holland, 'Robić film. Rozmowa z Agnieszką Holland', interview by Wilhelmina Skulska, *Przekrój* no. 2035, 1989, 8–9.
9. To attract young filmmakers to his unit, Wajda approached the film school students and announced a script competition for making a short film in his unit. The result was the omnibus film *CDN* (1975), consisting of three novels made by Paweł Kędzierski, Zbigniew Kamiński and Radosław Piwowarski (the latter's novel was not accepted for distribution). The two novels were independent in terms of the characters and story, yet they both featured female protagonists experiencing difficult situations. The directors were responsible for their own parts, however, they also helped one another, working as director's assistant or helping with editing. This model of collective filmmaking that merged artistic autonomy with professional collaboration has been practised in many later film projects realised in the unit 'X'. It is worth mentioning that Polish socialist realist cinema explored the possibilities of collective authorship in the film *Two Brigades* (*Dwie brygady*, 1950) made by six filmmakers.
10. Imre quotes the opinion expressed by the authors of the comprehensive volume *A European Television History*: 'In most Western European countries, television developed into a medium for the propagation of consumption, leisure and individualism; in the Eastern countries, it became a medium for the political socialization of the individual and the subtle implementation of ideology and political values' (quoted in Imre 2016, 18).
11. As Holland explained to John Tibbetts, 'We have in Poland the Theatre for Television, which is a little like your own television movies – classical and contemporary plays shot with three cameras' (Tibbetts and Holland 2008, 134). For more detailed examination of this television genre, see Sordyl 2010.
12. Polish television theatre can be compared with American 'quality drama' that, as Jane Feuer explains, 'existed in the form of the live "anthology" teleplays of the 1950s. Written by New York playwrights, appealing to an élite audience and financed by individual sponsors as prestige productions' (Feuer 2007, 146).
13. Agnieszka Holland, email message to the author, 15 December 2022.
14. In the survey conducted among the former members of the film unit 'X', Holland listed three scripts that were not accepted by the film authorities: *Konarski* (for TV), *Behind Glass* (*Za szkłem*, for TV), and *I Do Not Care about a Big Man* (*Nie zależy mi na dużym mężczyźnie*); (Andrzej Wajda's Archive, henceforth AWA; the Andrzej Wajda Archive in Kraków is located in the Centre for Japanese Culture Mangha; the collection is not yet catalogued).
15. Agnieszka Holland, email message to the author, 15 December 2022.

16. Irena Bołtuć, 'Różne oblicza kariery', review, *Przyjaźń*, no. 24, 1974, 14–15.
17. In 1975, Holland directed another television project, *Homemade Wine* (*Wino domowej roboty*), by the Czech writer Pavel Hajny, who authored several scripts for Polish movies made in the 1970s and 1980s.
18. Bolesław Michałek, the literary director of the unit 'X', also encouraged the young filmmakers to adapt Iwaszkiewicz's works (see Szczepańska 2017, 133).
19. The location is presented in static long shots with careful frame composition that transform the landscape into tableau-like images reminiscent of Bruno Schulz's *shtetls* described in *The Street of Crocodiles*. The cross-border location that often serves as a spatial metaphor for ambivalent identities will return in Holland's later film projects such as *Europa, Europa* (1990), *In Darkness* (*W ciemności*, 2011) and *Spoor* (*Pokot*, 2017).
20. Alienation from the surrounding reality characterises many of Holland's protagonists, for example Leon from *Fever* (*Gorączka*, 1980), and Catherine Sloper from *Washington Square* (1997).
21. For more detailed analysis of the film see; Jankun-Dopartowa 2000, 75; Bobowski 2001, 32–8; Mazierska and Ostrowska 2006, 186–8.
22. Songs are prominently used in Holland's later films, *Sunday Children*, *Something for Something*, *To Kill a Priest* and *Washington Square*, always providing ironic or affective commentary on the depicted action.
23. Agnieszka Holland, 'Potrzeba intensywności wyrazu', interview by Marek Pawlukiewicz, *Kultura*, no. 50, 1979, 11.
24. In 1974, a television production company Poltel was established, and a new Film and Television School in Katowice was opened, whose main aim was to provide training in filmmaking and television work. In the 1970s many prominent filmmakers worked for television, with Krzysztof Zanussi and Krzysztof Kieślowski being the most notable examples. Dorota Ostrowska and Małgorzata Radkiewicz comment on Wajda's *Man of Marble* (*Człowiek z marmuru*, 1977) as being a self-reflexive reference to the powerful position of television in Polish cinema in the 1970s. As they note, a story of a film student who uses television resources to make her graduation film is 'reflecting the role of television as a producer of films in Poland' (Ostrowska and Radkiewicz 2007, 109). It is added that the protagonist of Wajda's film was partly shaped after Holland who participated in the collaborative projects of the film unit 'X' made for television.
25. The film's critical reception was lukewarm and occasionally entirely negative. The most frequent complaints were that the script was weak and the style inconsistent (see for example: Marek Wieroński, 'Pozory życia, pozory twórczości', *Ekran*, no. 14, 1976, 20; Janusz Skwara, 'Dyrdymałki z teki kibica', *Barwy* no. 5, 1975, 6; Czesław Dondziłło, '"Coś" z życia, coś z filmu', *Film*, no. 13, 1976, 10–11. In her review, Ewa Nurczyńska criticised both the general idea of the omnibus film as a chance for young filmmakers to make a short movie as well as the film itself (Ewa Nurczyńska, '*Obrazki z życia*', *Odgłosy*, no. 11, 1976, 5). Maciej Karpiński expressed more positive opinion and noticed certain consistency in the film (Maciej Karpiński, 'Czy ciąg dalszy rzeczywiście nastąpi', *Kino*, no. 2, 1976, 19–24. None of the reviews mentioned Holland's novella *Girl and 'Aquarius'*.
26. Although the film did not offer any explicit critique of socio-political reality, some members of the Approval Commission criticised it during the meeting on 28 May 1975 and they requested some changes (Andrzej Wajda's Archive, Notes from making *Pictures of Life*).
27. In his review published in *Ekran* (*Screen*), the film magazine following the official cultural politics, Wieroński suggested that the omnibus film was realised in the film unit 'X' because Wajda used almost all allocated money for his own film projects (Wieroński, 'Pozory życia'). Such rumours were disseminated in various circles.

28. Ryszard Bugajski confirms that the TV cycle *Family Situation* was proposed to Wajda by Holland who had a 'big authority' in the film unit 'X' (see Wojtczak 2009, 221).
29. Holland was a kind of model for Krystyna Janda of how to play the protagonist, a young and aggressive female filmmaker. Wajda sent the actress to the film set where Holland was making *Sunday Children* to get some inspiration, which means that he based the brave filmmaker on her (see, for example, Michalak 2016, 183, 185).
30. The most unexpected resolution came from Wajda who offered to adopt Holland and give her his name. Of course, she did not accept the offer as she deliberately kept her father's name even after getting married to manifest her loyalty to him and also as an act of political provocation against the authorities who had kept the circumstances of his death secret (Michalak 2016, 182–3).
31. It is worth noting that neither Wajda nor Holland were loyal to the communist authorities and they disobeyed the ban on Holland's employment on *Man of Marble*. As Katarzyna Mąka-Malatyńska reports, she was his 'secret advisor' who would frequently appear on the film set, and collaborated on the script, authoring several scenes. Yet her contribution could not be documented in the film credits (see Kornatowska 1990, 57; Mąka-Malatyńska 2009, 22).
32. For detailed and feminist-oriented analysis of Holland's Polish works see Monika Talarczyk-Gubała 2013, 205–239.
33. Krystyna Wachelko-Zaleska is one of Holland's regular collaborators; she was also cast in *An Evening at Abdon*, *Something for Something* and *Provincial Actors*. After a long break in their collaboration, she cast Wachelko-Zaleska in the first episode of the Netflix original TV series *1983* (2018).
34. Polish critics have noted the similarity, as did Polish film historians (see Jankun-Dopartowa 2000, 94; Bobowski 2001, 51; Mąka-Malatyńska 2009, 56).
35. In her book *Women, Communism, and Industrialization in Postwar Poland*, Fidelis discusses young working women's sexual emancipation; especially in Chapter 'Women Astray: Debating Sexuality and Reproduction during the Thaw' (Fidelis 2010, 170–202).
36. Polish film historians also classified *Sunday Children* as belonging to the Cinema of Moral Concern (Dabert 2003, 24). Sławomir Bobowski considers the Cinema of Moral Concern as the main framework for Holland's films made in Poland between 1975–1981 (Bobowski 2001, 13–27).
37. Czesław Dondziłło, 'Dzieci, rzeczy i szczęście', *Film*, no. 13, 1977, 6.
38. Dorothea Holloway, '*Niedzielne dzieci (Sunday children)*', review, *Variety* 18 May 1977.
39. Agnieszka Holland, 'Rozmowa z Agnieszką Holland', interview by Elżbieta Królikowska, *Tydzień*, no. 17, 1977, 14.
40. Agnieszka Holland, 'Emancypacja? Coś jest nie tak', interview by Jerzy Pawlas, *Głos Wielkopolski* no. 86, 1978.
41. Her daughter, Kasia Adamik, was born in 1972.
42. Dobrochna Dabert does not see *Something for Something* as representing the Cinema of Moral Concern, while she includes in it *Sunday Children* (Dabert 2003, 25).
43. It is worth mentioning that Holland co-authored a script for the film *Unwanted Man* (*Mężczyzna niepotrzebny*) made in 1982 for Polish television by her then husband Laco Adamik. It tackles the theme of abortion, while also depicting its procedure in graphic fashion. For a more detailed description, see Talarczyk-Gubała 2013, 233.
44. Agata Chałupnik uses the film to discuss the socio-cultural changes resulting from the availability of contraception pills; the protagonist of *Something for Something* is a conspicuous example of it (Chałupnik 2008, 240–1; see also Talarczyk-Gubała 2013, 227).
45. In his review, Tadeusz Szczepański claims that most of the cultural products authored by women are kitschy and sentimental, yet Holland avoids this. He argues that the ending

of her film shows that, for women, choosing a 'male' professional career is inappropriate. He concludes that 'true' femininity means to have children (Tadeusz Szczepański, 'Być kobietą po męsku', *Odgłosy*, no. 49, 1977, 10). Similarly, in her monograph on Holland, Jankun-Dopartowa claims that the protagonist of the film loses because she took on a male role (Jankun-Dopartowa 2000, 338).
46. In her review, Elżbieta Królikowska finds the female character solely focused on her professional career to be 'cold' and suggests that having a baby would probably fix her (Elżbieta Królikowska, 'Coś za nic', *Ekran*, no. 48, 1977, 10) Likewise, Czesław Dondziłło describes the protagonist as not a real woman and suggests that women should balance their professional and family life (Czesław Dondziłło, '"Coś" z życia, coś z filmu', *Film*, no. 13, 1976, 10–1). Aleksander Jan Wieczorkowski wrote that the film is 'antifeminist or perhaps even misogynist' (Aleksander J. Wieczorkowski, 'Pretensje do struktury', *Ekran*, no. 52, 1977, 17). Andrzej Baszkowski also claims that the alternative between professional career and happy family life is artificial and does not reflect reality (Andrzej Baszkowski, 'Kłopoty pani docent', *Fakty*, no. 47, 1977, 11). Hanna Samsonowska examines the whole cycle *Family Situation* and claims that the films accurately reflect the socio-demographic changes occurring in Poland, arguing that these are similar to those that happened in Western world (Hanna Samsonowska, 'Rodzina – portrety z natury', *Kino*, no. 10, 1977, 14–19).
47. See Małgorzata Karbowiak, 'O młodzieży serio', *Głos Robotniczy*, no. 118, 1977, 4; Wiesław Saniewski, 'Jeśli chcesz zostać reżyserem', *Opole*, no. 7, 1977; Kałużyński 1986, 76.
48. Zygmunt Kałużyński notes the similarity of the scene of Anka's sexual initiation with the scene from Miloš Forman's *Loves of a Blonde* (Kałużyński 1986, 76).
49. Anna Lechicka finishes her brief review with a comparison between the film's ending and Wajda's *Everything for Sale* (Anna Lechicka, 'Zdjęcia próbne', *Szpilki*, no. 23, 1977), whereas Małgorzata Dipont entitles her review 'Everything for Sale '77' (Małgorzata Dipont, 'Wszystko na sprzedaż '77', *Życie Warszawy*, no. 123, 1977, 4; finally, Wiesław Saniewski notes that both films use self-reflexivity (Wiesław Saniewski, 'Jeśli chcesz zostać reżyserem').
50. It is worth noting here that from the beginning of her professional career, Holland often employed her relatives and friends in small episodes or cameos; for example, in *Sunday Children* her nanny and her first boyfriend's wife appear.
51. Dorothea Holloway, '*Zdjecia Probne* (Screen Tests)', *Variety*, 25 May 1977.
52. Kleyff also appeared in Holland's novel *Girl and 'Aquarius'* as the girl's father.
53. Importantly, Wajda and Holland's professional relationship extended long after the 'X' unit was resolved in 1983; she wrote scripts to many of his films – *Without Anesthesia* (*Bez znieczulenia*, 1978), *Danton* (1982) and *Korczak* (1990) – and advised on many other scripts in the future.
54. Maciej Wojtyszko, another member of the 'X' unit, also mentioned that Holland and Janusz Zaorski wanted to 'rule the souls' and, thus, they were very active in organising meetings and acted as mediators between the group and Wajda (Szczepańska 2017, 122). Holland's strong position was also recognised by the filmmakers supporting the communist authorities such as Bohdan Poręba, the artistic director of the film unit 'Profil', who called her his 'biggest enemy' hostile to his unit's programme (in Wojtczak 2009, 59).
55. Talarczyk-Gubała uses it as a subheading of the section of her essay discussing Holland's position in the Polish film industry in the 1970s (Talarczyk-Gubała 2013, 203; see also Wiśniewska 2012, 30–5).
56. Krzysztof Mętrak, '*Zanussi w spódnicy*', *Kultura*, no. 48, 1977, 14.
57. Monika Talarczyk-Gubała claims that Holland's adaptation in male film units was for her 'a transgender experience and experimenting with mainstream culture' (2013, 217).

58. For more information on the Cinema of Moral Concern (also called 'the cinema of moral unrest') see Haltof 2002, 146–159; Iordanova 2003, 108–115.
59. Holland co-authored the script for *Without Anesthesia*, for which she was harshly admonished by her mother who thought that her daughter used her marriage with her father when she wrote the script for Wajda (Pasternak 2022, 94).
60. During this period, Holland also directed on her own *Wheel Breaking* (*Łamanie kołem*, 1979), the play by a then contemporary playwright, Maciej Bordowicz.
61. The reviewers noted the parallels, yet they could not express it in a direct form. In his brief review published in a local Kraków daily *Echo Krakowa*, Maciej Szybist claimed that the television project was comparable in terms of artistic quality to Andrzej Wajda's television production *November Night* (*Noc listopadowa* by Stanisław Wyspiański), while also mentioning that Agnieszka Holland was Wajda's apprentice ((masz.) [author] Maciej Szybist, '*Lorenzaccio*', *Echo Krakowa*, no. 279, 1978, 2). Another two reviewers compared the interpretation of the play to the Polish romantic drama by Juliusz Słowacki *Kordian* whose protagonist was unable to assassinate the Russian Tzar (BOB (Jacek Bober), '*Lorenzaccio*', *Gazeta Południowa*, no. 283, 1978, 2; Władysław Orłowski, 'Renesansowy Kordian', *Odgłosy*, no. 51, 1978, 14). Orłowski made direct comparisons between the historical situation depicted in Musset's play and contemporary reality: 'It was a statement made by contemporary directors on the universal and thus also contemporary times', while also making a comment on the futility of individuals attempting to change the political situation since history is created by collectives only; admittedly, the last statement was in tune with the official (and simplified for that matter) version of Marxism (Orłowski, 'Renesansowy Kordian').
62. Bober and Orłowski's reviews, see note 61.
63. The scene, which is rarely noted by the critics (see Mąka-Malatyńska 2009, 71–2), is of paramount importance in regard to the cinematic representation of female sexuality in Polish cinema, and world cinema for that matter, especially since *Screen Tests* belonged to mainstream rather than avant-garde cinema.
64. In *Provincial Actors* there is an episode with an old man taking his own life by jumping out of the window as a silent protest against the injustice he experienced from the local militia. Jankun-Dopartowa sees it as an autobiographical reference to the allegedly suicidal death of Holland's father (Jankun-Dopartowa 2000, 87).
65. She directed George Büchner's *Woyzeck* in Stefan Jaracz's Theatre in Olsztyn, premiere 11 June 1978.
66. See Jankun-Dopartowa 2000, 117.
67. Among these female filmmakers are Maria Kaniewska, Anna Sokołowska and Hanna Bielińska (see Talarczyk-Gubała 2013, 319–76).
68. In their brief analysis of *Provincial Actors*, Bolesław Michałek and Frank Turaj reproduced this national-patriarchal script in that they did not even mention the character of Anka (Michałek and Turaj 1988, 78).
69. Polish critics claimed that Holland represented women in an excessively negative way; see Jan F. Lewandowski, 'Obserwacje Agnieszki Holland', *Dziennik Zachodni*, no. 243, 1979, 4.
70. A similar situation occurs in *Kung-fu* made in 1979 by Janusz Kijowski who coined the term of Cinema of Moral Concern.
71. Interestingly, in his review published in *Ekran*, a film magazine supportive of the communist politics, Henryk Tronowicz also calls the male protagonist 'hysterical' (Henryk Tronowicz, 'Bez wyjścia?' *Ekran*, no. 35, 1979, 21).
72. Only a few Polish reviewers noted this 'dual narrative' (see Ewa Nurczyńska, 'Nie tylko o aktorach', no. 38, *Odgłosy* 1979, 12), whereas others were divided in their opinions of who was the protagonist. Some of them claimed it was Anka (for example, Krzysztof

Kreutzinger 'Wariacje nie na temat', *Film*, no. 35, 1979, 11), who was presented from a 'feminist' perspective (Anon. '*Aktorzy prowincjonalni*', *Razem*, no. 35, 1979), whereas others opted for Krzysztof (see Cezary Prasek, 'Młoda kobieta za kamerą', *Kobieta i Życie*, no. 39, 1979). In her monograph on the Cinema of Moral Concern, Maria Kornatowska acknowledged the film's misogyny, while claiming that it was the only work of the movement that employed male and female perspectives as equal (Kornatowska 1990, 191).

73. Unlike most of the Polish critics, Bronisława Stolarska claims that in *Provincial Actors* Holland takes up a position of a moralist, yet this is not clearly articulated due to the abundance of observational details (Bronisława Stolarska, 'Powiedzieć coś ważnego', *Czas*, no. 38, 1979, 27). Similar claim is made by Janusz Zatorski ('Stajnia Augiasza', *Kierunki*, no. 37, 1979, 11).

74. Zygmunt Kałużyński, one of the most controversial Polish film critics, noted this, negative in his opinion, evolution of Holland's work from astute analysis of women's issues to schematic films criticising social reality, as exemplified by the Cinema of Moral Concern (Zygmunt Kałużyński, 'Smutek papierowy', *Polityka*, no. 41, 1979, 10).

75. In her interview with Czerkawski, Holland also mentions this interference in the festival award (Czerkawski 2019, 152).

76. Distribution of the film was also limited; the local dailies in Łódź and Katowice complained on the poor distribution of the film; see: Sl., 'Kopie nas kopią', *Dziennik Popularny*, no. 204, 1979, 2; Jan F. Lewandowski, 'Obserwacje Agnieszki Holland', *Dziennik Zachodni*, no. 243, 1979, 4.

77. Dina Iordanova also considers Holland's Polish films as representing the Cinema of Moral Concern (2003, 122).

78. At that time Poland was partitioned by Russia, Prussia and the Austro-Hungarian Empire (1875–1918).

79. For detailed analysis of the film, see E. Ostrowska 2021.

80. See for example: Krzysztof Kłopotowski, 'Gorączka rewolucji', *Tygodnik Solidarność*, no. 26, 1981, 14; Jan F. Lewandowski, 'Brzydota rewolucji', *Panorama*, no. 42, 1981, 34.

81. In her interview in 1981, Holland herself suggested parallels between the 1905 revolution and contemporary political events, yet without delving into the issue (Agnieszka Holland, 'Sierpień pokazał, że może być inaczej', interview by Jerzy Pawlas, *Kurier Polski*, no. 197, 1981, 2).

82. For an extended analysis of the political contexts of the film see E. Ostrowska 2021.

83. As Holland said many years later, at that time feminism was perceived as a Western luxury Polish women could not afford (Pasternak 2022, 126).

CHAPTER 3

European exilic cinema

When martial law was introduced in Poland on 13 December 1981, Holland was in Sweden to participate in the premiere of *Provincial Actors*.[1] Many Swedish journalists asked her for comments on the political events in her home country. Initially reluctant, soon she furiously criticised the decision of the communist authorities, calling it fascist and comparing it to the actions of the Chilean junta (in Pasternak 2022, 206). Polish officials responded to her accusatory statements by immediately charging her with breaking the decree on martial law. She knew that if she returned to Poland, she would be interned and not allowed to make movies for a very long time, if ever. Very shortly after martial law was announced, Holland's mother, Irena Rybczyńska, came to Barbara Pec-Ślesicka, the production director of the film unit 'X', with a piece of paper on which was her daughter's signature. They decided to use it to type on her behalf a request for a period of unpaid leave. On 30 December 1981, the letter was sent to Leon Bach, the director of the 'Film Units' ('Zespoły Filmowe'). The letter explained that, during her unpaid leave, Holland would work in Paris on the script for the film about Korczak for the American film producer Larry Bachman (Michalak 2016, 267). Holland's application was supported by an official letter signed by Pec-Ślesicka, who confirmed that, among the film projects planned for the film unit 'X', was Andrzej Wajda's film *Doctor Korczak* (*Dr. Korczak*), for which Holland was assigned to write a script. The authorities denied the request in the official letter sent to Holland on 15 February 1982, terminating her employment in the film unit 'X'. The letter was resent in April 1982 to confirm the finality of the decision.[2] Holland had no other option than to stay in Paris where she had relocated in the meantime.

This chapter discusses Holland's professional activity between 1981 and 1992 during her exilic stay in Europe,[3] while looking at it against Hamid

Naficy's concept of 'accented cinema' (2001) and transnational cinema (Hjort 2010). As Naficy explains, this model of cinema is made by exilic and diasporic filmmakers who are film *auteurs* working outside of their home country, and for whom most often the decisions regarding location are not economically motivated (Naficy 2001, 25). Despite being spatially separated from their home country, exilic filmmakers remain connected to it, as is demonstrated by Holland's European works.

I examine her exilic output in chronological order to show her progressive distantiation from the national culture,[4] with a simultaneous shift towards subnational identities. It starts with an examination of her participation in Polish émigré culture, then it discusses *Angry Harvest* (*Bittere Ernte*, 1985), *To Kill a Priest* (1988), *Europa, Europa* (1990) and *Olivier, Olivier* (1992). The main aim of the discussion that follows is to demonstrate how Holland's transition from socialist to Western modes of film production resulted in a thematic and stylistic versatility in her exilic work which is especially evident when compared to her Polish works produced by the unit 'X' which examined contemporary subject matters in realistic form. Ultimately, it will be argued, her exilic European output showed a gradual dispersion of her authorship, which was paralleled by the narratives of the films featuring protagonists who frequently questioned or resisted any singular identity project.

While looking at Holland's time on exile period in the context of her life trajectory the Deleuze's concept of three lifelines proves illuminating (Deleuze and Guattari 2019, 234). Leaving Poland in 1981 marked a break line designating a new segment in her life, while her subsequent exile experience mobilised the 'crack line', as demonstrated by her participation in a – for her – new, non-socialist production culture that resulted in her Holocaust films, which depart significantly from the Polish hegemonic discourse on the issue. The film *Olivier, Olivier* marked her ultimate exit from the realm of national cinema and vernacular culture, and as such can be seen as the last point on the 'line of flight' that relocated her from the realm of European (exilic) cinema to global Hollywood cinema. Finally, her status as *auteur* of national cinema gradually changed to that of transnational filmmaker.

POLISH EXILIC CULTURES

In 1981, Holland had a strong position within Polish cinema. She was a prolific director whose work was an important part of the Cinema of Moral Concern. Her last film *A Woman Alone*, made during the Solidarity carnival period, was shelved, which solidified her status as dissident artist.[5] While living in exile in Paris, initially she continued contributing to the national culture. In a way, she carried on with the tradition of the Polish Romantics such as the poets Adam

Mickiewicz and Cyprian Kamil Norwid, and the composer Frédéric Chopin, who also spent many years in Paris and whose art was significantly fuelled by nostalgia for the lost country.[6]

The noble affinity with the Polish cultural tradition did not help advance Holland's career abroad. For a long time, she had to struggle to stay active in filmmaking. As she recalled,

> I felt knots in my stomach whenever I passed a film crew on the street [. . .] People from French film circles were not interested in immigrants, they treated them as potential competition, somebody who wants to take away their job. With every day, I would realize that I was in a position where my Polish output is worthless to people I would like to persuade to work with me. (Pasternak 2022, 225)

In this professionally uninviting environment, Wajda proved to be once again Holland's 'man of providence'.[7] Initially, she worked on the scripts of his transnational film projects such as *Danton* (France-Poland-West Germany, 1983) and *Love in Germany* (*Eine Liebe in Deutschland*, West Germany-France, 1983).[8] Before leaving Poland she had acquired extensive experience in scriptwriting, paradoxically because, being personally subject to censorship, she submitted many scripts for approval, however, nearly all of these were rejected (see Chapter Two). She authored or co-authored scripts for all the films she made in Poland, while also writing or co-writing scripts for *Without Anesthesia* (*Bez znieczulenia*, Andrzej Wajda, 1978), *Winners* (*Zwycięzcy*, Andrzej Zajączkowski, 1978), *A Shattered Mirror* (*Okruchy lustra*, Andrzej Zajączkowski, 1979), *Unwanted Man* (*Mężczyzna niepotrzebny*, Laco Adamik, 1982). While in Poland, scriptwriting had contributed to Holland's authorship; in Paris, it allowed her to stay active in the film industry and earn some money.

Wajda and his wife, Krystyna Zachwatowicz, also helped Holland to settle in France (Mąka-Malatyńska 2009, 22). In the 1982 diary entry, Wajda described one of their arrivals in Paris to their rented apartment in the 8ème arrondissement on the Rue de Beaume, where 'Agnieszka waits for them, longing for news from home' (Lubelski 2006, 206). Holland appreciated the help: 'I was in a rather difficult situation: a penniless single mother in a strange country without knowledge of the language or the people. They tried to support me materially. I was living in their apartment for several months' (Holland and Kornatowska 2012, 194). Further financial support came from Henryk Baranowski, a Polish émigré theatre director,[9] who, in 1983 run a film directing seminar in West Berlin Internationale Regieseminare für Film and Theatre (Baranowski 2013, 84). As Holland reported, he asked her first and she agreed on condition that she would do this with Kieślowski, who was then jobless and considered working as a cab driver (Socha 2018, 190).[10] Baranowski accepted the offer, and they delivered occasional film workshops for foreign students. The seemingly unimportant episode is worth mentioning as it sheds light on Holland's difficult professional situation during the first years of her exile as well as on the support that she received from the informal network of Polish diasporic community of artists who were at that time working abroad. Although scant, these precarious jobs were crucial for her survival during the first years of exile.

Besides the occasional jobs, Holland also contributed to Polish exilic cultures centred around the Literary Institute in Paris and the influential periodical *Culture* (*Kultura*), both important hubs of the postwar Polish anti-communist emigration.[11] Admittedly, it was not Holland's first contact with these circles, as years earlier in Prague she had helped in smuggling the samizdat literature from Paris to Poland, for which she was imprisoned (see Chapter One). In the 1980s, she made two documentaries together with her friend Andrzej Wolski: *Culture* (*Kultura*, 1985) and *Czapski* (1985). The films were produced by the Video Studio Kontakt in Paris,[12] an independent émigré company that was established in 1984 by Mirosław Chojecki, a prominent dissident in socialist Poland.[13] *Culture* presented people connected with the legendary eponymous periodical located in the equally mythical Maisons-Laffitte. The documentary featured the iconic figures of Polish émigré intellectuals and artists: Jerzy Giedroyć, Gustaw Herling-Grudziński, Józef Czapski, Zofia Hertz, Konstanty Aleksander Jeleński and Czesław Miłosz.[14] *Czapski*, a cinematic portrayal of the eponymous writer and painter, was one of many of Kontakt's documentaries presenting Polish émigré artists and politicians (see Więch 2015, 364). In 1988, Holland and Wolski made *KOR*, devoted to the legendary Workers' Defence Committee (Komitet Obrony Robotników), the most prominent dissident organisation in socialist Poland.[15] All Holland and Wolski's documentaries were smuggled into Poland and distributed on VHS through various underground networks. With her brief collaboration with Kontakt, Holland contributed to the sector of the national culture, whose aim was to mobilise the political subjectivity of its participants, as was the case with the Cinema of Moral Concern. Notwithstanding these ideological continuities, Holland made the documentaries within the radically different production culture. While in Poland she had had state funding for her films though they were subject to censorship, in Paris she had an unlimited creative freedom but a very limited budget coming from private pockets.

During her stay in Paris, Holland made great efforts to remain connected with the national culture. In 1982, she published an article, 'A Few Remarks on Recent Polish Cinema' ('Kilka uwag o młodym kinie polskim') in an émigré literary periodical, *Literary Letters* (*Zeszyty literackie*, published in Paris since 1982) (Holland 1982). It commented on the situation in the Polish film industry during the martial law period. In this, as she called it, 'obituary' of Polish cinema, Holland pointed out an empty space vacated by the filmmakers who decided to stay abroad (Janusz Kijowski, Andrzej Wajda, Krzysztof Zanussi, Wojciech Marczewski), which was instantly taken over by their mediocre colleagues whom she also named. She was alarmed that Polish national cinema would vanish if proper measures were not taken. Responses to her tirade came from Zbigniew Klaczyński, a film critic supporting the communist authorities,[16] and Jerzy Urban, the journalist, whose columns were adapted for the television omnibus film *Pictures from Life* in which Holland had participated seven years earlier. In 1981, Urban accepted the position of press secretary to the communist government. In the article signed with his literary namesake Jan Rem, he fiercely attacked Holland and accused her of disseminating fake information and hatred towards her native country.[17] Thus, although lonely and separated from her daughter Kasia – which was an unbearable experience for her – Holland was still part of the Polish 'imagined community'.

Holland's immersion in the Parisian *Culture* circle kept her connected with Polish national culture, yet some irreversible mutations were occurring that eventually formed a Deleuzian 'crack line'. Although she stayed connected with the vernacular cultural production, she was also slowly setting herself apart from it. The initially imperceptible changes in the general direction of her professional trajectory eventually led to the more definite transformation. In the latter, her scriptwriting collaboration with Wajda proved to be crucial, especially her contribution to the script for *Love in Germany*, the film that was produced by Artur Brauner.[18] Soon, he produced Holland's first film made in exile, *Angry Harvest* (*Bittere Ernte*, 1985). The film marked her entrance into the realm of transnational cinema.

ANGRY HARVEST: FIRST ENCOUNTER WITH ARTUR BRAUNER AND FIRST OSCAR NOMINATION

Artur Brauner,[19] a Jew born in Poland who survived the Holocaust, moved to Berlin after the Second World War, and in September 1946 he established the Central Cinema Company (CCC). Its first project, *King of Hearts* (*Herzkönig*, 1947), was a box-office success, however his next production, loosely based on his biography, *Morituri* (1947/48), about a group of prisoners escaping from a concentration camp, was a financial flop. As Brauner recollected: 'I had to pay debts for next five difficult years. However, I have never regretted making the film. Alas, I have learned that cinema was a space for entertainment, not for reckoning with the past' (quoted in Klejsa 2015, 117). Despite its critical and financial failure, *Morituri* remains an important film in Brauner's output as it initiated the universal or international approach to the experience of the Second World War and the Holocaust that is present in his later films on the subject. In *Morituri*, the characters of various nationalities and ethnicities – Polish, French, Jewish, German, Canadian, Serbian, Italian, Danish, Dutch (there is also one stateless person) – speak German (mostly), Polish, English, Russian and French, and this multilinguality does not obstruct their communication. None of the victimised group is privileged, and thus, the film offers a 'universalization of victims' (Kramer, quoted in Klejsa 2015, 113).[20] Arguably, the film foreshadowed, albeit in a rudimentary fashion, the concept of 'multidirectional memory' as theorised decades later by Michael Rothberg (2009).[21] This approach to the Holocaust hardened into a more manifest form in Brauner's later productions on the topic, including two films directed by Holland: *Angry Harvest* and *Europa, Europa*.

After the failure of *Morituri*, Brauner's company produced a whole variety of films. Although specialising in popular genre cinema (Loewy 2010, 175), he was also investing in more ambitious projects: 'Balancing the demands of art and commerce, Brauner experimented repeatedly with European coproductions featuring international stars such as Maria Schell, Lilli Palmer, and Curd Jürgens' (Hake 2002, 97). Most importantly, he engaged in making low-budget films on the Holocaust. As Ronny Loewy claimed, Brauner's Holocaust films were made to tell 'the stories of the victims of the extermination of Europe's Jews and to denounce the German responsible for these crimes' (Loewy 2010, 174), which was not sufficiently recognised or emphasised in other German films on the Second World War experience. As he goes on, 'West German cinema tended towards self-pity', whereas 'East German fiction film systematically transformed Jewish victims into antifascist resistance fighters when not busy complacently denouncing the ex-Nazis who were able to make careers for themselves in the capitalist FRG' (Loewy 2010, 176). Brauner's films' alternative approach to the Holocaust experience was facilitated by employing non-German directors from countries such as Poland (Aleksander Ford, *Sie sind frei, Dr. Korczak/The Martyr*, 1974; Jerzy Hoffman, *After your Decrees/Wedle wyroków Twoich*, 1984; Agnieszka Holland, *Angry Harvest/Bittere Ernte*, 1985 and *Europa, Europa/ Hitlerjunge Salomon*, 1991; Janusz Kijowski, *Warsaw – Year 5703 – Der Daunenträger*, 1992),[22] Yugoslavia (Žika Mitrović, *Witness out of Hell/Zeugin aus der Hölle*, 1967), Italy (Vittorio de Sica, *The Garden of the Finzi-Continis/Il Giardino dei Finizi Contini*, 1970), Hungary (István Szabó, *Hanussen*, 1988), Russia (Dmitry Astrakhan, *From Hell to Hell/Iz ada v ad*, 1997), and the US (Jeff Kanew, *Babiy Yar/Babij Jar*, 2003). Frequently, these films were made with international crews and were co-financed by international or other national funds. Due to their transnational production frameworks, they inevitably involved various cultural transactions that contributed to the process of constructing transnational and 'multidirectional memory' (see Rothberg 2009) of the Holocaust.

Wajda's *Love in Germany*, the script of which Holland co-authored, was part of a cycle of films commemorating the Second World War that Brauner decided to produce in the 1980s (see Bock and Bergfelder 2009, 60–1). As a follow up to his first meeting with Holland when she worked on the script for Wajda, he posted to her a large package containing the literary works about the Holocaust he had purchased copyrights for. One of them was the novel *Angry Harvest* (*Okiennice*, 1958) by Stanisław Mierzeński and Hermann Field. The member of the Polish anti-communist Home Army (Armia Krajowa) and an American architect who came to Poland to look for his brother were both arrested by the communist authorities and spent five years in the same cell of a Polish prison. There they wrote a novel together, in German because this was their common language though not the native language of either of them. Later, the novel was translated into English and Polish, as well other languages (see Insdorf 2003, 103). The novel exemplifies a particular example of collaborative authorship, and also of the kind of supra-national cultural production to which both Brauner and Holland significantly contributed years later. Like the original novel, Holland's script also underwent several translations and transpositions. As she reported, she wrote it in Polish, then her friend Dorota Paciarelli translated it into German, and this version was amended by Paul Hengge, a scriptwriter who had worked on Brauner's other projects. Holland

Figure 3.1 Agnieszka Holland and Artur Brauner on the set of *Angry Harvest* (*Bittere Ernte*)
© CCC Filmkunst GmbH

disapproved of these changes and requested that the earlier version be restored (in Zamysłowska and Kuźmicki 2013, 118). When it was finally accepted for production, its budget was exceptionally low, which was Brauner's strategy to reduce the financial risk. As Holland reported, there was no air conditioning in the sound stage; and they would reuse some parts of the set constructed for Wajda's *Love in Germany*. The natural location of the street was not adjusted to the historical period and they had to use the impromptu methods of hiding the anachronistic street lamps, and so on.[23] Holland's film also reused the actors employed for minor characters in Wajda's film: Armin Mueller-Stahl and Elisabeth Trissenaar.[24] They were both associated with German art cinema due to their appearances in films by Rainer Werner Fassbinder and Alexander Kluge. Furthermore, Mueller-Stahl, who emigrated in 1980 from the GDR (where he began his acting career) to West Germany, evoked the tradition of Eastern European cinema.[25] Because of all these production strategies and contexts, the German film *Angry Harvest* marked Holland's entrance into transnational European art cinema that can also be approached as 'exilic cinema' that as Naficy claims employs often artisanal mode of production.[26]

Angry Harvest tells the story of the Polish farmer, Leon Wolny[27] (Armin Mueller-Stahl) who hides an Austrian Jewish woman, Rosa (Elisabeth Trissenaar). She has survived an escape from the transport to the extermination camp, while her little daughter died, and her husband's fate is unknown. Leon and Rosa are different, not only in terms of their ethnicity and nationality but also in the social class each represents. The upper-middle-class woman is well educated, possessing a remarkable cultural capital that Leon is evidently lacking. However, the Holocaust destabilises their identities: Rosa's Austrian citizenship becomes obsolete, and her persona is reduced to a vulnerable, racialised female body, while his economic and social position improves. Both are displaced subjects, which is not due to migration as usually in 'accented cinema'. Leon projects his oscillation between superiority and inferiority, having power and being powerless, onto Rosa. He simultaneously worships and degrades her. As Paul Coates notes, 'Leon's duality corresponds to the chronic partiality of all his actions: neither priest or layman, rich nor poor, "good" nor "evil," he is always riven, locked in a position in between' (Coates 2005, 170). Rosa responds to her existential situation in an equally dual manner: Leon revolts her, yet she also has affectionate feelings for him; she feels entrapped, but also safe in the basement of his house; she finds sex with Leon both degrading and comforting. (see Fig. 3.2) When Leon has a chance to marry an impoverished Polish noblewoman, he decides to get rid of Rosa, for whom he secures another hiding place. In response to the situation, Rosa commits suicide, the only means available to her to protest his decision.

Annette Insdorf examines Holland's film as representing the 'In Hiding/ Onstage' narrative strategy employed by several films about the Holocaust,

Figure 3.2 *Angry Harvest* (1985)

while asking the question: 'if the noble act of saving a Jew from the Nazis is inspired by lust, is the action less noble?' Instead of providing a definite answer which would hardly be possible, she emphasises the film's ambiguity, especially in its portrayal of the victim and the victimiser (Insdorf 2003, 102–3). She also considers the possibility that the relationship is not only specific to the Holocaust experience, as suggested by Holland herself, who claimed that the literary original dealt 'with more universal questions of human beings in extreme situations of danger and dependence – especially between a man and a woman' (quoted in Insdorf 2003, 103). Contrarily, Ingrid Lewis argues that the specific historical contexts of the film affected its politics of representation. As she explains, Holland's film epitomises a broader tendency in European Holocaust cinema emerging in the 1970s that 'brought to the fore unconventional images of female victims: characters who were variously temperamental, depressed, suicidal, mentally unstable, troubled or in crisis' (Lewis 2017, 162). In her opinion, these troublesome portrayals are also products of the women's movement and the backlash against it: 'This "age of ambivalence" resulted in [. . .] introduction of explicit elements of sexual abuse within the narratives' (Lewis 2017, 163, 165).[28] Finally, Lewis asserts that *Angry Harvest*, like many other films, is 'dominated by a male gaze', in which 'the crisis of the female figure is configured as self-destructive, and in most cases these films end with her death' (163). She supports her argument with a detailed description of the formal devices used in the film:

> Held captive in the cellar, humiliated, sexually and verbally abused, with no one to trust, the story of Rosa illustrates one of the many possible scenarios of women's vulnerability and sexual exploitation during the Holocaust. A key scene of the film shows Rosa anguished at the thought of having to leave her cellar and move to a different hiding place. Halfway out of the cellar, she is positioned both literally and symbolically at Leon's feet while beseeching him to be allowed to remain in the same hiding place [. . .]. This scene highlights how, after months of seclusion and abuse at the hands of the alcoholic farmer, Rosa has become totally dependent on her abuser. (Lewis 2017, 167)[29]

The politics of the gaze in *Angry Harvest* is more complex than Lewis claims, and as such the film does not offer a singular spectacular identification. The penultimate scene of *Angry Harvest*, when Leon discovers that Rosa has committed suicide in a cellar, presents a multiplicity of point of view (POV) shots that cannot be attached to a singular subjectivity.[30] It begins with a low-angle shot from the camera that is placed inside the cellar, thus simulating (dead) Rosa's gaze. We see Leon's boots from above, as he stands next to the cellar door, that metonymically represent him as her executioner rather than saviour. When he gets no response from her, he kneels, and then, in the same long take, we see his face as he looks into a dark hollow space of the cellar. Within one continuous shot, an instant transformation of Leon's persona occurs: from powerful master over Rosa's life and death to frightened (or perhaps abandoned) lover. After he buries her body in the cellar, there is a moderate high-angle shot of him lying curled on a heap of soil. This closing image of the scene is a reversal of its opening low-angle shot. Within the feminine space of Rosa's basement hideout – as dark and closed as a womb – Leon experiences a regression, becoming a helpless child. In the scene, as in the whole film, Leon's gaze does not provide a privileged perspective; initially he is shown from (dead) Rosa's point of view and his POV shots are used only later. The simulation of a visual perspective of the dead Rosa signifies the symbolic power that she has acquired through her decision to take her own life. As paradoxical as it sounds, her suicide resisted Leon's decision concerning her persona. As Insdorf put it: 'Here the Jew is not submissive but intransigent about her values, not meek but masterly' (Insdorf 2003, 103). The film does not establish a privileged perceptual perspective and it alternates between Leon's and Rosa's gaze. In consequence, the viewer's alignment to both characters is equal, and thus one is unable to develop a full allegiance to either. The film itself does not offer a moral or an emotional centre. As Insdorf concludes: 'no character is shown to be completely heroic or villainous' (2003, 103). Instead of the binary division into victims and victimisers, *Angry Harvest* establishes what Michael Rothberg calls an 'implicated subject' (Rothberg 2019) that will reappear in Holland's other films interrogating the Holocaust theme.

Rothberg's concept of the implicated subject refers to the situation in which an individual does not occupy a position of power and does not perpetrate any harm either, yet his or her proximity to the victimisers results in various forms of benefits. More specifically,

> An implicated subject is neither a victim nor a perpetrator, but rather a participant in histories and social formations that generate the positions of victim and perpetrator, and yet in which most people do not occupy such clear-cut roles. Less 'actively' involved than perpetrators, implicated subjects do not fit the mold of the 'passive' bystander, either. Although indirect or belated, their actions and inactions help produce and reproduce the positions of victims and perpetrators. [. . .] The implicated subject serves as an umbrella term that gathers a range of subject positions that sit uncomfortably in our familiar conceptual space of victims, perpetrators, and bystanders. (Rothberg 2019, 1, 13)[31]

The concept of the 'implicated subject' is particularly relevant to the Holocaust experience in Eastern Europe to which the clear Western division into victims, perpetrators and bystanders does not apply (see Himka and Michlic 2013, 4).[32] More importantly, Rothberg's concept proves useful in undermining the communist discourse on the Holocaust that is presented in Polish socialist cinema solely as a Nazi war crime, while the Polish nation is largely constructed as a helpless and passive witness in the face of the Holocaust. Produced by the German Jew Artur Brauner, and directed by a Polish-Jewish female filmmaker, *Angry Harvest* departed radically from the hegemonic (male) Polish discourse on the Holocaust.[33]

Leon in *Angry Harvest* embodies the implicated subject in the most conspicuous way, something which was implicitly noted by Karen Jaehne in her review: 'The whole story has built toward this peasant's coming to an awareness of his own contribution to the persecution of Polish Jews during the Second World War', while the film revealed 'the psychological mechanisms of self-deception practiced by the Poles in the Holocaust'.[34] Although not directly involved in the Holocaust, Leon profits from it in many ways, which eventually elevates his status in the local community, as proved by the possibility of marrying a noblewoman. Consequently, *Angry Harvest* stands in a strong opposition to the Polish hegemonic discourse on the Holocaust that would equate Polish and Jewish victimhood. Those Poles who collaborated with the Nazis in the extermination of Jews and gained material profit out of it were considered for a long time a marginal group of criminals within the nation. Leon is not a criminal, and he provides Rosa with a shelter, yet he expresses anti-Semitism in several scenes, while also being implicated in the death of several Jews. Holland made the film two years before Jan Błoński's essay, 'Poor Poles Look at the Ghetto' (Błoński 1987/1990), was published in the Catholic weekly *Tygodnik Powszechny*. This essay initiated a prolonged and heated public debate on Poles' involvement in the Holocaust. *Angry Harvest* has never been included in the debate, largely because the film has never been granted distribution in Polish cinemas, even after the collapse of communism. There were several special screenings and eventually, in 1997, the film was broadcast by public television. One of these screenings took place during the Festival of Jewish culture in Łódź in 1990, and as such it was seen by the reviewer of the local daily. She described Leon as a rescuer and Rosa as his reluctant lover. His implication in the Holocaust was not even alluded to.[35] In his monograph on Holland, Bobowski noticed this critical void around *Angry Harvest*, which he explained in relation to the film's uncomfortable theme (Bobowski 2001); the authors of the other two Polish monographs examined the film as a psychological-existential drama, while not paying attention to Leon's implication in the extermination of Jews (Jankun-Dopartowa 2000; Mąka-Malatyńska 2009). The Polish critical discourse around the film is scant to say the least, and this has not changed since 1989, when discussion of the Holocaust was liberated from the former constraints. Polish film critics did not engage with the motif of sexual exploitation either as it was presented in too ambivalent a way. Unlike *Night Porter* (Liliana Cavani, 1974), Holland's film did not present the sexual relationship between the victim and victimiser as a perverse sado-masochistic entanglement, but rather as a disturbing imitation of quotidian marriage. *Angry Harvest* demonstrates the easiness with which the act of sexual exploitation is normalised and masquerades under the familiar emotions of infatuation and gratitude. Rosa's suicide brutally annihilates these safe narratives and reveals the emotional terror of the situation.

As in Poland, although for different reason, the German distribution of *Angry Harvest* was also limited as the co-producer, the television channel ZDF, refused to distribute Holland's final cut, over which she had to struggle. Fortunately, the film found its way to the film festivals in Montreal and New York, which was decisive in its nomination for the Oscar for the Best Foreign Language Film. Holland self-ironically said that the Germans nominated *Angry Harvest* because they did not have anything better (Holland and Kornatowska 2012, 223). Some critics did not welcome this decision. For example, Roger Ebert complained that the nomination revealed a flawed selection process: '*Angry Harvest* [. . .] was nominated. Meanwhile, Kurosawa's *Ran* sits on the shelf. Until the best foreign film nominees are chosen on the basis of art, not geography and politics, they won't mean very much.'[36] Notwithstanding the critical opinions on the selection process, the Oscar nomination prompted Brauner to continue his collaboration with Holland, although she was not enthusiastic about it (Holland and Kornatowska 2012, 257). Despite Holland's difficulties in adjusting to the different mode of production practised by an experienced independent film producer, *Angry Harvest* marked her entrance into transnational cinema, which was also a departure from the hegemonic national discourse on the Holocaust.

TO KILL A PRIEST: RETURN TO POLISH CINEMA?

The Oscar nomination for *Angry Harvest* made Holland recognisable in the US and was instrumental in Columbia's offer to co-finance her next project, *To Kill a Priest*, a film about Father Jerzy Popiełuszko, a Catholic priest who supported the Solidarity movement and was murdered by the secret security forces in 1984.[37] The film was Holland's first international co-production, although, due to its subject matter, it also formed a part of Polish exilic culture. The liaison with the national culture was later reinforced by the exhibition strategies and critical reception in Poland. In a paradoxical way, *To Kill a Priest* was a symbolic return, and at the same time an exit from Polish national cinema.

Holland received the offer to make the film first from Jean-Pierre Alessandri, a French producer, and then the offer was seconded by Columbia, led at the time by David Puttnam, a British film producer famous for ambitious entertainment films such as the Oscar-winning *Chariots of Fire* (Hugh Hudson, 1981). During his brief tenure as CEO of Columbia, Puttnam advocated for the production of moderate budget films that would 'elevate moral and social sensibilities of the audience'. He publicly disparaged the commercial projects expected by the Coca Cola consortium, the owner of the film studio since 1982 (Prince 2000, 54). A movie about a political assassination in a communist country would perfectly fit Puttnam's agenda of 'a moral responsibility to the audience' (Prince 2000, 54). Notwithstanding differences in terms of scale and recognisability of the production enterprises, Brauner's Holocaust projects and Puttnam's idea of the cinema of moral obligations are somehow comparable. Both producers were advocating for 'in-house' production, which was a reasonable and efficient strategy in the case of an independent European film company such as Brauner's CCC. Yet it proved to be disastrous for Columbia when they rejected expensive star projects intended to be realised by directors of star-like status. As Puttnam himself admitted, he was trying to do business differently: 'smaller films, smaller risks' (Prince 2000, 56). *To Kill a Priest* embodies Puttnam's vision of cinema in that the story had the potential to 'elevate moral sensibilities' of the audience, while its assigned budget was a moderate sum of six million dollars. However, the film did not resonate with the world critics or with international audiences.

To Kill a Priest was made by a truly international crew whose most significant members were all Polish émigrés: Agnieszka Holland – director, Adam Holender – director of photography, Anna Biedrzycka-Shepard – costume designer, and Wojciech Pszoniak and Eugeniusz Priwieziencew – actors in supporting roles. The main parts were played by the popular American actor, Ed Harris, and a star of French cinema, Christopher Lambert; a few then-unknown yet later prominent British actors such as Pete Postlethwaite, Timothy Spall and Tim Roth made appearances in supporting roles. The international cast used English in the dialogue, yet with different accents that marked the transnational aspect of the production, although not necessarily in the intended way. The soundtrack included compositions by Georges Delerue (who authored music for *Hiroshima Mon Amour*, Alain Resnais, 1959), Zbigniew Preisner (later famous due to his collaboration with Krzysztof Kieślowski on the *Three Colours* trilogy) and Joan Baez (the ballad 'Crimes of Cain'). The technical crew included mostly French personnel. *To Kill a Priest* represented a kind of Euro-American cinema popular in the 1980s that, according to Peter Lev, merged two different modes of filmmaking: popular genres attracting the audience with stars and spectacular action, and art cinema of ambiguity and stylistic sophistication (Lev 1993). Specifically, the film merged the genres of political thriller and psychological drama.

To Kill a Priest begins with a brief sequence presenting the brutal introduction of martial law in Poland in 1981. The film then presents the story of the preparation and final execution of Father Popiełuszko (Christopher Lambert) by the secret militia forces supervised by Stefan (Ed Harris). Although the narrative develops in chronological order and is unambiguous in its goal, it departs from the conventions of popular cinema in that it wavers between various characters without establishing any of them as a proper protagonist. The priest is static and flawless and as such does not encourage spectatorial identification, whereas the secret militiaman experiences existential dilemmas comparable to Dostoyevsky's characters, which prevents him from functioning as a typical antagonist (see Fig. 3.3). As Paul Coates notes,

> If one portion of Holland's film offers a two-dimensional characterisation that is indeed hagiographic, Alek's main antagonist – the secret policeman Stefan (the Ed Harris character) – is dark, complex and intriguing [. . .] Holland's Stefan may be interpreted as an image of a Saul unable to become a Paul. (Coates 2003, 139, 140)

The non-orthodox characterisation that oscillates between generic clarity and art cinema ambiguity is reflected in the variable style. On the one hand,

Figure 3.3 *To Kill a Priest* (1988)

To Kill a Priest employs stylistic transparency to present the narrative in an unobtrusive fashion, yet it also includes several instances of narrative and stylistic excess that foreground cinematic form.[38] The film's stylistic and generic ambivalence has been noted by critics, who often attributed it to the American-European co-production framework. The reviewer of *Variety* wrote:

> Polish by subject and director, French by official production and shooting locations, American by soundtrack and partial financing, and transatlantic in casting, *To Kill a Priest* is an ambitious political thriller emptied of substance by its heterogeneous components and hybrid dramaturgy.[39]

In her review in *Monthly Film Bulletin*, Sylvia Paskin claimed that the film which 'had all the markings of a gripping political thriller, has succumbed to the weight of its heterogeneous components and the exigencies of international coproduction', and as a result, it 'offers no social or political context within which the character can develop'.[40] Roger Ebert commented on what he saw as the disastrous results of using an international cast:

> The central characters are surrounded by many others, too many others, in an international cast. The movie might have seemed more convincing if it had been made in Polish and subtitled in English, but instead we get a bewildering array of accents. Lambert sounds vaguely French, Harris is American and his son is so British he sounds like a parody ('Please, father, may I have a dog?'). Couldn't they find an American kid for the role? No

one sounds Polish in the movie except when they sing the Solidarity hymn, which is in Polish (but not subtitled, of course).[41]

One of the most crushing reviews was published by Rita Kempley in *The Washington Post*, who claimed that the movie was 'like some sadistic communist buddy movie in which persecution complex meets Jesus complex'.[42] These critical assessments of the film indicate that the mode of American-European co-production almost inevitably involves an artistic risk. Mark Betz commented on the issue from a larger cultural perspective:

> the ubiquitous coproductions of European art cinema are, in the case of their backing by American coin, read as rather unnatural hybrids, as compromises of the auteur's vision or as cautionary examples of the damage brought upon Western European cinematic traditions by the commercialism and manifest destiny inherent in Hollywood's colonizing interests in Europe. (Betz 2009, 54)

Polish critics also noted these artistic compromises in Holland's film, yet they were much more appreciative of it than their Western colleagues. Arguably, these differences in critical assessment resulted from the different distribution and exhibition strategies employed in the West and in Poland. In the latter, none of distribution agencies – that were still controlled by communist authorities – were allowed to purchase the film. Unlike in France – where the film had its premiere in two prime-screen movie theatres located on the Champs-Élysées with appearances by Christopher Lambert, Agnieszka Holland and other members of the crew – in Poland, the first screening took place at the annual convention of the cine-clubs (DKF) – the same cine-clubs that the young Holland frequented in her youth (see Chapter One) – in Gorzów Wielkopolski in November 1988. In December of the same year, another screening of the film was organised by Roman Gutek (who then worked in the Student Club 'Hybrydy' and today is one of the most prominent independent film distributors) in Warsaw for invited guests only. The event was reported by John Tagliabue in *The New York Times* as politically important due to the presence of many Solidarity activists, including Adam Michnik and Jacek Kuroń. For both screenings, the French Embassy provided the copy of the film which was sent via diplomatic post. Later, the film was distributed by the underground publisher NOWA on VHS.[43] As Piotr Sitarski noted, one of the most important characteristics of early video screenings in Poland that were organised outside of the official distribution networks was:

> the sense of freedom [. . .] Even if a film was not overtly political, the mere fact of participating in a public screening, of watching with others a film

that was banned (or at least not approved) by the authorities, was community-forming. The lack of physical comfort or perceptual comfort viewers might have experienced was rewarded with a sense of independence and belonging [. . .] For some people, it was an extension of their politics or religion. (Sitarski 2020, 87–8)

The alternative channel of distribution that was traditionally associated with politically engaged cultural production by dissident artists and cultural workers instantly located *To Kill a Priest* within the realm of Polish national cinema contesting communism.

Polish film criticism also contributed to the 'nationalisation' of Holland's film, in which of crucial importance was Andrzej Wajda's article published in the Catholic weekly *Tygodnik Powszechny* – the same that published Błoński's article on Polish responsibility for the Holocaust – entitled 'I was in the cinema. . . To Agnieszka Holland on her brief visit to the country'.[44] The article was a critical assessment of the then recent film production in Poland, while expressing a nostalgic longing for the splendid period in Polish film history of the Polish Film School. Towards the end of the article, the respected director made a confession: 'I am desperately looking for a movie that would be a farewell to the Polish Film School [. . .] and the French-American film made by Agnieszka Holland is such a film'.[45] With the statement, he symbolically appropriated transnational film production into the realm of national cinema and its history, while simultaneously consecrating Holland as a national artist. Wajda's opinion has provided a critical matrix for film critics and scholars. For example, Tadeusz Lubelski wrote: 'In her film, Agnieszka Holland referred to the most valuable traditions of our cinema that is the Polish Film School. [. . .] Although it was made abroad, it says a lot about us'.[46] Holland did not deny this affinity; in the interview given to a Polish journalist, she said she was pleased with the comparison: 'while I was making *To Kill a Priest* I was thinking a lot about Wajda's *Canal* [. . .] In the Polish Film School I was especially fascinated with the merger of the historical and the personal'.[47] Years later, the authors of all three Polish monographs on Holland set the seal on the nationalisation of *To Kill a Priest* which consequently erased its transnationality. Bobowski presented the most radical opinion: '*To Kill a Priest* [is] one of the most important Polish films [. . .] despite it being made in France with foreign actors, it could be considered a Polish film because of its Polish subject matter and Polish *auteur*' (Bobowski 2001, 156). Likewise, in his monumental history of Polish cinema, Tadeusz Lubelski claimed that 'The French-American film with English dialogues, featuring international stars, was nevertheless Polish in its spirit' (Lubelski 2009, 453). In contrast to Western film criticism that located the film within the framework of American-European co-production, Polish auxiliary discourses placed it within the frameworks of national, *auteur* and exilic cinema. The international critics questioned Holland's reputation, while the cultural workers from her native country enhanced it.

EUROPA, EUROPA: SECOND ENCOUNTER WITH ARTUR BRAUNER AND NO OSCAR NOMINATION FOR FILM OR DIRECTOR

Europa, Europa was Holland's first European co-production. The film's script was based on the real-life story of Salomon Perel, who, during the Holocaust, hid his Jewish identity in order to survive. First, in the Soviet Union, he joined the communist youth organisation Komsomol, and then, after being relocated to Germany, he became a member of Hitlerjugend. After the end of the Second World War he emigrated to Israel, and for years he did not share his story out of shame. Only years later, on returning to his place of birth, did he share his story with a journalist who published an article on this astonishing tale of survival. Brauner instantly became interested in it and purchased the copyright for the story from Perel for very little money. The producer added it to the large pile of the Holocaust testimonies he was considering for filming. He assigned writing a script to Paul Hengge, who had authored the original script for *Angry Harvest* that Holland disliked and rewrote. Brauner approached many filmmakers with the offer to make the film from Hengge's script, yet in vain. Eventually, Holland accepted the proposition, albeit reluctantly.[48] She was hesitant because of the poor production conditions provided by Brauner for *Angry Harvest* and his lack of support in her struggle with ZDF over the final cut. Luckily, she managed to interest Margaret Ménégoz, the French producer, who had collaborated earlier with Andrzej Wajda on *Danton*, in the project. In 1988, during her first visit to Poland after seven years in exile, Holland explored the possibility of making the film in Poland using some of the amenities of the domestic film industry.[49] Eventually, *Europa, Europa* was made as a German-French-Polish co-production with an international crew and cast. The participation of Poland was possible due to the post-1989 changes in the country. The film industry and distribution agencies were quickly and often chaotically adjusting to the rules of the free market, hence the eagerness to participate in international co-productions. Within the framework of transnational production, Holland was able to exercise more control over various stages of the project implementation compared to her first collaboration with Brauner, thereby manifesting her authorship agency.[50] For example, she requested permission to change the original script by Hengge, who eventually decided to withdraw his name from the project as the new version radically differed from his original ideas.[51]

Locating her collaboration with Brauner within the framework of Bruno Latour's theory of network-actors, it can be seen as a fluctuating system with a shifting centre of power. In their first work, *Angry Harvest*, Brauner had played the role of a super-actor, which Holland recollected as a rather frustrating experience:

> My German producer interfered at all levels of making the film – the choice of actors, the choice of locations, and so on. This was very difficult for me, because I was used to making all the decisions myself – after getting advice from others, of course. With *Angry Harvest*, it was always a battle. (Holland and Brunette 1986, 17)

Within the co-production framework of *Europa, Europa*, the role of a super-actor was no longer accessible to Brauner. Accordingly, Holland gained more agency, which is proved in her selection of collaborators, whom she recruited mostly from the film circles she was a part of before emigrating. Jacek Petrycki, who photographed most of her Polish films (*Something for Something*, *Provincial Actors*, *Fever* and *A Woman Alone*) and was also a regular collaborator of Krzysztof Kieślowski, was employed as director of photography. The score was composed by Zbigniew Preisner, who was then already famous due to his score for Kieślowski's TV series *Decalogue* (*Dekalog*, 1988), while also collaborating with Holland's sister, Magdalena Łazarkiewicz. The position of production designer was offered to Allan Starski, who frequently teamed up with Andrzej Wajda, including production design for *Love in Germany*. Furthermore, the second unit directors' team included among others Laco Adamik, Holland's husband (although at that time they were already separated), and Marcin Latałło, a son of her late best friend Stanisław Latałło. Finally, Barbara Pec-Ślesicka, a former production director in the film unit 'X', was an executive producer. Holland was able to recreate to a certain extent a creative-production team she worked with in Poland. Furthermore, she increased her authority over the content of the fictional reality and its ideological aspect, which eventually resulted in her further detachment from the hegemonic Polish discourse on the Holocaust.

Like *Angry Harvest*, *Europa, Europa* undermines the dichotomous model of the Holocaust experience where a clear line separates perpetrators from victims, presenting instead the whole range of 'implicated subjects' (Rothberg 2019) representing various ethnicities and nationalities. Neither the Poles who demonstrate anti-Semitism[52] nor the German youth who support the Nazi doctrine participate in the genocide, yet they both benefit from it, not necessarily materially, but through buttressing their self-worth and the feeling of supremacy. Most importantly, the protagonist of the film, Sally (Marco Hofschneider), while hiding his Jewish identity in order to survive the Holocaust, temporarily also occupies the position of the 'implicated subject'. When he pretends to be a German orphan and becomes a member of the Hitlerjugend, he becomes

Figure 3.4 *Europa, Europa* (1990)

implicated in the ideological system aimed at the extermination of the Jews. The scene of him taking a tram ride across the Łódź ghetto and secretly observing the horror of his people dying on the streets reveals his liminal position as a potential victim who temporarily occupies an insulated spatial location – here the closed space of the tram separating him from the space of genocide – and establishes him as a passive bystander (see Fig. 3.4). A similarly ambiguous position is also given to the character of the German officer Robert Kellerman (André Wilms), a gay actor forced to hide his sexual orientation, a punishable crime for the Nazis. Being himself in danger of persecution, he nevertheless is a member of the German army, the Wehrmacht. Their symbolic encounter, during which they reveal to each other their respective Jewish and gay identity, betrays their ambivalent positioning in relation to the Holocaust.[53] Robert could denounce Sally, and vice versa, and this power over the other human being implicates them both in the totalitarian system.

In its exploration of the issue of identity, *Europa, Europa* questions common gender politics in that it establishes the male rather than the female body as an object of camera's gaze, which is at odds with the visual logic of the classical model of cinema as described by Laura Mulvey (Mulvey 1975). As William Collins Donahue claims in his comments on Holland's film, 'Some will undoubtedly find satisfaction in this very appropriation of the gaze, seeing it perhaps as a kind of feminist assumption of male privilege' (Donahue 2000, 115). However, the film's politics of the gaze is not entirely subversive as Sally is presented as an adolescent boy whose masculinity is still in the formation stage. When he forcefully tries to recreate the foreskin on his penis, he symbolically prevents his phallus to, so to speak, fully emerge to manifest his power. Due to his fear of his Jewishness being discovered, he cannot release his libidinal energy through sex with Leni (Julie Delpy), a German girl he is in love with. She questions his virility and by extension his masculinity. Finally, his adolescent boyish body, along with delicate facial features, may invoke a gender ambivalence, and as such it may serve as a source of visual pleasure for the viewers of any gender and sexual orientation. Ruth Johnston astutely summarises the film's engagement with the issue of identity:

> the film documents the hero's engagement in a series of masquerades that call into question different aspects of identity: nationality, religion, race, class, linguistic capability, genetic inheritance, sexuality, and finally, the one tangible sign of difference – his circumcision. Not only do these categories often conflict with one another, but each category is itself unstable and subject to deconstructive pressures. (Johnston 2003, 5, 6–7)

However, in the ending of the film, the real Salomon Perel appears and proclaims his Jewishness, declaring that it was a linchpin around which he constructed his postwar life in Israel. The statement undermines the fictional play with various identities as noted by Johnston and many other critics. The extra-diegetic ending of the film contradicts its diegetic discourse on the protagonist's selfhood. If the fictionalised story puts into doubt – or perhaps even destroys – the notion of a singular and coherent identity, the ending solidifies the category in presenting the real Salomon Perel as finally discovering his 'true self'.[54] In this context, all Solly's previous masquerades do not reveal the performative aspect of identity but instead hide and protect the true self that he recovers in the post-Holocaust era.[55] The tension between the fictionalised life of the filmic Solly and the narrative coda provided by Salomon Perel can be seen as a retreat from the progressive identity discourse into the conservative position of singularity based on ethnicity and nationality. This symbolic katabasis is not dissimilar to Holland's Polish films that also explored emancipatory possibilities in terms of gender only to finally embed these within the larger project of national identity.

Unlike *To Kill a Priest* and *Angry Harvest*, *Europa, Europa* had a nationwide distribution in Poland. Its premiere was a prestigious cultural event preceded by an extensive promotional campaign that capitalised on Holland's newly acquired cultural capital. While several years earlier she had been persona non grata, now she was welcomed as a filmmaker of international reputation whose films were nominated for the Oscars and awarded the Golden Globe.[56] Arguably, Holland's accelerating career and the international success of *Europa, Europa*, a European co-production, epitomised post-communist changes in

Poland and the country's 'return to Europe', as declared by the popular political slogan used during the first democratic election in 1989.

While Poland proudly celebrated its participation in the successful European co-production, German cultural politics responded to *Europa, Europa*'s 'Europeaness' with reserve, if not overt hostility. Firstly, the film was officially selected by the Bundesamt für Wirtschaft (Federal Office for the Economy) as the German candidate for the Oscar for the Best Foreign Language Film in 1991, yet soon the process of submission was halted. Manfred Steinkühler, business manager for the German Film Export Union which approves the selection, claimed on behalf of all its members that the film was not German due to being co-produced by France and directed by Holland, a Polish filmmaker.[57] The German press defended the committee's decision, arguing that the film was of poor quality, while also highlighting its alleged biased portrayal of the Germans and their anti-Semitism.[58] Holland was disappointed with the German committee's decision: 'I was close to getting an Oscar for the film. [. . .] I believe that the Germans made a mistake. They failed the film, the producers, their own cinema industry, and to some extent, me as well' (in Zamysłowska and Kuźmicki 2013, 130). In her interview for *The New York Times*, she accused the Germans of 'hating the subject', meaning the Holocaust. In response, thirty acclaimed German filmmakers, including Werner Herzog, Margarethe von Trotta and Wim Wenders, wrote an open letter published in *Variety* protesting the German Export Film Union's decision. As Donahue concluded, 'The effort to gain Oscar recognition for this film became a cause célèbre, and as the controversy gained steam, Holland's view appeared to prevail' (Donahue 2000, 109).

Film scholars did not engage in the public debate concerning the decision of German film authorities, however, they interrogated it to comment on the German national discourse. Susan Linville claimed that 'lacking pure German bloodlines, *Europa, Europa* came to be seen as the product and expression of a kind of cultural miscegenation as a film body trying to pass as German, and as impostor not unlike Solly himself' (Linville 1995, 40–1; see also O'Sickey and Van 1996, 231–50).[59] Donahue argued that 'What may ultimately account for the German audience's rejection of this film is [. . .] that Germans are denied any substantive opportunity to identify themselves as victims of any kind' (Donahue 2000, 116).[60] Finally, Sabine Hake claimed that it was Holland's use of humour that the committee found objectionable, while arguing that the 'playful exploration of the performativity of identity resonated with some of the projections and displacements that continue to haunt German-Jewish culture and complicate the situation of Jews living in post-unification Germany' (Hake 2002, 215). Whether affirmative or critical, opinions on *Europa, Europa*'s ambivalences all prove the primacy of the concept of national identity that needs to be either protected or interrogated, especially when it intersects with other identity factors such as race or sexual orientation.

Ultimately, the withdrawal of *Europa, Europa* from the Oscar competition uncovered discriminatory aspects of the concept of national identity as it operated within German culture. It could be argued that the situation is partly comparable with the Polish critical reception of *To Kill a Priest*. While the German export commission rejected the submission of *Europa, Europa* to the Oscar competition because of its 'impure' representations of national identity, Polish film criticism assimilated the equally 'impure' *To Kill a Priest* into the system of national cinema, erasing or diminishing traces of its transnational Otherness. In both cases, the films were embedded within the totalising body of national cinemas, being respectively rejected by, or absorbed into it, as if in a symbolic act of annihilating the films' transnationality because it was deemed 'cultural miscegenation', as Linville called it. However, Thomas Elsaesser indicates a way to liberate films like *Europa, Europa* from the discourse of national cinema, calling them

> 'films without a passport' – stateless, in-between, one-offs, happy accidents or near disasters, forming new spaces of collectivity and solidarity, and thus symptomatic for the 'margins' and the different kinds of metabolism they invoke for the circulation and consumption of European film culture. (Elsaesser 2005, 28–9) [61]

All the films Holland made since she left Poland in 1981 occupy a marginal position between various models and genres of cinema. As such, they are often marginalised by hegemonic critical discourses developed around such concepts as national cinema, *auteur* cinema, women's cinema and genre cinema, as they do not provide convenient material for case studies illustrating or supporting certain methodologies or theoretical concepts. As transnational productions they do not aim at a specific national audience either and, consequently, they do not establish 'interpretive communities' to use Stanley Fish's concept (Fish 1980). Despite this frequently unfavourable positioning within cultural networks, Holland's films made in Europe enhanced her visibility within screen cultures and established her international reputation.

While the withdrawal of *Europa, Europa* from the Oscar competition was unfortunate for Holland, it did not harm her reputation. The scandal around Andrzej Wajda's *Korczak* (1990), for which she wrote the script,[62] was, however, a serious threat to it. The Polish-British-German co-production presented the final days of Janusz Korczak and the Jewish orphanage run by him in the Warsaw ghetto before he and the children were gassed in Birkenau. Its screening at the Cannes Film Festival in 1990 met with a standing ovation, yet Danièle Heymann's review published in *Le Monde* the following day nearly destroyed the positive reception. She accused the film of promoting an anti-Semitic perspective and not acknowledging the Polish participation in the Holocaust.[63] Her comments on the film's ending were especially harsh:

> The liquidation of the ghetto is underway. Under the Star of David, the children and Dr. Korczak enter the sealed carriage singing. And then the doors swing open – a coda to a sleepy, disgusting dream on the edge of revisionism – and we see how the little victims, energetic and joyful, emerge in slow-motion from the train of death. Treblinka as the salvation of murdered Jewish children. No. (Haltof 2012, 198)

Heymann's attack was soon seconded by Claude Lanzmann, the director of *Shoah* (1985). In response, a large group of French intellectuals such as Alan Finkielkraut, Simone Veil and Elisabeth Badinter, as well as many others, defended *Korczak* and its creators. Heymann's attack was also criticised by Marek Edelman, one of the leaders of the Warsaw Ghetto uprising, and his wife, Alina Margolis-Edelman (see Preizner 2012, 390). Holland decided to write a letter to *Le Monde* responding to Heymann's accusation, yet it was never published in its complete form. For Holland – half-Jewish herself and a director of two films presenting the Poles as 'implicated subjects' in the Holocaust – being implicitly accused of taking up an anti-Semitic approach to the Holocaust was difficult to accept.[64]

Presumably, the attack on *Korczak*, the script of which she contributed to, affected her subsequent professional decisions. Since then, for a significant period of time, she avoided the themes of historical experience in Europe, especially that pertaining to the Second World War. The German decision not to nominate *Europa, Europa* for the Oscar and the smear campaign around *Korczak* instigated in France undermined her European success and most likely prompted her later decision to accept the offer from Hollywood. Before leaving for the States, Holland made for French television an adaptation of Václav Havel's play *Largo desolato* (1991) and *Olivier, Olivier* (1991), an intimate domestic drama for which she authored the script and found producers (Oliane Productions Films, A2, Canal+) to finance it. The film focused on psychological issues and made generous use of visual symbolism, thereby fitting the framework of art cinema, while also referencing Polish cinema.[65]

OLIVIER, OLIVIER: EXIT FROM HISTORY

Inspired by the true events, *Olivier, Olivier* tells a story of the mysterious vanishing of a little boy, the eponymous Olivier (Emmanuel Morozof), and the subsequent deteriorating of his family life. Several years later, an amnesiac teenager

(Grégoire Colin), a petty thief and male sex worker living on the streets of Paris, is identified as Olivier. He joins the family, whose members variously respond to his persona. Olivier's vanishing functions as a narrative caesura dividing the film into two parts that tell, respectively, the story of the boy's vanishing, and of his 'return'. The first part ends with Olivier's mother, Elisabeth (Brigitte Roüan), falling asleep, hence the second part – that ultimately reveals that the real Olivier was murdered by the neighbour Marcel (Frédéric Quiring), a paedophile – can be interpreted as her dream. The film examines different approaches to the traumatic experience. Elisabeth and her husband Serge (François Cluzet) are unable to face or accept the loss of their child. He takes up an offer to work abroad in Africa, whereas she lives in denial, surviving with the help of large doses of tranquillisers. Due to their denial, they easily recognise their missed son in the teenager, whereas Nadine (Marina Golovine), their daughter – who, unlike her parents, has accepted the death of her brother – is highly suspicious of the new Olivier, while being also attracted to him. Ultimately, they have sex that may be incestuous as she is still unsure about his identity (see Fig. 3.5). When the truth eventually comes to light, the parents, especially Elisabeth, do not change their attitude to the false Olivier. When, at the end of the film, he enters the family home, she says to him with a relieved smile: 'You are back', and it is unclear whom she welcomes with these words: an impostor or the newly found son that she believes him to be. Then, there is a shot of an empty swing that is the ultimate symbolic proof of Olivier's absence. Emma Wilson insightfully argues that 'The swing imitates the double movement of disavowal, swinging between acknowledgement and denial', while concluding that '*Olivier, Olivier* is finally most radical and unsettling in its call to think through disavowal

Figure 3.5 *Olivier, Olivier* (1992)

as a mode of survival' (Wilson 2003, 63, 64). Indeed, in Holland's film, Nadine recognises and accepts the loss, while for her mother, disavowal is the only possibility to survive. For her, denial is not a stage in the process of mourning but the only accessible form of it. Her case indicates that a positive resolution of a post-traumatic scenario is not always a viable option.

Due to its theme, *Olivier, Olivier* reveals an affinity with Holland's earlier films whose protagonists decided to live in denial of traumas that were either inflicted on them or by them. The couple from *Sunday Children* refused to take responsibility for abandoning the baby they had planned to adopt; Anka from *Screen Tests* repressed her traumatic sexual initiation and humiliated Paweł instead, while perpetuating her trauma. Anka from *Provincial Actors* accepted living in a toxic marriage out of a moral duty she felt towards her weak husband. In *Angry Harvest*, both Rosa and Leon denied the exploitative aspect of their sexual relationship, and finally, Sally suffered from being separated from his family and attempted to relinquish his Jewish identity through an act of self-mutilation. The ending of *Olivier, Olivier* is somehow perverse in its evocation of trauma being both acknowledged and denied, which prevents its complete healing and subsequent renewal.

Olivier, Olivier is also similar to Holland's films made in the film unit 'X' due to its family theme,[66] while privileging the female characters who often struggle with their maternity.[67] Elisabeth is not able to get over the loss of her son, and consequently, she abandons her daughter Nadine, who is forced to play the role of mother to her mother. The (emotionally) abandoned daughter can be compared to the newborn baby from *Sunday Children* and Boguś from *A Woman Alone*, both left by their mothers in orphanages. Furthermore, after losing her son and abandoning Nadine, Elisabeth becomes figuratively childless like Anna in *Something for Something*, Barbara in *Sunday Children*, and Anka in *Provincial Actors*. Finally, *Olivier, Olivier* features a violent scene of sexual intercourse that is forced by Elisabeth on her protesting husband, which marks the eventual destruction of their marriage.[68] As in many earlier films by Holland such as *Screen Tests*, *Fever*, *Angry Harvest*, *To Kill a Priest* and *Europa, Europa*, sex is not associated with intimacy and affection but is presented rather as a violent fatal force that destroys relationships.[69]

Critics located *Olivier, Olivier* within the framework of *auteur* cinema rather than national cinema as was the case with *To Kill a Priest*. Holland contributed to this 'authorisation' discourse in that she frequently called *Olivier, Olivier* her most personal film:

> Like the mother in the film, I know what it's like to be forcibly separated from a child, my daughter, when I was in Paris during the martial law back in Poland. And I know that my daughter must have felt that I had vanished from the world. When I finally got her out of Poland, she didn't speak to

me for a while. She told me she had thought I had died. (Tibbetts and Holland 2008, 136)

Holland herself suggests a 'biographical-fictional pact' (Erhart 2019) which is a signpost of *auteur* cinema. In her essay, Wilson also commented on the director's self-authorising discourse: 'Agnieszka Holland herself has not avoided the association of *Olivier, Olivier* with aspects of her own experience of maternity and loss', and writes that she 'signal[s] some awareness of the ways in which her involuntary exile and her circumstances as a Polish director filming in France, may transform and inflect her treatment of a missing child drama' (Wilson 2003, 55). Wilson is cautious to admit the 'biographical-fictional pact', yet she recognises the 'personal' flair to the film, which she implicitly locates within the mode of *auteur* cinema. Her essay on *Olivier, Olivier* is a chapter in her book *Cinema's Missing Children* that examines exclusively films representing art/ *auteur* cinema. The author also points out that several other films by Holland feature the motif of 'loss in childhood', which can be associated with the director's loss of her father, whose death has remained a mystery for more than forty years. Another possible biographical reference in *Olivier, Oliver* was suggested in the recently published biography of Holland by Karolina Pasternak (2022). Pasternak reports that Holland was abused as a teenager for almost five years (see Chapter One). When asked about *Olivier, Olivier* as possibly reflecting the experience, the director responded vaguely, as if to prevent the film being approached with an all-too-obvious biographical key. Notwithstanding Holland's evasive comments, the 'biographical-fictional pact' emerges here forcefully and links *Olivier, Olivier* with *auteur* cinema.[70]

Although frequently located within the framework of *auteur* cinema, *Olivier, Olivier* was also approached from the perspective of national cinema(s). When commenting on the film's lukewarm critical reception in France, Holland speculated that perhaps it was because the film 'looked French', yet it was not (in Zamysłowska and Kuźmicki 2013, 144).[71] Wilson made a similar observation: 'Critics have read *Olivier, Olivier* in its French filmic context', specifically comparing it to *Le Grand chemin* (1987) and *Les Jeux interdits* (1952), and consequently:

> In such references, in its setting, language and in the (French) nationality of its cast and crew, *Olivier, Olivier* claims identity and reference as a French film. Yet it also recalls certain Polish filmic images of a pastoral landscape of childhood, as found, for example, in Andrzej Wajda's *The Birchwood* (1970) or, more recently, in the films of Dorota Kędzierzawska. (Wilson 2003, 56–7)

In a more elaborate fashion, Wilson reiterated Holland's intuitive opinion on the film's 'imperfect Frenchness'. She commented on how 'Holland makes the national context of the film subliminally significant' (Wilson 2003, 56).[72] However vague and general these comments are, they refer to the film's ambiguous national identity and thereby somehow echo the German cultural officials' claim concerning the 'insufficient Germanness' of *Europa, Europa*.

Holland's disappointment with the mostly indifferent critical response to *Olivier, Olivier* deepened when she learned that the film was considered for a prestigious prize, yet was blocked by a critic from *Le Monde*, which, as she put it, 'Has entirely repulsed me from France. I told myself: I don't want to have anything to do with these people. I told myself: This is not my territory, though the French film audience is the most intelligent' (Holland and Kornatowska 2012, 270). Arguably, the average performance of *Olivier, Olivier* in movie theatres and a somewhat lukewarm critical reception in France – that were preceded by the German withdrawal of *Europa, Europa* from the Oscar competition and the massive attack on *Korczak* – were crucial in helping Holland decide to try her chances in Hollywood when the opportunity arose.

To conclude, Holland's exile in Europe was a transitional period in her professional career in that it was a gradual, yet not linear, process of relocating from the realm of national to transnational cinema. Initially, she joined the Polish intellectual and artistic émigré circles, while making efforts to maintain professional connections with her native film networks through writing scripts for the films of her colleagues working abroad and subsequent collaboration with other creative film personnel from Poland. Simultaneously, she was gradually adjusting to independent production modes as established by Artur Brauner in Germany or Margaret Ménégoz in France, who, on the one hand, facilitated her entrance into European transnational cinema, yet on the other hand limited her thematic and generic choices. Gradually, she distanced herself from the Polish national discourse, as demonstrated in her Holocaust movies that significantly departed from the then hegemonic narratives equating Jewish and Polish victimhood and erasing anti-Semitic acts, to acknowledge instead some Poles' position of 'implicated subjects'. In turn, her one-time collaboration with David Puttnam during his brief post in Columbia marked her first encounter with global Hollywood.

Ultimately, during her stay in France Holland established herself as a travelling filmmaker whose position necessitated constant negotiations between available projects and her own aesthetic preferences. As a result, her European output from the 1980s and the early 1990s presents diversity in terms of genres and aesthetic, and as such it exemplifies authorship as a 'space of dispersion', to use Dana Polan's concept. While some Polish film critics noted the absence of Holland's authorial signature,[73] most of them made every attempt to reintegrate her European films into *auteur* cinema, 'nationalising' it whenever possible.[74] Holland herself also participated in the 'authorisation' of her works, presenting them as related to her own personal life experience. Her authorship established by her European work and auxiliary public discourses around her persona is somehow paradoxical in that the 'authorial signature' is rarely if ever visible in the films, whereas her agency in terms of exercising her directorial authority within new production models and different socio-cultural circumstances is indisputable.

NOTES

1. Agnieszka Holland, email message to the author, 28 November 2022. In her interview given to John Tibbetts, Holland said she went there to promote *A Woman Alone* (Tibbetts and Holland 2008, 136).
2. All these letters are available in Andrzej Wajda's Archive (AWA).
3. Formally, Holland was in exile until 1988 when she visited Poland for the first time after spending seven years abroad.
4. In her interviews from the early 1990s, Holland admitted her distance from Polish reality; see for example: Mariusz Miodek, 'Zawistnicy i film z Coppolą', *Film*, no. 8, 1992, 5.
5. In 1981, she was a member of the executive committee of the Association of Polish Filmmakers, while Andrzej Wajda was its president. As Mieczysław Rakowski, a deputy prime minister between 1981 and 1985, noted in his diary, the conservative circles of the communist parties attempted to persuade them to withdraw from these bodies (Rakowski 2004, 370, 375). Holland's status as dissident artist was also reinforced by playing a secondary role in Ryszard Bugajski's *Interrogation* (*Przesłuchanie*, 1982), a brutal representation of the Stalinist prison, that was also shelved until 1989. Ironically, Holland played a zealous communist activist who eagerly admitted the accusation of treason despite being innocent.
6. In his essay on Polish filmmakers working abroad, Paul Coates noted the parallel: 'It is assumed that sooner or later the director of integrity will be compelled to go into exile, re-enacting the primal drama of a Mickiewicz or a Miłosz – or, at the very least, to do some work abroad' (Coates 1990, 104). Likewise, Izabela Kalinowska considers exile a key notion for Polish culture, while examining its presence in both Polish Romantic literature and contemporary cinema (Kalinowska 2002).
7. Holland addressed Wajda a 'man of providence' in one of her interviews (Agnieszka Holland, 'Robić film. Rozmowa z Agnieszką Holland', interview by Wilhelmina Skulska, *Przekrój*, no. 2035, 1989, 8–9).
8. Subsequently, she also collaborated on the scripts for Wajda's *Demons* (aka *The Possessed*, *Les Possédés*, France 1988), and, eventually, *Korczak* (Poland-Germany-UK, 1990), which was made in Poland.
9. In 1983, Baranowski established the International Film and Theatre Seminars that he organised until 1992. He invited prominent Polish film and theatre directors such as Erwin Axer, Wojciech Marczewski, Filip Bajon, Tadeusz Łomnicki, Andrzej Wajda, Andrei Tarkowsky, Anatoli Vassiliev, Jan Kott, Edward Żebrowski, Robert Wilson and Yuri Lyubimov. Baranowski is also known for playing the protagonist in the first episode of Krzysztof Kieślowski's *Decalogue* (1988).
10. In his autobiography, Baranowski reports that he invited together Holland and Kieślowski to teach the seminars which gave them a chance to meet on a neutral ground for the first time since she left Poland. He admits that it gave him a satisfaction to help people who were separated due to political reasons to reunite and to help them financially (Baranowski 2013, 84).

11. For detailed information on *Kultura* and its political and cultural significance, see Bolecki 2009; Labov 2019, 147–52.
12. For detailed information on the Video Kontakt Studio, see Nowakowski 2019, 103–30.
13. Expelled from university due to his participation in the student protests in 1968, in the 1970s Mirosław Chojecki founded NOWA, an independent underground publishing house in the Poland of state socialism. A prominent activist in the Solidarity movement, he left Poland in 1981 to avoid imprisonment for his anti-communist political activity. Encouraged by Jerzy Giedroyć, the editor-in-chief of *Culture*, to establish a publishing house, in 1982 he was able to secure financial sources for Kontakt from a Polish businessman who, in turn, prompted him to open a film section in 1984 (Nowakowski 2019, 116–18).
14. The film consists mostly of brief statements made by the people linked to *Culture*, while also presenting the villa at Maisons-Laffitte. The filmmakers refrain from using sophisticated formal devices, aiming at representational transparency. The only aesthetic intervention is adding a song with the lyrics by the Romantic poet Seweryn Goszczyński; for more details see Nowakowski 2019, 116–22.
15. The film is similar to *Culture* and *Czapski* in that it also presents KOR's founders and members as they recollect the history of the organisation, see Nowakowski 2019, 123–5.
16. While attacking Holland for hypocrisy, Klaczyński summarised the whole article, which might have been useful for those readers who did not have access to samizdat publishings (Zbigniew Klaczyński, 'Paranoja jako program', *Film*, no. 13, 1983, 3–5).
17. Jan Rem, 'Pozycja wyjściowa', *Tu i Teraz*, no. 9, 1983, 3. A similarly hostile comment on an allegedly anti-Polish interview Holland gave to *Liberation* was included in the article: Anon. 'Ach, gdyby nie ci urzędnicy', *Perspektywy*, no. 8, 1984. Two years later, the same magazine, *Perspektywy*, published another hostile comment on Holland's article, 'A Few Remarks on Recent Polish Cinema' – that was reprinted in a Polish samizdat periodical *Kurs* – on the crisis of Polish cinema at that time (GEM, '"Gwiazda" w szczelinach "hołoty,"' *Perspektywy*, no. 5, 1986, 9).
18. *Love in Germany* was not Brauner's first Polish–German collaboration. The company had collaborated earlier with the Polish film industry and its filmmakers. The first collaboration was in 1958 when the company covered 30 percent of the costs of production and international distribution of *Eight Day of the Week* (*Ósmy dzień tygodnia*), directed by the Polish-Jewish director Aleksander Ford.
19. For a comprehensive overview of Artur Brauner see Dillmann-Kühn 1990.
20. Another Polish scholar, Andrzej Gwóźdź, focuses on the (low) artistic quality of the film, while not sufficiently recognising its historical significance (Gwóźdź 2018, 262–3).
21. Rothberg considers multidirectional memory as 'subject to ongoing negotiation, cross-referencing, and borrowing; as productive and not privative'. His book on the subject 'considers a series of interventions through which social actors bring multiple traumatic pasts into a heterogeneous and changing post–World War II present' (Rothberg 2009, 3, 4).
22. Janusz Kijowski recollected his collaboration with Brauner as one of the worst professional experiences in his life. He said it was not accidental that directors such as Andrzej Wajda, Agnieszka Holland and Jerzy Hoffman did not want to continue collaboration with him: 'Mr Artur treated us as poor relatives whom he would exploit as if they worked illegally on the construction site' (Janusz Kijowski, 'Dlaczego Kijowski nie nakręcił "Listy Schindlera"', interview by Bogdan Sobieszek, *Dziennik Łódzki*, no. 293, 1994, 3).
23. As Holland reported, the production conditions provided by the Western independent film producer were not better than those she was supplied with by the state film industry in Poland but rather the opposite. See Holland and Brunette 1986, 17.

24. Some of the German reviewers objected to her casting as she was 'too beautiful' to play a devastated Jewess (Andreas Kilb, 'Klage mit Belcanto', *Frankfurter Allgemeine Zeitung*, 11 January 1986, 2).
25. In their essay on Armin Mueller-Stahl, Claudia Fellmer and Jon Raundalen noted 'his exoticism [that] was marked as "Eastern Europeanness", an association that his roles have retained ever since' (Fellmer and Raundalen 2020, 152).
26. As Fellmer and Raundalen noted, playing in *Angry Harvest* was also decisive for Armin Mueller-Stahl's transnational career: 'Mueller-Stahl's breakthrough beyond domestic filmmaking in the mid-1980s was grounded in the international attention garnered by both Istvan Szábo's *Oberst Redl* (Colonel Redl, 1984) and Agnieszka Holland's *Bittere Ernte* (Angry Harvest, 1985) when they were nominated for the Oscar for Best Foreign Language Film. The actor's high visibility, gained through appearing in films directed by Fassbinder, Achternbusch, and Kluge, had attracted the attention of other European directors. For his performance in *Bittere Ernte*, Mueller-Stahl won the Best Actor award in Montreal in 1985. These nominations and awards opened doors in North America, and Mueller-Stahl's career became more international in the process' (Fellmer and Raundalen 2020, 152).
27. Some of the German reviewers identified the character of Leon as *volksdeutsch* whose socio-economic advancement was facilitated by the Nazis (see Andreas Kilb, 'Klage mit Belcanto'), however the film does not provide such a definite hint. He is introduced as an opportunist Pole who is ready to collaborate with the underground movement yet is also obedient to the Nazi administration whose laws make it possible to take over Jewish properties.
28. For detailed analysis of women's position in Holocaust discourse, see Waxman 2017.
29. Joanna Stimmel also interprets the relationship between Leon and Rosa as sexual exploitation: 'Rosa becomes his slave, forced by the circumstances to fulfill her master's urges whenever he pleases. Still worse than the sexual slavery is the psychological torture Rosa has to endure: she remains hidden in the dark cellar, unable to see the daylight, and depending entirely on Leons's moods and caprices. The film's mise-en-scene corresponds to the woman's perspective' (Stimmel 2005, 87).
30. The analysis of *Bitter Harvest*'s gender politics develops on ideas presented in my essay on Holland's films published in 2014 (Ostrowska 2014).
31. Rothberg uses the concept of 'implicated subject' to interrogate examples of contemporary social injustice caused by various factors such as racism, sexual abuse, the exploitation of the natural resources, and so on. However, his starting point is Primo Levi's 'The Grey Zone' of the Holocaust, where 'we find multiple implicated subject positions, multiple figures of implication' (Rothberg 2019, 12).
32. Stimmel also notices the film's reconsideration of the Holocaust discourse: '*Bittere Ernte* deconstructs established notions of victimhood, perpetration, and collaboration, clearly condemning the choices Poles made when faced with the genocide' (Stimmel 2005, 84).
33. However, as Stimmel notices, because of its focus on a Polish–Jewish relationship and actual absence of German characters, the film '"de-Germanizes" the Holocaust by moving it beyond Germany's border. In this way, at least for the German viewer, the film undoes mourning by placing "the site and origin of loss elsewhere" in a foreign country and among foreign people' (Stimmel 2005, 97).
34. Karen Jaehne, '*Angry Harvest*', Review, *Cinéaste*, no. 15, 1, 1986, 39–40; Stimmel interprets the character of Leon as bearing a multiple guilt: 'Holland clearly points to Leon's multiple layers of guilt. He is not only responsible for Rosa's mental torture and her subsequent suicide, but also guilty of lying about the details of his "rescue" efforts and having later assumed the role of a Righteous Gentile. Most importantly, by thus

appropriating Rosa's perspective, he, in a way, erases the memory of the victim and her plight' (Stimmel 2005, 91).
35. Małgorzata Karbowiak, '*Gorzkie żniwa* Agnieszki Holland', *Głos Poranny*, 6 May 1990, 4. According to my archival query, there were no other reviews of the film published in Polish press.
36. Roger Ebert, 'Angry Harvest', Review, 21 March 1986, https://www.rogerebert.com/reviews/angry-harvest-1986 (accessed 30 March 2022).
37. In my article 'Duma i uprzedzenie – krytyczne dyslokacje filmu "Zabić księdza" Agnieszki Holland' I present a detailed analysis of ancillary discourses around the film. I use some of the parts of the article in this section of the chapter (E. Ostrowska 2021).
38. A manifest example of such a stylistic and narrative excess is provided by a disconcerting scene of Stefan kidnaping the priest Alek's dog, named a Secret Agent (*tajniak*). When the dog accidentally jumps into his car, the militiaman drives off quickly, while the disoriented animal tries to leave the car through a half-opened window. The man furiously closes the window, almost decapitating the terrified dog, and after a brief while, equally unexpectedly, he stops and lets the animal go. The close-up of the dog's head and his howl on the soundtrack do not only represent the violence committed to the animal but also make the image itself violent towards the viewer.
39. '*To Kill a Priest*' by Variety staff, *Variety Movie Reviews*, 1987 https://variety.com/1987/film/reviews/to-kill-a-priest-1200427392/ (accessed 7 March 2022).
40. Sylvia Paskin, '*To Kill a Priest*. Review', *Monthly Film Bulletin*, 1 November 1988, 342.
41. Roger Ebert, '*To Kill a Priest*. Review', 13 October 1989. https://www.rogerebert.com/reviews/to-kill-a-priest-1989 (accessed 7 March 2023).
42. Rita Kempley, '*To Kill a Priest*. Review', *The Washington Post*, 1 December 1989. https://www.washingtonpost.com/wp-srv/style/longterm/movies/videos/tokillapriest.htm (accessed 7 March 2023).
43. *To Kill a Priest* was released on the tape no. 021 (see *Ludzie Nowej* 2007).
44. Andrzej Wajda, 'Byłem w kinie . . . Agnieszce Holland z okazji krótkiej wizyty w kraju', *Tygodnik Powszechny*, no. 39, 1988, 4.
45. Wajda, 'Byłem w kinie'.
46. Tadeusz Lubelski, 'Morderca i ofiara', *Film na Świecie*, no. 366, 1989, 9. In similar vein, Jerzy Uszyński argued that *To Kill a Priest* reflected on Polish reality in a way the films made in Poland did not (Jerzy Uszyński, 'Archetyp polskiego sporu', *Kino*, no. 8, 1989, 5). However, it needs to be added that the positive reviews were to a certain extent a response to a negative critical campaign run by the critics supporting the communist authorities. For example, the review published in an official weekly of Polish military forces, *Żołnierz Wolności* (*Freedom Soldier*), reported the box-office failure in Western Europe and the Western journalists' opinions regarding the film as politically implausible. The author called the film 'political propaganda' (Tadeusz Mitek, 'Święci i rój szatanów', *Żołnierz Wolności*, no. 30, 1989, 14).
47. Agnieszka Holland, 'Lekcja historii. Rozmowa z Agnieszką Holland', interview by Janusz Wróblewski, *Kino*, no. 8, 1989, 12.
48. Brauner's note on their meeting in Paris on 5 March 1988 mentions some of the issues to be negotiated (Artur Brauner's Archive in the DFF – Deutsches Filminstitut & Filmmuseum).
49. Holland discussed the options as well as Margaret Ménégoz's participation in the project with Brauner during their meeting on 11 July 1988 (the minutes of the meeting are available at Artur Brauner's Archive in the DFF – Deutsches Filminstitut & Filmmuseum; see also Holland and Kornatowska 2012, 257–60).
50. Her control is also evidenced by the fact that her right to determine the final cut was respected by Brauner (as mentioned in his note reporting their conversation on the subject

on 20 September 1991, Artur Brauner's Archive in the DFF – Deutsches Filminstitut & Filmmuseum).
51. The conflict between Hengge and Brauner is described in the article by Gerhard Beckmann, 'Der lange Streit um den *Hitlerjungen Salomon*' published in *Die Welt*, 16 January 1992. According to Hengge, as the article reports, the director changed the script in such a way that he could not identify with it any longer. He protested the use of comedy in it as inappropriate with regard to the victims of the Second World War.
52. Apart from Ewa Mazierska, Polish film critics did not mention the film's acknowledgement of Polish anti-Semitism, see: Ewa Mazierska, '*Europa, Europa*', *Twórczość*, nos. 4–5, 1992, 211; For an extensive examination of the Polish–Jewish relationship in *Europa, Europa* see Pakier 2013.
53. Ruth Johnston makes a direct link between Jewish and gay identity that are both 'closeted' in Holland's film (Johnston 2003).
54. Cynthia Fuchs indirectly corroborates such an interpretation of the character of Solly when she claims that all of women who were fascinated with him did not know his 'true' self (Fuchs 1999, 52).
55. Some Polish reviewers saw Sally's changes of identity as immoral and opportunistic (see Michał Danielak, untitled column, *Dziennik Bałtycki*, no. 39, 1992, 2).
56. In 1991, *Europa, Europa* received the Golden Globe Award for Best Foreign Language Film. The association of film critics in Boston and New York selected it as the best foreign language film of the year.
57. Brauner made some attempts to extend the German contribution, listing some collaborators who had not been credited, such as Frank Beyer, a GDR-based director who was involved in the work on the original version of the script (Brigitte Desalm, 'Salomon und die Scharfrichter', *Kölner Stadt-Anzeiger*, 12 February 1992, 3). Somehow paradoxically, Joanna Preizner, the author of the Polish monograph on Polish Holocaust films, does not include *Europa, Europa* either, for reasons similar to those given by the German committee. She limits her discussion to 'Polish' films only, defined as films produced in Poland and made by Polish filmmakers and crews (Preizner 2012, 9).
58. *Frankfurter Allgemeine Zeitung*, 7 February 1992, 4.
59. The journalists also discussed the 'national deficiency' of the crew (see 'Das Team ist nicht Deutsch', *Rheinischer Merkur*, 19 February 1992, 4).
60. The author of the first script on Perel's story, Hengge, vehemently criticised Holland's film as, according to him, the film omitted to use the opportunity to show that it was not eighty million Germans who killed Jews because among these eighty million were many victims (quoted in Gerhard Beckmann, 'Der lange Streit um den *Hitlerjungen Salomon*', *The Welt*, 16 January 1992, 5).
61. A similar comment is presented in Jonathan Rosenbaum: 'technically speaking, no single country can claim it; it spreads too wide a net, with French and German financing and Polish, Russian, and German dialogue, to have a nationality of its own' (Jonathan Rosenbaum, 'What Is a Jew?' *Chicago Reader*, 7 November 1991, https://chicagoreader.com/film/what-is-a-jew/)
62. When Holland lived in Paris, Wajda received a warning letter from Kazimierz Żygulski, then the Minister of Culture, that no script with Holland's signature would be accepted for production (Notes Wajdy, 15 April 1983, AWA). For a detailed history of the project, see Preizner 2012, 364–74.
63. Danièle Heyman, 'Korczak.' Review, *Le Monde*, 13 May 1990, 87.
64. Interestingly, Czesław Pilichowski, a member of the Script Committee (Komisja Scenariuszowa), claimed in his review of Holland's 1983 script that it presented a Polish anti-Semitism that in fact did not exist (Preizner 2012, 369). In her letter to Wajda written

in Paris after the film's premiere, Holland included the negative comments on the allegedly insufficient representation of Polish anti-Semitism; she suggested the necessity to show an example of a *szmalcownik* (Poles who blackmailed Jews or denounced them to the Gestapo) that was an epitome of this during the Second World War (Preizner 2012, 379).
65. The affinity between *Olivier, Olivier* and the Red Riding Hood fairytale was noted by the Polish critic and film historian Tadeusz Lubelski (Tadeusz Lubelski, 'Czerwony Kapturek u państwa Duval', *Kino*, no. 12, 1992, 6).
66. Maria Stalnaker claims that the theme of family is central to the films Holland made abroad, something which is frequently overlooked by Western critics who habitually approach Eastern European cinema as always tackling political issues (Stalnaker 2003, 320).
67. According to one of the Polish reviewers, *Olivier, Olivier* features strong females and weak or degenerate males, while also making a disclaimer that Holland is not a militant feminist (Jacek Łaszcz, 'Z punktu widzenia babci', *Morze i Ziemia*, no. 8, 1994, 6).
68. Some of the reviewers claimed that observing intimate family life may cause spectatorial discomfort (Maria Malatyńska, '*Olivier, Olivier*', *Echo Krakowa*, no. 44, 1994, 5).
69. Notwithstanding the thematic similarities with Holland's Polish films, stylistically, *Olivier, Olivier* differs from them. Instead of gritty documentary-like realism, *Olivier, Olivier* offers stylish and eye-pleasing imagery. This stylistic turn towards mysterious themes in Holland's work parallels Krzysztof Kieślowski's oeuvre transformation from narrative and visual realism towards sophisticated photography and metaphysical themes, as demonstrated in his first Polish-French film *The Double Life of Veronique* (*La double vie de Véronique/Podwójne życie Weroniki*, 1991). The similarity was noted by film critics such as Maria Kornatowska (in Holland and Kornatowska 2012, 142; see also Mąka-Malatyńska 2009, 140). The similarity was also signalled in the title of the review by Kathleen Murphy 'The Double Life of Olivier' (*Film Comment* 28, no. 6, November–December 1992, 66). Furthermore, the score for both films was composed by Zbigniew Preisner, which added to the stylistic and thematic parallel. Tellingly, Holland and Kieślowski, two Polish filmmakers originating from the cinematic movement of the Cinema of Moral Concern, who were also very close friends, in their films made abroad that both premiered in 1991, told stories featuring the motif of a double. This was perhaps a veiled comment on their own 'double occupancy', to use Elsaesser's term (2005), in European cinema. In his review of *Olivier, Olivier*, Jonathan Romney commented on the 'double' titles of the last two films Holland made in Europe: 'The subject of *Olivier, Olivier* could hardly be more different from [. . .] the historical picaresque *Europa, Europa*. But it could be seen as a variation on the doubling – and the rhyming of both films' titles is no accident' (Jonathan Romney, 'Olivier Olivier', *Sight and Sound*, no. 2, 1992, 54). One of the Polish reviewers compared the title of *Europa, Europa* with Elia Kazan's *America, America* (1963), which also tackled the theme of the journey and of dislocation (see Mieczysław Borkowski, '*Europa, Europa* – opowieść prawdziwa', *24 godziny – Gazeta Kielecka*, no. 34, 1992, 4; Kazimierz Witkowski, '*Europa, Europa*', *Ekran*, no. 8, 1992, 3).
70. Polish film critics and scholars have described *Olivier, Olivier* as one of the finest achievements of Holland's *auteur* cinema; for example, in her monograph, Mariola Jankun-Dopartowa claimed that in the film, 'We witness how elements originating in popular culture are transformed in an existential metaphor comparable to the finest achievements of film art' (Jankun-Dopartowa 2000, 244). Although other critics were more restrained in their opinions, they prized the film in unison as a fine example of art cinema.
71. Holland was sceptical about the possibility to make *auteur* cinema in France as early as 1984, which she expressed in her letter to Wajda of 1 January 1984 (AWA).
72. The Polish film critics did not contextualise the film within either French or Polish cinema but located it solely within Holland's own work or a broad tradition of European culture.

73. See Mirosław Przylipiak, '*Europa Europa* trochę jak komiks', *Gazeta Gdańska*, no. 219, 1991, 5; Tadeusz Lubelski, 'Cztery wcielenia Salomona Perela', *Kino*, no. 4, 1991, 16.
74. In his essay on post-communist Eastern European cinema, Paul Coates claimed that Holland along with some other filmmakers was capable of adapting to new modes of film production, while continuing her previous work: 'Krzysztof Kieślowski, Emir Kusturica, and Agnieszka Holland [. . .] are ones whose success beyond their countries of origin indicates an ability fruitfully to exploit the coproduction imperatives that prevail across a Europe otherwise unable to compete with the massive investment in production that is one of the keys to American global dominance (the other being, of course, a frequent near-monopoly of distribution). This involves a capacity for self-transformation while simultaneously retaining the vital impetus and preoccupations of their earlier, pre-1989 work, and inevitably entails confrontation with the ways in which individual identity interfaces with that of the native cultural sphere' (Coates 2005, 265).

CHAPTER 4

Transatlantic journey/adventure, or the re-phase

In her discussion of eighteen different multimedia versions of Frances Hodgson Burnett's *The Secret Garden*, Margaret Mackey consistently refers to Agnieszka Holland's adaptation (1993) as a 'Warner Brothers movie';[1] the director's name appears in the filmography section only. Admittedly, Mackey does identify an authorial agency, but this is the film's producer rather than its director (Mackey 1996).[2] American film critics only occasionally recognised Holland's authorship, while in her native Poland by contrast the film was consistently located within her authorial work and celebrated as her first Hollywood success. A similar polarisation is noticeable in the critical reception of her other films made in North America, *Total Eclipse* (1995), *Washington Square* (1997), *The Third Miracle* (1999), *Julie Walking Home* (2002), and *Copying Beethoven* (2006). This discrepancy among critics over Holland's authorship testifies to its further evolution and also sheds some light on the concept itself. To use Deleuzian terms, her American experience, whether with big studios or smaller independent production companies,[3] created further 'cracks' on her professional timeline that eventually led her to move from (art) cinema to global television and streaming platforms.

In this chapter, I examine Holland's North American works, demonstrating how these adapted within the constraints of the Hollywood model of popular cinema and the European tradition of art cinema. Accordingly, Holland's position gradually evolved from that of an *auteur* working in (trans)national cinema into a filmmaker-for-hire active in global Hollywood. Four of these six films are costume dramas or adaptations of classical literature, and as such they can be located, albeit somehow problematically, within the framework of heritage cinema largely identified with European cultural production. In these subgenres, multidirectional transfers between European and American cinematic traditions occurred, which resulted in an aesthetic merging of popular and art cinema. A similar ambiguity characterises the gender and ethnic politics of these films as they neither condoned nor subverted American hegemonic discourses. Some of them, for example *Washington Square* and *Copying Beethoven*, included feminist emancipatory impulses, yet these were embedded within conservative ideologies. Consequently, the American[4] period in Holland's career demonstrates both her further engagement in issues of identity politics and a dilution of her authorship, which may be linked to working within the structures of sojourn cinema. As will be explained, American film criticism argued that her authorship had been diluted, whereas Polish cultural workers, especially film distributors and critics, saw it as consolidated, arguing for her American films' affinity with European art cinema.

'HOLIDAY FROM HISTORY' AND HERITAGE CINEMA

Vincent LoBrutto and Harriet R. Morrison introduce Francis Ford Coppola's decision to produce *The Secret Garden* in the following way:

> Francis had been drawn to a talented Polish director, Agnieszka Holland, who was mentored by the revered director Krzysztof Kieślowski. In the United States she was best known for *Europa, Europa*, which had been distributed widely in America. Coppola asked her to direct the film. (LoBrutto and Morrison 2012, 195)

As they further explain, in the early 1990s, Coppola did not plan to direct any movies at all; instead he was eager to help those filmmakers who wanted to realise more risky projects that did not fit easily into the agendas of the big studios: 'From the beginning he had lent support to creative ideas that needed assistance in order to see the light of day' (LoBrutto and Morrison 2012, 188). LoBrutto and Morrison imply that Holland owes her Hollywood debut to Krzysztof Kieślowski, her mentor, and Francis Ford Coppola, who provided her with financial support as an executive producer of *The Secret Garden*. However, Holland developed a different narrative concerning the circumstances of her first Hollywood production: she reported that the script for *The Secret Garden* was one of many sent to her at that time, and she decided to accept it as the book was one of her childhood favourites (Holland and Kornatowska 2012, 278).[5] These two contradictory accounts establish two different actor-networks (Latour 2005): the first narrative constitutes Coppola as a super-actor, whereas the second grants this position to Holland. These two networks correspond with, respectively, the producer- and director (*auteur*)-centred models of cinema which Holland has been negotiating throughout her career. *The Hollywood Reporter* provided a third narrative on Holland and Coppola's collaboration. It reported their meeting on the occasion of her visit to Los Angeles when she came to talk about Germany's refusal to submit *Europa, Europa* for the Oscar award. It was after watching the controversial film that Coppola decided to produce Holland's next project, and she accepted the offer because the project 'was devoid of the polarizing "cultural obstacles" that she had addressed in *Europa, Europa*'.[6] *The Hollywood Reporter*'s narrative reconciles the other two, while simultaneously demonstrating the instability of the position of super-actor that can shift between different subjects.[7] Accordingly, the authorship emerges as fluid and dispersed between various agents participating in film projects.

The Secret Garden was made in 1993 during the post-Cold War period declared by Francis Fukuyama as 'the end of history' (Fukuyama 2006). Contrarily, Derek Chollet and James Goldgeiger claimed that in 1989, history did not end, but stopped momentarily: 'the era of uncertainty and opportunity that began with the fall of the Berlin Wall on 9 November 1989, or 11/9, ended violently on September 11, 2001, the day known in America simply as 9/11' (Chollet and Goldgeiger 2008, x). George W. Bush called these times 'years of sabbatical', while George Will, a conservative political commentator, dubbed it a 'holiday from history'; finally, the journalist Frank Rich described it as 'a frivolous if not decadent decade-long dream' (all quoted in Chollet and Goldgeiger 2008, x–xi). Initially, the post-Cold War period in the US caused disorientation, yet it quickly transformed into a lethargic stagnation, affecting the cultural production of that time. The 1990s brought not only systemic changes in the Hollywood film industry, mostly entailing the fusion of film studios into big media conglomerates, but also unprecedented technological development, especially CGI, that changed film aesthetics. In the introduction to the anthology on Hollywood cinema of the 1990s, Chris Holmlund commented on all of these factors: 'The movies and the moods of the 1990s depict a period that most Americans experienced as both peaceful and prosperous'. Henceforth, the vernacular audience favoured pure entertainment represented by popular genres, especially action movies, horror films and romantic comedies (Holmlund 2008, 1, 16), while '[c]inema as art, expression, and social statement filled in the margins' (Kleinhans 2008, 112–13).[8] Between these two tendencies, there was a significant 'middle' segment of film production offering less spectacular special effects and professional performers rather than stars, but still attractive narratives and appealing visuals (see Kleinhans 2008, 96).

With its moderate budget of $15 million, *The Secret Garden* represented the middle sector of Hollywood film production in the 1990s. It was one of hundreds of middle-budget films produced at that time and a typical product of Hollywood employment policies. As Christine Lane commented, assigning film projects in Hollywood was evidently gendered at that time, in that middle-budget 'non-event' movies were 'assigned to women directors struggling in Hollywood, which impede[d] their access to the industry', hence 'most women directors [. . .] find themselves "pigeon-holed" into either the "teen-film" or relationship-oriented/family projects' (Lane 2000, 37). After the 1980s, the opportunities for female directors to participate in film production increased, due mostly to an agreement signed by the Directors Guild of America in 1981 pledging to hire more women and people from minorities (Lane 2000, 37). These specific regulations facilitated Holland's debut as much as her personal taste for Burnett's novel and Coppola's film production company profile.

The Secret Garden received a 'G' MPAA rating, which secured it a worldwide audience, eventually grossing of $40 million internationally.[9] The premiere took place on 13 August 1993, in the US and Canada, in 1,319 cinemas.[10] The film was classified as a children's or family movie, a category that, along with action movies, was at the time third in audience popularity, occupying 15.77 percent of the 1990s film market (Litman 1998, 56). Among children's films, adaptations of classical children's literature were especially popular and 'remained a commercially successful venture for the corporate studios in the 1990s' (Wojcik-Andrews 2000, 109–10). As the most successful of this genre, Ian Wojcik-Andrews cites *The Secret Garden* made by 'by acclaimed Polish director Agnieszka Holland' (Wojcik-Andrews 2000, 110), and Steven Spielberg's *Hook* (1991).[11]

Financed by the Americans, *The Secret Garden* was a transnational film project. It was made in British film studios with the participation of British film artists and professionals. Stuart Craig was the art designer, while Roger Deakins was employed as director of photography. The interior scenes were mostly filmed at Pinewood Studios, whereas exterior scenes were shot at Fountains Abbey in North Yorkshire, Allerton Hall in Merseyside, Eton College in Windsor and a chamber at Harrow School in London. Deakins transformed realistic mise-en-scène into painterly compositions with a masterly use of low-key lighting in the interiors and soft-focus high-key lighting in exterior scenes. Casting consisted predominantly of British actors who were using different accents from each other, while some of the characters spoke regional dialect (of Yorkshire). The film quickly gained popularity with British audience that taken it as a 'product made in England' (Królikowska-Avis 2001, 73). It was not only British viewers who misidentified Holland's *The Secret Garden* as a British production, for the British scholar Karen Wells also examined the film as a British 'heritage film for children' and criticised it accordingly for the oppressive representation of class and race (Wells 2009, 123).[12] As was the case with *Europa, Europa* and *Olivier, Olivier*, the 'national identity' of Holland's first Hollywood movie also proved ambiguous. Although this misidentification can be classified as a factual error, it has its merits as the film does fit the framework of 'heritage cinema' that is associated mostly with British films.[13]

The term heritage cinema,[14] as Richard Dyer explains, refers to

> period films made since the mid-1970s' in Europe with the following characteristics: canonical source from the national literature, generally set within the past 150 years; conventional filmic narrative style, with the pace and tone of (European) art cinema but without its symbolism and personal directorial voices; a museum aesthetic, period costumes, décor and locations carefully recreated, presented in pristine condition, brightly or artfully lit; a performance style based on nuance and social observation. (Dyer 1995, 204; see also Dyer and Vincendeau 1992)

The first spectacular success of heritage cinema was the 1981 film *Chariots of Fire*, directed by Hugh Hudson and produced by David Puttnam, however its international appeal was due to the Merchant-Ivory productions such as *A Room with a View* (1986), *Howards End* (1993) and *The Remains of the Day* (1994).[15] Following Andrew Higson's critique of heritage cinema (Higson 1993), British film critics and academics used the term as a pejorative, admonishing these works for an overly academic aesthetic and a conservative ideological message.[16] They claimed the films offered museum-like pictorialism, exploited the cultural prestige of their literary sources, and restrained from a critical interrogation of the past (Higson 1993, 1995, 2003; Hill 1999; Voigts-Virchow 2007). Heritage cinema was also rebuked for using the national past (or rather its specific components) as a marketable commodity in the international film market dominated by corporate Hollywood (Higson 1995).

Paradoxically, these 'quintessentially British' films were mostly transnational cinematic productions aimed at a global audience:

> 'British' period film successes are repeatedly made by non-British personnel with non-British money, and measured in terms of their reception and commercial performance abroad. Indeed, a case could be made that they have *characteristically* been products of international funding, migrancy or collaboration. (Monk 2002)[17]

Holland's *The Secret Garden* in an example of such a 'British' film that was a Hollywood production made by an international crew. Although her other American films, such as *Total Eclipse* (1995), *Washington Square* (1997) and *Copying Beethoven* (2006), do not invoke British cultural heritage, they still belong to the genre of heritage film as they all are historical costume dramas with carefully designed mise-en-scène that, along with stylised cinematography, produce picturesque images. Holland's access to heritage cinema was not exceptional as other travelling filmmakers also eagerly contributed to the sub-genre. For example, Alfonso Cuarón began his Hollywood career with an adaptation of Burnett's novel *A Little Princess* (1995), which was followed by Charles Dickens' *Great Expectations* (1998). Similarly, Jane Campion's first Hollywood movie was a costume drama, *The Piano* (1993), about a Scottish woman travelling to New Zealand, and her next film, made three years later, was an adaptation of another novel by Henry James, *The Portrait of a Lady* (1996).[8] Finally, Shekhar Kapur, an Indian director, gained international recognition due to *Elizabeth*, a costume drama made in 1998. In the 1990s, heritage cinema provided a relatively safe space of transition from national to global Hollywood cinema for travelling filmmakers.

In one of her interviews, Holland admitted that making movies about contemporary life in the States would be not feasible: 'It's true that I will never feel so free in the description of this society, of these subjects, as I felt doing *Provincial Actors* or *A Woman Alone*, when I really knew everything about it', while also expressing her self-confidence in adapting literary classic for cinema: 'I think that in some ways I may understand James better than some American directors. I am a reader and certainly know him better and have a deeper connection to him that many American directors' (Crnković and Holland 1998–9, 4). It is also worth noting that, for her two heritage films, she selected novels by Frances Hodgson Burnett and Henry James, writers who can be considered transnational authors: the former moved from England to the States and the latter travelled in the opposite direction. They both experienced displacement, which in Burnett's novel is echoed in nostalgic images of the English countryside and the recurrent motif of abandonment, while in James's work in a multiperspective narration that constantly shifts points of identifications. In both novels, the trope of transatlantic travel – in *The Secret Garden* Mary travels from India to England, while in *Washington Square* Catherine goes with her father on a European trip – is instrumental in the female characters' development. Holland's relocation from Europe to Hollywood was similarly instrumental in the development of her professional career.[19]

THE SECRET GARDEN AND *WASHINGTON SQUARE*: ADAPTATIONS, ALTERATIONS AND ASSIMILATIONS

Holland's *The Secret Garden* is a coming-of-age story that explores the themes of abandonment and the healing power of nature. These perennial motifs are embedded within a meticulously recreated Edwardian England including then current norms of social class, gender roles and ethnicity. The film was classified as heritage cinema for children and as such subjected to the customary ideological critique. Karen Wells admonished the film not only for perpetuating the ideological conservatism of the novel but even for occasionally reinforcing it. She claimed that the changes from the novel 'have the effect of heightening the representation of whiteness [. . .] and diminishing or erasing the novel's critique of class inequalities and its implicit critique of imperialism' (Wells 2009, 125). Admittedly, the film does not interrogate the politics of the British Empire, however, it does not condone the imperialist project either. The narrative content of the first shots presenting the protagonist, Mary (Kate Maberly), as she is dressed by the East Indian servant women, reproduces the racial and class hierarchy of the British Empire, however, the cinematography and editing disturb this ideological structure. First, the static shots emphasise the immobility of Mary's body as well as her blank facial expression, and as a result she is transformed into a puppet-like figure deprived of any kind of subjectivity. Although she occupies an elevated position in the frame with the East Indian women located below her, she appears as almost an ossified remnant of the Empire rather than a lively and active force subordinating the colonised land.

One of the next shots showing her trying to grow a plant in an ash-like soil lends itself to two readings: it may show her impotence with regard to cultivating the (Other) land, or it may allude to its past exploitation by the coloniser that resulted in its infertility. The shot belongs within a larger sequence that employs the principle of discontinuity in terms of editing and narrative structure. The disjointed images are connected through Mary's voiceover narration that is far from a nostalgic return to the so-called glorious days of the British Empire.[20] It reveals rather her disorientation and loneliness. The lighting design used in the India sequence employs minimal fill-light, resulting in the unnaturally sharp look of the environment. The replacement of the novel's cholera epidemic with an earthquake in the film compresses the India sequence into a brief traumatic event, while also eliminating the parts of the literary original describing Mary's tyrannical behaviour. Therefore, while agreeing with Wells' insightful analysis of the film's coalescing of whiteness with Britishness, I argue that the film's visuals and narration do not articulate an imperialist position as coherently as the author claims.[21]

The opening scene of *The Secret Garden* was also subjected to criticism on the grounds of its problematic sexual politics. Máire Messenger Davis compared it to the opening of *Pretty Woman* (Garry Marshall, 1990), due to the use of fetishising close-ups that sexualise Mary's body (Davis 2001, 48). However, the critic overlooked that – in contrast to the smooth movements of Julia Roberts's body that are emphasised by 'gliding' camera movement – Mary's body remains disconcertingly static or mechanical in its movement, something that is reinforced by the motionless camera shots. Therefore, I would argue that the sequence demonstrates Mary's alienation from her body rather than her body's sexualisation. In her analysis of what she calls the film's exploitative sexual politics, Davis also draws attention to the shot of Mary and Colin (Heydon Prowse) sleeping in the same bed surrounded by scattered

Figure 4.1 *The Secret Garden* (1995)

photographs of his pregnant mother, and the scene in the garden when he photographs his cousin with a country boy, Dickon (Andrew Knott), as they are sitting at the swing and tenderly look at each other (see Fig. 4.1). While admitting the sexual undertones here, I would question whether these scenes are exploitative.[22] The first scene, when put in the narrative context of Colin's prior subjugation to torturous medical practices, can be seen as him reclaiming his body, from which he has been alienated for a long time. The photos of his pregnant mother may also signify a symbolic reconnection with the maternal body, from which he was separated due to her death. The second scene, with an adolescent couple being photographed, lends itself to being read as a self-reflexive enunciation of the potentially exploitative voyeuristic camera gaze.

Notwithstanding Davis's acute comments on sexual motifs in *The Secret Garden*, her interpretation of these as sexualising children requires more attention. Arguably, it evokes a deep-rooted anxiety towards children's sexuality in Western culture which was displaced in the Victorian cult of the child. As Vicky Lebeau explains, it:

> continues to help to shape our sensibilities towards children. In particular, the compulsion to render the child sexless, to present her nudity as symbol

of her primordial innocence – the Edenic ignorance of procreation, of sexual desire – tends to have the effect of sexualizing the child through the look that comes at her or him. Repudiated in the object of vision, sexuality, that constant reference in notions of childhood innocence, can only rebound on the one who wants to look: to paint pictures, to make drawings, to take photographs and, now, to make films. (Lebeau 2008, 98)

The sexual undertones in *The Secret Garden* disrupt the Victorian cult of the innocent and sexless child, yet the film does not offer an alternative to mainstream cinema's hegemonic politics of the gaze that would acknowledge children's sexuality without transforming it into the object of visual pleasure. Nevertheless, the film employs certain narrative devices that work against the objectification of Mary's body and the voyeuristic gaze of the camera. The opening objectifying sequence of shots of Mary's body is followed by her voiceover narration that is momentarily accompanied by her POV shots as she voyeuristically looks at her parents from her hiding place under their bed. Instantly, she changes from the object of the look into its subject. The scene evokes 'the pleasures of female looking' that Claire Monk considers one of the most important characteristics of heritage cinema, but one which is usually overlooked by the hegemonic British film criticism (Monk 2002).

Mary's gaze remains active throughout the film, and ultimately is reconnected with her voiceover narration in the film's ending that serves as a narrative frame articulating her subjectivity. There are two endings: a 'proper' resolution of the narrative conflict, in which Colin is reunited with his father, and a 'feminist coda', presented as Mary's voiceover monologue along with the sequence of disconnected images. The former is filmed in a transparent style, while the latter uses discontinuous sound and image. In the soundtrack, we hear the girl's voice, whereas the image shows the close-up of the hand of an adult woman whom in a while we see as a blurred silhouette in a long shot as she walks away. Susan Smith astutely claims that the sequence establishes the garden as a feminine space (Smith 2010).[23] Thus, the first film's ending presents the symbolic moment of patriarchy regaining its hegemonic position, but the second ending subverts the patriarchy by giving the voice back to Mary and destabilising the system of cinematic representation. The double ending epitomises the film's 'mixture of conservatism and progressiveness' that was characteristic of Holland's earlier works but is also typical of heritage cinema (Monk 1995, 122). As Monk argues, heritage films establish 'spaces in which identities (whether those of characters and nations within the film or the spectators viewing it) are shifting, fluid, and heterogeneous' (Monk 1995, 122; see also Pidduck 2004). The film's ending, with its double coding, substantiates shifting subjective positions between patriarchal and feminist identity projects. Likewise, any stylistic transparency is ruptured with discontinuities that momentarily foreground cinematic form. In other words, in *The Secret Garden*, visual pleasure is rarely, yet persistently, corrupted, or at least temporarily destabilised by narrative or visual excesses. These ideological contradictions and aesthetic surplus demonstrate the complexity of heritage cinema as conceptualised by Monk, while also revealing antinomies characteristic of Holland's Polish films, oscillating between progressive and conservative gender politics.

The ambivalent gender politics of *The Secret Garden* has been recognised by some critics, however it has never been subjected to closer scrutiny, maybe because of the film's middle-ground position within the film production of the day. As Monk succinctly observes:

> Branded as middlebrow cultural products, heritage films have been disparagingly associated – rightly or wrongly – with middle-class, middlebrow, middle-aged and largely female audiences [. . .]. Precisely because of their 'quality', the hierarchies of film/critical culture have assigned them very low status as cinema. (Monk 2002, 100)[24]

Although such an influential film critic as Roger Ebert praised *The Secret Garden* as 'a work of beauty, poetry and deep mystery', and said that 'watching it is like entering for a time into a closed world where one's destiny may be discovered',[25] Western academic critical discourse located the film exclusively within the familiar frameworks of heritage cinema, family film genre, literary adaptation or Warner Brothers (American Zoetrope) productions. Rarely if ever was the film approached by Western critics as belonging to *auteur* or women's cinema. Pigeonholed within the customary critical concepts that implied ideological conservatism per se, the film's emancipatory potential, in terms of narrative and visual strategies, has never been properly recognised. Although for different reasons, Polish critical discourse also overlooked these aspects and, as will be discussed, located *The Secret Garden*, like all Holland's other Hollywood works, within the framework of global Hollywood *auteur* cinema.

Four years after completing *The Secret Garden*, Holland made *Washington Square* for Walt Disney Studios from the novel by Henry James, whose prose gained a special popularity among filmmakers in the 1990s.[26] As Laurence Raw reported, 'There is little doubt that Disney conceived *Washington Square* as a prestige production, in spite of its comparatively modest budget ($15 million)' (Raw 2003, 71).[27] *Washington Square*, like many other heritage films, and Holland's previous works for that matter, was a truly transnational project. The crew included several Poles: Jerzy Zieliński (director of photography), Jan A. P. Kaczmarek (composer), Allan Starski (production designer), Anna Shepard (costume designer) and Holland's daughter, Kasia Adamik (storyboard artist). The American actress Jennifer Jason Leigh played the protagonist Catherine Sloper, while British actors were cast as other main characters: Albert Finney played Dr Sloper, Catherine's father, Maggie Smith – who appeared in *The Secret Garden* as Mrs Medlock, and at that time was well known to American audiences due to her iconic role in the heritage film *Room with the View* (James Ivory, 1984) – played Auntie Lavinia, while Ben Chaplin performed the role of Morris, Catherine's mercenary lover. Holland's film was preceded by the novel's earlier transposition into a play by Ruth and Augustus Goetz, who subsequently rewrote it as a script for William Wyler's *The Heiress* (1949), the epitome of Classical Hollywood Cinema, starring Olivia de Havilland and Montgomery Clift. Although closer to the literary original than its predecessors, Holland's film offered a revisionist reading.

Holland's *Washington Square* follows the original novel, reconstructing meticulously James's descriptions of nineteenth-century material culture, especially the urban setting, interior designs and costumes. Despite its faithfulness to the Jamesian narrative, the script, co-authored by Holland and Carol Doyle, adds several scenes to the original that introduce new meanings and affective structures. The film begins with a brief glimpse into the backstory reported in the first chapter of the novel by the omniscient narrator. The opening shows idyllic images of a lazy afternoon in the affluent Washington Square area; at some point, the camera sneaks through the window into the apartment of Dr Sloper, to discover the family tragedy that has just occurred. We see a man, who is grieving over the body of his wife, who has died while giving birth to their daughter, Catherine. Thus, unlike in the novel, Dr Sloper's character is introduced, not as a respected representative of the medical profession and local celebrity, but rather as a grief-stricken widower. The scene provides a psychological explanation for his later cold demeanour towards his daughter. On the one hand, this emotionally charged reading of the character of Dr Sloper fits the 1990s gender discourse,[28] which validated male emotions; on the other hand, the scene is also typical of heritage cinema, which explored the emotions suppressed by Victorian ideologies. This emotional investment goes awry in the next scene that presents the adolescent Catherine as she fails in her performance of a song at her father's birthday party. Desperate for her father's approval,[29] she becomes paralysed with stage fright and wets herself in front of the embarrassed guests. The camera shows this ruthlessly, in a slow tracking-down movement. The scene is painful to watch for both the viewers and the fictional characters witnessing the humiliating occurrence. The audience is subjected to the forceful voyeuristic sight of the vulnerable girl unable to control her bodily functions. It can be argued that she is as alienated from her body as Mary was in the opening sequence of *The Secret Garden*.

Catherine's wetting herself in front of other people exemplifies the 'intriguing "bodily" twist' that Anne-Marie Scholz notes in other filmic adaptations of James's works made in the 1990s (Scholz 2013, 166), however it also echoes similar situations in Holland's earlier films. In *Sunday Children*, an adolescent girl wets herself on the carpet, much to her father's disapproval and embarrassment. *Europa, Europa* features a scene of Jupp's painful urination due to a forceful tightening down of his circumcised foreskin with a string knot. In *Total Eclipse* there is a scene about a gathering of Parisian poets, during which Rimbaud provocatively urinates on one of the presented manuscripts to express how much he despises traditional poetry. All these 'urinating moments' in Holland's works – transgressive gestures per se in that they violate social and cultural norms concerning human body excretions – are invariably associated with humiliation, pain, and, in Julia Kristeva's analysis, abjection (Kristeva 1982). These affects are reinforced by camera work and editing: the shots presenting these bodily acts are not integrated into a shot-reverse-shot system; thus, they are dis-attached from the fictional characters' subjectivity that the viewer might otherwise identify with. The camera's look remains separated from the audiences' bodies. Leo Bersani proposes to see such a cinematic structure as mobilising what he calls 'affectless sadism':

> It is our inviolability that film protects in assuring us that we can approach, know, even take possession of the real by an act of pure apprehension in which we need not be implicated. Here is an appropriation of objects in which the subject remains untouched [...] From this perspective, the aesthetic medium of film would almost miraculously realize the analytic fantasy of nonerotic sadism, the sadism of an affectless mastery of the world. (Bersani and Dutoit 1992, 15)

The camera's 'affectless sadism' is reinforced in Holland's films in that the protagonists and antagonists do not mobilise emotional structures which would contain the scenes of violation and humiliation that originate in their bodies inadvertently. Such an affectlessness is also used in the erotic scenes: for example, in *Screen Test*, *A Woman Alone*, *Fever*, *To Kill a Priest* and *Angry Harvest* (and in many later films that will be discussed in due course) the acts of sexual intercourse are filmed mostly with a static camera in relatively long takes and often from angles that cannot be taken as the characters' POV. The bodies move spasmodically, and the faces are contorted with grimaces that may express either pleasure or pain. The characters emit non-verbal sounds that bolster these ambiguous emotions. The erotic scenes rarely employ ambient music to provide the viewers with an emotional clue.[30] These cinematic techniques are consistently used to block spectatorial affinity or allegiance with the characters that are subjected to the 'affectless sadism' of the camera's gaze. The only available position for the viewer is that of an alienated observer exposed to affective images of the fictional reality rather than emotional narrative structures. The viewer is displaced from the position they are customarily given within the system of signification of the dominant model of cinema.

Washington Square, by contrast, employs music for creating an emotional affinity between the viewers and the female protagonist. It marks the stages of Catherine's character's development from psychological dependency towards autonomy and self-awareness (Chandler 2015, 186–70; Raw 2003, 71). Each of the songs used in the film serves as a 'musical moment' that, according to Estella Tincknell and Ian Conrich, creates a 'particular point of disruption, an isolated musical presence in a non-musical film which is most notable for its potential to disturb the text through its unexpectedness or at times excessiveness' (Tincknell and Conrich 2006, 1–2). The first, and failed for that matter, performance of 'The Tale of the String' marks the point of rupture in Catherine's relationship with her father, whereas its last performance with the children in the film's ending signifies her ultimate breaking up with the past. In the mid-section of the film, she performs, together with Morris, the song 'Tu Chiami Una Vita',[31] which evokes their emotional connectedness, while also liberating her from fatherly authority. Unlike in the scene of her failed performance during the birthday party, during the duet performance, her father is not in the centre of the informal audience but is a distant observer. She is not an object of his controlling gaze either, which demonstrates her emotional dis-attachment from his authority. Instead, she exchanges tender gazes with her lover, Morris. The song returns in the film's ending, yet it is now used non-diegetically as a background for the last shot showing Catherine smiling and looking off-screen. The song, performed with English lyrics under the title 'Please Don't Come Here Again' by April Armstrong, ultimately marks the protagonist's unchaining from emotional dependency on both her father and her lover.[32]

The emotionally charged music contrasts with the emotionless acting in the last scene that does not offer a conventional narrative resolution. In the last close-up, Jennifer Jason Leigh's inexpressive face remains mostly inscrutable (see Fig. 4.2), and as such it radically opposes the grand finale of *The Heiress* in which Olivia de Havilland performed with royal dignity an act of revenge on her treacherous ex-lover. Although the critics admitted that Catherine from Wyler's film reproduced masculine patterns of behaviour, whereas Holland's heroine represents a feminist consciousness in her rejection of patriarchal values (see Chandler 2015),[33] the audience did not fully embrace these feminist interventions, as proved by the film's moderate box-office results (it grossed $1.9 million).[34] The lukewarm reception of *Washington Square*[35] can also be explained by its generic ambivalence which made it difficult to target a specific audience sector.[36] Belén Vidal observes that Holland's film along with a number of other period dramas made by international directors 'produce an image of

Figure 4.2 *Washington Square* (1997)

women's cinema at the crossroads, poised between a feminist tradition and a post-feminist popular culture' (Vidal 2012, 126). This contradiction is also noticeable on the formal level; on the one hand, as an adaptation of the classic novel offering laboriously created mise-en-scène, the film represented heritage cinema, on the other hand its 'affectless sadism', conveyed by the camera's gaze directed at the female body, compromised the female spectatorial pleasure that, according to Monk, was usually provided by the sub-genre. Most importantly, developing the character of Catherine towards her feminist-oriented self-consciousness did not result in her increased narrative agency.[37] She remained passive, whether a victim of patriarchy or a self-conscious (feminist) subject. However, some critics have noted a strong emancipatory potential in her character. In his analysis of Holland's film and Campion's *The Portrait of a Lady* (1996), John Carlos Rowe claimed that both films were revolutionary calls for changing gender and sexual relations across geopolitical borders. These changes, as he argues, need to be transnational endeavours (Rowe 2006).

However, *Washington Square* did not offer an aesthetic radicalism that is usually associated with revolutionary cinema. Similarly to *The Secret Garden*, the film oscillates between conventions of mainstream and art cinema. Dianne F. Sadoff noticed the tension:

> While the film scrutinizes the middlebrow cultural question of a woman's marital choice and its consequences, however, Holland's mise-en-scène and montage identify *Washington Square* as 'highbrow'. The opening sequence's establishing shots of *Washington Square* betray the film's bid for an art house audience. (Sadoff 1998, 294)

Furthermore, the transparent visual style and clear narrative logic are juxtaposed with disturbing imagery and an inconclusive story. Neither a blockbuster nor a quirky independent production, *Washington Square*, like Holland's other American films, was not easy to promote.[38] Besides, the female audiences of the 1990s, struggling with the backlash against feminism while also enjoying postfeminist freedom, would prefer the rebellious heroines of *Thelma and Louise* (Ridley Scott, 1991) who embodied female agency regardless of the film's ambiguous ending. Catherine's newly acquired self-awareness is not attested through her actions undermining patriarchal power, and as such the film does not facilitate the customary spectatorial alignment expected by female viewers. Accordingly, the film's feminist potential remained underdeveloped. For Catherine's decision to run a daycare centre for the neighbourhood children can be seen as her attempt to create an alternative world to the patriarchal system, leaving the latter intact. Not unlike Holland's earlier films, *Washington Square* leaves emancipatory discourse hanging in the air, marking this time the ideological uncertainty around Holland coming to terms with the feminism that she previously rejected.

TOTAL ECLIPSE AND *COPYING BEETHOVEN*: FROM REBELLION TO SUBORDINATION

Total Eclipse – a film adaptation of Christopher Hampton's play of the same title, presenting the turbulent homosexual relationship between the two French poets, Arthur Rimbaud and Paul Verlaine – and *Copying Beethoven* – a portrayal of the last years of the genius composer – are not typical of the biopic, yet the category provides a useful framework for a critical examination of the two films. As Hila Shachar noted, the sub-genre of literary biopic, to which *Total Eclipse* belongs, was especially popular in the 1990s, when it was viewed 'as a cursory "subgenre" within the more established and general biopic and heritage screen genres [. . .] tied to a patriarchal past and present' (Shachar 2019, 1, 3). Holland's biopics play aggressively with generic conventions and dominant ideological structures to reclaim these unexpectedly from time to time as if marking her hesitancy in embracing the principles of popular cinema. Holland commented that, after making *The Secret Garden* for a big studio, which meant being under the tight control of a producer, she opted for the next project having a smaller budget, and therefore less supervision and fewer interventions. *Total Eclipse* was made as a transnational project financed by several European production companies, while the Hollywood financial input came from Fine Line Features, a division of New Line Cinema that specialised in indie films. The film fitted the filmmaking cycle she designed for herself: one film for money and one for her own pleasure and satisfaction. *Total Eclipse* was the latter. She frequently presented the film as her personal project, while admitting her attachment to both characters: 'Rimbaud is me when I was sixteen-seventeen-eighteen, whereas Verlaine is me now' (Holland and Kornatowska 2012, 81; see also Turk 1998, 263). While 'personalising' the film, Holland dislocated it from the realm of popular genre into art cinema.

Total Eclipse begins with a greyish scene of the old Verlaine (David Thewlis) meeting Rimbaud's sister, Isabelle (Dominique Blanc), who came to Paris to reclaim any manuscripts of her late brother. However, she does not want to preserve them for the future but to destroy the ones defying Christian morality. When Verlaine starts recollecting his relationship with Rimbaud, the first flashback scene emerges on screen presenting picturesque imagery of the French countryside and then equally pleasing images of Paris. The saturated colours and soft lighting beautify the past in the way typical of heritage cinema. Similarly, the scenes that follow, set in Verlaine's household, offer comforting images of an affluent bourgeois apartment that is tastefully decorated, protecting its inhabitants from the unpredictability of public life. Played by Leonardo DiCaprio, the character of young Rimbaud embodies energy, charm and beauty. A young rebel, he soon disturbs both the mundane life of the French middle-class and the Parisian bohemian habitat of smoky bars and cafes. His destructive power is manifested through his bodily performances. Upon his arrival at Verlaine's house, he announces to his mother and wife that 'he needs to piss'. Later, while dining with them, he eats with his fingers, belches and plays with his saliva, drooling it down his lips and sucking it back. During the gathering of Parisian poets, he provocatively disrupts a somewhat pompous event (see Fig. 4.3), calling a poem recited by its author 'shit' and finally urinating on one of the manuscripts.

Figure 4.3 *Total Eclipse* (1995)

By repeating the word 'shit', referring to 'man's juices' and, finally, urinating, Rimbaud is forcefully injecting corporeality into the realm of sublime poetry. His excessive bodily performances can be seen as a desperate attempt to reconnect with his body, from which he feels alienated by the social conventions of bourgeois life and bohemian style.

Holland's narrative and visual emphasis on the poets' excessive bodily performances, along with their violent and destructive homoerotic relationship, put the film at odds with middle-class social norms that in the 1980s and 1990s had been adopted by gay culture. Not surprisingly, numerous critics vehemently criticised the film's presentation of Rimbaud and Verlaine's liaison. In his review in *Variety*, Todd McCarthy complained, '[a]ccording to this film, the exchange of bodily fluids, not of intellectual and artistic ideas, was the important thing between these two legendary poets'.[39] Other critics were similarly disapproving of the film.[40] The critical reception of the film does not only reflect the dominant aesthetic and ideological discourses but also reveals certain aspect of film culture in the 1990s. As Christina Lane notes, at that time, 'The role of reviewers has slowly been colonized by studio marketing departments. This phenomenon means that the ability to shift a negative tide surrounding a particular film is now, more and more, out of the hands of Kael-style critics' (Lane 2000, 35). Produced outside of the corporate Hollywood and violating the sensibilities of the middle-class audience, the largest and most important sector of the global audience, *Total Eclipse* was rejected by the film critics who spoke from the position of this socio-cultural formation.

Total Eclipse violates the principle of good taste in its visual presentation of bodily excess, and also on the level of characterisation: Rimbaud is obnoxious and cruel, Verlaine is mean and ugly, Verlaine's wife is pitiful, her parents are narrow-minded, as is Isabelle Rimbaud, the poet's sister. The protagonists destroy each other, and there is no redemption for them. These utterly despicable characters were not a rarity in cinema of that time; for example, two years before working with Holland, David Thewlis appeared in Mike Leigh's *Naked* (1993) as a sexually violent character who was destroying his own life and the lives of those he encountered on his way. However, unlike *Total Eclipse*, *Naked* consistently employed the conventions of gritty realism, while also referring to the familiar figure in British culture of 'angry young man', which returned in a more radical form in the 1990s to express the contemporary crisis of British masculinity. In contrast, Holland's film offers the elaborate and often picturesque mise-en-scène typical of heritage cinema, while populating it with characters whose behaviour transgresses the social norms of the era and occasionally are blatantly misogynistic. Moreover, the film employs the non-chronological and episodic narration typical of art cinema, yet it does not establish a consistent subjective perspective nor produce psychological depth. Finally, Holland's exploration of homoerotic desire is not 'timid and restrained' as it is usually in heritage cinema (Hill 1999, 94, 98),[41] but excessive and abject.

In *Total Eclipse*, homoerotic desire serves as a destructive force that binds the two men in a sado-masochistic relationship, as conspicuously demonstrated in the scene where they have sex; the film lands the viewer in it *in medias res* without any lead-in showing emotionally charged gestures or passionate kisses. Instead, there is a sequence of alternated close-ups of the men's contorted faces, expressing aggression – on the part of young Rimbaud – and submission, on the part of Verlaine. The erotic scene employs an unattractive mise-en-scène, with dim lighting, drab colours and an austere interior. It is appalling in every possible way, and viewers are most likely to respond with disgust that, as Colin McGinn usefully explains, 'is an aesthetic emotion in that its primary focus is the *appearance* of its object, not what the object can do or has done in the way of harm' (McGinn 2011, 6). Accordingly, images of male frontal nudity also appear as 'disgusting' (McGinn 2011, 6). First and foremost, usually they are placed in an unfavourable narrative context of violent relationship between the men. Secondly, the mise-en-scène de-beautifies the bodies through unflattering lighting, unsaturated colours and the grim setting. Thirdly, the absence of POV shots prevents the integration of the images of naked bodies into emotional structures of desire. Instead, these images are most frequently connected with the negative affects of shame and humiliation, as demonstrated in the scene of Verlaine's medical inspection at the police station; it begins with a long frontal shot of his naked body (see Fig. 4.4) and then the doctor lubricates his gloved palm prior to conducting with an anal examination. The scene is

Figure 4.4 *Total Eclipse* (1995)

presented from the objective perspective, and, in consequence, the viewers cannot identify with Verlaine's torment and humiliation. They are forced to observe it as they had been forced to watch the adolescent Catherine wetting herself in *Washington Square*. *Total Eclipse* does not embed homoerotic desire within the familiar structures of the romance (a genre that often reflects the patterns of heterosexual relationships), and as such it did not offer a familiar means of identification for the global audiences of 1990s, something that was reflected in the film's poor box-office results.

In his insightful essay on *Total Eclipse* as a contemporary 'film maudit', Edward Baron Turk persuasively explains that 'Creative works sometimes fail to find a substantial audience for reasons that have less to do with artistic quality than with the ideological climate prevailing at the time of their appearance' (Turk 1998, 260). Holland's film is such a case. Turk claims that audiences and film critics rejected *Total Eclipse* because of its 'deviation from prevailing norms of American gay cultural politics' (Turk 1998, 264). The representation of homosexual desire in *Total Eclipse* as a destructive force was at odds with then dominant conservative gay discourse. In the 1990s, AIDS had been decimating the gay community, which was seen by some as a punishment for promiscuity. To oppose this negative narration around homosexuality, affirmative images were needed like those offered by *Philadelphia* (Jonathan Demme, 1993) or *In and Out* (Frank Oz, 1997), which, however, replicated hegemonic heterosexual norms.[42] Similarly, independent cinema also remained bound by this ideological conservatism, as exemplified by Ang Lee's *The Wedding Banquet* (1993).[43] Accordingly, both mainstream and independent film productions in the 1990s successfully integrated the gay movement into middle-class ideologies, which Leo Bersani predicted as early as in 1987 in his seminal essay 'Is the Rectum a Grave?' As he wrote, 'many gay men could, in the late '60 and early '70s, begin to feel comfortable about having "unusual" or radical ideas about what's OK in sex without modifying one bit their proud middle-class consciousness or even their racism' (Bersani 1987, 205). Bersani's diagnosis proved valid during the AIDS period and aftermath when the gay movement consolidated around family values traditionally cherished by hetero-normative middle-class people. In his discussion of the conservative grip on gay discourse, Bersani commented on its 'sanitisation', which is owed to a great extent to academics who performed 'a frenzied epic of displacements in the discourse on sexuality and on AIDS. Among intellectuals, the penis has been sanitized and sublimated into the phallus as the originary signifier, the body is to be read as a language' (Bersani 1987, 220). In a way, the academic discourse alienated the penis from the male body. With its visual emphasis on the body, *Total Eclipse* works against such sublimation of gay sexuality, however, it does not further interrogate the fetishism of cinematic signifying practices. Eventually, Holland's film did not meet the expectations of either experimental/art cinema spectatorship or the wide audience of global heritage cinema.[44] Although the film was later distributed on VHS and DVD, and presented on various streaming platforms, most likely '[i]t's best remembered now by DiCaprio completists'.[45] Besides, the figure of the rebellious Rimbaud that was idolised by the counterculture, with Jim Morrison being his most zealous devotee, lost its appeal during the conservative 1990s, as testified by Oliver Stone's *The Doors* (1991), which embedded Morrison's self-destructive rebellion within the structure of a cautionary tale.

In the conclusion of his article on *Total Eclipse*, Turk noted that 'Holland's commitment to risky art cinema has not hurt her credibility with Hollywood's major studios, as her recent mega-budgeted adaptation of Henry James's *Washington Square* (1997) makes clear' (Turk 1998, 263). Indeed, *Total Eclipse* did not destroy Holland's career, yet it hampered it. Yvonne Tasker commented on differences in how a failure affects the professional position of male and female filmmakers: 'men have repeated opportunities to recover from the commercial (and even critical) failures that can seriously hamper a woman's career' (Tasker 2010, 217).[46] Although Holland was given an opportunity to make several more films in North America, these were invariably mid-budget productions that never got sufficient promotion or the critical hype needed to raise her career to the next level.

Copying Beethoven (2006) was Holland's last Hollywood project. The film was produced by Metro-Goldwyn-Meyer and distributed in US cinemas only. The script was authored by Stephen J. Rivele and Christopher Wilkinson, who earlier scripted another two biopics: *Nixon* (Oliver Stone, 1995) and *Ali* (Michael Mann, 2001). As Holland recollected, the script on Beethoven drew her attention because it told:

> a story of a great artist who creates his work despite all unfavourable circumstances. No one wants to pay for his music – it is too revolutionary for those times. But despite that – although he struggles with his physical impairment, his progressing deafness, he is cursed and hated – he creates. It is a story that, despite appearances, is very contemporary. Beethoven was the Mick Jagger of his times. (quoted in: Zamysłowska and Kuźmicki 2013, 190)[47]

Copying Beethoven presents the last years of Beethoven's (Ed Harris) life when, practically deaf, he is working on his Ninth Symphony and the late string quartets. Anna Holtz (Diane Kruger), a fictional character, is working for him as a copyist. The film meticulously and sensually records this process, connecting it with the body:

> Richly textured, loving close-ups of hand, pen and ink moving across handmade paper as it is inscribed with notes (whose musical realization we

hear on the soundtrack) dominate the film's mise-en-scène, reminding us that the inscription and ultimately the sounding of music is never far from the body's physicality and the materiality of the writing instruments and paper. (Kumbier 2010, 647)

Unlike in *Total Eclipse*, where the body remains somehow detached from the process of writing and creating, *Copying Beethoven* grasps the bodily sources of artistic creation. The bodily dimension of music is fully revealed in the long scene of the premiere performance of the Ninth. Beethoven, by then completely deaf, conducts the orchestra on the podium, while Anna, concealed in the middle of the orchestra, reads the score and conveys it with her hand movements as well as her facial expression. She uses her body to mediate the score, a transcript of Beethoven's creation, back to him. Cinematic devices employed in the performance scene establish Anna and Beethoven's relation as equal rather than hierarchical. Although initially he is presented mostly from a low angle, and she from a high angle, these merely reflect their position within the narrative space. As these varied camera angles are not integrated into POV sequences, they do not establish any hierarchy between them. Moreover, as the scene proceeds, both characters are more frequently filmed from neutral, head-on angles from the same camera distances; there are also several swish pans that frantically move back and forth between Beethoven and Anna as if visualising the flow of creative energy passing between them. The visual parallel established by the camerawork shows them as mirroring each other. At some point, there are shots of their hands moving in a balletic way, as if using an alternative language. Although some details of gender-coded clothes are visible, the shots soon become unfocused and create an almost abstract image of bodily performances.[48] Finally, the twelve-minute-long scene is devoid of any dialogue, which is itself a temporary retreat from the regime of logocentric and, by the same token, patriarchal culture. In its place there opens up a cinematic space for bodily and purely visual sensations.

Notwithstanding the non-hierarchical gender politics developed visually in the musical moment of the Ninth performance, the narrative logic of the scene prompts the viewer to see Anna's role here as a sign of her ultimate subordination and de-subjectivisation.[49] In the story, she is reduced to the vehicle of Beethoven's music, becoming a kind of a ghost-conductor, as she remains as invisible to the audience as was Kathy in *Singing in the Rain* (1952). In Gene Kelly and Stanley Donen's classic Hollywood musical, male characters open the curtain and reveal the fakery of the on-stage performance to the audience, showing instead the actual female singer. Clearly, woman's creative potential needed male mediation to be recognised in the public space. By contrast, in *Copying Beethoven*, the female character is provided with such agency. At the ending of the conducting scene, Anna steps up to the podium and

Figure 4.5 *Copying Beethoven* (2006)

turns the composer towards the audience to let him see the massive applause he was oblivious to due to his impaired hearing (see Fig. 4.5). At that moment, Beethoven regains his superior position, shown in the shot of him being carried on the arms of his fans, whereas Anna leaves the scene. The gender hierarchy that was momentarily obliterated during the musical moment is re-established within the narrative, aided by the dialogue and mise-en-scène. Although the character of Anna serves as a pivotal narrative point, a feminist transported into the past,[50] her screen existence is limited to her collaboration and relationship with Beethoven. The last scene of the film conveys a contradictory ideological message: it first shows Anna in her own room, composing – thus she is presented outside the limits of symbolic patriarchal culture[51] – then she leaves her room and walks across the pastoral meadow landscape towards the horizon to eventually dissolve in it, as if embodying Beethoven's vision of religious eternity that he shared with her before dying. Yet it could be also argued that Anna Holtz continues her own journey towards independence and creativity.

While *Total Eclipse* and *Copying Beethoven* represent global Hollywood cinema, they also link with Holland's earlier Polish films featuring artist figures, specifically actors and filmmakers, namely *Screen Tests* and *Provincial Actors*. Protagonists of all these films struggle with unfavourable circumstances and, more importantly, with their own limits posed either by their minds or bodies. Their rebellion is appealing and appalling, whereas their position is constantly shifting from subservience to exploitation. The aspiring actress Anka, from *Screen Tests*, is first sexually abused by her would-be boyfriend, but then she harms Paweł when she 'sells out' details of their intimate encounter. Importantly, she is encouraged to do this by the director, played by Holland herself. In *Provincial Actors*, neither Anka nor Krzysztof can fulfil their artistic aspirations, for which they compensate by humiliating each other. Verlaine is a victim of the cruel and possessive Rimbaud, while simultaneously brutalising his wife. Finally, in *Copying Beethoven*, the genius composer is a victim of conservative society's non-response to his revolutionary music, but he also ruthlessly criticises and humiliates Anna. The artists in Holland's films are both vulnerable and cruel. Following Lucy Fischer's discussion on the on-screen presence of authors as 'the film creator's "body double" – a version of him- or her-self personified onscreen' (Fischer 2013, 15), one may assume that these relatively frequent figures of artists in Holland's films are narrative equivalents of an authorial signature that is not manifest in her visual style.

The relationship between Beethoven and Anna in *Copying Beethoven* can also be seen as an example of 'fictional-biographical overlap' (Erhart 2019, 68) in that it recalls Holland and Wajda's long-lasting professional collaboration that gradually transformed into friendship. She suggested this analogy on several occasions: 'While making this film, I was thinking about my first meeting with Wajda. [. . .] He was a master that helped me to emancipate' (Holland and Kornatowska 2012, 378).[52] A useful perspective on Holland and Wajda's collaboration and friendship is offered by Katarzyna Maciejko-Kowalczyk in her documentary *How He Looks from a Close Distance?* (*Jaki jest z bliska?*, 2004). The film features three women talking about Wajda, the master of Polish cinema: Krystyna Zachwatowicz, his wife and costume designer of many of his films, Krystyna Janda, an actress who created the iconic character of Agnieszka in *Man of Marble* (*Człowiek z marmuru*, 1973), and Holland, who authored or consulted on many of his scripts. The stories they tell imply that the figure of 'the master of Polish cinema' was to a significant degree sculpted by these three women. Holland and Wajda's relationship is also well documented in the letters they had been exchanging throughout their long friendship.[53] They demonstrate how Wajda's initial protection gradually changed into a dependence on Holland's expertise in scriptwriting and knowledge of trends of contemporary cinema. The later professional Wajda's reliance on Holland is figuratively echoed in Beethoven's eventual realisation of his dependency on Anna that is epitomised in a dramatic scene when he asks her on his knees to work with him again. Their interdependence in the process of creation emerges as one of the most significant topics of the film, which gains a special meaning in the context of Holland's approach to filmmaking as a collective enterprise.

Admittedly, all the artists in Holland's films are somehow unable to work on their own as solitary creators. In *Screen Tests* and *Provincial Actors*, the actors belong to theatrical and filmic collectives; Rimbaud establishes an intensive relationship with Verlaine in the hope of fuelling his creativity; and, finally, Beethoven needs Anna to witness his struggles with God and assist him in composing and conducting. This fictional preference for collective creation implicitly refers to Holland's past collective film projects and her later dispersed authorship. In her interview given on the occasion of the premiere of *Copying Beethoven*, she said that 'it would be difficult to call us [film directors] creators in the full sense of the word, we are rather makers or co-ordinators'.[54] Her early participation in collective projects produced in Poland in Wajda's film unit 'X' and her later collaboration with the regular team of mostly Polish film artists and professionals substantiate the abstract concept of 'dispersed' authorship. At the same time, Holland's attempts to work with the same collective might have been for her a strategy to 'domesticate' the initially unknown terrain of European and Hollywood cinema. Her authorship, perceived from Latour's actor-network theory, emerges as a changeable constellation of many participants that establishes various internal hierarchies. Jerzy Zieliński worked as a cinematographer for *The Secret Garden* (additional cinematography), *Washington Square* and *The Third Miracle*; Jacek Petrycki, who did the cinematography in many of Holland's films made in Poland and Europe, collaborated with her in *Shot in the Heart* and *Julia Walking Home*; Anna Biedrzycka-Sheppard, who designed costumes for *To Kill a Priest*, did the same for *Washington Square*; Zbigniew Preisner composed music for *The Secret Garden*; Jan A. P. Kaczmarek did the same for *Total Eclipse* and *Washington Square*; and last but not least, Kasia Adamik, Holland's daughter, participated in all the Hollywood films, working first as her mother's personal assistant (*The Secret Garden*), and then as a storyboard artist (*Total Eclipse, Washington Square, The Third Miracle, Copying Beethoven* and *Julia Walking Home*). Holland herself frequently emphasised the contribution of Polish artists and professionals to her films, however she located this collaboration within the framework of friendship rather than any professional relationship.[55] Polish film critics adopted this approach too, for example Mąka-Malatyńska calls some of these relationships 'intellectual falling in love' (2009, 38), which is a manifest example of an attempt to transpose the professional network into an affective structure that opposes the institutional frameworks of the film industry. Holland's collaboration with the Polish film artists and professionals in transnational film projects also secured her a continuity with her earlier Polish works.[56]

THE THIRD MIRACLE AND *JULIE WALKING HOME*: POST-SECULAR JOURNEYS TO (EASTERN) EUROPE

In 1999, Holland made *The Third Miracle*, produced by Coppola's American Zoetrope and two small independent film production companies, Haft Entertainment and Franchise Pictures. It was a contemporary drama indebted to European art cinema, exploring metaphysical issues as represented by Robert Bresson and Carl Theodor Dreyer, while its content offered a brief foray into the realm of Eastern Europe. Its action begins in Bystrica, Slovakia, during the Second World War when the Americans were bombing the Nazi

Figure 4.6 *The Third Miracle* (1999)

arms factories located in the area. A little Roma girl prays to the Holy Mary statue to stop the raid (see Fig. 4.6). And it stops. Many people's lives are saved. Then, the action leaps several decades ahead to Chicago, where another statue of the Holy Mary cries with bloody tears of healing power. The miracle is ascribed to Helen O'Regan (Barbara Sukova), a pious woman, a healer, who has spent her last years in a convent, abandoning her teenage daughter. The priest from the local parish, Frank Shore (Ed Harris), is given the task of verifying the miracle. While embarking on the mission, he struggles over his own crisis of faith that is fuelled by his infatuation with Roxane (Anne Heche), the daughter of Helen, the would-be saint. 'The killer of miracles', as he is called, eventually finds out that Helen, as a child – the little Roma girl from the opening sequence – performed a miracle of stopping the bombing, which is the 'second miracle' required for the beatification procedure. In the film's ending, that lapses forward in time, Frank Shore is a devoted priest again, Roxane is a happy mother, whereas Helen's beatification is still hanging in the air. The realistic plots are resolved, while the religious one concerning the issue of miracles is left open. Paul Coates noted the contradiction: 'Holland's objectivism and tact appear to clash with the populism of the material she has taken on, reflecting a tension between her "European" and her "Hollywood" identities' (Coates 2003, 138).

The cinematic 'miscegenation' of *The Third Miracle* was noted by Coppola,[57] who claimed 'The film [was] very much Eastern European', while the Polish critic, Tadeusz Sobolewski, claimed it was Polish and indebted to vernacular Romanticism with its supernatural worlds and metaphysical themes.[58] With its explicit religious theme, the film can be linked with Holland's diploma film *Jesus Christ's Sin*, although the tonality is radically different as the erstwhile absurdity has changed to seriousness and occasionally even solemnity. Supernatural and religious motifs have also appeared in several of Holland's films. For example, in the ending of *A Woman Alone* – which consistently used gritty realism – there is a brief fantasy sequence in which the dead Irena drops from heaven a letter for her son. *To Kill a Priest* presents the character of the secret service functionary who is seduced by religion. The male protagonist of *Angry Harvest* is a would-be priest whose attitude to Rosa, the Jewish woman, is almost exemplary for both Christian charity and Christian anti-Semitism. In *Olivier, Olivier*, inexplicable occurrences and coincidences blur the line between the real and the supernatural.[59] In one of the scenes of *The Secret Garden*, children perform a magical ritual to call Colin's father back home, which unexpectedly works. In 1999, directly after completing *The Third Miracle*, Holland directed Ansky's *The Dybbuk* (*Dybuk*), the epitome of Jewish mysticism, for the Polish Television Theatre.

Metaphysical motifs appear also in the 2002 *Julie Walking Home*, which tells the story of Julie (Miranda Otto), a daughter of Polish immigrants in Canada, whose peaceful family life with her Jewish husband, a professor, and their two children is unexpectedly ruined when she learns that her husband, Henry (William Fichtner), has cheated on her, while their little son Nicholas (Ryan Smith) is diagnosed with a cancerous tumour. When she learns about a Russian healer, Alexy (Lothaire Bluteau), operating in Poland, she travels there to get help for her son. After the first session, Nicholas feels better, and Julie follows Alexy from town to town to get healing treatment for her son. At the same time, she develops an intimate relationship with the man. Once they have sex, Alexy loses his healing power. Although pregnant by him, Julie returns to her husband to face the painful and unavoidable reality.

For the roots of religious themes in Holland's films, one can search in her biography, specifically her youthful fascination with religion despite her atheist upbringing (Holland and Kornatowska 2012, 73, 338; see also Chapter One).[60] However, they can also be located within the broader context of more general phenomenon of post-secularism that 'emerges as a dissatisfaction with the influential tradition of militant atheism and rationalist secularism built on the Manichean opposition between reason and faith, emancipation and religion' (Ungureanu 2014, 4). As Camil Ungureanu notes, many contemporary thinkers and artists:

> questioned the secularist opposition between religion vs. modernity, faith vs. reason, and looked for a new common ground shared by atheists and faithful alike. Jürgen Habermas, Charles Taylor, John Caputo, Jacques Derrida, Ronald Dworkin, Thomas Nagel, Jean-Luc Nancy, Gianni

Vattimo, José Casanova, Peter Berger, Rajeev Bhargava, Partha Chatterjee, Bruno Dumont, Michael Haneke – to name but a few – form a complex constellation of contemporary thinkers and artists who search for alternatives beyond religious conservatism and a secularism which is hostile to religion. (Ungureanu 2014, 1)[61]

Several of Holland's films have participated in this post-secular debate,[62] yet in *The Third Miracle* and *Julie Walking Home* the conflict between faith and reason is pushed to the foreground and this discord defines the relationship between the characters. In the former film, Frank Shore initially performs the role of the 'miracle killer' in that he tries to demystify the supposedly miraculous occurrences, yet soon he becomes a zealous supporter of Helen's beatification. Similarly, initially sceptical, Cardinal Werner (Armin Mueller-Stahl), an eyewitness of the miracle performed in Bystrica, experiences a metaphysical revelation. *Julie Walking Home* also juxtaposes rationality, represented by Julia's Jewish husband and his parents, with the irrationality expressed by Julie's Polish father, Mietek (Jerzy Nowak) and his compatriots living in the diaspora and attached to the Roman Catholic Church. As a genuinely transnational subject, Julie lives in-between faith and rationality. The film's evasive ending does not question the supernatural, yet it does not affirm it either. The only thing beyond any doubt is Julie's pregnancy. As in other of Holland's films, the body is the only anchorage in the everchanging world of history and politics.

While connecting to the global phenomenon of post-secularism, *The Third Miracle* and *Julie Walking Home* locate traditional religiosity in Eastern Europe which is contrasted with the West that is portrayed as materialist and devoid of spirituality. The female protagonists, Helen O'Regan and Julie, and Holland herself for that matter, travel across these two regions. Coates noted the parallel in *The Third Miracle*: 'Polish-born, she [Holland] herself, like Helen O'Regan, originates in what was long known as "the other Europe," while Helen's Chicago itself represents the American "other Poland"' (Coates 2003, 138). *Julie Walking Home* presents the Polish diaspora living in Toronto, Canada, that also stands for the 'other Poland'. The cultural East believes in divine protection and the supernatural power of the 'chosen' such as Alexy, whereas the West trusts in medical expertise and scientific rationalism. Unlike professional doctors, Alexy, the Russian, considers healing people to be his destiny and duty, not a gift he may use or not. He refuses any remuneration for his work and lives in poverty, as testified by his worn shirt. He is surrounded by young volunteers who are as selfless as is he. Julie, who initially worries about how to pay for the service with her credit card, soon becomes a member of the affectionate community centred around Alexy. The contrast between the West (Canada) and East (Poland) is conveyed by mise-en-scène; as Ewa Skoczowska, the production designer, explained, the Canadian part is 'bright, clear, geometric [. . .] Poland is supposed to be chaotic and a bit weird'.[63] Although this visual contrast reinforces the stereotype of Eastern European backwardness,[64] it still suggests the metaphysical mysteriousness of reality. Julie's journey to Poland expresses a Western post-secular longing for spirituality.

As Holland reported, it took several years to secure funds for *Julie Walking Home*. Eventually the film was made as a Canadian-German-Polish co-production without any contribution from American studios.[65] As Krzysztof Zanussi and his film unit 'Tor' was the Polish co-producer of the film, it could be said that Holland symbolically reconnected with the beginnings of her career in Poland as he was the first director she worked with after returning from Prague. The Polish part of the narrative was filmed on location in Poland with significant participation from Polish personnel, including actors such as Maciej Stuhr and Maria Seweryn. Like *Europa, Europa*, the film uses multilingual dialogues: English spoken with different accents, Russian and Polish. It also employs the motif of travel, yet in the opposite direction than it is usually featured in transnational tales on a journey of desire from East to West. Julie travels from Canada to Poland in the hope of curing her terminally ill son. Initially, the hope is fulfilled, as little Nicholas's health improves. Whether it is an act of gratitude or amorous fascination, her intimate relationship with Alexy also heals the wounds inflicted by her husband's infidelity. Once the double process of healing is complete, she returns to Canada. The healer follows her, yet after a brief joyful consummation of their passionate relationship that takes place in the serene Canadian wilderness (see Fig. 4.7), he loses his

Figure 4.7 *Julie Walking Home* (2002)

supernatural gift, as proved by his inability to heal Nicholas, whose state suddenly deteriorates. It remains unclear whether it is the West, with its secularism, or his sexual activity that has caused this loss. Although in the ending, Julie keeps her pregnancy with Alexy, she is also reunited with her family, who take care of Nicholas. The ambivalent closing scene does not indicate whether the encounter with Eastern spirituality was a transformative experience or a temporal detour from the path of Western rationality.

Julie Walking Home, like all Holland's films made in North America, employs the motif of the intercontinental journey. In *The Secret Garden*, Mary leaves India for England; in *Total Eclipse*, the characters first travel across Europe, and then Rimbaud leaves for Africa; in *Washington Square*, Dr Sloper takes Catherine to Europe in the hope that it will cure her from her infatuation with Morris Townsend; in *The Third Miracle*, Helen O'Regan escapes Europe for the States; and finally, in *Julie Walking Home*, Julie travels from Canada to Poland. None of these journeys is presented as a positive experience, although some are presented as having transformative potential. In Holland's last film made in Hollywood, *Copying Beethoven*, Anna Holtz travels back and forth between her and Beethoven's homes. In the last scene, she composes music in her own room, yet she leaves it and walks towards the horizon. Unlike Catherine from *Washington Square* and Julie from *Julie Walking Home*, Anna leaves the safe and familiar space of her room and moves in the direction of the unknown. It could be said that the film foreshadowed Holland's future retreat from American cinema and her turn, first to global streaming television platforms, and then European co-productions.[66]

Holland's 'Hollywood adventure' brought neither spectacular successes nor grave failures. *The Secret Garden* was a box-office and critical success, while *Total Eclipse* was a fiasco; *Washington Square* and *Copying Beethoven* were appreciated, yet they did not reach a large audience.[67] Most of the American film critics approached these four movies as standard mid-budget global Hollywood film productions with international financial and creative input (only *Washington Square* was entirely financed by American money). They rarely identified Holland as a film *auteur* due to the generic and stylistic diversity of her American films and the critics' unfamiliarity with her Polish works. Lane usefully explains the difficulties involved in obtaining the status of *auteur* in global Hollywood. Firstly, it is achieved 'through complex processes of reputation-building, self-promotion, and the approval of certain media gatekeepers, such as producers, curators, and critics' (Lane 2000, 218).[68] Secondly, she noted the unwillingness of film critics to grant the status to so-called directors-for-hire (220). Arguably, these factors are as important in hampering the authorial discourse around Holland's American works as is the stylistic and thematic diversity of the works. For, as Lane goes on, '[a]uteurism pretends to derive meaning from directorial themes and social messages, but its criteria are, more often than not, governed by the commercial and critical reputation a director is able to garner' (Lane 2000, 222).

Upon her arrival in Hollywood in the early 1990s, Holland, a newcomer from Eastern Europe who had spent several years in exile in France, became a director-for-hire working in sojourn cinema who did not have the proper resources to manage the mechanisms of reputation-building. Like many other female filmmakers, Holland worked for big studios and independent companies, which meant, as Lane noted, 'simultaneous subscription to and rejection to auteurism' and eventually she followed other female filmmakers active in Hollywood cinema, who 'hang onto certain threads [. . .] and leave others to dangle' (Lane 2000, 221). Consequently, Holland did not establish a long-term contract with any specific audience sector. *The Secret Garden* and *Total Eclipse* were aimed at two radically different audience sectors. Made from a moderately feminist angle, the adaptation of *Washington Square* may have been unsatisfactory for both the conservative and the progressive audience in that, for the former, the film was too modern, whereas for the latter, it was not subversive enough. With each film, Holland broke her contract with the target audience won over by the previous work. With her mid-budget films, she achieved neither genuine commercial success nor significant critical reputation. Feminist themes remained underdeveloped or contradicted the regressive gender discourses, and as such her films were not considered to represent women's cinema. The transnationalism of her films concerned more their production mode than their aesthetic strategies. In consequence, the ancillary discourses developed around her American works positioned her as a director-for-hire, whose expertise guaranteed good-quality cinematic products.

By contrast, Polish film critics approached Holland's work from the *auteur* cinema perspective, and they constructed her persona accordingly. They welcomed *The Secret Garden* with unquestionable enthusiasm and pride, although they soon became confused and disappointed as her next American films did not match up to the achievements of her Eastern European fellows, Roman Polanski or Miloš Forman. Since the Oscar nomination for *Angry Harvest* and Holland's successful Hollywood debut, the Polish film critics had been waiting for a master stroke.[69] The occasional scepticism and criticism expressed by some of her compatriots were counterbalanced with ancillary discourses developed through distribution, exhibition and critical practices that maintained her status as film *auteur* that she had achieved earlier with her Polish and European films.

'NOBLE COMMERCIALISM', OR POLISH RECLAMATION OF HOLLAND'S AUTHORSHIP

In discussing the Polish reception of Holland's American films, I take inspiration from Rick Altman's concept of the cinema event. As he explains, 'the cinema event is constituted by a continuing inter-change, neither beginning nor ending at any specific point. No fixed trajectory characterizes this interchange, nor is it possible to predict which aspect of the system will influence which other aspect' (Altman 1992, 4). Retreating from the text-centred analysis, he advocates looking closely at the specificity of each cinematic experience that mobilises different meanings and emotional structures for the viewers. Admittedly, the Polish and North American experiences of Holland's films were different. The Polish screenings were celebrated as cultural events and widely promoted by the media. *The Secret Garden* was first presented as a special screening at the Polish Film Festival in 1993, along with Holland's earlier film *Olivier, Olivier* and Krzysztof Kieślowski's *Three Colours: Blue* (1993). I participated in this festival and still remember the hype around these films that celebrated the international success of Polish filmmakers. The Polish distributor of *The Secret Garden*, the Solopan company, organised the so-called 'continental premiere' of the film as a spectacular cultural event. It took place in Warsaw on 25 January 1994, in the 'Kultura' movie theatre.[70] Invited guests included Tadeusz Mazowiecki, the first post-communist prime minister, and Maja Komorowska, a famous actor who supported the anti-communist dissident movement, both with their granddaughters. There were also many film directors and other representatives of artistic circles. In 1995, Warner Home Video released the film on video cassettes that were sold in a package with the book *Reżyseria: Agnieszka Holland* (*Directed by: Agnieszka Holland*), edited by Stanisław Zawiśliński, that included interviews with Holland and her collaborators as well as excerpts from the reviews of her films. All these distribution strategies increased the cultural capital of the film and its director. For all Holland's other American films similar, although not such spectacular distribution strategies were employed.

The Solopan company that also distributed Holland's next film, *Total Eclipse*, was established and managed by Jacek Szumlas, a Polish émigré, who decided to return to Poland in the 1990s. It soon built up a reputation as a distribution company purchasing art films that were controversial content-wise or formally innovative. Its most contentious decision was to distribute in Poland Antonia Bird's *Priest* (1994) that was aggressively criticised as anti-Catholic and thus condemned by the Church. Before the Polish premiere of *Total Eclipse* that arrived in Poland surrounded by the aura of the film's negative critical reception in the States, Szumlas said: 'After *Priest* I am not afraid of anything'.[71] Like *The Secret Garden*, *Total Eclipse* was also presented at a special screening at the Polish Film Festival in 1995 to the delight of the cultivated film audience. Its official premiere was organised by the Film Centre Graffiti in the arthouse 'Wanda' cinema in Kraków.[72] The promotional campaign included publishing a small volume of Rimbaud's poetry featuring Leonardo DiCaprio on its cover and a CD with the soundtrack composed by Jan A. P. Kaczmarek. *Washington*

Square, which had had its premiere at the Toronto Film Festival in 1997, was first presented in Poland at the Polish Film Festival in Gdynia in 1997, and was rewarded with standing ovation.[73] There was also a special screening of the film for the students of the famous Łódź Film School, where it was also received enthusiastically.[74] Furthermore, the International Film Festival of the Art of Cinematography Camerimage hosted pre-release screenings of Holland's several films: in 2000 it presented *The Third Miracle*, while *Copying Beethoven* was selected to open its 2006 edition. The official premiere of *Copying Beethoven* took place in the Warsaw Philharmonic as one of the events accompanying the Beethoven Piano Festival. As the Polish journalist, Mirosław Winiarczyk, reported, the screening was preceded by the concert of Beethoven music and then the presentation of the crew welcomed by a standing ovation from the audience, as requested by Elżbieta Penderecka, the organiser of the festival.[75] The distribution of Holland's American films by a company that specialised in art cinema, film festival (and classical music in one case) presentations, and exhibition in arthouse movie theatres built up their cultural prestige.

Holland supported these distribution strategies with her participation in special screenings and promotional events. As one journalist reported, at the banquet following the premiere of *The Secret Garden*, the director appeared in an evening gown, while the invited guests enjoyed champagne and exotic fruits.[76] When *Total Eclipse* was released in Poland, she travelled with the film to promote it, often with Jacek Szumlas, the owner of the Solopan company, and her daughter, Kasia Adamik, who at that time regularly worked with her mother.[77] When she came to Kraków to participate in the Polish premiere of *Washington Square*, she was treated with a birthday cake celebrating the fifth premiere of her films organised by the Kraków Film Centre 'Graffiti'.[78] At the premiere of *Julie Walking Home* in the Warsaw cinema 'Relax' in 2003, Holland was decorated with the Knight's Cross of the Order of Polonia Restituta, given to her by the state secretary, Barbara Labuda.[79] Her participation in all these events not only promoted the films but also increased her visibility as a film *auteur*.

Numerous interviews further solidified Holland's status of film *auteur*. First and foremost, she often personalised her film projects; as she confessed, *The Secret Garden* was her favourite book from childhood; the protagonists of *Total Eclipse* were her respectively younger and older alter egos, *The Third Miracle* reflected her own dilemmas concerning religion and metaphysics, *Julie Walking Home* told a story of her close friend,[80] and finally, the relationship between Anna and Beethoven in *Copying Beethoven* reflected to a certain extent her own relationship with Wajda. These personal narratives stamped the Hollywood film industry products with her authorial signature. Interviewed, she would talk from the position of a film *auteur* whose work did not fit the standard film production and thereby was not popular with American audiences. While commenting on the financial failure of *Total Eclipse*, she said that her films were 'too difficult for a mass audience',[81] and she reiterated this negative opinion later:

> Americans are undereducated and usually they treat film as entertainment, not as an intellectual adventure. Today's audience does not stimulate the filmmakers. During the screenings of the film [*Washington Square*], I would sneak into the screening room and look at the people. Among five hundred people there, there were at least one hundred I would not be able to stand if I'd met them. I was thinking, do I want them to like the movie? No, I don't. I have understood to what extent I did not fit this world. Heads of the big film studios love movies that everyone likes. In my films there is a lot of myself, and I cannot be liked by everyone as I am too distinct and provocative.[82]

When the journalist conducting the interview asked Holland why she would return to Hollywood despite having such a critical opinion on it, the director answered that there was no other place for her to escape to. She presented her North American career not as a 'journey of desire' but rather as a kind of 'last resort'.[83] She had difficulties in getting her projects accepted for financing because they were neither blockbusters favoured by big studios nor avant-garde independent projects fitting the profile of independent companies. Despite all these unfavourable circumstances, in the 1997 interview she considered her position in world cinema to be strong and comparable to the standing of Jane Campion.[84]

Polish film critics debated Holland's in-between position in cinema and some of them emphasised her Hollywood success, while others argued for her belonging to art cinema. For example, one film critic claimed that, with *The Secret Garden*, Holland 'has conquered Hollywood',[85] another announced that she was 'better than Spielberg',[86] while others argued that, due to its aesthetic sophistication and metaphysical content, the film belongs exclusively to art cinema.[87] Usually, the Polish critics were more appreciative of her work than their American counterparts, which was especially evident in the case of *Total Eclipse*. While reporting the negative reception of the film in the States under headings such as 'West offended',[88] the Polish film critics responded positively to it and found it 'very European' in terms of style and content.[89] The most radical defence of the film was given by the reviewer of the regional daily from Szczecin, who accused the American audiences of being infantile and thus unable to appreciate the film that was made by the 'the first lady of world cinema'.[90] In their comments on *Washington Square*, some Polish film critics suggested that, since many members of the crew were Polish, the film was somehow 'Polish',[91] while others found it 'too Hollywood'.[92] A similar complaint was directed at *The Third Miracle*.[93] *Julie Walking Home* met with the most reservations; for example, Michał Lenarciński claimed that Holland aimed at a

Kieślowski-like metaphysical tale, yet what she produced was a 'pretentious TV soap opera'.[94] Another Polish journalist reported that the audience of the Venice Film Festival responded to the film with both booing and applause.[95] Finally, Tomasz Jopkiewicz claimed that *Julie Walking Home* continues a regression in Holland's work that started with *Total Eclipse*.[96] Despite these harsh remarks, the film was announced as Holland's symbolic return to Poland. Krzysztof Zanussi, one of the film's producers, stated at the press conference in Venice: 'We are proud that Agnieszka returned home'.[97] Although this return has never really happened in terms of working exclusively within the Polish film industry, the 2006 *Copying Beethoven* ended Holland's 'Hollywood adventure'.

As demonstrated, for American film critics Holland was an accomplished director-for-hire, whereas in Poland she was identified as a film *auteur* who had to adjust her artistic visions to the expectations of producers and global audiences. It could be said that the former produced a deficient *auteur* discourse around Holland's work, while the latter its excessive variant. It is not my intention to suggest that *auteur* discourse is in any way measurable but rather to emphasise the plurality of ancillary *auteur* discourses that are developed locally. Arguably, this difference in Holland's reception in the States and her native Poland can be linked with respectively the absence and presence of an 'interpretive community', to use Stanley Fish's concept (1980). Although many of Holland's films made in Poland and Europe were presented at various film festivals, only *Europa, Europa* was known to a larger audience in the States, hence American critics used familiar frameworks of genre cinema and heritage cinema rather than the *auteur* cinema that was established in Poland as a critical habitat for her films. Despite her impressive productivity (within the span of thirteen years, she made six full-length feature films), she did not settle down in any distinctive sector of film production. Made within different production frameworks and generic scripts, the American films mark the gradual dilution of Holland's *auteur* persona, while also strengthening her professional brand name. This reputation as a true professional that she achieved in Hollywood inflicted some Deleuzian 'cracks' on her lifeline as film *auteur*, yet eventually it mobilised the 'flight line' that initiated the long and fruitful collaboration with television streaming platforms that was to follow. Moreover, as will be demonstrated shortly, her auteurism, that was obscured by the critical discourse that developed in the USA around her feature films, has been somewhat revived by her work for quality television.

NOTES

1. For discussion of the corporate studio authorship in Hollywood, see Christensen 2011.
2. Other critics employed a similar strategy; Paul H. Frobose in his discussion of Holland's film mentions first Francis Ford Coppola – the film's executive producers – and only then provides the name of its director (Frobose 2006, 142); in her article comparing three

adaptations of the novel, Julaine Gillispie introduces Holland's film as 'the 1993 Warner Brothers film (American Zoetrope) movie' (1996, 133).
3. As Jon Lewis notes, the independent film studios are dependent on the big ones and there is not such a big difference in their aesthetic as was maintained for a long time (Lewis 2001, 7).
4. I use 'American' in its customary meaning, as in fact I refer to North America.
5. One of the Polish reviewers claimed that it was Holland who persuaded Coppola to produce the film (anon. '*Tajemniczy ogród w Kosmosie*', *Głos Szczeciński*, no. 23, 1994, 2).
6. *The Secret Garden*, AFI Catalogue. https://catalog.afi.com/Film/59653-THE-SECRETGARDEN?sid=79bf0536-6cf2-4519-890f-691b91ec16e1&sr=7.9564786&cp=1&pos=2 (accessed 28 March 2023).
7. One of the Polish reviewers of *The Secret Garden* claimed it was a hybrid form between Holland and Coppola's styles, specifically the review referred to lighting used in *Dracula* and music in *The Godfather* ((ab) [author], 'Ogród wśród ruin', *Kino*, no. 11, 1993, 14).
8. Jon Lewis also notes a retreat from politics in American cinema of the 1990s: 'A commitment to political correctness at the studios and at the MPAA led to a watering down of content. This was less a political than an economic strategy, as inoffensive films can be marketed to the largest possible audience' (Lewis 2001, 5).
9. In 1993, Warner Brothers, the producer of *The Secret Garden*, had 18.5 percent of the film distribution market in the US (Litman 1998, 23).
10. *Gazeta Krakowska*, 1993, no. 286, 2.
11. For a detailed analysis of *The Secret Garden* and broader contextualisation of the presented facts, see Ostrowska-Chmura 2013.
12. Wells provides the following information on the film: '*The Secret Garden*, UK, 1993, dir. Agnieszka [sic] Holland' (Wells 2009, 123).
13. The similarity of *The Secret Garden* to British 'heritage culture' was also noted by Polish film critics; for example, Mirosław Winiarczyk compared Holland's film to British TV series based on Victorian literature (Mirosław Winiarczyk, 'Dziewczynka i ogród', *Prawo i Życie*, no. 42, 1994, 5).
14. The term 'heritage cinema' was coined by Charles Barr in reference to a group of films from the 1940s that evoked 'national heritage' (Barr 1986, 12).
15. These 'quintessentially English films' were directed by James Ivory, a Californian, produced by Ismail Merchant, an East Indian Muslim, and usually written by Ruth Prawer, a Polish-Jewish woman married to an East Indian.
16. Claire Monk points out 'the heritage film is a genre defined exclusively by those who professionally mediate films, not by those who produce or consume them' and, thus, as she claims, '"heritage cinema" is most usefully understood as a critical construct rather than a description of any concrete film cycle or genre' (Monk 2002, 101).
17. The transnational dimension of heritage cinema represents a more general tendency of an ongoing internationalisation of Hollywood cinema in the 1990s: 'The movie business in the nineties was characterized by an increasing concentration of industrial power among a select group of multinational players [. . .] Nineties Hollywood was dominated by five companies that controlled the industry more completely than the old studio trusts ever did. This conglomeration was accompanied by growing internationalization' (Lewis 2001, 2).
18. Anne-Marie Scholz notes that two of the three adaptations of Henry James's novels were made by two 'foreign' female directors who could be 'overly intimidated by so illustrious a modernist as James' (Scholz 2013, 164).
19. Jayson Baker claims that displacement is the main theme in Holland's adaptation of *Washington Square*: '*Washington Square* (Agnieszka Holland, 1997) stands out among Jamesian adaptations produced in the so-called global age by reimagining established domestic communities grappling with feelings of displacement' (Baker 2013, 1).

20. Garret Stewart considers Holland's film as critical reconsideration of imperialism, while also noticing its erotic undertones: 'Holland's film not only highlights this imperial aspect of the text but also inserts into the story [. . .] a photographic subtext not found in the novel, one that serves directly to eroticize the frustrated yearnings of the characters in a manner that also "updates" the book' (Stewart 1995, 167).
21. In this context, it is worth mentioning Holland's recollection of the film's test screening organised for children; as she reported, black American children displayed a vehement hostility towards the white world depicted in the film, whereas their Caucasian peers were delighted with it (Holland and Kornatowska 2012, 248). The way in which Holland reported this, testifies to her then not full awareness of racial tensions in the United States, which changed with time, as demonstrated in her later American projects, especially those made for television and streaming platforms that are examined in the next chapter.
22. Polish critics also noted the sexual undertones in *The Secret Garden*. One of the reviewers suggested that *The Secret Garden* was not an adaptation of Burnett's novel, but of *Lady Chatterley's Lover*, with all erotic motifs being erased ((eko) [author], 'Prawdziwa Holland', *Gazeta Olsztyńska*, no. 177, 1993, 4); interestingly, in her article published in 1994, Judith Plotz has noted the same parallel (Plotz 1994). Tadeusz Sobolewski observed that Holland has added to the original some knowledge about children's sexuality that was not acknowledged in the romantic ideal of the child (Tadeusz Sobolewski, 'Ogród uczuć', *Gazeta Wyborcza*, no. 23, 1994, 3; see also: (ab) [author], 'Ogród wśród ruin', *Kino*, no. 11, 1993, 14). In one of her interviews, Holland mentioned the erotic symbolism in the novel (Agnieszka Holland, 'Happy end jako katharsis', interview by Tadeusz Sobolewski, *Kino*, no. 1, 1994, 4–5).
23. Arguably, this progressive ending has its more pragmatic reasons; as Gillispie explains, Hollywood has accepted the fact that women buy tickets for 'family films' and their expectations concerning gender politics needed to be properly responded (Gillispie 1996, 143).
24. Andrew Higson also identified heritage films as a 'middle-class quality product' (Higson 1996, 232–3), as did Richard Dyer: 'The market research is not available, it seems likely that they [heritage films] are especially popular with middle-class audiences' (Dyer 1995, 205).
25. Roger Ebert, '*The Secret Garden*', review, 13 August 1993. https://www.rogerebert.com/reviews/the-secret-garden-1993 (accessed 8 August 2022).
26. In his review, Edward Guthmann admonished the film for being 'one of the many [. . .] coming as it does on the heels of so many chaste Merchant-Ivory costumers and all the other well-appointed adaptations of Jane Austen, Edith Wharton, and E.M. Forster, "Washington Square" suffers, inevitably, from arriving late at an already overcrowded gathering' (Edward Guthmann, 'Cast Gives Character to the "Square"', *SFGATE*, 10 October 1997).
27. In addition, as Raw informs: 'A television documentary, "On the Set of *Washington Square*," was commissioned for broadcast on cable television. The director Agnieszka Holland had attracted considerable critical attention, both in America and her native Poland' (Raw 2003, 71).
28. Jayson Barker claims that Holland's adaptation privileges narratively Dr Sloper: 'Thus, the film places the spectator in a privileged social position to stress anxiety with thinning lines of division within the nation' (Baker 2013, 1).
29. Anne-Marie Scholz analyses Catherine's 'psychological dependency' on her father (Scholz 2013, 175).
30. *Total Eclipse* employs ambient music for Rimbaud's and Verlaine's acts of intercourse, yet it is minimal and without the significant changes of tempo and volume that are usually used to mark sexual climaxes.

31. The lyrics are by the Italian poet Salvatore Quasimodo who was born in 1908, thus, the song that is stylised as a period piece, is anachronistic in both its score and lyrics.
32. Holland would frequently mention that she read the character of Catherine through the prism of Witold Gombrowicz's work, especially his play *Yvonne, the Princess of Burgundy* (*Iwona, księżniczka Burgunda*, 1935), whose heroine is constantly performing herself to meet expectations of other people, while finally rebelling against this (Holland and Kornatowska 2012, 294). Some Polish critics also indicated parallels with Gombrowicz (AWANGARDA, '*Plac Waszyngtona*', *Gazeta Warmii i Mazur*, 28 November 1997, 3). Holland often pointed out that the main theme of her films was the issue of identity understood in Gombrowiczian way: 'To what extent can we be ourselves? Do we exist only through the gazes of other people?' (Agnieszka Holland, 'Nie mieszczę się w tym świecie', interview by Barbara Hollender, *Rzeczpospolita*, 29 October 1997, 4).
33. During the question-and-answer session following the film's screening at the New York Film Festival, Holland herself admitted: 'I think my touch was a bit feminist' (Agnieszka Holland, '*Washington Square* Director Draws Parallels To Today', interview by David Sterritt, *The Christian Science Monitor*, (https://www.csmonitor.com/1997/1024/102497.feat.film.1.html 24 October 1997). The reviewers also noted this; for example, in his review published in *Newsweek*, David Ansen stated that the film gave James 'a feminist spin without diminishing the men in the tale', while also claiming the film was closer to the spirit of Jamesian prose than any previous adaptation (David Ansen, 'An Heir to *The Heiress*', *Newsweek*, 20 October 1997, 18). Similarly, many Polish film critics admitted the film's feminist perspective on the literary classic (for example Mirosław Winiarczyk entitled his review 'Feminism in costume'; Mirosław Winiarczyk, 'Feminizm w kostiumie', *Kurier Polski*, 18 November 1997, 2); see also Przemysław Wielgosz, 'Bunt w krynolinach', *Wiadomości kulturalne*, 2 November 1997, 4), however, usually they would claim that identifying the film as feminist would be a simplification as 'the director had much more to say than repeat feminist slogans' (Piotr Wojciechowski, 'Przełamując chłód klasyki', *Film*, no. 11, 1997, 18). Notwithstanding sceptical or unappreciative remarks on the film's feminism, the film has not been attacked for it as Holland claimed (Holland and Kornatowska 2012, 299).
34. Holland claims that the unremarkable box-office results were due to the intricacies of the distribution market in the States in the 1990s. As she reported, in the same year, Iain Softley made *The Wings of the Dove* from Henry James's novel, which was produced by Miramax. Holland speculated that most likely, Miramax, infamous for its ability to promote their productions, had made an agreement with Disney to promote Softley's film at the expense of *Washington Square*; moreover, she mentions their reproachful practice of 'buying' critics (Holland and Kornatowska 2012, 298). These claims sounded like pure speculation in 2012; however, now, after all the crimes of Henry Weinstein have been revealed, they resonate as true. Christina Lane commented on the promotion strategies of the Weinsteins: 'Harvey and Bob Weinstein transformed Miramax into a "giant" through the creation of controversy around films' (Lane 2000, 32).
35. In his review published in *National Review*, John Simon wrote: '*Washington Square*, comes as an anticlimax, even though it sticks closer to James's text. That is its first mistake. Miss Holland, a Polish filmmaker working in the West, always struck me as overrated' (John Simon, 'Climbing, Social and Mountain', *National Review*, 10 November 1997, 61).
36. Dianne F. Sadoff commented: 'Holland's *Washington Square* and Campion's *Portrait* betrayed their artistic ambitions and so, unlike Softley's *Wings of the Dove*, failed to cross over into modest mass popularity and so to be screened at mainstream exhibition outlets' (Sadoff 2002, 41).

37. Irving Singer noted the development of the character of Catherine: 'By the end of the movie, she is fully in control of her destiny as someone who does not have to have the affiliation of either a husband or a demonstrative lover. She can manage very well by herself' (Singer 2008, 130).
38. Kate Newell comments on various generic frameworks that can be used for *Washington Square*: 'it may be evaluated as a Holland film, a period piece, or a romantic drama, but it is evaluated primarily according how well it compares or contrasts to other James adaptations' (Newell 2006, 206).
39. Todd McCarthy, '*Total Eclipse*', review, *Variety*, 10 September 1995. https://variety.com/1995/film/reviews/total-eclipse-1200442933/ (accessed 15 August 2022).
40. For a detailed analysis of the film's reception, see Turk 1998. The article explains how the film's failure was caused by its incompatibility with the then dominant gay discourse.
41. Hill claimed that 'the heritage film not only deals explicitly with homosexuality [. . .] but also invests many of its male relationships with a clear homo-erotic dimension' (Hill 1999, 94).
42. Holland admitted that her film violated the rule of 'political correctness' in that it presented the homosexual relationship as destructive, whereas there was a socio-cultural pressure to show these as counterparts of happy, middle-class marriages (Holland and Kornatowska 2012, 239).
43. This similarity in the politics of representation links with the emergence in the 1990s of a 'centrism of independent cinema, [. . .] that configures "independent" films that are more and more similar to the products from the major distributors' (Wyatt 2001, 67). Likewise, Lane noted, 'As the boundaries between independent companies and studios become more indefinite [and] the division between film criticism and film promotion also becomes less certain' (Lane 2000, 34).
44. In 1995, when *Total Eclipse* was released, the wide audience preferred typical Hollywood entertainment; the highest-grossing films of 1995 were: *Die Hard with Vengeance* ($366 million), *Toy Story* ($363 million) and *Apollo 13* ($355 million); the only film that offered entertainment 'with a flair of art cinema' was *Seven* ($327 million). Distributed by New Line *Total Eclipse* earned $339,889.
45. LGBT Movies: Total Eclipse (1995). https://the-avocado.org/2021/11/08/lgbt-movies-total-eclipse-1995/ (accessed 14 June 2022). In the beginning of his career, Leonardo DiCaprio claimed, 'The role of Rimbaud is one of the most important roles in my career. As well one of the best to be played by a young actor [. . .] when working on the film I learned not to mind what others thought of me. That was not simple, but that experience changed me' (quoted in Zamysłowska and Kuźmicki 2013, 154). However, since being elevated to the position of a global star due to his success in *Romeo + Juliet* (Baz Luhrmann, 1996) and *Titanic* (James Cameron, 1997), he has mostly omitted it when talking about his career.
46. Shelley Cobb corroborates Tasker's point: 'The elusive track record for women directors can be derailed at any point, whether it is that crucial second film or after long breaks between features or after critical or box-office failures' (Cobb 2015, 51).
47. It is noteworthy that in both of her Hollywood biopics Holland looks at the esteemed European artists through the lens of popular culture.
48. Robynn J. Stilwell argues that the conducting scene is a substitute for sexual intercourse between Beethoven and Anna (Stilwell 2007, 202).
49. Stilwell also claims that the music used in the film is gender coded: 'A simple schema operates in which the symphony, especially the Ninth Symphony, represents the public face of Beethoven, the late quartets signify his decline and interiority, and the solo piano works stand in for the domestic and feminine' (Stilwell 2007, 199).

50. Polish film critic, Andrzej Kołodyński, called Anna a 'feminist transported in the past era' (Andrzej Kołodyński, 'Kopia mistrza', review, Kino, no. 12, 2006, 59). Mirosław Winiarczyk suggested that Holland wanted to employ a feminist angle, while also paying homage to Beethoven and his genius which did not work well together (Mirosław Winiarczyk, 'Ania i Beethoven', Czas, no. 49, 2006, liv). Likewise, the reviewer of the *Seattle Times* was sceptical about the feminist filter: 'To introduce the notion of feminism in a movie set in 19th century Vienna (Budapest makes a convincing stand-in) seems kind of silly, especially when it's so obviously filtered through a 21st century sensibility' (Moira Macdonald, '*Copying Beethoven:* Masterful performance, electrifying music', *The Seattle Times*, 10 November 2006. https://archive.seattletimes.com/archive/?slug=copying10&date=20061110 (accessed 6 August 2022).
51. This dis-attachment from the patriarchal culture echoes the final scene of *Washington Square*.
52. See also Agnieszka Holland, 'Muzyka Beethovena teraz jest we mnie', interview by Piotr Śmiałowski, Kino, no. 12, 2006, 20–4.
53. Their correspondence is available in Wajda's Archive in Kraków, at Manggha, the centre of Japanese art and culture founded by Wajda.
54. Holland, 'Muzyka Beethovena teraz jest we mnie'.
55. Agnieszka Holland, 'Między Jane Austen a Czechowem', interview by Monika Madurowicz and Krzysztof Lipka-Chudzik, Cinema, no. 11, 1997.
56. During her meeting with the audience after the special screening of *Total Eclipse* in Kraków, Holland stated that it would be feasible to make a film in Hollywood with an exclusively Polish crew, and 'it would be an excellent crew' (quoted in Jerzy Armata, 'Poezja Rimbauda też wielu bulwersowała – przypomina Agnieszka Holland', Gazeta w Krakowie, no. 87, 1996, 4).
57. Paula Kane also commented on the aesthetic hybridity of the film: 'The film is a combination of romance, detective story, legal drama, melodrama, and western showdown between Father Harris and the pompous German Archbishop Werner of the Vatican tribunal. There is also an element of urban sociological comment as well' (Kane 2001, 90).
58. Tadeusz Sobolewski, 'Drobne kroki', Gazeta Wyborcza, no. 134, 2000, 14.
59. In her review of *Olivier, Olivier*, Kathleen Murphy calls the film 'deeply religious' (Kathleen Murphy, 'The Double Life of Olivier', Film Comment, 28, no. 6 (November–December), 1992, 66).
60. In her article discussing *The Third Miracle*, along with other two films dealing with religious theme, Paula Kane misidentifies Holland as a 'Polish Catholic' (Kane 2001, 81).
61. For discussion of post-secular turn in Eastern European cinema, see Berezhnaya and Schmitt 2013.
62. Kane interprets *The Third Miracle* as an expression of 'a kind of postmodern nostalgia for the fifties as the last real Catholic decade and an aesthetic identification with the European Catholic Renaissance' (Kane 2001, 89).
63. Quoted in: Joanna Pogorzelska, 'Podróż na Wschód', Film, no. 12, 2001, 91.
64. Andrzej Bukowiecki, a Polish reviewer, accused the film of presenting an anachronistic portrayal of contemporary Poland that reinforced the stereotype of Eastern Europe as backward and primitive (Andrzej Bukowiecki, 'Wypadek przy pracy?' Życie Warszawy, 4 September 2003, 4).
65. In her *Reel Women: An International Directory of Contemporary Feature Films about Women*, Jane Sloan included the film under the title *The Healer* in the section on Canadian cinema (2007, 26).
66. When asked by a journalist at the occasion of the Polish premiere of *Julie Walking Home* whether the film marked her return to Poland, she answered that it was unlikely she would

'return home' soon because of the difficulties of financing her film projects in Poland ((RS) [author], 'Lustro tajemnicy losu', *Dziennik Polski*, 3 September 2003, 3).
67. Roger Ebert expressed a moderately positive opinion of *Washington Square* (Roger Ebert, *Washington Square* – https://www.rogerebert.com/reviews/washington-square-1997, 10 October 1997 (accessed 8 August 2022)), whereas Stephen Hunter called *Copying Beethoven* 'hugely enjoyable' (Stephen Hunter, 'Oh, the Joy of 'Beethoven', *Washington Post*, 17 November 2006, https://www.washingtonpost.com/wp-dyn/content/article/2006/11/16/AR2006111601636.html (accessed 6 August 2022). Some critics located the film within the larger body of Holland's work; for example, Morris Wesley called Holland an 'estimable' director who is 'no stranger to informal period dramas, having tackled the Holocaust in "Europa Europa," Rimbaud and Verlaine in "Total Eclipse," and Henry James in "Washington Square." She's also familiar with the ways of Ed Harris, having guided him to one of his best performances as a priest suffering a spiritual breakdown in "The Third Miracle." And most of her work contains a related philosophical strain' (Morris Wesley, 'Harris Gives "Beethoven" Its Beat', *The Boston Globe*, 10 November 2006 http://archive.boston.com/ae/movies/articles/2006/11/10/harris_gives_beethoven_its_beat/ (accessed 23 March 2023). There were also utterly negative reviews; for example, Dennis Schwartz called *Copying Beethoven* an 'earnest but lackluster period biopic' (Dennis Schwartz, 'Copying Beethoven: COPYING BEETHOVEN', *Dennis Schwartz Movie Reviews*, 5 August 2019, https://dennisschwartzreviews.com/copyingbeethoven/ (accessed 6 August 2022)). In his review of *Copying Beethoven*, Emanuel Levy lamented: 'What has happened to the gifted director Agnieszka Holland, the Holland we admired based on films like *Europa, Europa, Olivier, Olivier,* and *The Secret Garden*. She can't seem to find proper subjects to which to apply her considerable skills and thus moves from one disappointing project to another. The latest, *Copying Beethoven*, is arguably one of Holland's worst films, worse than *Total Eclipse*, the literary portrait of the French poets, which was both an artistic and commercial flop. A shallow, clichéd portrait of Ludwig van Beethoven as an old, deaf man, the new movie comes across as bargain-basement *Amadeus* (about Mozart and Salieri) and not only because the two films were Euro-centric, shot in Budapest and Prague, respectively, by European directors (Holland is Polish, Milos Forman, who staged *Amadeus*, is Czech)' (Emanuel Levy, '*Copying Beethoven*: Agnieszka Holland's Portrait of Composer Beethoven', https://emanuellevy.com/review/copying-beethoven-6/ 2 September 2006 (accessed 6 August 2022)).
68. Lane refers to Robert E. Kapsis' book on Hitchcock (Kapsis 1992; see also Hicks and Petrova 2006).
69. For example, in his review of *Washington Square*, Piotr Wojciechowski wrote that the film testified to Holland's ability to make a masterpiece, however 'It's a pity that we still need to wait for this masterpiece – beautiful and masterfully made *Washington Square* is not the one' (Piotr Wojciechowski, 'Przełamując chłód klasyki', *Film*, no. 11, 1997, 18). Zygmunt Kałużyński was more ironic: 'Holland is attempting to make a career abroad, yet for a genuine cinephile it is difficult to support her efforts' (Zygmunt Kałużyński, '*Plac Waszyngtona*', *Polityka*, 1 November 1997, 10).
70. This is one of the most famous arthouse movie theatres located in the Warsaw old town.
71. Quoted in: anon. 'Zuchwała i prowokująca', *Dziennik Polski*, no. 75, 1996, 2.
72. 'Zuchwała i prowokująca'.
73. Alina Kietrys, 'Europejska premiera', *Głos Wybrzeża*, 21 October 1997, 4.
74. Anna Płażewska, 'W Kanadzie, Rosji i w Polsce', *Gazeta Łódzka*, 29 October 1997, 6.
75. Mirosław Winiarczyk, 'Ania i Beethoven', *Czas* 2006, no. 49, liv.
76. Małgorzata Karbowiak, 'Europejska premiera *Ogrodu*', *Głos Poranny*, no. 22, 1994, 2.
77. See 'Zuchwała i prowokująca'.

78. Artur Szklarczyk, 'W kolejce czeka Polska', *Gazeta Krakowska*, 31 October 1997, 2.
79. Paweł T. Felis, '*Julia wraca do domu*', *Cogito*, no. 15, 2003, 61.
80. Felis, '*Julia wraca do domu*'.
81. Agnieszka Holland, 'Dlaczego ten film Pani Agnieszko?' interview by Elżbieta Podolska, *Express Poznański*, no. 64, 1996, 4.
82. Agnieszka Holland, 'Nie mieszczę się w tym świecie', interview by Barbara Hollender, *Rzeczpospolita*, 29 October 1997, 4.
83. Holland, 'Nie mieszczę się w tym świecie'.
84. It is noteworthy that both directors stopped their Hollywood film career in the first decade of the twenty-first century, however for Campion it was a substantial pause (after *Bright Star*, 2009, she also directed the TV series *Top of the Lake*, 2013–17), whereas Holland remained active in directing for television streaming platforms and feature film projects made in Europe. In 2021, Campion returned triumphantly with *The Power of the Dog* that won the Oscar for best director and solidified her position as one of the world's best directors.
85. Anon. '*Tajemniczy ogród* A. Holland', *Gazeta Krakowska*, no. 286, 1993, 3.
86. (ber) [author], 'Holland lepsza od Spielberga', *Kurier Polski*, no. 184, 1993, 2.
87. Bożena Sycówna, 'Ogród wewnętrzny', *Kino*, no. 1, 1994, 10–12; Agnieszka Baranowska, 'Sekretne przejścia', *Kobieta i Życie*, no. 1, 1994, 18. The authors of the Polish monographs of Agnieszka Holland also employed this perspective (see Jankun-Dopartowa 2000; Bobowski 2001; Mąka-Malatyńska 2009).
88. Anon. 'Zachód oburzony', *Gazeta Krakowska*, no. 258, 1995, 2.
89. Hanna Pasek, 'Miłość straceńców', *Echo Krakowa*, no. 63, 1996, 4; Zdzisław Beryt, 'Europejskie zaćmienie', *Gazeta Poznańska*, no. 74, 1996, 6.
90. ADL, 'Ciemny pokój', *Kurier Szczeciński*, no. 65, 1996, 3.
91. Holland denied this classification saying that if a movie was made in the States for American money then it cannot be considered 'Polish' (Agnieszka Holland, 'Między Jane Austen a Czechowem', interview by Monika Madurowicz and Krzysztof Lipka-Chudzik, *Cinema*, no. 11, 1997).
92. Małgorzata Dipont, 'Niekochana', *Trybuna*, 7 November 1997, 4.
93. Jerzy Wójcik, 'Kontakt z Najwyższym', *Rzeczpospolita*, no. 134, 2000, A10; Tomasz Jopkiewicz, 'Dotkliwy głód wiary', *Życie*, 11 July 2000, 4; Barbara Kosecka, 'Wielebny detektyw', *Film*, no. 6, 2000, 75.
94. Michał Lenarciński, 'Miało być jak u Kieślowskiego', *Dziennik Łódzki*, 8 September 2003, 2; see also: Andrzej Bukowiecki, 'Wypadek przy pracy?' *Życie Warszawy*, 4 September 2003, 4.
95. Wojciech Orliński, 'Gwizdami i oklaskami', *Gazeta Wyborcza*, no. 208, 2002, 2.
96. Tomasz Jopkiewicz, 'Pokusa azylu', *Kino*, no. 9, 2003, 59.
97. Barbara Hollender, 'Agnieszka wraca do domu', *Rzeczpospolita*, no. 236, 2001, A12.

CHAPTER 5

From cinematic *metteur en scène* to television *auteur*?

In one of her interviews, Holland commented on her collaboration with television:

> Occasionally I deliver guest lectures in various film schools [. . .]. In both the States and Europe, the young people who see their future in film directing are often more impressed with the fact that I made several episodes of *The Wire* than with my several Oscar nominations. For the students, this is a cult series, while Oscars are the symbol of the old and archaic world. (Pasternak 2022, 362)

On another occasion, she admitted that working for television was instrumental for her professional development: 'The great American television series *The Wire*, *Treme* and *The Killing*, in which I participated, were for me a school in fictional storytelling. They enhanced my craft and gave me more confidence' (Bittencourt and Holland 2014, 46). Contemporary TV series – which offer the psychological complexity and narrative innovativeness customarily associated with cinema and literature – have, in the new millennium, been attracting many esteemed filmmakers such as David Fincher (*House of Cards*), Steven Soderbergh (*House of Cards*) and Todd Haynes (tv mini-series *Mildred Pierce*, 2011).[1] Holland, as discussed in Chapter Two, began her collaboration with television much earlier, under state socialism in Poland. She may have used this experience while working for the global television stations and streaming platforms like HBO and Netflix in that she was familiar with the small screen format and participating in collaborative projects. As her authorial debut, *An Evening at Abdon*, demonstrated, television provided her with space for formal experimentation in terms of both narrative structure and visual qualities. In her subsequent Polish works made for both television and cinema, she consistently employed the mode of realism combined with the conventions of art cinema, a merger which was typical of the most acclaimed products of 'quality television' like *The Sopranos*, *The Wire*, *Six Feet Under*, and many more (see Feuer 2007, 157).[2] Furthermore, Holland's American television works can also be linked with the Cinema of Moral Concern; as explained in Chapter Two, the main aim of this movement was to represent the aspects of corrupted Polish socialist reality that were absent from the propagandistic cultural production. A similar representational gap characterised Hollywood cinema of the 1990s which was dominated by action blockbusters and romantic comedies (see Chapter Four). In contrast to the New Hollywood cinema represented by such filmmakers as Martin Scorsese, Francis Ford Coppola and Arthur Penn, the cinema of the last decade of the twentieth century turned away from American socio-political realities. Once *Star Wars* and *Indiana Jones* took control over the big screens, the small screens of television opened up for explorations of the everyday experience of a diversified and divided American society.

In this chapter, I examine Holland's television work as an integral part of her oeuvre that reveals her authorship, albeit often in a dormant form. First, I discuss *Red Wind* (1995), an episode of the TV series *Fallen Angels* (1993–6, Showtime), and two feature films made for American television stations: *Shot in the Heart* (HBO, 2001), and *A Girl Like Me: The Gwen Araujo Story* (Lifetime Movie Network, 2006). These three television projects examine urgent socio-political issues pertinent to then contemporary American society and as such they contrast with Holland's feature films that she made during this period that were either costume or metaphysical dramas (see Chapter Four). Then I examine Holland's selected works made for the global streaming platforms (episodes of *Cold Case*, *The Wire* and *Treme*), demonstrating how these developed her storytelling skills, while also continuing certain themes of her earlier work. Finally, the chapter presents Holland's collaboration with Polish post-communist private television and Eastern European divisions of the global streaming platforms. These projects can be seen as her eventual 'return home', however, they belong as much to national/regional as to transnational cultural production in terms of financing, the participation of international creative personnel, and intertextual embedding within global genres.

SMALL SCREEN, BIG THEMES

'That was my best experience of working with producers in America' commented Holland on her work on *Red Wind* (1995) (Zamysłowska and Kuźmicki 2013, 160), an episode in the neo-noir anthology television series entitled *Fallen Angels* (1993–5). The series was produced by Propaganda Films for the Showtime cable television network with Sydney Pollack as its executive producer. The first season was aired in 1993, and the second in 1995. Among the directors of the first season were Steven Soderbergh, Tom Hanks, Tom Cruise and Alfonso Cuarón. Holland joined the directorial crew of the second season, along with Kiefer Sutherland, Peter Bogdanovich and others. She chose a short story by Raymond Chandler, *Red Wind*, featuring the iconic protagonist, Philip Marlow. The cultural tradition of film noir, with its staple characters of hardboiled detective and *femme fatale* as well as highly stylised iconography, can be approached as an American variant of heritage cinema that Holland had been working within at that time. Not unlike in her cinematic projects, in *Red Wind* she also contravened one of the most solid ideological pillars of hardboiled fiction:

> I did a thing which an American director would not do. I made Chandler's main character Philip Marlow, a private detective previously played by famous American actors like Mitchum and Bogart, black. It was very interesting. It also explains many things which are in the novel and which are today not very understandable. Marlow is always beaten up by the police, is always in love with this rich white client but he cannot fuck her; all these are more understandable if he is black. (Crnković and Holland 1998–9, 4)

Holland's brave decision to cast the Afro-American actor Danny Glover as Marlow,[3] whose character is the epitome of troubled white Anglo-Saxon masculinity, can be seen as a colour-blind casting and as such open to critique on the ground that the film erased the racial conflict that existed in the States of the 1940s when the action of the film takes place. Contrary to Todd Haynes's *Far From Heaven* – made in 2002 – in which the mixed-race heterosexual romance between a Caucasian woman and an Afro-American man was the main dramatic conflict, *Red Wind* acknowledges only the racism of the policemen towards black Marlow, while presenting his romantic involvement with a white woman as controversial not because of its potential miscegenation threat but on the grounds of her being married (see Fig. 5.1). Unintentionally, Holland – who admitted that at that time she was not fully aware of the cultural taboos around sexual relationships between Caucasians and Afro-Americans (Holland and Kornatowska 2012, 321) – participated in the post-racial discourse that is frequently criticised for its 'inability to represent characters' lives amid social realities, structural imbalances, and injustices' (Aymar 2018, 112). In *Red Wind*, visual stylisation, especially theatrical mise-en-scène and highly saturated colours, isolates its fictional reality from the social and cultural tensions and the conflicts inherent to the depicted era.

However, Holland's casting decision relates also to the revisionist approach to the tradition of film noir emerging in neo-noir film production in the 1990s.

Figure 5.1 *Red Wind* (1995)

Red Wind re-reads Chandler's original foregrounding of the latent ethnic/ racial diversification of the characters. Black Marlow evokes the genre's hidden 'sense of the intimate proximity of racial Others to American national identity' (Lott 1997, 562). While *The Secret Garden* coalesced whiteness with Britishness, as denounced by Máire Messenger Davis (2001), *Red Wind* implied the 'Blackness' of American identity or rather racial conflict as its core. Danny Glover's Marlow was not the only black detective in American cinema of the 1990s. In her article 'Black Faces, White Spaces' examining the presence of black actors in film noirs, Angelica Jade Bastién discussed two neo-noirs, *Deep Cover* (1992) and *Devil in a Blue Dress* (1995), featuring black protagonists and directed by black directors, respectively Bill Duke and Carl Franklin. *Devil* provides an especially interesting point of comparison for *Red Wind* as its action takes place in 1948 in Los Angeles, which approximates to the time and place of the action of the episode directed by Holland. Bastién emphasised – as did the Polish director in the statement quoted earlier – the importance of casting a black actor in the role of the staple detective character: 'It's a classic *noir* world, but instead of Robert Mitchum or Humphrey Bogart we find Denzel Washington – a star with more than enough charisma, skill and internal complications to authentically inhabit the role of *noir*'s most enduring archetype: the detective' (Bastién 2016, 44).

In *Red Wind*, besides Marlowe, the secondary character of a bartender is also played by an Afro-American actor, Tyrin Turner. Importantly, in the first scene, they both are passive witnesses to the murder involving Caucasian men being both perpetrator and victim, which connects violence with white masculinity. The most violent character in the film is detective Copernic (Dan Hedaya), who is blatantly racist towards his partner, Ybarra (Miguel Sandoval), who is of Spanish origin, and Marlowe. Towards the end of the opening scene, Copernic uses a racial slur to his partner, saying he is in a company of 'spic and nigs', the line being added to Chandler's original. The short story presented ethnic diversification in neutral terms, while its adaptation transposes it onto the brutal discrimination that is associated with while masculinity and by the same token with hegemonic American society.

According to Bastién, the character of the black detective reveals these discriminatory social structures, yet without making any significant intervention into them:

> Black detectives [. . .] feel like they are traversing the line between two Americas – the one white people experience, and a second that only people of colour know. They're asked to move between both worlds, an experience that isolates them from everyone. (Bastién 2016, 45)

Danny Glover's Marlow corroborates Bastién's conclusion. His involvement in 'white people's business' is only temporary, and eventually he needs to suppress his desire for a white woman. His emotional withdrawal and denial of his affection expedite a reconciliation between the white middle-class heterosexual couple which is presented in the iconic shot of their affectionate embrace. Yet Holland follows this clichéd Hollywood image with a coda that shows Marlowe going towards darkness while pondering in his voiceover narration whether to pay a visit to Eugenia Kolchenko (played by Italian actor Valeria Golino), who he thinks is as lonely as him. In the last line of dialogue, he asks: 'What name is it, Kolchenko, Russian, or maybe Polish?', which may well be Holland's self-reflexive joke to be spotted only by those viewers who are aware of the director's Polish origins. Likewise, only Polish viewers would catch its latent sarcasm concerning the customary 'throwing' of Poles and Russians into the same 'Slavic pot' to which the former respond with an almost irrational irritation. Finally, this closing line can be seen as Holland's peculiar authorial signature stamped on the standard product of American television. It may also be a self-referential gesture indicating her alienation within Hollywood cinema not dissimilar to the one experienced by Marlow and Kolchenko within the symbolic structure of film noir.[4]

Unlike the highly stylised world of *Red Wind*, Holland's two next television productions examined vital social issues in a more direct fashion: *Shot in the Heart* (2001, HBO) pertains to the heated debate around the death penalty and domestic violence, while *A Girl Like Me: The Gwen Araujo Story* (2006, Lifetime) explores the subject of transgender people and ethnic minorities. Both films were based on real stories and as such they can be linked with Holland's explorations of the biopic genre. When she first read the script for *Shot in the Heart*, written by Frank Pugliese (who also wrote a couple of scripts for the TV series *Fallen Angels* to which Holland contributed with *Red Wind*) and based on the book by Mikal Gilmore (1994), she did not know it was based on a true story. The autobiographical novel portrayed the author's dysfunctional family terrorised by the criminal father whose violence passed on his older brother, Gary, who killed two innocent men. For the crime, he was sentenced to capital punishment, which was not carried out due to its suspension by the Supreme Court in 1967 as too cruel and thus unconstitutional. In 1977, the death penalty was reinstated, and Gary Gilmore demanded it be carried out, which had been widely publicised. According to the American law, Mikal, as Gary's brother, had the right to stop the execution. However, he accepted his brother's decision as his only option to exercise his free will and escape the vicious circle of violence.

Shot in the Heart records Mikal's (Giovanni Ribisi) meetings with Gary (Elias Koteas) in prison, during which he gradually comes to terms with the family history that he has been repressing for a long time. Accordingly, the film's narrative mixes scenes of the present and the past: the in-prison conversations are punctured with flashbacks recovering various memories, such as the father (Sam Shepard) violently destroying the Thanksgiving dinner, or their Mormon mother's (Amy Madigan) oneiric visions of a white horse that she saw as the nemesis of her family. In these images of the past, the camera's long shots mark the remoteness of the family situations or ambiguous visions, while close-ups are used for the brief moments of emotional shock experienced by little Mikal witnessing the violence and cruelty of his father. The present scenes of his meetings and conversations with his older brother initially employ long and medium long shots to convey the distance between the siblings who practically have not known each other due the age gap and their subsequent escapes from the family. Gradually, the camera distance shrinks to mostly close-ups that are edited at a slow pace into prolonged shot-reverse-shot sequences to transmit the emerging intimacy and mutual understanding. At some point there is a two-shot of the brothers while one of them is shown through his mirror reflection in a glass pane and thus they are both seen within one shot as they talk to each other.[5] This visual effect and others used in *Shot in the Heart* are results of Holland's collaboration with the director of cinematography, Jacek Petrycki, who worked on many of her Polish films such

FROM CINEMATIC *METTEUR EN SCÈNE* TO TELEVISION *AUTEUR?* 163

Figure 5.2 *Shot in the Heart* (2001)

as *Something for Something*, *Provincial Actors* and *Fever* (see Chapter Two). His lighting design used for portraying the grim reality of socialist Poland in the 1970s, with its preference for subtle underlighting and unsaturated colours that made the small apartments of socialist housing projects look even tinier and more depressing than they were, proved instrumental for depicting the claustrophobic space of the American prison that was gradually, and somehow unexpectedly, transforming into a space of intimacy between the two initially estranged brothers (see Fig. 5.2).

Produced by HBO, *Shot in the Heart* was praised by many critics for its sensitivity in telling the personal story relevant to the important political issue of capital punishment. For example, Tim Goodman started his review in *San Francisco Chronicle* with this preamble:

> Only the brother of a killer about to be executed could take the death penalty as a topic and have it be a movie not so much about the death penalty as about life. Only a writer as talented as Mikal Gilmore could tell a story that punches you in the gut about every five seconds and yet leaves you hoping for more. And only HBO could make 'Shot in the Heart' one of the least sensationalistic, least obvious, least formulaic movies about a hot-button issue.[6]

Later in his review, Goodman praised the producers of the film: 'Executive producers Barry Levinson and Tom Fontana[7] have crafted what amounts to a subtle, sad punch in the nose. No wasted movement. No need to spice up the story'.[8] Implicitly, the critic ascribed authorial agency to the producing company, HBO, and the executive producers of the film, while not even mentioning its director.[9] By contrast, Polish film critics all addressed Holland as author of the film. Although made for the small screen format, in Poland, *Shot in the Heart* was screened at the Warsaw Film Festival in 2001 as its opening event. On this occasion, the respected daily *Gazeta Wyborcza* published a set of relevant materials: the review by a renowned Polish critic Tadeusz Sobolewski,[10] excerpts from Mikal Gilmore's book, an interview with him[11] and an interview with Holland.[12] In his review, Sobolewski contextualised *Shot in the Heart* within Holland's earlier work that, as he claimed, explored the evil aspect of human nature, while also acknowledging the contribution of the cinematographer Jacek Petrycki. Furthermore, the critic compared the film to Krzysztof Kieślowski's *A Short Film about Killing* (*Krótki film o zabijaniu*, 1988) and *Dead Man Walking* (Tim Robbins, 1995), while also suggesting an affinity between cinematic Gilmore siblings and the Karamazov brothers which is a symbolic gesture recognising the film's cultural significance.[13] Finally, a public debate on the film held at the Faculty of Law at the University of Warsaw with participation of three scholars, a politician, and Holland herself added to the film's reputation.[14]

The special screening of *Shot in the Heart* at the Warsaw Film Festival in a regular movie theatre is worth mentioning, not only because it reveals how specific distribution strategies contribute to aesthetic classifications and hierarchies, but also because it exemplifies the ambiguation of the distinction between cinema and television and their respective genres. The Warsaw screening of Holland's film can be seen as an almost perfect realisation of the HBO slogan 'It's Not TV, It's HBO' and their exemplary strategy of 'distancing the channel from what television "is", moving closer to a style regularly dubbed by critics as "cinematic"' (Gray and Johnson 2021, 100). Screened in movie theatres, *Shot in the Heart*, with its aesthetic excess – criticised by some of the American critics while appreciated by their Polish colleagues – questions the difference between the cinematic and the televisual. Holland is well aware of the process:

> My approach to television is that it's not such a big difference from making movies. Sometimes you have more freedom because you don't have to worry about ticket sales. Today you can find material on television more courageous and with more edgy content than on the big screen. (Tibbetts and Holland 2008, 140)

Holland's next television work, made for the Lifetime television channel *A Girl Like Me*, about a transgender woman (see Fig. 5.3), is a stellar example of such courageous content. Like *Shot in the Heart* it is based on a true story

FROM CINEMATIC *METTEUR EN SCÈNE* TO TELEVISION *AUTEUR*? 165

Figure 5.3 *A Girl Like Me: The Gwen Araujo Story* (2006)

that is also presented in a non-chronological order. It centres on the trial of the four men who murdered the transgender woman Gwen Amber Rose Araujo in 2002 in Newark, California. Prior to the murder, they were partying with her for several days and allegedly making sexual advances towards her. The young men committed the murder after forcibly exposing her genitals and discovering she was a trans person. After torturing her to death over several hours, they wrapped the body in a blanket and disposed of it in a shallow grave in a field. The body was discovered after three weeks because of the help of one of the perpetrators (he later accepted a lesser charge from the Almeda County district attorney). The defence lawyers attempted to justify the criminal deed on the grounds of 'trans-panic', however it was deemed second degree murder. The trials were extensively covered by the media and later used in social campaigns against transphobia. As Francisco J. Galarte reported:

> Araujo's murder sparked activism for transgender rights in the San Francisco Bay Area. The activism took various forms, including attendance at Araujo's memorial service, documentation of the murder retrial through the court-watch blog *Justice for Gwen Araujo*, and the beginnings of what would become the San Francisco Trans March, an annual event that takes

place on the Friday night of San Francisco Pride Week [. . .] Araujo's death [was] a pivotal moment in trans Latina/o/x history and politics. (Galarte 2021, 24-7)

A Girl Like Me was aired at 8.00 p.m. on 19 June 2006, on Lifetime television. Its executive co-producer was the famed attorney Gloria Allred – who represented the Guerrero family at the trial and brought the movie to Lifetime (Davis 2006).[15] It attracted a large audience of five million people. As Galarte noted, 'The premiere was scheduled during Pride Month and aired continually over the next few months as California state lawmakers prepared to vote on the Gwen Araujo Justice for Victims Act' (Galarte 2021, 28). The film proved instrumental in the galvanising of activism for the rights of transgender people (Franklin and Lyons 2016). The film was also significant because of the expanding media space for Chicano actors. Galarte recognised the importance of casting an Oscar winner, Mercedes Ruehl, as Gwen's mother, a well-known Hollywood actor, Lupe Ontiveros, as her grandmother, and less popular Chicano actors in secondary roles as family member who played an important role in the whole story (Galarte 2021, 28). They were typical members of the traditional Latino family practising strictly defined gender roles who gradually accepted Gwen's transition. However, according to Galarte, the film perpetuated negative stereotypes of Latino families as patriarchal, dysfunctional structures that served as an oppressive ideological framework within which transgender identity was presented as deviancy that could either be accepted or rejected.

> In the film, transsexuality and Chicano culture become limitations to overcome, and the lack that is associated with the two is only resolvable through Araujo's death [. . .] The film effectively allows most spectators to maintain a distance from the violence Araujo and other trans women of color endure and to ignore how these women are marginalized socially, culturally, and politically. Representing Araujo and her mother as culpable for her death reassures a white cisgender American spectator of the truth of the tropes about Chicano/Latino culture they have been exposed to in film and television. (Galarte 2021, 44)

While Galarte's criticism concerning the film's ethnic bias is valid, the statement concerning Araujo and her mother's guilt is one-sided as their behaviour and decisions were conditioned by the socio-cultural norms they were subjected to.

Furthermore, the film's politics of representation need to be related to the profile of the television station which produced it. In 1993, Lifetime was announced as a 'Television for Women', and accordingly it aired material pertinent to women's issues such as, for example, breast cancer awareness, but also entertaining programmes such as talk-shows and television series. For the creators and producers of *A Girl Like Me*, rising political awareness was a priority which explains the decision to make the extended family the pivotal point in its narrative as it was potentially the emotive structure within which a wide range of viewers representing various genders, social classes and ethnicities could find something to identify with. In 2006, *A Girl Like Me* was awarded the GLAAD (Gay & Lesbian Alliance Against Defamation) award for outstanding television film, which testifies to its socio-political impact. As the GLAAD awards website reads:

> The GLAAD Media Awards honor media for fair, accurate, and inclusive representations of LGBTQ people and issues. Since its inception in 1990, the GLAAD Media Awards have grown to be the most visible annual LGBTQ awards show in the world, sending powerful messages of acceptance to audiences globally.[16]

Directing *A Girl Like Me* exposed Holland to the activist potential of audiovisual media that she then capitalised on in the future (see Chapter Seven).

Although the topic of transgender identities may seem very distant from Holland's earlier works, it is worth noting that these also featured non-hegemonic sexualities, albeit always locating these on the margins of fictional realities. In *Provincial Actors*, the gay character evokes the ambiguity between homoerotic desire and homosocial bonds.[17] *To Kill a Priest* features a gay secret service officer whose sexual orientation is not narratively significant yet is made visible. *Europa, Europa* examines totalitarian oppressiveness towards racial minorities and gay people. Finally, *Total Eclipse* foregrounds a gay relationship while presenting it as being at odds with the then dominant gay discourse. While indicating Holland's attempts to include in her films non-normative sexual identities and behaviours, it is worth mentioning that in her two Polish films, *Screen Tests* and *Provincial Actors*, there are episodes of female masturbation – a manifest recognition of (frustrated) female sexual desire – the representation of which in cinema was taboo for a long time in contrast to male masturbation, frequently presented on screen in more or less explicit fashion. *A Girl Like Me*, directed for the American family television channel, provided Holland with an opportunity for a more radical exploration of the issues of gender and sexual identities to which she has always been sensitive.

To conclude, Holland's television productions, *Red Wind*, *A Shot in the Heart* and *A Girl Like Me*, examined sensitive social issues pertinent to American society, concerning racial diversification, the death penalty and transgender identities. Despite all the differences between her Polish and American television works, they are similar in that they explored vital social and political issues. Although made in different geopolitical locations, ideological systems and television production cultures, Holland's television projects investigated marginal areas of social realities often overlooked in mainstream cinema.

FROM 'MORAL CONCERN' TO 'MORAL MIDGETRY' – OR VICE VERSA?

Holland often proudly talked about her contribution to *The Wire*: 'I made three episodes of this cult serial which you watch as if you're reading a classic twentieth-century American novel. There's a huge social spectrum – police and criminal dealers, unions, the school and politics. The Polish community is also shown' (Zamysłowska and Kuźmicki 2013, 188). While working for 'quality television', Holland revisited, albeit in a radically different format, the model of socially and politically engaged cinema that she practised in her films belonging to the Cinema of Moral Concern (see Chapter Two). Unexpectedly, she was also able to mark her authorial agency in these collective television projects, albeit in a tacit and non-conspicuous fashion.

Holland directed her first episode for *The Wire* in 2004 (S3 E8),[18] when she also started contributing to the TV series *Cold Case* (2004–9, CBS). As she explained, the latter provided her with opportunities to develop her narrative skills and visual strategies (Holland 2008, 156). As its title indicates, the series is centred around 'cold cases' (a separate one for each episode) that are reinvestigated by the detective teams in which the female character of Lilly Rush (Kathryn Morris) plays the most prominent role. Accordingly, a significant part of the narrative is presented in flashbacks that need to be visually differentiated from the present action. The first episode Holland directed for *Cold Case*, 'Hubris' (S1 E11), tells a story of a once respected academic teacher whose career was ruined when he was suspected of the murder of a student with whom he had had an affair. The episode employs two distinct visual designs for the past and the present parts of the narrative: the former uses warm and well-saturated colours and soft lighting, and the latter, cold hues of blue and grey as well as low-key lighting that obscures certain elements of reality, keeping them beyond visual exploration. In effect, the past looks transparent and appealing, while the present is hostile and impenetrable. The flashbacks often begin with chaotic camera movements, as if replicating the disorientation of entering the past, which is gradually replaced with more stabilised set ups to convey increasing control over it.

Prior to directing the episodes for *Cold Case*, Holland did not have much experience with non-chronological narratives; there was only a brief flashback used towards the ending of *Olivier, Olivier* to explain the circumstances of the murder of the eponymous character, while *Shot in the Heart* used the flashback structure to resurface the family traumatic past. Working on 'Hubris' and other episodes of *Cold Case* provided Holland with a training ground for excelling in visual codes used for marking various temporalities and relevant affective structures. These experiences were useful in working on *A Girl Like Me*: the scenes of the trial are greyish and not well illuminated, whereas the scenes from the past, especially those in which Gwen was joyfully experiencing her female identity, used vibrant colours and high-key lighting. The past scenes of Gwen's mother struggling with her child's transgender identity and her family's hostile response to it are also low-key lighted and darkish in mise-en-scène. Throughout her work for American television stations and global streaming platforms, Holland was refining her cinematic abilities and gradually solidified her position as a highly skilled professional filmmaker-for-hire.

Other episodes Holland directed for *Cold Case*, 'The Plan' (S1 E22), 'Justice' (S5 E10) and 'Lotto Fever' (S6 E12), are aesthetically consistent with 'Hubris' in that they also employed a different lighting design and colour palette for the present and the past parts of the narrative, yet the most significant formal devices are editing and cinematography, which are used to blur the difference between these two different temporalities. Often, in the scenes of conversations or interrogations, like, for example, in 'Justice', the shot-reverse-shot sequences present a character simultaneously in the past and in the present (two different actors play the same role); sometimes such a change occurs within one shot by means of panning movement. The editing transitions between the past and the present rarely use straight cuts; instead, fade in and outs or special effects are employed to obscure the distinction between these two temporalities. These formal devices are especially suitable for the first three episodes directed by Holland, 'Hubris', 'The Plan' and 'Justice', as they concern traumatic experiences of sexual violence and abuse. As trauma always functions in both the past and the present, the cinematic devices aimed at creating a peculiar amalgam of various temporalities added to the meanings conveyed by the narrative. These three episodes are consistent in terms of formal devices and narrative content, while the latter gains a special significance in the context of Holland's recent disclosure that she was sexually molested as a teenager (Pasternak 2022, 155–6). Furthermore, 'The Plan', which focuses on a paedophile's victims, can be related to *Olivier, Olivier*. Thus, rather unexpectedly, the thematic and stylistic consistency that is customarily associated with *auteur* cinema, resurfaced, in the case of Holland, in the television work she made as a reputed filmmaker-for-hire. This 'inconspicuous' authorship can be seen as parallel to the masquerade strategy she had developed in Poland in the 1970s when she adopted a masculine idiom as the only viable option to function in the film industry. In the episodes directed for TV series, she also hides herself behind the story arc and general formal design.

Despite its inconspicuousness, Holland's televisual authorship was recognised by critics in relation to her work for *The Wire*, which she considers her most important television experience. The acclaimed series, the action of which takes place in Baltimore, depicts a wide spectrum of crime permeating life in all social milieus of contemporary American society, presenting it from the dual perspective of the drug dealers' organisations and the police forces attempting to reveal the criminal networks. Gradually, the difference between those who break the law and those who protect it diminishes to the point of chaos. Holland's first episode directed for the series, 'Moral Midgetry' (S3 E8), denounces the moral debasement of all social relationships that are reduced to monetary gain. The lord of the drug empire, Russell 'Stringer' Bell (Idris Elba), ruthlessly sentences to death all those who are obstacles on his way to fortune, even if they are from his closest circle of friends and extended family. In the collection volume devoted to the series, there is an essay authored by Kevin McNeilly 'Dislocating America: Agnieszka Holland Directs "Moral Midgetry"' (2009).[19] The title explicitly recognises her authorial agency in the collective HBO project,[20] while the author suggests that Holland's experience of being an expatriate Pole living in the States could be related to the main themes of *The Wire*. As he notes:

> As a non-American helming a television program that is, as its creator David Simon puts it, 'rooted in the logic and ethos of a second-tier city, of a forgotten rust-belt America' [. . .], Holland is admittedly out of place, a foreigner. But this sense of unresolved displacement closely informs her directorial approach to the fraught American content of *The Wire*. (McNeilly 2009, 203)

Although the characters featured in 'Moral Midgetry' are connected in complex networks of crime or legal structures, they all are alienated from their social habitats. That also concerns 'Stringer' Bell, whom his friend and collaborator confronts in the following line: 'I look at you these days, String, you know what I see? I see a man without a country. Not hard enough for this right here and maybe, just maybe, not smart enough for them out there . . .'. Although scripted by David Simon, the character of Stringer is akin to many of Holland's protagonists, whose in-between position alienates them from mainstream society, and perhaps he is somehow similar to Holland, who, at that time, could be described as a woman without a cinematic country, as evidenced in the stylistic and narrative diversity of her works. McNeilly noted that the theme of alienation is present throughout Holland's work made for both television and cinema, while also comparing the characters from *The Wire* to the protagonists of *Olivier, Olivier*, *Europa, Europa* and *Washington Square*. Due to theme of dislocation and displacement the episodes of *The Wire* can be linked with her exilic films made in Europe.

Contextualising 'Moral Midgetry' within Holland's biography and her works is a critical strategy customarily used for *auteur* cinema; McNeilly dislocates it into the field of quality television where the authorial agency is usually attributed to the persona of the series creators, such as David Simon in the case of *The Wire*:

> If her work studies situations of moral or existential compromise, Holland rarely compromises her own hard-eyed vision, and never turns her lens away from those troubling moments of selling oneself short; it is toward such moments, in fact, that Holland's interest as a filmmaker is most forcefully directed. Her approach, she says, is to 'try to capture an original, sensual, visual truth that works for each story.' Because her subject matter often intensifies the loss of various cultural, social, or moral bases upon which any claims to truth can be made by her characters, the nature of that 'visual truth' needs to be carefully understood as predominantly a kind of critical scrutiny: an objectification of the crumbling of various objective grounds of knowing. (McNeilly 2009, 205)

Most importantly, McNeilly recognises 'Holland's visual style' that he identifies with the 'incommensurability of perspectives'; as he further explains '[h]er visual practice concentrates small points of revelation, when we have our way of seeing instrumentally reoriented' (2009, 209, 211). Holland's usual avoidance of providing a stable point of spectatorial identification proved an especially well-suited strategy for *The Wire*, the narrative of which reveals a multilayered social structure that resists moral diversification due to the all-encompassing corruption and struggles for power. In his analysis of 'Moral Midgetry', which is one episode in the five-season TV series, McNeilly recognises Holland's authorial agency, which was mostly obscured in the critical reception of her films made in Hollywood (see Chapter Four).

Holland's televisual authorship was implicitly confirmed when she was offered the chance to direct a pilot episode for *Treme* – a series that was also the brainchild of David Simon – which was both a prestigious and responsible task as the television station uses the pilot to test the potential popularity of the planned series with audiences. As Holland recollected, while on the set, her daughter Kasia asked the consultant on New Orleans culture whether Spike Lee – who was also considered for directing the pilot episode – would not be a better choice as he had made a famous documentary about post-Katrina New Orleans and was very familiar with the Afro-American culture depicted in the script. The consultant responded, 'What does Spike know about suffering? Agnieszka knows much more' (Holland and Kornatowska 2012, 402). As Holland explained, she was constructing the story as if she were making a film about Poland after the end of the Second World War: 'The world here was also destroyed and the people [. . .] were betrayed by the federal government'.[21] She conceived the collective trauma inflicted by disastrous events as an affective link between the Polish and the New Orleans' experiences.

Treme can also be contextualised within Holland's Polish films due to their social engagement. Martha P. Nochimson claimed that *Treme* was built on David Simon and Eric Overmyer's pre-Katrina idea of juxtaposing a unique arts culture with a severely wanting civic structure (Nochimson 2019, 126). Similarly, the Cinema of Moral Concern was a cultural formation connected to the civic structure of Polish society desperately fighting the communist oppression from which the Solidarity movement emerged. Holland's personal and professional experiences from the 1970s matched the authorial vision of Simon and Overmyer. Analogously to her script collaboration with Andrzej Wajda which remains hidden behind his well-established *auteur* persona, in her episodes directed for *The Wire* and *Treme*, Holland performed a kind of authorial ventriloquism, expressing her own agenda through the more powerful and widely recognised authorial voices of Simon and Overmyer. Nochimson discusses the collective authorship of *Treme*: 'Simon rejects the notion that he is an auteur [. . .] saying that he depended on many of his co-workers as much as he depended on himself for creative decisions'. She later identifies Simon and Overmyer's collaboration on the teleplay for *Treme* as 'a strong and vital Creole partnership' (Nochimson 2019, 127). However, the 'Creole authorship' contains not only work of the two creators and writers but also contributions from the large personnel who are not always easily discernible as they are integrated in the general concept of the series.

The term 'Creole authorship' can be used to describe Holland's works made since leaving Poland in 1981 as she had to adjust to various models of screen cultures and collaborative networks which facilitated or suppressed authorial agency. From the perspective of the *Cahiers du Cinéma* circle, Holland is a (mere) *metteur en scène*, 'a competent, even highly competent, film-maker, but lacking the consistency which betrayed the profound involvement of personality' (Caughie 1981, 9–10); however, from a contemporary perspective, this concept appears obsolete. For personality, or identity if you wish, is not a solid and static set of components, but rather a liquid – to use Zygmunt Bauman's favourite metaphor for modernity (Bauman 2000) – constellation of dispositions and currents, with some being hidden below for a prolonged period of time. By the same token, Holland has developed a 'liquid authorship' that emerges as series of thematic and stylistic adjustments to the constantly changing screen formats and modes of production. She epitomises the experience of global (female) filmmaker-for-hire who needs to adjust and adapt to sundry circumstances in order to remain professionally active. Nevertheless, while working in these everchanging circumstances and collective projects, Holland finds a small and often hardly noticeable space for her own personal voice.

Directed by Holland, the pilot episode of *Treme* presents a vast panorama of the New Orleans inhabitants as they deal with the disaster caused by the hurricane Katrina in New Orleans in 2005. As if to reflect on the general theme of displacement and hybrid culture, the pilot episode was conceived in the teleplay as a mosaic of many characters from a variety of backgrounds who all struggle with the traumatic experience. Everyone feels displaced: in a physical sense (as many people lost their houses or apartments), emotional (many lost their relatives and friends) and existential (they suddenly acquired an awareness of the fragility of life, in both its material and spiritual aspect). In a way, everyone in post-Katrina New Orleans had to find a new place for themselves, as did Holland during her personal and professional journeys. Being of mixed Polish-Jewish origins, while living in the American melting pot, she had a strong personal disposition to create a portrayal of 'a city that fuses European and African cultures and also the newly integrated Latino culture'. She also expertly implemented 'a narrative structure that fuses the multiplicity of personal heritages and contextual influences with a rapidity that embodies the vitality of the feeling of fusion' (Nochimson 2019, 133).

The episodic narrative structure and non-continuity editing are confusing for the viewers – most likely expecting standard television storytelling – who may feel as displaced as the fictional characters themselves. Instead of a protagonist whose aims and deeds would establish a continuous storyline, the first episode of *Treme*, and all the others for that matter, offers a fragmented narrative presented as a free flow of rhythmic images.[22] Nochimson acknowledges that the first episode establishes the stylistic mode of the whole series: 'The opening of the first episode embodies the rhythms of narrative and visuals to follow. We move quickly among a collage of images, often at the expense of the kind of narrative clarity that is obligatory in formulaic entertainment' (Nochimson 2019, 133). The viewer is not provided with the important narrative information about what Second Line is or who the Indians represented by the character of Albert Lambreaux (Clarke Peters) are, the 'Big Chief', whose appearance in his spectacular costume is as shocking as it is astonishing (see Fig. 5.4). The excessive stylisation of the 'Big Chief's performance on the level of both mise-en-scène and cinematography breaks up the realistic mode established in the previous sequences. In her close analysis of the scene, Stefanie Hofer directly connects it to Holland's *auteurism*: 'The Polish filmmaker Agnieszka Holland directed the series' first episode. Because I was quite familiar with the director [. . .] I expected high aesthetic quality. Like a sponge I soaked up these aesthetics of which the mentioned scene was a stellar example' (Hofer 2017, 57–8). Although Nochimson does not mention Holland's name as the director of the first episode, she examines the cinematic devices employed in the pilot episode as establishing a specific aesthetic pattern which implies the creative (authorial) contribution of the director.[23]

Figure 5.4 *Treme*, episode 1, 'Do You Know What It Means' (2010)

In 2014, Holland was offered the chance to direct a four-hour mini-series, *Rosemary's Baby*, for NBC. The mini-series format has proved attractive for many recognised filmmakers such as Lisa Cholodenko who, in the same year, directed *Olivia Kitteridge* for HBO featuring Frances McDormand and Richard Jenkins. The cast of *Rosemary's Baby* was equally impressive: Zoe Saldaña – who was then a well-established star due to her role in James Cameron's *Avatar* (2009) – played the eponymous character of Rosemary; Jason Isaacs – who gained popularity in the *Harry Potter* franchise – played Roman Castevet; Carol Bouquet – who made an appearance in Luis Buñuel's *That Obscure Object of Desire* (1977) and was also one of the Bond girls in *For your Eyes Only* (1981) – played Margaux Castevet; and Patrick J. Adams – who was known mostly due to his roles in TV series such as *Cold Case* (2003–10), and *Pretty Little Liars* (2010–17) – played Guy Woodhouse, Rosemary's treacherous husband. In a secondary role, the Polish actor Wojciech Pszoniak, whom Holland had cast earlier in *Angry Harvest*, also appeared. There were also French actors who played secondary characters and extras. Thus, the cast was truly international, representing the tradition of art as well as popular cinema. Finally, Saldaña's Dominican-Puerto Rican origins expanded the ethnic spectrum of casting that was reflected also in the content in that the previous victim of the Castevets, Nena, was of Egyptian origins (she was played by a French actor, Victoire Bélézy). Another alteration to Ira Levin's novel and Roman Polanski's famous adaptation was locating the action in Paris instead of New York and changing Guy's profession from actor to a writer experiencing writer's block.[24] The change of the place of action displaces the couple not only socially and economically, as presented in the literary original, but also culturally and linguistically. Importantly, the Castevets and their social circle speak English, while Rosemary and Guy do not possess a sufficient command of French, which alienates them in many situations. As in Roman Polanski's *Frantic* (1988) and Paweł Pawlikowski's *The Woman in the Fifth* (2011), Holland's *Rosemary's Baby* reverses the joyful stereotype of 'the American in Paris' as created by Vincente Minelli in his famous musical (*American in Paris*, 1951).

The most significant change to the literary original and Polanski's adaptation concerns the eponymous character of Rosemary, specifically her recent miscarriage from which she hopes to heal in Paris. We also learn about her professional achievements as a ballet dancer and being the breadwinner in their marriage for a long time. She is introduced as both a vulnerable and an independent woman, which seems to resonate with the experiences of many contemporary young women. A quintessentially female traumatic experience of miscarriage makes her potentially prone to the predatory intrigue of the Castevets, yet she is also capable of resisting the exploitation of her (maternal) body. As Holland explained, her aim was to show:

> how complex and complicated motherhood is, and pregnancy, and how difficult it is for women to accept this growing thing inside her body [. . .] The notion of postnatal and prenatal depression, and the feeling that you don't own yourself anymore, that you're not yourself anymore, it's a quite important subject of 'Rosemary's Baby'. [25]

With *Rosemary's Baby* Holland revisited the subject matter of pregnancy and motherhood that she has explored throughout her career since her diploma film made at FAMU, *Jesus Christ's Sin* (1969). Unlike her Polish films on the subject which explored it in the context of socialist realities, the TV series offered a 'post-feminist meditation'[26] on it. In both socio-cultural environments, women are not in control of their bodies and are subjected to various ideologies constructed around motherhood. In the ending of the last episode of *Rosemary's Baby*, the protagonist is pushing the pram with her baby who is attracting admiring looks from passers-by (see Fig. 5.5). To one of them, she replies, 'Yes, he is perfect'. As we saw the child in the previous scene, we know he is anything but perfect, hence her delight is puzzling to say the least. Has she accepted the child despite its monstrosity, or has she internalised the perspective of the Satanist sect on becoming its member? Is it a rational and as such desirable pragmatism or a surrender to the will and perspective of others? With the ambivalent ending, *Rosemary's Baby* continues Holland's exploration of the pregnancy and motherhood theme present in her earlier works.[27]

Holland's work for American television networks and streaming platforms has continued certain strands of her earlier output, while also engaging with

Figure 5.5 *Rosemary's Baby* (2014)

new themes and genres. First and foremost, she started working within classical cinematic genres that were accommodated for the needs of TV series and as such provided space for various modifications and experiments. In *Red Wind*, she tested the conventions of film noir with the non-orthodox casting of an Afro-American actor as Philip Marlow, the epitome of troubled white masculinity; in *A Girl Like Me*, she mixed family melodrama and court drama to interrogate the social oppression of transgender people; in the episodes she directed for *The Wire*, she worked within a crime drama deprived of the customary (moral) genre's logic; in *Rosemary's Baby*, the horror genre is used to explore the issues of pregnancy and motherhood in the era of post-feminism; finally, in the episodes she directed for *The First* (2018, S1 E1, S1 E2, Hulu), the genre of science fiction emerges as a narrative promise rather than the actual organisation of the plot which focuses on preparation for the mission to Mars that never happens. While exploring classical genres, Holland's television works expanded on the themes of racial/ethnic difference (*Red Wind*, *A Girl Like Me*, *Treme*, *The Killing*), sexual exploitation (*A Girl Like Me*, *Cold Case*, *The Killing*), displacement (*A Girl Like Me*, *The Wire*, *Treme*), and the pathologies of societal life (*A Shot in the Heart*, *A Girl Like Me*, *The Wire*). In *The Wire* and *Treme* she excelled in cinematic realism; both series provide subtle psychological characterisation and sharp analysis of the local communities as diversified due to race, ethnicity and social class. The TV series format and collage narratives facilitated the exploration of multiracial and multiethnic communities featured in both series.[28] The theme of displacement and trauma permeates all the above works but is also examined in the episodes of *Cold*

Case and *Shot in the Heart*. Finally, *The Wire*, *The First* and *House of Cards* (to which Holland contributed by directing four episodes) explore the moral decay of American society where the political elites and criminal aristocracy blend together to secure their political and economic power. All these themes were examined in Holland's earlier works, yet it was only in her American television works that they emerged with the clarity and affective intensity typical of generic forms developed within popular culture.

POST-SOCIALIST TV AND 'PROFESSIONAL INTIMACIES'

After eighteen years of working as an exilic and travelling filmmaker, Holland decided to reconnect with the Polish screen industries. In 1999, she directed for the Television Theatre (see Chapter Two) *The Dybbuk*, a play by S. Ansky (Shloyme Zanvl Rappoport), which was her first work on a Jewish theme made in her native country. She presented it as her personal project: 'It was no accident that I reached out to Ansky's play. A half of my family was Jewish.'[29] She also admitted that living abroad had changed her perspective on her partly Jewish identity. Initially, she approached it exclusively through the Holocaust experience, yet her later contacts with the Jewish communities in the States significantly expanded and deepened her attitude to it.[30] Due to its mysticism, *The Dybbuk* also links with her American films made at that time such as *The Third Miracle* (1999) and *Julie Walking Home* (2002) (see Chapter Four).

In contrast to *The Dybbuk* – that was Holland's return to the format of television theatre and Eastern European cultural tradition – her next television project, the political fiction TV series *The Crew* (*Ekipa*, Polsat, 2007), originated from American television culture, which she had been contributing to for some time (by then she had directed *Red Wind*, two episodes of *The Wire* and three episodes of *Cold Case*). As she reported: 'We drew our inspiration [the series was directed by Agnieszka Holland, her sister, Magdalena Łazarkiewicz, and her daughter, Kasia Adamik] from the American serial *West Wing* [1999–2006], whose authors proved that it was possible to portray political processes in an interesting way'. She also explained that they decided to embark on the project in response to the political apathy of Polish society as demonstrated in the very low turnout (40.57 percent) in the 2005 Polish parliamentary election (Zamysłowska and Kuźmicki 2013, 202). Łazarkiewicz and Adamik also saw it as a kind of civic duty: 'The motivation for filming *The Crew* was in some sense patriotic and pro-citizen' (Łazarkiewicz quoted in Zamysłowska and Kuźmicki 2013, 205); and '*The Crew* was born out of a sense of responsibility as citizens of the country' (Adamik quoted in Zamysłowska and Kuźmicki 2013, 205). Although inspired by the American TV series, *The Crew* revived the idea of cultural production as mobilising political awareness and creating a desire for change, as practised years earlier in the films of the Cinema of Moral Concern.

Initially, public television accepted the project for financing, yet when the right-wing Law and Justice party came to power in 2005, it withdrew from it. Instead, the commercial free-to-air Polsat Television funded its production. It was aired weekly between September and November 2007, while its DVD edition was released two weeks after the premiere of the first episode, which most likely negatively affected audience ratings but was also a pioneering strategy in terms of distribution: 'Holland and Adamik along with the Polsat network had been precursors of immediate content availability without the need to wait for a scheduled broadcast' (Majer 2021, 272). The series was moderately popular with the viewers,[31] while receiving positive critical assessments from the prominent media critics that were published in esteemed magazines and newspapers. Some journalists compared *The Crew* to the Cinema of Moral Concern, indicating that the series also explored the theme of civic responsibility for political life.[32] The first episode of the series was screened in the movie theatre 'Muranów', owned by Gutek Film[33] that had organised earlier screenings of Holland's *To Kill a Priest* and *Europa, Europa*. The DVD edition was released by the Agora consortium that owned *Gazeta Wyborcza* of which Adam Michnik was the chief editor. *The Crew* was contextualised within the national cultural tradition that by then was gradually merging with liberal ideology, while incorporating strategies and forms of cultural production typical of global neoliberalism. In a sense, *The Crew* participated in the complex and prolonged process of political, economic and cultural transformations occurring in post-1989 Poland.

The Crew is Holland's first family project realised together with her daughter, Kasia Adamik, and her sister, Magdalena Łazarkiewicz. Kasia has been working with her mother since *The Secret Garden*, first as her assistant, then as a storyboard artist, and finally as a second director. As for Holland's sister, it was their first and only collaboration to date. The family collaborative authorship was widely publicised as an element of the promotional campaign. In one interview concerning *The Crew*, Holland jokingly referenced Wajda's definition of a film director as being a combination of a soldier and poet, and identified herself as the former and her sister Magda as the latter.[34] When the renowned Polish journalist Teresa Torańska asked Holland whether they argued on the set, she admitted it happened two or three times, which she attributed to their profession-related need to rule and control. As she confessed:

> I have a nasty personality and try to be the loudest. Nothing dramatic happened though. The girls stood against me, and I corrected myself. I wish our politicians collaborated in such a way. It does not need to be a hierarchical structure.[35]

In contrast to Holland's collaboration with her sister that proved a one-off enterprise, her professional bonds with Kasia have become even stronger. The 2018 TV series *1983*, made for Netflix, was an intergenerational family project that brought together the mother (two episodes), the daughter (five episodes), the daughter's partner Olga Chajdas (two episodes), and a friend, Agnieszka Smoczyńska (one episode). The four women have also collaborated in various configurations on other projects, creating an (in)formal network, the dynamic of which has been constantly changing and has been adjusted to the specificities of any given project. Frequently, Holland has taken the most prominent position; for example, she was an executive producer of *The Offsiders* (*Boisko bezdomnych*, 2008, directed by her daughter, with Chajdas working as Adamik's assistant), an artistic supervisor of Smoczyńska's *Lure* (*Córki dancingu*, 2015) and Chajdas's *Nina* (2018). Holland has also collaborated extensively with her nephew, Antoni Komasa-Łazarkiewicz, who composed the music for several of her films. Recently, her niece Gabriela Łazarkiewicz-Sieczko has joined the 'family team' as a co-author of the script *The Green Border* (*Zielona granica*, 2023) about the immigration crisis on the Polish-Belorussian border in 2019. Throughout the years of her professional activity, Holland has created an extended cinematic family, including many regulars, as noted throughout this volume such as Jacek Petrycki, Zbigniew Preisner, Jan A. P. Kaczmarek, Tomasz Naumiuk, to name only a few. It can be argued that this relatively stable team of collaborators counterbalanced the accidental and temporary professional relationships Holland has had as a filmmaker-for-hire working within various screen cultures and modes of production. With her family, friends and regulars she created a kind of cinematic *Heimat*.

Holland's professional circle of family and friends can be considered within several frameworks, with the concepts of collaborative and collective (or multiple) authorships being the most relevant here. However, it can also be approached from the perspective of nepotism that is commonly deemed anti-democratic and discriminatory, while being more widespread than it is commonly thought. In their study 'Indirect Nepotism: Network Sponsorship, Social Capital and Career Performance in Show Business Families', Yasaman Gorij, Michael Carney and Rajshree Prakash have examined data provided by the International Movie Database (IMDB) and analysed 150 showbusiness families and 3,500 relationships among their members as developed between 1970 and 2015. The research confirmed 'the influence of show-business family social capital on relatives' career performance in the hypercompetitive Hollywood movie industry'. As the authors claimed, the 'show business families' can be beneficially transferred to succeeding generations and with temporally increasing effects' (Gorji, Carney and Prakash 2020). In their analysis, they distinguished between direct and indirect meritocratic nepotism; the former refers to family preferment in granting positions and employment, while the latter to positing competence as a condition to attain a valued occupation. As the authors argue, indirect nepotism involves 'dynastic strategies' that are aimed at transferring of social and cultural capital to facilitate the descendants to succeed in highly competitive markets of cultural production (Gorji, Carney and Prakash 2020). Indirect nepotism occurs frequently in the cultural and creative industries where there is no consistent and objective system of evaluation, while taking up the form of 'sponsorship, suggesting that individuals must develop competence and skills before they can benefit from their family's social capital' (Gorji, Carney and Prakash 2020). From the perspective of the described research, Holland's family professional network is nothing unusual in the entertainment business. It has developed its own forms of collaboration with fluctuating horizontal and/or hierarchical structures depending on whether she works with them (as a co-director of the episodes of TV series) or monitors them (as an executive producer and artistic supervisor). Her supervision can be seen as both controlling and caring. On the one hand, with her reputation she is able to secure sources for implementing film or television projects and as such she acts as 'the archetypal neoliberal subject [that] is the entrepreneurial individual whose only relationship to other people is competitive self-enhancement' (Chatzidakis et al. 2020, 13), while on the other hand her monetary value allows her to care for her extended family and to help them to flourish and thrive in their professional fields.

Holland's family team consisting mostly of women can be seen as responding to Claire Johnston's call for a collective work of women in cinema as an efficient way to overcome male hegemony:

> The development of collective work is obviously a major step forward; as a means of acquiring and sharing skills it constitutes a formidable challenge to male privilege in the film industry as an expression of sisterhood, it suggests a viable alternative to the rigid hierarchical structures of male-dominated cinema and offers real opportunities for a dialogue about the nature of women's cinema within it. (Johnston [1973] 1985, 217)

Although the multiauthor collaborative television and film projects made by Holland's female circles (with participation of male creative and technical professionals) do not necessarily implement counter-cinema strategies as envisioned by Johnston, they efficiently undermine male hegemony in the Polish screen industries. Most importantly, they have enhanced the visibility of female filmmakers in the public space.

GLOBAL NETWORKS AND LOCAL HISTORIES

Once global streaming platforms expanded their operations to Eastern Europe, Holland became one of the most suitable filmmakers to be assigned to the local projects. On the one hand, she had experience of working on the most acclaimed American TV series, on the other hand she was expertly familiar with the political nuances and cultural specificities of the region. She directed episodes for three Eastern European productions for global platforms: *Without Secrets* (*Bez tajemnic*, HBO, Poland, 2013, four episodes), the mini-series *Burning Bush* (*Hořící keř*, HBO, Czech Republic, 2013, three episodes), and *1983* (Netflix, Poland, two episodes). I will focus on *Burning Bush* as it is an exemplary collaborative work 'that ultimately enhances not diminishes, the primary author' (Carringer 2001, 377) and an instrumental project in HBO Europe's strategic plans of acquiring new markets.

In his comprehensive essay on HBO Europe, Petr Szczepanik[36] writes that the so-called Visegrad countries (Hungary, Czech Republic, Poland and Slovakia) were the first strategic region in HBO's plans for expansion into Europe. In 2004, HBO opened four original programming departments in Budapest, Prague, Warsaw and Bucharest which were responsible for providing local content for streaming and on demand services. As Szczepanik claims, special credit for boosting production of the local content is to be given to Ondřej Zach, who in 2008–12 was the vice-president of programming for HBO Central Europe. He realised that limiting streaming to Hollywood-produced content at the time when piracy was a common practice in the former Eastern Bloc was not a viable option; instead, he saw original programming as a useful alternative. '[U]nder Zach's management, HBO Europe stopped communicating primarily Hollywood movies and instead geared the focus of marketing campaigns and public relations towards original productions' (Szczepanik 2021a, 246). While HBO Europe still had access to the HBO US production, it focused 'on a handful of original programmes per year which were carefully selected, meticulously developed and well financed' (Szczepanik 2021a, 247). Another person who contributed to boosting HBO Europe original production was Marc Lorber, who was hired in 2009 as the first senior vice-president of original programming and production. One of his first strategic decisions was 'to test local markets with new versions of well-proven fiction formats' (Szczepanik 2021a, 248). The first project was an Israeli drama, *Be' Tipul*, the episodes of which were structured around psychotherapeutic sessions run by the protagonist. As demonstrated by its American version *In Treatment* (2007), the series proved easily transferable to other localities and consequently Czech, Polish, Hungarian and Romanian versions were made. All Eastern European adaptations were directed by prominent directors and featured respected actors.[37] Holland (as well as her daughter, Kasia Adamik) contributed to the third season of the Polish version, titled *Without Secrets* (*Bez tajemnic*, 2011–13), that brought a somehow unexpected turn of action as the leading character of the psychotherapist, Andrzej Wolski (Jerzy Radziwiłowicz), is shifted to the position of a patient analysed by his younger and talented colleague, Tomasz (Maciej Stuhr). Holland's first collaboration with HBO Europe was soon to be followed by the larger and more prestigious project, *Burning Bush*, a perfect implementation of the strategies of development envisioned by the creative personnel of the platform.

Burning Bush is a flagship product of the HBO Europe strategy of local programming and its first 'event mini-series', as termed by Szczepanik (2021a, 249). Its production was facilitated by the strategy envisioned by Anthony Root – in 2011, he replaced Lorber in the position of senior vice-president of original programming and production – who implemented the politics of protecting the local professional capital, especially in helping the directors 'realize their true authorial vision' (Szczepanik 2021a, 254). The aim of HBO Europe was to create 'US-style muscular storytelling in television form married with auteur cinema' (Steve Matthews quoted in Szczepanik 2021a, 254). In its supporting of local resources, HBO Europe developed an alternative trajectory of development than Netflix (at least initially) or Amazon in that it gave away financially motivated international co-productions and runaway productions, while investing in local labour resources and shooting local stories in local languages. 'In HBO Europe's original programming, local appeal still comes first, while transnational appeal plays second fiddle. [. . .] "problematic" aspects of national history, politics, and culture [. . .] are mined to create nationally specific spectacles' (Szczepanik 2021a, 256). Anikó Imre calls the local programming strategy of HBO Europe (after Zala Volčič and Mark Andrejevic) 'commercial nationalism', claiming that 'HBO Europe has very successfully incorporated small nations' preexisting brand loyalties into its own brand, creating a uniquely European quality' (Imre 2018, 62). According to Szczepanik, using global narrative formulas for local content is characteristic of post-global corporations that exploit the recent upsurge of national sentiments, especially in the post-socialist countries (Szczepanik 2021a, 256).

HBO Europe decided to produce *Burning Bush* after its screenplay was rejected by the Czech public television (Szczepanik 2016, 98). It was written by the then-unknown Czech screenwriter Štěpán Hulík (b. 1984), a graduate of FAMU, who in 2011 published a book *Kinematografie zapomnění* on Czechoslovak cinema of the 'normalisation' period. The project of the three-part mini-series *Burning Bush* was initiated in 2010 and was co-produced by an independent film company Nutprodukce and by newcomer Tomáš Hrubý. *Burning Bush* – that had also its theatrical release[38] – demonstrates a successful merger between the accessible model of entertainment practised by the medium of television and the psychological subtleties of art cinema.[39] Accordingly, in his essay, Tadeusz Lubelski consistently addresses the mini-series as a film (Lubelski 2017) and his intuitive classification is convergent with the more general process of diminishing the difference between cinema and television.[40]

Burning Bush revisits one of the most dramatic episodes in post-Second World War Czech history, the self-immolation of the young student, Jan Palach, committed in 1969 as a protest against the Soviet suppression of the Prague Spring. The series reconstructs only briefly the historical event of Palach's immolation, while focusing on the young female lawyer, Dagmar Burešová (Tatiana Pauhofová) (see Fig. 5.6), who agreed to represent Palach's mother (Jaroslava Pokorná) and his brother (Petr Stach) in the trial against the communist politician Vilém Nový (Martin Huba) whom they accused of defaming Jan.

As explained in Chapter One, Holland witnessed the events of the Prague Spring and then the invasion of Czechoslovakia by the military forces of the Warsaw Pact, so directing the mini-series was for her a return to her youthful past. As she recalled:

> The Czech time was very important for me – I felt very close to this country and to its culture. My work on *Burning Bush* allowed me to return to those times and was for me one of the best professional and personal experiences I've had in recent years. I am the only well-known director who experienced the events of those times in Czechoslovakia directly and who additionally, has a dissident past. Thus, my personal experience adds credibility to the project. (Zamysłowska and Kuźmicki 2013, 236) [41]

Figure 5.6 *Burning Bush* (2013)

In Chapter One, I argued that, while studying at FAMU, Holland was somehow distanced from both the Polish and the Czechoslovak generational experiences of, respectively, March '68 and the Prague Spring. Paradoxically, this position of simultaneous closeness to and distance from the historical experience of the Prague Spring had made her, in the opinion of her young Czech collaborators, the writer and the young producers, the perfect director for their project. As Holland reported:

> I was the only person who could do it because I experienced it.[42] And at the same time I was an outsider and so I could look at the history without a sort of Czech complex. And by Czech complex they meant the aversion to talking seriously about the country's problems. You know, 'Let's make it funny.' And the young people behind this film had grown tired of a culture that was turning everything into some kind of joke. They saw that in some ways their parents and themselves were the victims of this silence. So they wanted to reconstruct or express their roots more seriously – and re-discover their roots for themselves.[43]

For Holland, making *Burning Bush* was a work of memory, while for Hulík it was a work of post-memory, or a symbolic act of recovering the collective memory. The visual design employed in the series structures the narrative as a work of memory; the colour palette ranges from the minimalist black-and-white photography used in the documentary footage, through monochromatic images that serve as a transition to the fictional reconstructions of the historical events, up to the saturated colours used generously in the family scenes in Burešová's home. Throughout the series, colour connotes the private life as a retreat from the oppressive and grim reality of the period of 'normalisation'.[44] Veronika Pehe identifies 'a muted colour palette in grays and browns [as] the main authenticating mechanism of *Burning Bush* [. . .] the fashions and styles of the film are not packaged to be consumed by a contemporary viewer, but to be enjoyed at a distance' (Pehe 2015, 249). The visual design emerged as an effect of creative collaboration with the cinematographer Martin Štrba, with whom Holland worked at *Janosik*. His 'transparent' cinematography respected reality, which was evoked by his predilection for natural lighting (if it was necessary to use additional sources of lighting, he would locate it close to the natural sources).[45]

Burning Bush's realism and visual design prompted Lubelski to discuss the similarity of the series with the Cinema of Moral Concern (Lubelski 2013, 70).[46] However, unlike the protagonists of the Polish films from the 1970s, the people who are depicted in the Czech series are heroic and determined in their struggle for truth. Palach's mother first despairs in an almost operatic fashion, yet after recovering from the first shock, she accepts her son's decision, and

Figure 5.7 *Burning Bush* (2013)

in a way, she continues his mission in that she demands punishment for the communist apparatchik who defamed her son's memory. She is almost a perfect incarnation of the mythical figure of the heroic Polish Mother (see Fig. 5.7) that Holland had been consistently distancing herself from in her Polish films from the 1970s (see E. Ostrowska 1998). The mother is supported by Palach's brother, whose character is introduced in his domestic space along with his wife as she is comforting their baby. Apparently, he is living his life far away from politics as if embodying the passivity and withdrawal of the Czechoslovak society during the period of 'normalisation'. However, he soon stands next to his mother and they both fight for historical justice for Jan. Likewise, Burešová is not introduced right away as a heroic figure. Although her first appearance demonstrates her professional efficiency, it is instantly juxtaposed with her image at home, where she is a caring mother and tender wife. A few scenes later, she joins her colleague in his search for his daughter who did not return home the previous night. In all of these roles of a lawyer, mother, wife and friend, she appears as a person who cares, and this care and sense of responsibility seem to be at the very core of her heroic yet doomed-to-fail battle against the communist legal system. This faithfulness to the 'lost cause' approximates Burešová to the model of the Polish patriot developed in Polish Romanticism but also to Agnieszka from Andrzej Wajda's film *Man of Marble* (see Chapter Two), who was allegedly modelled on Holland.

Burning Bush was an unquestionable success among Czech audience and the critics. It was intended as the Czech submission for the Oscar competition, yet it was not eligible due to its broadcasting on television prior to its theatrical release. However, it was nominated for fourteen awards from the Czech Film Academy and received four awards from the Czech film critics. One of them, Jan Gregor, wrote: 'If the Czechs didn't have Agnieszka Holland, they would have to invent her. Actually, it is quite significant that the first comprehensive film account of our communist past was made by a Polish woman who has personal experience of the period in Prague'. The critic also compared *Burning Bush* to the Cinema of Moral Concern to which Holland significantly contributed.[47] In turn, Mirka Spáčilová referred to the director's transnational experience: 'director Agnieszka Holland combines the experience of European totalitarianism with compelling American-style storytelling [. . .] From the sets to the music to the tricks, *The Burning Bush* maintains a professional level that is rarely seen here'.[48] Both reviews emphasise Holland's transnational authorship.[49] Szczepanik commented on *Burning Bush*'s success in the Czech Republic and abroad:

> the series proved to be an immense national success, being sold to dozens of foreign markets, including the US. What is more, its global reach made people outside the CEE region recognize the existence of HBO Europe for the first time. If *In Treatment* placed HBO Europe on the map of regional television culture, *The Burning Bush* did the same on the global TV series scene, playing at international festivals, being represented by the renowned German sales agency Beta Film, and finally making its way into the HBO US catalogue. (Szczepanik 2021a, 250)

While Holland was working on *Burning Bush*, Jacek Petrycki, her regular collaborator, and Krystyna Krauze made a documentary, *The Return of Agnieszka H.* (*Powrót Agnieszki H.*, 2013), recording the director revisiting the places from her youth in Prague. Polish film scholar, Mariusz Guzek suggested *Burning Bush* and *The Return of Agnieszka H.* can be seen as a kind of biographical study (Guzek 2019, 45). Lubelski entitled his essay on *Burning Bush* 'Defense against Homelessness', suggesting that the Czech Republic is as much her spiritual home as is Poland (Lubelski 2017, 287–99). Paradoxically, her return home – whether it is to Poland or to the Czech Republic – was facilitated by the global streaming platform HBO Europe.

While *Burning Bush* was a flagship of HBO Europe, *1983* (2018) was the first original Polish Netflix TV series also exploring the political past, yet in the formula of a dystopian science-fiction drama. The story was based on a hypothetical assumption that martial law in Poland did not end two years after its imposition in 1981 but lasted for another twenty years until 2003 when the action takes place. The series depicts a futuristic world controlled by a communist totalitarian regime, while some citizens organise in an underground movement. Two protagonists, a policeman Janów (Robert Więckiewicz) and a law student, Kajetan (Maciej Musiał) act together to discover the nation's past. Unlike *Burning Bush* that employed the mode of realism, *1983* uses a visual stylisation typical of neo-noir. Dark and enclosed spaces, low-key lighting and a dark-colour palette are visual codes used to present the 'never-ending' reality of communism that might be read as a metaphor of current political situation in Poland (see Borowski 2023). Both global streaming platforms, HBO Europe and Netflix, provided space for Holland for an exploration of local histories, while also operating within 'commercial nationalism' as saleable products.

In conclusion, Holland's television works that were made in the States, Poland and the Czech Republic can be seen as mobilising various transfers between cinema and television, global and local cultural productions, *auteur* and genre cinema, and individual and collective authorship. With their focus on socio-political issues, these projects can be related to her works made for Polish socialist television in the 1970s, while developing on the themes related to gender, sexuality and ethnicity. Under closer scrutiny, Holland's television output reveals thematic threads and stylistic preferences, with a non-singular perceptual perspective being the most significant, that can be attributed to authorial subjectivity. Most importantly, working for television and streaming platforms allowed her to further explore the possibilities of collective, often female, authorship that she had practised at the beginning of her professional career in Poland. Holland's television works are not insignificant margins of her oeuvre but an integral part of it, expanding and reconsidering traditional concepts of authorship. Not unlike in socialist Poland, global television networks provided Holland with an alternative creative space within which the cinematic myth of the individual (male) *auteur* who controls is replaced with a (collective) female author who *cares*.

NOTES

1. Andrew Stubbs discusses collaboration of indie *auteurs* such as David Fincher and Steven Soderbergh with global streaming platforms (Stubbs 2020).
2. As Jane Feuer explains 'HBO drama merges series or serialised TV with postmodern theatre or art cinema [...] there is nothing "new" or "original" generically between HBO drama and the television tradition of quality drama that cannot be ascribed to an equally generic tradition of art cinema' (Feuer 2007, 157). For discussion of the concept of 'quality television', see McCabe and Akas 2007.
3. Holland's casting decision can be contextualised within the racial motifs of Chandler's prose. As James Naremore reported: 'one of Raymond Chandler's earliest stories, "Noon Street Nemesis," originally published in *Detective Fiction Weekly* in May 1936, is set almost entirely in a black section of Los Angeles. When the story first appeared, the editors of the journal deleted all references to the race of the characters, but Chandler made sure that the deletions were restored for the reprinted version, "Pickup on Noon Street," in *The Simple Art of Murder*' (Naremore 2008, 233–4).

4. Holland herself suggested a kind of affinity between herself and black Americans. As she recollected, her visit to Glover's house reminded her of her own home in Poland in the 1960s: 'A crowd of young people, an old father, the wife cooking a lot of food for everyone, and everybody laughs, hugs, and shouts. Then I understood that Afro-Americans are my American homeland' (Holland and Kornatowska 2012, 321).
5. In his review, Steven Oxman criticised this device as exemplifying the film's aesthetic self-indulgence: 'The film tries, in a sense, to make the story poetically meaningful rather than powerfully honest, and that gives it an occasionally pretentious feeling [. . .] Holland, however, tends to latch onto the obvious image and force it almost to the point of corniness. When Mikal and Gary meet for the last time, the use of reflection to signal their deep connection is severely overdone, belaboring the very obvious' (Steven Oxman, '*Shot in the Heart*. Review.' *Variety*, 11 October 2001. https://variety.com/2001/tv/reviews/shot-in-the-heart-1200553402/ (accessed 27 December 2022).
6. Tim Goodman, 'Brother's Sad Tale / Gary Gilmore Focus of HBO's Fine "Shot"', *San Francisco Chronicle*, 12 October 2001. https://www.sfgate.com/entertainment/article/Brother-s-sad-tale-Gary-Gilmore-focus-of-HBO-s-2868907.php (accessed 27 December 2022).
7. Barry Levinson and Tom Fontana produced the TV series *Oz* for HBO.
8. Goodman, 'Brother's Sad Tale'.
9. However, some of the reviewers identified her as an experienced director yet not necessarily an *auteur*; for example, Nathan Rabin introduces *Shot in the Heart* as '[d]irected by veteran Agnieszka Holland' (Nathan Rabin, '*Shot in the Heart*', review, *The Onion A.V. Club*, 3 April 2002. https://www.avclub.com/shot-in-the-heart-1798196284 (accessed 27 December 2022).
10. Tadeusz Sobolewski, 'Przerwany łańcuch', *Gazeta Wyborcza*, no. 232, 2001, 11.
11. Mikal Gilmore, 'Strzał w serce'. Translated by Jacek Łaszcz, *Gazeta Wyborcza*, 10 January 2002, 4–5.
12. Agnieszka Holland, 'Człowiek za kratami', interview by Tadeusz Sobolewski, *Gazeta Wyborcza*, no. 232, 2001, 11.
13. In some promotional material for *Shot in the Heart* published in a Polish daily *Rzeczpospolita*, there is a quote from Holland who compared the Gilmore brothers' story to Dostoyevsky's *Crime and Punishment* and the biblical parable of Cain and Abel (anon. 'Początek z Agnieszką Holland', *Rzeczpospolita*, no. 233, 2001, 6).
14. 'Czy należy zabijać w majestacie prawa?' *Tele Świat*, no. 5, 2002, 42.
15. Andrew Davis, 'Gloria Allred: Talking about a Girl Like Gwen', *Windy City Times*, 21 June 2006. http://www.windycitymediagroup.com/lgbt/Gloria-Allred-Talking-About-a-Girl-Like-Gwen/11861.html
16. GLAAD website: https://www.glaad.org/mediaawards/32
17. As Holland admitted in one of her interviews, the motif was introduced by her gay friend Witold Zatorski with whom she co-wrote the script for the film (Holland 2021, 138).
18. She also directed 'Corner Boys' (2006, S4 E8) and 'React Quotes' (2008, S5 E5).
19. Holland's name was quite often mentioned by critics; in his essay on *The Wire*, Fredric Jameson also singles out Holland: 'There could also be an artistic bonus, owing to the fact that each of the episodes is written and/or directed by different people, some of them distinguished visitors (George Pelecanos, Agnieszka Holland)' (Jameson 2010, 360). Likewise, J. M. Tyree wrote in his review: 'The directors used in the series have included the Polish New Wave director Agnieszka Holland' ('The Wire: The Complete Fourth Season', *Film Quarterly*, 61, no. 3 (Spring 2008): 32–8).
20. While in Poland television production has been treated as an integral part of filmmakers' oeuvre since the late 1960s (see Chapter Two) and as such it was included in 'authorisation'

discourses, in the States this cultural 'uplift' happened much later, in the 1990s. In her book, *Television Rewired: The Rise of the Auteur Series* (2019), Martha Nochimson discusses the cultural elevation of television as exemplified by, among others, *The Wire* and *Treme*, while locating the authorial agency solely in the person of David Simon, the creator of both series and the author of the teleplay. She consequently omits the names of the directors, which testifies to the relocating of authorial agency from directors to the creators of the TV series.
21. Agnieszka Holland, 'Nasz kolega Jan Palach', interview by Tadeusz Sobolewski, *Gazeta Wyborcza*, no. 52, 2013, 34–5.
22. J. M. Tyree prises the opening sequence of the first episode: 'season 1 of *Treme* begins with a raucous "second line" street procession, filmed in a wonderfully confused riot of celebration by Agnieszka Holland', '*Treme* vs. *The Bad Lieutenant*', *Film Quarterly*, 64, no. 1, Fall 2010, 23–8.
23. As Holland claimed, while directing the pilot episode, she was allowed to introduce many 'authorial' ideas, which was no longer possible when she did the last episode (Holland and Kornatowska 2012, 403).
24. In that, he is similar to the protagonist of Paweł Pawlikowski's *The Woman in the Fifth* (2011) who is also an American writer arriving to Paris in the hope of reviving his family life and writing career.
25. Rachel Donadio, 'Bedeviled Anew by a Pregnancy', *The New York Times*, 8 May 2014, https://www.nytimes.com/2014/05/11/arts/television/agnieszka-hollands-post-feminist-rosemarys-baby-on-nbc.html (accessed 5 April 2023).
26. Donadio, 'Bedeviled Anew by a Pregnancy'.
27. American film critics have not linked *Rosemary's Baby* with Holland's other films concerning motherhood and as such contributing to her *auteur* work. It was located within genre cinema and approached as a (not so successful) remake of Polanski's film. In contrast, Jane Campion's BBC mini-series *Top of the Lake* (2013; she scripted and directed it), which was her first work since *Bright Star* (2009), was instantly incorporated by the critics to her *auteur* oeuvre and women's cinema.
28. Nochimson notes the parallel collage-like narrative structure of *The Wire* and its acute exploration of ethnic and racial tensions: 'The narratives of *The Wire* are a bubbling, steaming stew flavored by many races and ethnicities [. . .] a live mosaic of perspectives emanating from the essentially white middle/upper-class community and from the essentially black poor/lower class community. These multiple perspectives flow through the city, frequently at cross-purposes, often cancelling each other out, sometimes making some small inroads on the problems of Baltimore' (Nochimson 2019, 95–6).
29. Agnieszka Holland, 'Bez katharsis', interview by Feliks Platowski, *Teatr*, no. 11, 2020, 25–6.
30. Holland, 'Bez katharsis', 25.
31. The serial attracted an audience of 1.5 million viewers, and these represented mostly the well-educated middle-class (Karolina Pasternak, 'Dobry premier, choć fikcyjny', *Przekrój*, no. 43/44, 2007, 88).
32. See Helena Kowalik, 'Co wynika z rzecznika?' *Film*, no. 3, 2008, 74–7; Tomasz Plata, 'Political fiction bez popkulturowego luzu', *Dziennik. Polska-Europa-Świat*, no. 257, 2007, 18–19; Tadeusz Sobolewski, 'Odtrutka na Mordasy', *Gazeta Wyborcza*, no. 214, 2007, 14–15.
33. See '*Ekipa* w Muranowie. Premiera serialu o polskiej polityce', *Gazeta Wyborcza*, no. 207, 2007, 1.
34. Agnieszka Holland, Kasia Adamik and Magdalena Łazarkiewicz, 'Polska nas wkurzyła', interview by Aleksandra Krzyżaniak-Gumowska and Piotr Pacewicz, *Gazeta Wyborcza-Wysokie Obcasy*, no. 8, 2007, 38–41.
35. Agnieszka Holland, 'Ekipa jak marzenie', interview by Teresa Torańska, *Gazeta Wyborcza*, no. 214, 2007, 14.

36. All information concerning HBO Europe's enterprises in Eastern Europe come from Szczepanik (2021a).
37. Anikó Imre commented on HBO Europe's collaboration with renowned filmmakers and actors as an important strategy of maintaining its reputation for 'quality television': 'One important way in which HBO has legitimized its productions locally has been by recruiting for the small screen actors and directors who previously gained a reputation in feature films. [. . .] Having Agnieszka Holland direct the Czech HBO original series *Burning Bush*, Oscar-nominated Ildikó Enyedi direct the Hungarian adaptation of *In Treatment*, or Bogdan Mirica, winner of the 2016 Cannes Fipresci Award for his feature *Dogs*, direct the Romanian serial *Shadows* instantly distinguishes these productions from ordinary television' (Imre 2018, 57).
38. In Poland, the first screening took place on 25 February 2013 in the Warsaw Opera.
39. Imre noticed, 'HBO's quality dramas and documentaries issue a broader popular appeal – a kind of entertaining quality aesthetic and ordinary language that had not existed before due to the value gap assumed to separate art film and television' (Imre 2019, 176).
40. Imre commented on this convergence in relation to Eastern Europe: 'Paradoxically, "quality TV" enters the post-socialist milieu at a time when the media are so globalised, interconnected and convergent that some have questioned the very need for distinguishing between film and television any more' (Imre 2019, 179).
41. At the press conference preceding the first screening of the film in Prague, Holland said that the Prague Spring was a formative experience in that it shaped her understanding of the world (Aneta Kyzioł, 'Serial moralnego niepokoju', *Polityka*, no. 9, 2013, 76–7).
42. In fact, Holland was not in Prague when Palach committed his self-immolation, yet she was informed by a friend of what was happening in Prague (Barbara Hollender, 'Pochodnia numer jeden', *Rzeczpospolita*, no. 50, 2013, A12).
43. Agnieszka Holland and Joshua Sperling, 'In Conversation: Agnieszka Holland with Joshua Sperling', *The Brooklyn Rail*, 18 December 2013. https://brooklynrail.org/2013/12/film/agnieszka-holland-with-joshua-sperling (accessed 6 April 2023).
44. Agnieszka Holland, 'Normalizacja w kadrze', interview by Jolanta Tokarczyk, *Film & TV Kamera*, no. 1, 2014, 34–9.
45. Holland, 'Normalizacja w kadrze'.
46. Tadeusz Lubelski, 'Czeska gorączka', *Ekrany*, no. 2, 2013, 70.
47. Jan Gregor, 'Recenze: Hořící keř přináší patos bez sentimentu', *Magazin Aktualne*, 24 January 2013. Translated by Marek Čermák, https://magazin.aktualne.cz/kultura/film/recenze-horici-ker-prinasi-patos-bez-sentimentu/r~i:article:769355/ (accessed 22 July 2023).
48. Mirka Spáčilová, 'RECENZE: Hořící keř předvádí, jak točit vlastní dějiny bez plakatu', iDNES.cz, 28 January 2013. Translated by Marek Čermák, https://www.idnes.cz/kultura/film-televize/televizni-film-o-palachovi.A130127_172415_filmvideo_spm (accessed 23 July 2023).
49. Jan Čulík, a Czech journalist and lecturer at the University of Glasgow, published a very negative review of *Burning Bush*, accusing it of being historically inaccurate, psychologically shallow and boring. His opinion was not shared by other critics whether working in Czech Republic or abroad (*Hořící keř* je neuvěřitelně slabý film, Britské listy, 29 January 2014, https://blisty.cz/art/71956-i-horici-ker-i-je-neuveritelne-slaby-film.html (accessed 22 July 2014).

CHAPTER 6

'Back home' or 'There's no such place as home': post-communist political cinema revisited

In 2002, Agnieszka Holland and her daughter, Kasia Adamik, began working on *Janosik – A True Story*, their first fully collaborative project. Soon, the production was put on hold because the Slovak film producer, Rudolf Biermann, had miscalculated the budget, and the prospective American funding was withdrawn. It took six years for production to be resumed. The film, and its expanded version as a four-episode TV series, had its premiere in 2009. *Janosik*'s turbulent production history is exemplary of the complex process of transformation of the post-communist film industry in Poland and (Eastern) Europe occurring at the beginning of the twenty-first century. It also marks Holland's difficult return to European cinema. When the production was suspended, she continued her professional career in the States as a filmmaker-for-hire (see Chapter Four and Chapter Five), yet she also managed to complete a collaborative project, the TV series *The Crew* (*Ekipa*), for the Polish private TV station (see Chapter Five). The first decade of the 2000s was a transitional period in Holland's career in that she was working for both cinema and television within both American and (Eastern) European production models. This stage in her career develops into another Deleuzian 'molecular line' that includes segments of different creative and production materials emerging as 'blocs of becoming' and a 'combinations of fluxes' (Deleuze and Parnet 2007, 130). As she had been constantly travelling between North America and Europe, there was no apparent threshold that would demarcate the new stage. However, these incidental forays into European screen cultures put a crack in the trajectory of her American film and television career and increased her European transnational productions. The changes within the European film industry have expedited the process.

In this chapter, I discuss Holland's films made in the twenty-first century in the context of the changes in the European film industries resulting from the new geopolitical order, specifically the enlargement of the EU through the accession of several countries of the former Eastern Bloc. The films, *Janosik – A True Story*, *In Darkness* (*W ciemności*, 2011), *Spoor* (*Pokot*, 2017), *Mr Jones* (2019) and *Charlatan* (*Šarlatán*, 2020), are all European co-productions that examine historical or political issues relevant to the region. Except for *Spoor*, these films all depict the lives of real people, and as such they can be seen as a continuation of Holland's exploration of the genre of biopic in her American feature and television works. Simultaneously, they mark a further shift towards sub-national identities such as ethnicity (*In Darkness*), gender (*Spoor*) and sexuality (*Charlatan*). As I will argue, with the vital subject matters and moderate departures from the conventions of mainstream cinema, Holland's European transnational film productions represent socially engaged cinema designed for the specific sector of the film festivals circuit and exhibition in art movie theatres. While discussing these films, I take inspiration from Thomas Elsaesser's discussion of European 'festival films', especially his concept of 'double occupancy' (2019, 34). As he argues, directors of these films need to meet the expectations of both national and transnational audiences and hence they frequently employ contradictory politics of representation.

Expanding on Elsaesser's line of argument, I propose to see Holland's European films from the 2000s as producing the effect of the post-communist exotic that I adapt from Graham Huggan's concept of the postcolonial exotic that, as he explains:

> occupies a site of discursive conflict between a local assemblage of more or less related oppositional practices and a global apparatus of assimilative institutional/commercial codes. More specifically, it marks the intersection between contending regimes of value: one regime – postcolonialism – that posits itself as anti-colonial, and that works toward the dissolution of imperial epistemologies and institutional structures; and another – postcoloniality – that is more closely tied to the global market, and that capitalises both on the widespread circulation of ideas about cultural otherness and on the worldwide trafficking of culturally 'othered' artifacts and goods. [. . .] the postcolonial exotic is, to some extent, a pathology of cultural representation under late capitalism – a result of the spiralling commodification of cultural difference, and of responses to it, that is characteristic of the (post)modern, market-driven societies in which many of us currently live. (Huggan 2001, 28, 33)

In what I call post-communist exotic there are also contradictory ideological forces: on the one hand it is potentially a critical tool for an examination of post-communist identity, while also being embedded in the logic of late capitalism. Therefore, a critical representational strategy produces eventually a saleable product.

(EASTERN) EUROPEAN FILM PRODUCTION: FROM CRISIS TO SUCCESS

After 1989, the film industry in Poland, and in other Eastern European countries for that matter, remained for a significant period of time in a state of deep crisis and stagnation. The state funding of national film industries ceased to exist, while new forms of financing had not yet emerged. The production story of Holland and Adamik's *Janosik – A True Story* is a textbook example of the turbulent process of restructuring the Eastern European film industry.[1] *Janosik* was initially conceived as a Slovak project with American financial input, and it was launched in 2002 by the Slovak film producer, Rudolf Biermann. When 40 percent of the shooting material was completed, the American co-producers withdrew from the project, and it was abandoned for six years. It was resumed in 2008, which was made possible by the transformation of the Eastern European film industry that occurred at that time. The most important change concerned the establishment of the national film institutions, whose main aim was the distribution of state funding through official competition schemes. The pioneering programme was developed in Romania, where in 1999 the Romanian Law of Cinematography was introduced that eventually facilitated the production of the films that are now commonly identified as the Romanian New Wave. Its spectacular achievements, especially at the international film festivals, with the Golden Palm awards for Christian Mungiu and others, epitomised the rejuvenation of post-socialist Romanian and Eastern European cinema. In 2005, Poland introduced the Act on Cinematography that established the Polish Film Institute (Polski Instytut Sztuki Filmowej, PISF), whose primary task was distributing state funds among specific film projects on the basis of evaluations made by independent teams of experts.

PISF co-financed *Janosik*, yet the main credit for resuming the film's production goes to Dariusz Jabłoński's Apple Film Production, one of the first Polish independent film studios that secured co-financing from various sources. Polish and Slovak state funds came respectively from the Polish Film Institute as well as Polish Television and the Ministry of Culture of Slovakia. The project was also supported by the independent Hungarian Eurofilm Studio, the Czech Charlie's, and HBO Europe. Ultimately, the film was made as a Polish-Slovak-Czech-Hungarian co-production that was distributed under four different titles: *Janosik. Prawdziwa historia* (Polish); *Jánošík – Pravdivá história* (Slovak); *Jánošík – Pravdivá historie* (Czech); *Janosik – Egy igaz történet* (Hungarian). The crew were mostly Slovak (the scriptwriter Eva Borušovičova; the director of photography Martin Štrba; the art designer František Lipták) and Polish (directors Agnieszka Holland and Kasia Adamik, the composer Antoni Łazarkiewicz; the art designer Marek Zawierucha). The titular role was played by the Czech actor Václav Jiráček, while his antagonist, the bandit Huncaga, was played by the Polish actor Michał Żebrowski, who was then very famous due to his roles in Polish heritage cinema: Andrzej Wajda's *Mr Tadeusz* (*Pan Tadeusz*, 1999), and Jerzy Hoffman's *With Fire and Sword* (*Ogniem i mieczem*, 1999). The Slovak, Czech and Polish actors were cast in the secondary roles, while the film was made at locations in Poland. Due to the six-year gap in the shooting, the production of the film was a challenge. As Kasia Adamik recollected: 'It was quite an amazing puzzle because many of the scenes had not been completed and we had to match them all up to the new shots' (Zamysłowska and Kuźmicki 2013, 208). Jabłoński, the Polish film producer, concluded that 'despite all difficulties', the project was 'truly worthwhile' as 'a truly Central European film' (Zamysłowska and Kuźmicki 2013, 208).

The film revisited the legend of the 'Central European Robin Hood' – as Jánošík was often called – from a regional rather than a national perspective that subverted respective national myths created around his persona. Furthermore, the film's disrupted process of production resulted in some narrative and visual discontinuities that were reintegrated into a lyrical or ballad-like narration, which also included numerous action-driven scenes and episodes typical of costume adventures movies. As a result, the film was a hybrid of a folk tale and a Hollywood-type genre film. The narrative and visual discontinuities reflect the disrupted production course, but they may also symbolically evince the equally turbulent and prolonged process of the cultural emancipation of the countries of Central Europe from the previous Eastern Bloc and the following painstaking process of integration into the Western structures of democracy and the free market.

Holland's next film, *In Darkness* (2011), bridges her North American and post-1989 European career. The film was produced by the Polish film studio 'Zebra', the German Schmidtz Katze Filmkollektiv GmbH and the Canadian studio the Film Works that had co-financed her earlier film, *Julie Walking Home* (2002). The project was also financially supported by the Polish Film Institute, Canal + and the City Council of Łódź. The idea for the film came from David F. Shamoon, who read, in a Toronto newspaper, about the book *The Righteous* by Sir Martin Gilbert, which portrayed people who saved Jews during the Holocaust. As the scriptwriter confessed, one sentence drew his attention: 'A Polish Catholic thief hid a group of Jews in the sewers of Lvov, which he knew well because that was where he hid his loot and actually got a job as a sewer worker'.[2] Shamoon contacted Gilbert to learn more about this unorthodox hero and became aware of the book *In the Sewers of Lvov* by Robert Marshall, published in 1991. It describes the story of a petty thief who saved the lives of ten Jews, charging them at first for his help, then continuing for a long time after their financial resources ran out. Fascinated with the book, Shamoon purchased the rights for its screen adaptation, and wrote a script. As he reported: 'After I finished the script, a well-known Hollywood director and producer wanted to make it, but I felt strongly that this story should never be "Hollywoodized." A friend in Britain suggested the ideal director: Agnieszka Holland'.[3] Shamoon decided to send the script to the Film Works, which had produced Holland's *Julie Walking Home* (2002). The Polish and German producers soon joined the project. Yet Holland rejected it twice because of the producers' requirement to make the film in English. Instead, she insisted that the film should be multilingual for the purpose of realism and authenticity. Pre-war Lviv belonged to Poland, yet it was inhabited by many nationalities and ethnicities, as were most of the towns and villages in Central and Eastern Europe. Eventually, the producers agreed, and the film's dialogues were in Polish (not in its literary version but its Lviv dialect called *balak*) Yiddish, Hebrew, Ukrainian, Russian and German. Although the protagonist is Polish and the action takes place in the then Polish city, the linguistic polyphony de-nationalises the story. Simon Lewis claims that 'the film presents a vernacular cosmopolitanism [. . .] in a very literal sense: its mix of languages and dialects makes Lviv/Lwów hardly recognizable as a *Polish* city at all' (Lewis 2019, 536). Instead, the story is located in the expansive terrain of European history with the Holocaust being its critical moment.

Holland's insistence on making *In Darkness* with multilingual dialogues testifies to her authorial agency within the production network. Shamoon said: 'If we wished her to direct the film, and we really wanted that very, very much, then the film had to be shot in those languages' (Zamysłowska and Kuźmicki 2013, 220). Likewise, Mark-Daniel Dichant, the German co-producer of the film, emphasised that her participation in the project was the reason why his company joined it: 'Agnieszka Holland's work, her biography and her whole background made her an ideal director for the project. That is why we fought for her involvement' (Zamysłowska and Kuźmicki 2013, 220). He referred to both the professional reputation and biography that established her cultural and symbolic capital within European and Hollywood cinema. Holland's participation in the project secured a non-Hollywood approach to the theme of the Holocaust, while her North American experience in cinema and television guaranteed a high-quality cinematic product. As such, she perfectly fitted the European funding policy developed after 1989 that, as Dina Iordanova noted, favoured 'established "auteurs"' and created 'an emerging class of internationally renowned [. . .] bankable "auteurs" from Eastern Europe' (Iordanova 2002, 519). With her Hollywood reputation and the Oscar nominations, Holland's position within the new trans-European film production system was strong, ensuring her not only the realisation of the film projects for cinema, but also 'quality television' in Central Europe as discussed in the previous chapter.

Holland's next film project, *Spoor* (2017), an adaptation of Olga Tokarczuk's novel, *Drive Your Plough over the Bones of the Dead* (*Prowadź swój plug przez kości umarłych*, 2009), was made as an exemplary European co-production in that it involved local and European funds. It was produced by the Polish film studio 'Tor', German Heimatfilm, Czech Nutprodukce, Swedish Chimney, and Slovak Nutprodukcia. In Poland, it was co-financed by the Polish Film Institute, the National Audiovisual Institute, the local film fund Odra Film, HBO and the media consortium Agora. It was also financially supported by Eurimages (the Council of Europe's Fund) and MEDIA (the European Community Programme),[4] as well as the Polish-German Film Fund. The Eurimages contribution is especially worthy of note as it has been the most important institutional body financing film production in post-1989 Europe. Established in 1989, it has been providing vital support for European co-productions and the distribution of audiovisual works. Each of the member countries makes a contribution to the fund which is also supplemented from other sources. The interest-free loans are provided to the film projects that have already accumulated 50 percent of the planned budget (financing from the state and private sources cannot exceed 70 percent). These loans are repaid from the films' profits. Euroimages' mission is to facilitate cooperation between smaller and bigger players in the European film industry, and, as it is frequently emphasised, it

> has proved highly beneficial to the former countries of Central and Eastern Europe, whose previous total dependence on state subsidies left them in disarray once the state crumbled. Eurimages has become an important pan-European coproducing source that has kept alive a cinematographic output in countries where production otherwise would have stopped. (Rivi 2007, 62)

The European film funds were important for both economic and cultural reasons. They facilitated the rejuvenation of film production in the former Eastern Bloc and helped to integrate it with the European West, while also promoting projects supporting the idea of a democratic and inclusive Europe. As Iordanova explained:

> The establishment of such pan-European funding bodies as Media and Eurimages came as a reaction to the overwhelming triumph of commercialism in cinema. The share of international subsidies for filmmaking in

poverty-stricken Eastern European studios quickly increased as the concept of 'national cinema' gave way to a 'new European' one. (Iordanova 1999, 46)[5]

Although designed to rejuvenate Eastern and Central European cinemas and integrate these with the Western players, the funds implemented the policy of favouring low-risks projects, and hence the Eurimages schemes would allocate funding to the well-established filmmakers with remarkable cultural capital rather than unknown debutants. *Spoor* – that Holland jokingly identified as an anarchist, feminist and ecological crime movie with elements of black comedy – perfectly fitted the Eurimages programme. It features an old woman who vehemently fights for animal rights, which requires constant confrontation with the local authorities representing the patriarchal establishment. The author of the literary original, Olga Tokarczuk – the recipient of the 2018 Nobel Prize For Literature 'for a narrative imagination that with encyclopedic passion represents the crossing of boundaries as a form of life' – who also co-authored the film script, was a recognised writer.[6] Holland and Tokarczuk's cultural capital accumulated due to their work, and the circulation of their public personas was easily transferable into financial capital to support the production of *Spoor*.

With her international reputation and ability to adapt to the new mode of transnational European co-productions, Holland was one of the beneficiaries of the newly emerging schemes of film financing, which facilitated her reintegration with European screen cultures. Her films examined the topics that were important for Central and Eastern Europe, such as shared cultural heritage and the communist past (*Janosik*, *Mr Jones* and *Charlatan*), as well as global issues of the contemporary ecological crisis (*Spoor*). While being exemplary for the newly emerging model of transnational, or supra-national, European cinema, these films reveal certain characteristics of Central European post-socialist cultural production, in which, as Jessie Labov explains,

> there is still a distinct profile to the countries once designated 'Central European', whether they are labeled 'postsocialist' by scholars or 'new/aspiring member states' by pundits. For all the variation and divergence in political regimes and policies since 1989, these countries are still grouped together as an object for comparative analysis. (Labov 2019, 188)

Holland's transnational European films demonstrate such a 'regional' identity in that they recognise the cultural and political distinctiveness of Central and Eastern Europe, yet they do not interrogate or subvert the region's cultural and geopolitical marginal position. To conclude, her European co-productions demonstrate that Central European film industries were integrated into larger system of European cultural production, while their representational politics maintain the Otherness of the region.

BIOPICS, OR EASTERN EUROPEAN HISTORY REVISITED?

Four out of five of Holland's European transnational co-productions made in the 2000s feature historical figures – Juraj Jánošík (1688–1713) in *Janosik – A True Story*, Leon Socha (1909–46)[7] in *In Darkness*, Gareth Jones (1905–35) in *Mr Jones* and Jan Mikolášek (1889–1973) in *Charlatan* – and as such, the films can be linked to her unorthodox American biopics *Total Eclipse* and *Copying Beethoven* (see Chapter Four). *Janosik* also represents Central European heritage cinema, or rather post-heritage, as the film revises the myth of the (in)famous Slovak highwayman. The script was written by Eva Borušovičova, who started working on it while a student. As she recollects, 'It took seven years to write the script. [. . .] Working on the script meant spending vast amounts of time researching documents and text sources. [. . .] the film is based mostly on historical sources and not on the legend' (Zamysłowska and Kuźmicki 2013, 208). Jánošík's legend has traversed across various regions of Central Europe, while being incorporated in different national cultures.[8] In Slovak, he is called Juraj Jánošík, in Polish, Jerzy Janosik and in Hungarian, Jánošík György. The folk hero was born in 1688 and died in 1713. In the early 1700s, he joined Francis II Rákóczi's war against the Habsburgs. After a lost battle, he was conscripted into the emperor's army; as a guardian at one of the imperial castles, he helped Tomáš Uhorčík, a leader of highwaymen, to escape from prison. After completing his military service, Jánošík took over the leadership of the bandit cohort that operated in the region of the Carpathian mountains of today's Slovakia, Hungary, Poland and the Czech Republic, which explains the 'transnationality' of his legend. Its appeal was due to the bandits' exceptionally noble behaviour as they robbed mostly rich merchants to share their loot with the poor. They did not kill their victims either. Jánošík was the most recognisable hero of the region whose figure was monumentalised in many poems, paintings, songs, legends and eventually films.[9]

In Poland, in 1973, Jerzy Passendorfer[10] made a thirteen-episode TV series, *Janosik*, then in 1974 compiled a full-length feature film from the selected parts of it. It was an adventure action movie with many comedic elements, employing spectacular mise-en-scène including natural locations of the Tatra mountains, colourful costumes and skilfully choreographed scenes of folk rituals such as weddings and religious festivities.[11] Intentionally or not, Holland and Adamik's film is a polemic against Passendorfer's version, beloved by the Polish audience, which was signalled by the title itself: *Janosik – A True Story*.[12] It was an attempt to see beyond the nationalistic legends around the mythical figure of Jánošík and to present him as a 'cross-border' hero (Hames 2014, 115). The film represents a rather unique example of Central European heritage cinema in that it does not mobilise the national sentiments as typical of the sub-genre.[13] The film's dialogues were recorded in Slovak and Polish accordingly, yet as

Figure 6.1 *Janosik – A True Story* (2009)

most of the actors were Slovak, they were dubbed in the Polish version, which de-naturalised the Polish language to a certain extent, as always occurs in the practice of dubbing. Furthermore, whether Polish or Slovak, the language of the dialogues sounds very contemporary, which is appropriate for the characterisation of the protagonist who does not fight national or social oppression but rather expresses existential dilemmas and incompatibility with any collective project of identity (see Fig. 6.1).

Not unlike Rimbaud in *Total Eclipse*, Janosik stands for a Western figure of a youthful rebel, as conceived within the framework of the 1960s counterculture. Adamik compared Janosik to Leonardo DiCaprio in that he was prematurely transformed into his own legend,[14] which had occurred previously to many iconic figures such as Jim Morrison and Jimi Hendrix. Holland herself also identified Janosik as a rebel, indicating that such a figure was frequently featured in her films. She saw his character as very contemporary and compared him to a young man returning from the war in Iraq or Afghanistan. 'Infected' with evil and violence, he cannot adapt to civilian life and thus he joins structures of organised crime.[15] Holland and Adamik's Janosik is a truly cross-border hero: he has been de-Polonised, yet his original Slovak identity has not been clearly articulated either, which is historically legitimate as he lived well before the nineteenth-century mobilisation of national sentiments. As if to reflect on this nationally ambivalent portrayal of the protagonist, the film depicts his environment as distinctively Central European. As Holland said, the Tatra region interested her as a space where Slovak, Czech and Polish elements cross over, establishing regional rather than national identities. When asked by the journalist whether the protagonist of their film will be Polish or Slovak, she responded: both, and first and foremost, he will be the Tatra region hero.[16] In *Janosik*, Holland and Adamik decided to explore sub-national identities, while simultaneously destroying the popular myth of the figure of Janosik manufactured by Polish socialist nationalistic culture.

Similarly, *In Darkness* also engages in sub-national identities, manifested through multilingual dialogues. Although ethnically Polish, the protagonist, Socha (Robert Więckiewicz), represents the Lviv local community rather than the Polish (hegemonic) nation. He speaks the local dialect of Polish called *balak*, as does his wife, Wanda (Kinga Preis), and their daughter Stefcia (Zofia Pieczyńska). Ignacy Higer (Herbert Knaup) – one of the Jews hidden by Socha in the Lviv sewers – who represents the educated middle-class, speaks perfect literary Polish, while also demonstrating a good command of German and Yiddish. His multilingualism connotes Jewish cosmopolitanism, but also questions the concept of a native language as a marker of national identity. Furthermore, *In Darkness* does not present the city landmarks that would evoke the town's 'Polonised' history that is often exploited by the politics of national nostalgia. On the contrary, in Holland's film, Lviv 'is deterritorialized from the national imaginary' (Lewis 2019, 538).

The protagonist of *In Darkness*, Socha, is as morally ambiguous as Leon Wolny from *Angry Harvest*[17] (see Chapter Three), and he is also an 'implicated subject', as defined by Michael Rothberg (2019), in that he benefits financially (to a certain point) from helping Jews. However, unlike Wolny, Socha finally experiences redemption; this happens when he leaves his daughter's First Communion ceremony to help the Jews who are in danger of drowning due to the heavy storm. Eventually, he transforms into a selfless and lonely hero. His cinematic friend and helpmate Szczepek (Krzysztof Skonieczny) at one point withdraws from helping the Jews out of fear, which is at odds with the historical records, according to which Stefan Wróblewski helped Socha until the end of the Second World War, and both of them, along with their wives, were recognised as Righteous Among the Nations. Leaving Socha in *In Darkness* as the Jews' only helper spectacularised the action of saving the Jews from drowning, while contributing to the romantic myth of an individual hero risking his own life to save others. Eventually, as we learn from the closing credits, he died prematurely: in 1946, Socha was fatally hit by a Red Army truck, while he was trying to rescue his daughter. Allegedly, as the final credits read, at his funeral somebody said that his death was a punishment for helping Jews. This information acknowledges Polish anti-Semitism, yet it is relegated to the non-diegetic coda.

Unlike the murky morality of *Angry Harvest* and *Europa, Europa*, *In Darkness* offers a story that is embedded within traditional Christian morality based on the concepts of sin and redemption. The shift from 'implicated subjects' to the figure of the 'righteous' hero is at odds with the 'after Jedwabne' debate on the Polish contribution to the Holocaust initiated by the publication of Jan Tomasz Gross's book *Neighbors* (2000), which depicts the massacre of the Jewish inhabitants of the village Jedwabne by their Polish neighbours. This hotly debated publication marked another turning point in the Polish discourse on the Holocaust, the first being Błoński's article (see Chapter Three), in that it demonstrated that Poles were not merely passive observers, selfless helpers or 'implicated subjects', but that some of them also acted as perpetrators. In one of many discussions concerning art's response to the change in the Polish discourse around the Holocaust, Holland said 'I do not see anything especially new that was added [to the subject] after 1989' (in Sariusz-Skąpska 2009, 35). Krzysztof Warlikowski – a renowned theatrical director, whose work has resolutley interrogated repressed Polish historical experiences – disagreed with her, claiming that it was only after 1989 that the historical debate reached wide circles of society instead of being confined to the elitist group of intellectuals and artists as it was during the period of state socialism. On other occasion, Holland admitted that Gross's and other historians' books on the Polish participation in the Holocaust did change the public discourse on the matter,[18] however, *In Darkness* seems to be outside this debate. Although the film does break with the stereotypical image of Jews as innocent victims, presenting them in a more diversified and nuanced fashion[19] and admitting the financial motives of the Polish helpers, it still condones the modernist ethical system, with the concepts of good and evil remaining intact.[20]

The redemption of the character of Socha is justified in historical sources and the testimonies of survivors. The gravity of his deed was recognised on various occasions, for example, Linda Zagzebski used his story, among others, to explain her exemplarist moral theory (Zagzebski 2017), which establishes an ethical framework for an individual acting in specific historical circumstances. Holland's film approaches Socha's story from a similar perspective. It symbolically counterbalances Polish responsibility for the Holocaust with an act of individual redemption (see Fig. 6.2). Tomasz Łysak claims that *In Darkness* involves a 'stereotypical perception of the trajectory of survival that usually occurs thanks to the help of a flawless hero or a redeemed villain' (Łysak 2020, 364). Polish anti-Semitism is acknowledged when local people are loitering in the liquidated ghetto, or in the character of the shop owner who decides to profit from Socha once she discovers he is hiding Jews. However, violent anti-Semitism is located in Bortko, once Socha's fellow criminal, now an auxiliary Ukrainian policeman. Compared to Władysław Pasikowski's film *Aftermath* (*Pokłosie*), released one year later, which presented Polish participation in the Holocaust in an uncompromising fashion, Holland's film, with its uplifting presentation of Polish–Jewish relations, appears to belong to the 'before Jedwabne' era.[21]

In his essay on *In Darkness*, Tomasz Żukowski claims that the film perpetuates the Polish phantasm of the 'Righteous' that he believes has

Figure 6.2 *In Darkness* (2011)

anti-Semitic undertones. The phantasm is based on the concept of the symmetry between Polish and Jewish suffering and the stereotype of a 'good anti-Semite' (Żukowski 2012, 1) developed within Polish culture to address those who helped Jews despite their biases and hostility towards them. Somehow paradoxically, the character of Socha, whose 'Polishness is peripheral' (Lewis 2019, 537), reproduces the redemptive phantasm produced at the centre of the Polish 'imagined community'. Lewis insightfully notices the modification of the national in the film's ending, claiming that its 'vision of nationhood [. . .] is unapologetically extroverted: it looks beyond the ambivalent peripheries and Lviv/Lwów to seek recognition from further afield, from Israel'. As he later claims, 'nationness itself becomes a cosmopolitan stance' as 'Lviv/Lwów is unburdened of its ethnocentric symbolism' (Lewis 2019, 538–9). While agreeing with Lewis, it needs to be noted that 'cosmopolitan nationness' refers to the politics of space and language only, while the deep structures of the narrative content recuperate the national phantasmatic scenario of redemption that mobilises national rather than cosmopolitan frames of memory.

'A LONELY WOMAN': FROM VICTIMISATION TO EMPOWERMENT

As discussed in the previous chapters, Holland's attitude to feminism, and gender issues more broadly, has been evolving from initial indifference and occasionally even enmity to its ultimate embracing. Her European films from the 2000s, especially *Spoor*, demonstrate the final stage of this change.

Although *Janosik* does not significantly depart from heteronormativity, it does undermine hegemonic gender patterns. The relationship between the bandits is based on homosocial bonds which manifests in their mutual and bodily expressed affectivity, exemplified in the warm friendship between Janosik and Tomáš Uhorčík (Ivan Martinka), and the passionate hostility between the former and Huncaga. Despite his position as the bandits' leader, Janosik does not represent a macho type, partly due to the casting of Václav Jiráček, who is not very tall and rather slim, while his facial expression does not convey stereotypical strength and roughness.[22] Importantly, Janosik's opponent in the bandits' cohort, Huncaga, who disobeys its moral code, represents masculinism in both his muscular body and his aggressive and frequently uncontrolled behaviour. The protagonist defies hegemonic gender discourse, while the antagonist adheres to it. In contrast to the dichotomous model of masculinity, all female characters do not act in accordance with normative gender roles. Jánošík's first love, Anusia (Tatiana Pauhofová), who makes love with him – 'as she could not resist it' – while being already engaged to somebody else is not punished for her deed, nor is she redeemed. Another girl, Zuzanna (Katarzyna Herman), drugs Janosik in order to have sex with him, which, according to her confession, she often does.[23] Barbara (Sarah Zoe Canner), Janosik's true love, makes him an object of her desiring gaze long before he notices her (see Fig. 6.3). Finally, she rescues him from committing suicide by drowning. Janosik functions as the object of female desire, which defies the gender politics typical of classical cinema. Furthermore, many of the female characters are represented outside of the patriarchal institution of the family, yet they are not stigmatised as lonely women but rather provided with agency.

The most extreme and ambivalent embodiment of the empowered figure of 'a lonely woman' is the local witch, Margeta (Maja Ostaszewska) (see Fig. 6.4). She is a fortune teller and healer who lives in the middle of the forest outside

Figure 6.3 *Janosik – A True Story* (2009)

Figure 6.4 *Janosik – A True Story* (2009)

the village. For her sex partner, she chooses Huncaga, whose immorality makes him a perfect match for her. When she gives birth to their baby boy, she does not express the tiniest trace of maternal instinct, which at first astonishes the bandit – when he witnesses her indifference to the baby's cry – and then terrifies him – when he discovers that she cut the baby's penis to use it as a necessary ingredient in one of her magical potions. On the one hand, Margeta can be seen as a radical transgression of normative femininity with maternal instinct being its vital attribute, while on the other hand her figure can be regarded as fitting the Western stereotype of the Eastern European woman. As Valentina Glajar and Dominica Radulescu note in their collection of essays about Eastern European women in Western cultural representations:

> Not fully Other, as Islamic or African women have been perceived, familiar because white and still European, Balkan and/or East European women form, in Western consciousness and imagination, the special category of what one critic has called 'the stranger in our midst'. (Glajar and Radulescu 2004, 3)

Their 'strangeness' is usually coded by their excessive sexuality and refusal, or, sometimes, inborn inability to perform the traditional feminine roles of a wife and mother. However, as a witch, Margeta has also emancipatory potential. As Adriana Madej-Stang noted, in the late twentieth century,

> The witch [. . .] is transformed into a symbol of a new woman defined in opposition to the patriarchal culture. In the eyes of feminists she became a role model to whom modern women could refer if they should want to gain personal independence and constitute themselves anew in the world. (Madej-Stang 2015, viii)

Holland's witches represent this emancipatory potential.

Charlatan also features a modern witch (Jaroslava Pokorná), an herbal healer, who lives at the margins of modernity and its medical discourse. She passes her secret knowledge to Mikolášek (see Fig. 6.5), a homosexual, who in future will use his expertise to heal everyone, from Nazis during the Second World War, through the powerful communist officials, to their powerless subordinates. Holland's film establishes a close link between non-normative models of femininity and sexuality. Mikolášek's apprenticeship with the healer opens his eyes to the world of nature and its poisonous and healing potential, which most likely facilitates the process of accepting his own 'natural' sexuality. In *Charlatan*, an old woman and a homosexual are integrated into the natural world, which is ruthlessly exploited by communist industrialisation and the collectivisation of agriculture.

Although in *In Darkness* and *Mr Jones* the female characters are overshadowed by the male protagonists, they also demonstrate the evolution of gender discourse in Holland's work. *In Darkness* recognises female sexual desire in the character of Chaja (Julia Kijowska) and in Socha's wife, Wanda. The former engages in an affair with a married man, Yanek (Marcin Bosak), who takes her instead of his wife and daughter to the hiding place in the sewers (Socha was able to hide a limited number of people only). Her behaviour can be deemed immoral, while her character qualifies as a stereotypical seducer or even 'a whore' who is heartlessly destroying another woman's family. She has sex with Yanek in the crowded ghetto room which Holland films in her customary affectless fashion without preceding it with an emotionally charged narrative context such as, for example, tender conversation or the exchange of

Figure 6.5 *Charlatan* (2019)

passionate gazes. The refusal to narrativise erotic scenes is nothing exceptional within Holland's work,[24] however, in this film it is embedded in the larger narrative of the Holocaust. The episode can be seen as 'bare sexuality' analogous to Giorgio Agamben's concept of 'bare life', 'in which life separates itself from its collective form of being' (Formis 2008, 189).

While in hiding, Chaja gives birth to her and Yanek's baby, yet she strangles it to death out of fear that its cry will betray their shelter. On the one hand, her infanticide ostentatiously marks the victimisation of a woman and her symbolic punishment for engaging in a sinful relationship. On the other hand, it can also be seen as a form of 'bare life' itself, and as such it would address a purely feminine experience of the Holocaust, something that is rarely recognised in world cinema or cultural production for that matter. As Joan Miriam Ringelheim noted in 1984:

> that women's experiences of the Holocaust were different from those of men; and that women had different survival capabilities, different work, roles, and relationships [. . .] all generalizations and gender-neutral statements about survival, resistance, the maintenance or collapse of moral values, and the dysfunction of culture in the camps and ghettos must be reassessed from the perspective of women. (Ringelheim 2003, 170)

While agreeing with Ringelheim's postulate to include women's perspective in Holocaust narratives, Pascale Rachel Bos advocates seeing them as emerging from many competing discourses such as gender, class, ethnicity and nationality (Bos 2003, 184). The narrative of *In Darkness* exemplifies such a discursive competition in which the masculine and national Polish perspectives gravitate towards a hegemonic position, while being momentarily sidelined by feminine subjectivities. Including the episode of infanticide inserts a feminine subject position into the masculine discourse, and as such it radically breaks with a gender-neutral perspective on the Holocaust experience.

The gender politics employed *In Darkness* have been subjected to criticism. For example, Deb Waterhouse-Watson and Adam Brown critique the film for 'a clear marginalization and disempowerment of women' (2016, 143), yet they overlook the complexity of its narrative and representational strategies. For example, they claim that Socha's wife, Wanda, is deprived of any agency and is occasionally even an obstacle to her husband's noble mission of hiding Jews, which, as the authors note, is at odds with the literary origin and historical facts as both of them were awarded the title of the Righteous Among the Nations in 1978. Waterhouse-Watson and Brown indicate that Wanda is shown as performing domestic duties without relating these to rescuing Jews. They conclude that the film 'reif[ies] dominative masculinity at the expense of femininity' (2016, 147–8, 150). Such a reading reduces the significance of the character of Wanda and perpetuates a devaluing of domestic space as the feminine domain.

Wanda does not represent passivity or a lack of subjectivity as she is instrumental in Socha's transformation from a petty thief into the 'righteous'. When her husband returns home after evacuating the Jews to the sewers, she fixes a bath for him and asks whether he saw the liquidation of the ghetto. He denies it, while she says matter-of-factly that Jesus, his Holy Mother and all Apostles were Jews (see Fig. 6.6). Unlike her husband, she seems to be free of the common Polish anti-Semitism based on the bias that the Jews killed Jesus Christ. Socha does not respond to this 'kitchen epiphany', yet this is a turning point in his attitude to the Jews he hides. The financial motivation gradually ceases and gives space to empathy that gradually takes over the erstwhile greed and calculation. Helena Goscilo and Beth Holmgren recognise the complexity of Wanda's character when they write that 'she is mercurial, quick to anger and forgiveness, but she is consistent in her sympathy for the Jews. She resists Socha's proposal to abscond with the Chigers' jewellery, make her a lady of leisure, and leave the Jews to perish' (Goscilo and Holmgren 2021, 130). Unlike her husband's path to redemption that is straightforward and linear, she experiences the whole spectrum of emotions from fear to hostility and selfless devotion. Her emotional imbalance may be seen as a sign of her unrecognised, yet affectively experienced, morally ambivalent position of 'implicated subject', as conceptualised by Michael Rothberg (2019; see Chapter Three). Her husband conveniently solves the moral problem when he asks the Jews to pretend to pay him for his help. Wanda is not privy to this staged

Figure 6.6 *In Darkness* (2011)

performance, and she believes Socha still benefits from it, thus, she faces up to her involvement in the Holocaust. Although pushed to the margins of the story, the female characters of Chaja and Wanda are important in that they embody (marginalised) gendered experience of the Holocaust that contrasts with the customary (masculine) script of wartime heroism, evoking instead the murky (im)morality of 'bare life' and implication in the Holocaust.

Like Wanda in *In Darkness*, the character of Ada Brooks (Vanessa Kirby) in *Mr. Jones* is also overshadowed by the male protagonist, yet she demonstrates her independence and prioritises her own professional ambitions over supporting Jones, the man she is emotionally involved with. Although her investment in communism can be seen as short-sighted, especially in the context of Jones's reports on famine in Ukraine, she is presented as attached to her own ideological agenda rather than passively adopting the other people's perspective.

The most progressive gender politics is developed in *Spoor*, a film that offers a truly feminist heroine who can also be seen as a modernised variant of the Central European witch as re-read by the feminist criticism. She does not only reject the patriarchal order but fights it, while transgressing the moral code of Western (patriarchal) culture. Duszejko (Agnieszka Mandat) is a retired civil engineer who has worked abroad. Now she lives her solitary life with two beloved she-dogs in a house on the outskirts of a small town located near to the Czech border. She works part-time as an English teacher in the primary school. One day, her dogs disappear, and it later transpires they were accidentally (?) killed by the local hunters, who, as it happens, represent the local establishment, consisting of the city major, an affluent businessman, the chief of the local police, and the Roman Catholic priest. They are cruel to animals, and they are abusive to women. Duszejko undertakes a secret plan to avenge her pets and all other animals killed by the hunters. She kills the men one by one, staging their deaths as murders committed by animals.

The protagonist of *Spoor* unmistakably refers to the ancient figure of a witch, and she is perceived as such. She lives outside of the local community and speaks a 'strange' language (English), and she is a vegetarian, which makes her an oddity in the hunting community. Unlike her neighbours, who are obedient Roman Catholics, she observes the cosmic universe in a search for the general principle that Magdalena Podsiadlo-Kwiecień interprets as a new animism and new paganism (Podsiadlo-Kwiecień 2021, 75). Duszejko is also a dedicated fighter for animals' rights. As Patricia Pisters notes, her opponents, the establishment men, 'consider her a crazy old woman, even a witch perhaps, but certainly not someone to take seriously' (Pisters 2020, 179). However, they are 'seriously' violent towards her. When, in the hunting sequence, Duszejko frantically tries to stop the hunters from shooting the animals, one man grabs her violently, while the priest delivers the most derisive remark: 'She is off her rocker'.

While fitting the ancient figure of a witch, Duszejko is surprisingly modern, especially when compared to the members of local community. She is familiar with the latest technology such as a laptop – that she uses to do astrological calculations and horoscopes – and a mobile phone. Her computer skills are contrasted with the local police chief's clumsiness and evident unfamiliarity with modern equipment. She 'loves' her SUV that allows her to move freely across the wilderness and, eventually, commit the acts of vengeance on behalf of animals. Furthermore, her clothes are strikingly modern, which visually distinguishes her from the local people. She wears a red bonnet and winter jacket in the same bright colour which contrasts the traditional hunters' green uniforms that look like museum artefacts. In her characterisation, Duszejko combines pre-modern and post-modern sensitivity, rejecting any human-imposed hierarchy of the natural world, while her opponents represent modern patriarchy oppressing anyone outside the privileged structure of power.

As Duszejko is a 'modern witch', her helpers are modernised as well. Although they are not provided with supernatural powers, their skills appear almost magical: her young friend Dyzio (Jakub Gierszal) is an exceptionally talented IT wizard, while Boros (Miroslav Krobot), an entomologist, is able to extract pheromones produced by insects that she uses in her vengeance plan. Duszejko establishes close and warm relationships with her friends and helpers, and, something that is especially important, she establishes a sexual relationship with Boros to the disappointment of her neighbour Batoga (Wiktor Zborowski), who is also attracted to her. In this peculiar 'love triangle', she is not presented as their object of desire but instead as an agent who can freely choose sexual partners. She is everything but a passive and submissive woman. This gender reversal is jokingly presented in the costume party at which Batoga shows up as a Little Red Riding Hood (which is especially humorous due to the fact that the actor, Wiktor Zborowski, is exceptionally tall), whereas Duszejko is dressed as the Wolf. This somewhat grotesque gender-bender can be seen as a carnivalesque masquerade, yet in the narrative context it becomes a self-evident metaphor for a genuine reversal of gender roles between the characters.

Her wolf-like behaviour is demonstrated in the church where a ceremony of naming the local school after St Hubert, the patron saint of hunting, takes place. When the priest – filmed from a low-angle – stands at the elevated pulpit, and says, 'Hunters are God's ambassadors to His creation', his overwhelming presence dominates the gathered people, who silently accept this shameless act of appropriating religion for the purpose of legitimising patriarchy and violence towards animals. Only Duszejko responds with righteous anger, shouting at him to get down from the pulpit (see Fig. 6.7). Disjunctive editing and a distorted soundtrack rapidly break with the film's codes of cinematic realism used earlier. These formal devices express Duszejko's disorientation and shock from seeing a wild boar's cadaver at the altar over which the boys'

Figure 6.7 *Spoor* (2017)

choir sings. The ceremony is a bloody, ritualistic performance of patriarchal power, not a customary Christian service. In this scene, as in many others, Duszejko responds to the oppressive and repugnant system with an intense affect that is perceived by others as a symptom of her psychological and emotional unbalance.

Gender politics in Holland's European transnational films reveal her complex approach to the issue. Except for Duszejko from *Spoor*, the other female characters do not fit a feminist, or post-feminist for that matter, agenda, yet they are not embedded within traditional patriarchal structures either. Most often, they function outside of these two ideological frameworks. Importantly, all these films recognise female sexuality, while its presentation wavers from a negative stereotype of it as a destructive force (*Janosik*) to a deconstruction of the cultural myth of the asexuality of older women (*Spoor*). Whether progressive or regressive, Holland represents female sexuality as not subordinated to reproduction, and locates it outside of the patriarchal framework of family. Duszejko from *Spoor* is a truly feminist heroine, however she is the only contemporary female character in Holland's films made in the 2000s, while the other are located in the past and their behaviour reflects the then dominant socio-cultural gender roles. The 'reluctant feminism' of the female characters – that might be seen as a drawback for the contemporary female audience – may originate from Holland's prioritising of global historical and political perspectives over gender issues.

The subordination of the gender and sexual issues to the political systems is especially visible in *Charlatan*, where the homosexual relationship is foregrounded as the main narrative focus, yet eventually is subordinated to the more general examination of Stalinist persecutions and atrocities. While the film attempts to balance the themes of gay romance and Stalinist oppression, they both remain underdeveloped. Although the eventual punishment of the homosexual characters is historically valid, a contemporary audience might object that this perpetuates the stereotype of the victimisation of gay people. Notwithstanding such objections, *Charlatan* testifies to Holland's struggles to examine simultaneously gender and sexuality issues as well as larger ideological systems of totalitarianism or authoritarianism. In her youth, Holland experienced political oppression, which seems to be still a driving force for her cinematic endeavours, while the awareness of gender oppression came much later when she lived abroad. In her youth, Holland was an emancipated anti-communist, while in her middle-age she became a feminist liberal. From national matters, she moved to the politics of identity. Only now does she demonstrate an awareness, as testified in *Spoor*, that these two are interconnected. The change in her attitude towards gender issues has been gradual, and for many hardly perceivable – as in a Deleuzian crack line – and her films reflect this. They offer seemingly consistent stories, yet the national identities crack under the pressure of gender factors that with time become more visible and prominent, while never appropriating the whole textual space.

FESTIVAL FILMS

Throughout her career, Holland's works have been acclaimed with various awards and distinctions. The first important recognition came with the FIPRESCI award for *Provincial Actors* at the Cannes film festival in 1980. In 1985, *Angry Harvest* was nominated for an Oscar, while in 1992, *Europa, Europa* received the Golden Globe for the best foreign film and was nominated for the Oscar for the best screenplay. In 1992, *Olivier, Olivier* was nominated for the Golden Lion at the Venice Film Festival and awarded at the Valladolid film festival. Her first Hollywood production, *The Secret Garden*, received, among others, the London Critics Circle Film Award for Kate Maberly in 1994. In 1995, *Total Eclipse* was nominated for an award at the San Sebastian Film Festival, and in 1999, *The Third Miracle* was nominated at the Mar Del Plata Film Festival. Finally, *Julie Walking Home* competed for the Golden Lion at the Venice Film Festival in 2002. Her last Hollywood production, *Copying Beethoven*, was screened at some film festivals, yet without successes. During her Hollywood career, Holland's presence in the international film circuit was rather limited and unsuccessful. Whether by coincidence or not, her transfer to transnational European cinema in the 2000s resulted in her more extensive participation in film festivals. *In Darkness* – which was also nominated for an Oscar in 2011 – was a turning point in her professional career. The film was nominated and won several awards at various film festivals such as in Mar Del Plata, Valladolid and Dublin. Although these are not as prestigious as the A-class film festivals, her works entered the transnational network of film circulation alternative to global Hollywood which was of paramount importance in boosting her reputation.

As recent research indicates, film festivals have increased the visibility of female authors whose films are frequently produced and distributed outside of the hegemonic mediascape. As Skadi Loist explained:

> Film festivals traditionally represent a wider range of film productions since their selection process is not based on the commercial potential of a film but the perceived quality and innovation of filmmaking. Here, small low-budget films, arthouse films, and art cinema as well as other thematic films find a platform. Festivals are especially important for small films with a small marketing budget in order to gain attention and visibility. The selection processes, positive film criticism, and awards at film festivals help films to gain awareness for further commercial exploitation and international distribution. (Loist and Prommer 2019, 104)

Loist's quantitative analysis of the participation of German filmmakers at the film festivals indicated that films made by women are more often included in the official competition and nominated for various awards than their male colleagues. They are also more successful (Loist and Prommer 2019, 104). As she further explained, various feminist organisations requested leading film festivals to reconsider their programming policy to 'sign the 50:50 by 2020 gender parity pledge, which aims for gender monitoring and inclusive programming'. Among the festivals that responded to this pledge was the Berlin International Film Festival, the Berlinale (Loist and Prommer 2019, 106). *Spoor* was submitted to the main competition at the 67th Berlin International Film Festival and it won the Artur Bauer Prize (Silver Bear) which is given to films that open new perspectives in cinema. Holland's next film, *Mr Jones* (2019), a Polish-British-Ukrainian co-production, was selected for the main competition at the 2019 Berlinale,[25] while *Charlatan* (2020), a Czech-Slovak-Polish-Irish co-production, competed at the 2020 Berlinale.

The Berlin festival belongs to the A-class film festival group, and it has its own profile and programming policy. Most importantly, it has established a strong platform for the presentation of Eastern and Central European films. As Marijke de Valck notes, it is 'a powerful media event, where local issues could become global concerns and politics reappeared on the festival agenda, albeit with a humanist and pacifist tint' (de Valck 2007, 74). The Berlinale implements the broader principle of establishing the space of encounter between the national and the global which facilitates a free flow of cultural production. Whether due to its gender politics or not, Polish female filmmakers' works are presented in Berlin more often than anywhere else. Małgorzata Szumowska and Agnieszka Holland are regulars, which has contributed to their *auteur* reputation. As Cindy Wong succinctly pointed out, 'within the festival context, it is difficult to separate the films from the auteur. With concerted efforts, auteurs and festivals have developed in a symbiotic relationship embodied by film, mediated by business concerns' (Wong 2011, 65). As the film festival circuit has recently rapidly expanded, Wong claims that successful 'festival films' might be nowadays seen as a semi-genre as it has several relatively stable characteristics: 'seriousness/minimalism in vision and sound; their open and demanding narrative structures; their intertextuality (including their use of "stars"); and, finally, their subject matter, including controversy as well as freedom' (Wong 2011, 68). These semi-generic conventions function as regulatory mechanisms for a significant sector of contemporary film production and distribution designated for the non-mainstream distribution network.

Holland's films made in Europe in the 2010s fit the model of the 'festival film' as proved by their submission to the events. They examine vital subject matters such as the Holocaust in *In Darkness*, animal rights in *Spoor*, the Holodomor in *Mr Jones* and Stalinist oppression in *Charlatan*. They were made in a minimalist style that opposes the generic conventions of historical films usually employing an epic perspective and spectacular mise-en-scène. Most of the action of these films takes place in tight interiors, such as the sewers and Sochas' small apartment in *In Darkness*, cramped offices, hotel apartments, crowded train compartments and poverty-stricken countryside cottages in *Mr Jones*, and finally, Mikolášek's dark offices and tiny prison cells in *Charlatan*. The occasional long shots of exterior spaces are brief and not aimed at spectacular visual effects. The colour palette is always toned down, while the settings and costumes are realistic. The lighting appears as the most expressive component of cinematic form: in *In Darkness*, Jolanta Dylewska, director of photography, uses it in a virtuoso way to create brighter and darker spots in the sewers that are pitch black anyway; in *Spoor* the lighting creates the effect of a halo around the character of 'Good News', a young woman who is sexually exploited by the local businessman, while taking care of her underage brother; in *Mr Jones* in the scene of the conversation between Jones and Duranty, the former is illuminated with bright yet soft lighting, whereas the latter's face is hidden in a total darkness, which symbolically signifies their relation to the truth about the Holodomor; finally, in *Charlatan* bright light is often used to signify Mikolášek's healing abilities and to distinguish the rare moments of freedom the lovers experience in the bucolic countryside (see Fig. 6.8), while darkness is used for showing the oppression of their closeted relationship.

Figure 6.8 *Charlatan* (2019)

Although the narrative structure of these films is usually linear and chronological, it is often episodic, with no well pronounced cause-and-effect relationship between consecutive scenes. The stories offer a standard exposition and resolution, however the climactic points are not clearly defined, and the ending is often left open, like *Spoor*'s oneiric scene that serves as a fantasy-like coda. In *In Darkness* and *Mr Jones*, the narrative resolution is complemented by the extratextual historical information concerning the deaths of both protagonists. Finally, all the films consider controversial subject matters and frequently transgressive imagery: *In Darkness* shows Jewish characters who are morally ambiguous and conflicted with one another, which is at odds with the dominant representational strategies employed in most Holocaust films; in *Spoor* an act of moral transgression occurs when an old woman kills four men as punishment for them killing animals; *Mr Jones* features episodes of cannibalism; *Charlatan* presents a gay character who collaborates with the Nazis and then with the communist regime for a long time until he becomes the latter's victim due to an unfortunate event. Eroticism is foregrounded in all these films – except for *Mr Jones* – even though there is no customary narrative justification for its presence; for example, in *Janosik*, in one scene the protagonist returns to his village from his military service, in the next one, he has passionate sex with a young girl who, as it transpires, is engaged to somebody else, which is followed by a scene of him joining the bandits. There is no sufficient information concerning their amorous relationship in the past (if there was any), and it is unclear whether his decision to join the gang was motivated by his unrequited love. The scenes are joined through the principle of sequential temporality rather than a narrative relationship of cause and effect. Similarly, the first sexual encounter between Mikolášek and his assistant occurs rather unexpectedly, and it starts with them violently slapping each other, which quickly leads to passionate sex. When Holland momentarily punctures the grand historical narratives with erotic excess it evokes the essence of Eastern European bodily discourse that established the body as subjected to pain instilled by totalitarian regimes but also as a source of (guilty/perverse) pleasure (see Mazierska, Mroz and Ostrowska 2016). Unadorned eroticism in historical dramas or biopics subverts generic conventions, which may be appealing to the film festival audiences who expect non-standard cultural production.

STRADDLING: INSIDE AND OUTSIDE OF EASTERN EUROPE

Aside from promoting *auteur* cinema, film festivals significantly contribute to the development of transnational discourses. As Dina Iordanova explains, '[f]estivals play a central, even if less recognised role, in transnational mediation' (Iordanova 2010b, 14). However, as Thomas Elsaesser notices, such a transnational mediation occurs within the clashing system of contradictory expectations:

> on one hand, to be on the side of resistance, struggle, activism, and thereby to represent the critical conscience of the nation; and on the other hand, to make the nation instantly identifiable through an appeal to a set of national (and often tourist) clichés: recognizable landscapes, mythologies, artifacts, architectural landmarks, or cityscapes, but also more subtly or insidiously through what one might call *autoexoticism* or *self-interpellation*, that is, the pressure to present one's characters (and one's nation) to the gaze of the other (the Big Other, or merely an international audience), in the terms that the other expects and demands. (Elsaesser 2019, 34)

Holland's transnational films made in Europe in the 2000s exemplify such self-interpellation which is manifest in the politics of representation of the region of Eastern Europe. They all question nationalism, yet they present the region as distinctly different from the Western part of the continent as might be expected by the international audience. On the one hand, these films advocate for inclusive and democratic societies, which can be seen as an attempt to integrate the region with modern (Western) Europe, yet simultaneously they foreground its Otherness by means of autoexoticising textual strategies. Holland's films reinvent Eastern Europe for the contemporary international audience, in a way not unlike what Western travellers did in the eighteenth century as described by Larry Wolff in his seminal book *Inventing Eastern Europe* (1994).[26] As a travelling filmmaker, Holland has developed an 'outside' look at her native country and region, while still sustaining an 'inside' perspective, which is an illustrative example of Elsaesser's concept of 'double occupancy'.

In *Janosik*, the narrative content and visual design recognise the cultural heritage of the region yet present it as distinctly 'other' to the Western tradition. The protagonist is a regional rather than a national hero, which is also historically justified as nationalism was non-existent in the eighteenth century when the action of the film takes place. Janosik, his cohort, and the locals inhabit the Carpathian mountains that spread across several contemporary countries. The numerous and prolonged long shots of the terrain demonstrate that in the world of nature there are no clearly demarcated borders that would separate one group of people from the other. The beginning of the film refers to the historical event of Rákóczi's War of Independence (1703–11), which was aimed at liberating Hungary from Habsburg rule. Although Slovak rather than Hungarian, Janosik takes part in the war, which foregrounds its anti-imperialist aspect as opposed to nationalistic one. Furthermore, when the bandits later discover that one of the robbed victims, a rich nobleman, Lani (Krzysztof Stroiński), is a Rákóczi supporter, they let him go free. Out of gratitude, or shared hostility to the Habsburgs, he invites Janosik and his friends to his estate where they dine and drink together, and the class difference seems to cease altogether. His sympathetic character is contrasted with the imperial officials who are presented as repulsive figures. Their obese bodies are squeezed into tight clothes, their wigs are often too small, which produces an effect of a mediocre masquerade rather than court sophistication and officialdom. When confronted with the bandits on the mountain roads, the stiffness of their bodies is especially visible and is contrasted with the swift and agile bodies of the assailants. With their clothes, wigs and formless bodies, they stand out in the pristine world of nature, whereas the highwaymen blend perfectly with their environment. The highwaymen's clothes – inspired by genuine folk tradition – are casual, unadorned and in toned-down colours that seamlessly mimic their habitat. The long braided hair of the locals is similar to the dreadlocks typical of Caribbean culture and contemporary counterculture, with both questioning hegemonic Western power. Janosik, with his slim body and delicate facial features, looks as androgynous as many rock stars from the 1960s and 1970s. In general, *Janosik* employs mise-en-scène to connote the Habsburg servants and supporters as representing oppressive culture and civilisation – or rather their grotesque caricature – and the bandits and the inhabitants of the Carpathian region as standing for nature. However, nature is not depicted in sentimental, bucolic terms but also as an often cruel and terrifying domain of primal instincts. Regardless of positive or negative connotations, the West stands for (oppressive) order and civilisation, whereas the East, here the Carpathian region, embodies the world of untamed nature that is simultaneously appealing and appalling.

Janosik shows various rituals and customs of the local folk culture. For example, there is a funeral ceremony during which people gather around the body exposed in the coffin to bid it farewell for the eternal journey (see Fig. 6.9). One person covers the male corpse's eyes and mouth with coins to provide for him in the afterlife and to keep his senses closed to prevent him from returning as a ghost to those who are still alive. The ritual of midsummer night appears as an enchanting drunken spectacle of a trance-like dance during which unleashed senses take over the mind. Interestingly, when Janosik and his cohort show up at the event, he sees his parents mixing with the young people in the frenzied festivity. His mother is visibly tipsy, whereas his father is sober, which may suggest women's eagerness to lose control over their conscious minds. Margeta, the witch, who also participates in the festivity, epitomises female connectedness to the supernatural that is as much captivating as it is fearsome.

Janosik, as the only male figure, has access to the unreal as visualised in the two fantasy scenes of him flying over the mountains and seeing the Holy Mother walking on the water. The second vision is designed as a primitive folk painting, while also using Frida Kahlo-like stylisation. These unrealistic inserts into the otherwise historically accurate story can be seen as examples of magic realism that Aga Skrodzka detects as a distinct trend in post-1989 East Central European cinema.[27] As she explains, many filmmakers of the region

> address in their films the monumental transition into the new, post-Wall era of capitalist democracy *without* sacrificing all of the old prejudices, lifestyles, ideas, spirits and things. That intention to preserve the past, whether nostalgically, superstitiously, grotesquely or simply out of habit,

Figure 6.9 *Janosik – A True Story* (2009)

is in itself constitutive of tradition. [. . .] While tradition usually refers to estimable and celebrated inheritance, the magic realist tradition, which is the subject of this narrative, embraces the shameful, parochial, wrecked, forgotten and naïve. Frequently uncanny, even abject, the characters, events and places [. . .] speak of the ways in which global political, historical and economic shifts affect local culture. Importantly, despite the local space of enunciation, the films refuse to glorify the indigenous. (Skrodzka 2012, xi)

While agreeing with Skrodzka that these films aim at preserving the tradition of the indigenous inhabitants of the region, I would argue that the presentation of the content in highly stylised form produces an effect of astonishment[28] that cannot be ascribed to the insider's perspective but must be attributed to those who are looking at it from the outside. Thus, the imagery revives the indigenous folk culture, yet it does it for the Western gaze. Janosik's gaze mediates the inside and outside perspective. As he returns home after many years of service in the imperial army, he finds it uncanny. Thus, he decides to leave again, this time as a bandit and vagrant who feels estranged everywhere. As most likely did Holland, who returned to East Central Europe after spending some time in the West only to discover the uncanniness of her affective home.

In *Mr Jones*, the Western gaze is somehow 'naturally' mediated by the protagonist, the eponymous Welsh journalist. During his journey across Ukraine, which is not authorised by the Soviet authorities, he observes the country, devastated and tormented by famine, and its inhabitants, whose existence is reduced to the Agamben's 'bare life'. The lowest point is the scene of the involuntary cannibalism Jones commits when he joins a bunch of orphaned children who have been nourishing themselves with chunks cut from their sibling who died from the cold and malnutrition (see Fig. 6.10). This episode, which was vehemently protested by the family of the late journalist, is also problematic due to its questionable reference to historical facts.[29] On the one hand, cases of cannibalism during the Holodomor did occur, as reported by the historian Timothy Snyder, who, however, emphasises that: 'People in Ukraine never considered cannibalism to be acceptable. Even at the height of famine, villagers were outraged to find cannibals in their midst, so much so they were spontaneously beaten or even burned to death' (Snyder 2012, 51). He also stated that,

> Cannibalism is a taboo of literature as well as life, as communities seek to protect their dignity by suppressing the record of this desperate mode of survival. Ukrainians outside Soviet Union, then and since, have treated cannibalism as a source of great shame. Yet while the cannibalism in Soviet Ukraine in 1933 says much about the Soviet system, it says nothing about Ukrainians as a people. (Snyder 2012, 51)

Figure 6.10 *Mr Jones* (2019)

I agree with the last statement wholeheartedly, yet cannot help but ponder whether a contemporary audience, especially from the Western world, while watching Holland's film, would think the same. Especially considering that the protagonist, after realising what he has done, involuntarily retches and expels the abject from his body, while the children remain catatonically stoic, as if incapable of the instinctual reaction of revulsion. Now, the question arises: does a non-Ukrainian filmmaker have the right to break the taboo that Snyder mentions? As a non-Ukrainian scholar, I will leave it unanswered.

Unlike *Janosik*, *In Darkness* and *Mr Jones*, *Spoor* is based on a literary fiction and as such it is not subjected to the test of 'historical truth'; however, it, too, mobilises the outside/inside look at the region of Central East Europe. Lewis prizes *Spoor* for its cosmopolitan approach to the world of nature inhabited by animals and the protagonist:

> In both the film's characterization and visual effects, border-crossing worldliness is directly opposed to national introspection and emerges as a principal theme of the film [. . .] Nature is colorful, expansive, and borderless, in contrast to the short-sighted parochialism of national culture, espoused by the corrupt and male-dominated hunting culture of the local community. (Lewis 2019, 539)

National myths and normative models of masculinity wield great power in contemporary Poland, so it may be seen as justified to critique them.[30] The film peeks beneath the surface of the strong prevailing socio-cultural norms to show their dark and violent underbelly by means of narrative and visual excess, as exemplified in the mentioned scene of the blasphemous church sermon or the episode of sexual exploitation of 'Good News' by the local businessman, Wnętrzak (Borys Szyc), not to mention all the bloody hunting rituals.

While denouncing the oppressive aspects of Polish patriarchal reality, these images fit the stereotype of Eastern European backwardness and savagery. Deliberately, I do not use the phrase 'Western stereotype' to emphasise that this representational politics originates from 'within' as a part of the process of 'autoexoticism' conceptualised by Elsaesser. The process involves internalising the perspective imposed by the powerful centre. As Graham Huggan explains in his seminal book *The Postcolonial Exotic: Marketing the Margins*:

> the exotic is not [. . .] an inherent *quality* to be found 'in' certain people, distinctive objects, or specific places; exoticism describes, rather, a particular mode of aesthetic *perception* – one which renders people, objects and places strange even as it domesticates them, and which effectively manufactures otherness even as it claims to surrender to its immanent mystery. (Huggan 2001, 13)

In *Spoor*, the hunters look exotic because Duszejko, an outsider to the local community, sees them as such. It is her perspective that the viewer is exposed to through the film.

Spoor reverses the customary relationship between the familiar and the exotic, as well as between the centre and the margin. Duszejko and her gang live at the margins of the local community, and they all are somehow 'foreign'. As already mentioned, Duszejko has worked abroad as a civil engineer and now she teaches English in the local school. The computer wizard translates William Blake's poetry from English to Polish. His love interest, 'Good News', works in a second-hand shop where she sells Western clothes and accessories. Duszejko's neighbour is of German-Polish origin, whereas her lover is a Czech entomologist. Estranged from the local community, they nonetheless represent familiar types within the field of Western modern culture in that they are well versed in modern technologies, they wear casual clothes, and they participate in global internet cultures. The scene of the outdoor marijuana party during which Duszejko, Matoga and Boros sing 'House of the Rising Sun' associates them with Western hippie counterculture, with which many young Polish people identified during the period of state socialism. By contrast, all the negative characters who represent the Polish nationalistic centre are presented as 'exotic'. The hunters wear traditional hunting uniforms and old-fashioned hats that look like theatrical costumes rather than comfortable and warm gear to be worn while exploring the wilderness. Their hunting rituals are cruel, ancient performances, while in everyday life they demonstrate uncivilised, according to social norms, behaviour, as exemplified by the chief of local police who sits in his office barefoot. Thus, Duszejko and her friends are characterised as familiar (Western) Europeans, while their opponents are exotic Poles who celebrate their collective identity in a rampant, cruel and domineering way.

The margins, as represented by Duszejko and her friends, are provided in the film with significant agency to resist the oppressive centre, a possibility which bell hooks recognised a long time ago:

> Marginality [is a] central location for the production of a counterhegemonic discourse that is not just found in words but in habits of being and the way one lives [. . .]. [Marginality is] a site one stays in, clings to even, because it nourishes one's capacity to resist. It offers the possibility of radical perspectives from which to see and create, to imagine alternatives, new worlds. (hooks 1990, 341)

In her works, Holland has explored various margins of dominant discourses, yet *Spoor* is the first film that presents the margin as equipped with agency and power. However, the empowerment of the margin coincides with the exoticisation of the centre, and these two aspects stand respectively for West and East, which solidifies the geopolitical division rather than subverting it. In *Janosik*, the subversive potential of the exotic vanishes once the collective regional myth is translated into the individual existential drama of the protagonist. Socha's lower-class character, representing the Eastern margins of the Polish nation, is familiarised through his inscription into the hegemonic heroic script and his experience of Christian redemption. The homosexual herbal healer's drama in *Charlatan* is embedded in a tale of communist oppression and the ethical system of Christianity (as demonstrated in the scene of the protagonist praying at the Cross). In Holland's transnational European films, the exotic is scrutinised by the Western gaze, and as such it often loses its subversive potential.

Holland's career in the 2000s is truly transnational and trans-medial as she has continued working for American and global television networks and streaming platforms, while being also active in transnational European politically engaged cinema. Her return to European cinema was possible due to the newly emerging funding schemes and programmes such as Euroimages. As these resources were aimed at rejuvenating European cinema to compete with mainstream Hollywood, the funds were mostly distributed among art cinema projects examining urgent issues concerning European past and present. Holland embraced these new opportunities, while responding to the aesthetic and thematic expectations, which in her case meant also returning to the model of political and socially engaged cinema that she had practised in Poland in the 1970s (Chapter Two), and to a certain extent during her European exile in the 1980s (Chapter Three). At the same time, her films made in the 2000s also continued certain strands of her American works, exploring the historical past through individual biographies. In her historical films, regardless of their genres, Holland has explored either the Victorian period or the totalitarian eras of the Second World War and communism. Although geopolitically distant, both epitomised bodily oppression, which explains Holland's emphasis on the body that is presented as either an abject or a tormented object.

While portraying the region of Central East Europe, whether in films made in North America or Europe, Holland does it from the position of 'double occupancy', in that the films present legitimate criticism of its sociopolitical and cultural realities, but at the same time they exoticise it and thus perpetuate the myth of the Otherness of Eastern Europe. Holland's films made in the 2000s present Eastern Europeanness from the perspective of the Western centre rather than the Eastern periphery and, thus, I consider them as manufacturing a post-communist exotic. They involve contradictory impulses of critical interrogation of the communist past and the following upsurge of the national ideologies, as well as the commodification of these realities and the transformation of them into a saleable product, which testifies to the assimilation of the Western gaze and its attendant ideological framework. Thus, the subversive potential of the post-communist exotic is ultimately embedded in the logic of late capitalism. In that, Holland's transnational European films can be seen as analogous to the literary migrant text that Subha Xavier sees as 'constantly caught in the lure of, and struggle against, exoticism and otherness' (Xavier 2016, 64). Holland's authorship emerges as contradictory in that the films made in the 2000s are consistent in terms of exploring vital subject matter related to the region of Eastern Europe, while using a transparent, self-effacing (authorial) style as if to prevent the content being overshadowed by the form. At the same time, her agency within the areas of film production, distribution and exhibition has significantly increased since re-entering European (transnational) cinema. For the last two decades she has been more visible in European screen cultures than ever. Her visibility and reputation are also increased due to her carefully performed public persona which is the subject of the next chapter.

NOTES

1. A comprehensive study of the transformation of the media industry in Central Europe is provided by Petr Szczepanik in his book *Screen Industries in East-Central Europe* (2021b); see also Iordanova 2002.
2. *In Darkness*, press kit. *In Darkness*, press kit. Available at https://www.sonyclassics.com/indarkness/In_Darkness_presskit.pdf (accessed 10 November 2022).
3. *In Darkness*, press kit.
4. For more information on the Media Programme that has been instrumental in developing film industries in unified Europe see Jones 2017, 29–61.
5. In a similar vein, Luisa Rivi noted, 'Eurimages has constantly prioritized the cultural relevance of the projects it has sustained because these were deemed to be vehicles of European identity' (Rivi 2007, 62). Eventually, the mechanisms of financing Eastern

European transnational film production supported a particular type of film that Ioana Uricaru defined as: 'low-budget, artistically important (as defined by critics and film festivals), auteur-driven by a strong director or writer-director who has confirmed repeatedly the originality and force of his [sic] vision, and placed in a market niche that does not overlap with commercial blockbusters' (Uricaru 2012, 443–4).
6. Nobelprize.org, https://www.nobelprize.org/prizes/literature/2018/tokarczuk/facts/ (accessed 11 November 2022).
7. See Leopold Socha. https://web.archive.org/web/20131006174759/http://www.sprawiedliwi.org.pl/pl/family/637,socha-leopold/ (accessed 15 November 2022).
8. For a comprehensive presentation of Janosik's figure see Raßloff 2009; Sroka 2004.
9. For a comprehensive survey of Janosik's portrayals in cinema and television, see Skoczek 2007.
10. Similarly to Holland, Jerzy Passendorfer also had connections with Czechoslovakia. He began studying film directing at the Film School in Łódź and then continued at FAMU in Prague, where he stayed for some time after graduating and made several educational films. After returning to Poland, he made many films supporting communist ideology, while using the conventions of genre cinema, especially war and action movies.
11. Passendorfer's *Janosik* exemplifies what Józef Burszta, a Polish ethnographer, called 'folklorism', which he defined as a modified variant of folk culture manufactured for mass audience' (Burszta 1974, 27). Folklorism adjusted folk culture to the ideological tenets of real socialism, while erasing ethnic differences and foregrounding social class identities. The protagonist, played by Marek Perepeczko, and his cohort were Polonised (see Piotr Burda, 'Janosik. Buntownik bez powodu', *Gazeta Wyborcza*, no. 214, 2008, 16), while the action was moved from the original eighteenth to the nineteenth century when Poland was partitioned by Russia, Prussia and Austro-Hungary. In consequence, the figure of the noble bandit who robbed the rich – the Austro-Hungarian administration or the loyal subjects of the *Kaiser* – and supported the poor – the Polish peasants from the Tatra mountains region – was conveniently imprinted into the socialist concept of class struggle, while also mobilising nationalist sentiments that were still alive after the 1968 anti-Semitic campaign. With its blatant nationalism and nostalgic presentation of the past, Passendorfer's TV series, along with other costume dramas and adaptations of classical literature, formed a peculiar model of socialist heritage cinema that adjusted the past to fit the ideological discourse developed in 1970s Poland. However, at the same time, as Anikó Imre noticed, the actor who played the eponymous character, Marek Perepeczko, was one of the 'movie actors who established a limited transnational fandom within the socialist bloc' (Imre 2012, 126).
12. Adamik said that in *Janosik* they wanted to recreate genuine folklore, not its commercialised version that could be called, after Burszta, 'folklorism' (Kasia Adamik and Agnieszka Holland, 'Janosik jak DiCaprio', *Przekrój*, no. 15, 2002, 42). Karolina Pasternak made a similar comparison (Karolina Pasternak, 'Janosik po liftingu', *Przekrój*, no. 35, 2009, 38).
13. The Polish film reviewer notes that Holland's film returns the mythical figure of Janosik to Slovaks (Lech Kurpiewski, 'Prawie jak Braveheart', *Newsweek Polska*, no. 35, 2009, 75).
14. Adamik and Holland, 'Janosik jak DiCaprio'.
15. Adamik and Holland, 'Janosik jak DiCaprio', 20, 21.
16. Agnieszka Holland, 'Cała prawda o Janosiku', interview by Cezary Polak, *Dziennik. Polska-Europa-Świat*, no. 63, 2008, 20.
17. Holland herself indicated this similarity (Agnieszka Holland and Jolanta Dylewska, 'Życie w piekle', interview by Dorota Paciarelli, *FilmPro*, no. 2, 2010, 36–41).
18. Agnieszka Holland, 'Zamiast przeklinać ciemności, lepiej zapalić świeczkę', interview by Jacek Rakowiecki, *Film*, no. 1, 2012, 48–50.

19. The reviewer of *Variety* noted that 'the director resists portraying her Jewish protagonists as purely sympathetic victims. Instead, the core group consists of con men, cheats and tight-fisted business owners who constantly fight and argue among themselves'. As he goes on '[h]istorically speaking, this harsh approach is the most honest [. . .] At the same time, in dramatic terms, it severely jeopardizes audience identification, making for long unpleasant stretches in which we resist the characters and wish they weren't so petty when bigger concerns' (Peter Debruge, 'In Darkness', *Variety* 424, no. 5, 2011, 27. https://search-1ebscohost-1com-10a01bj6r1a43.han3.lib.uni.lodz.pl/login.aspx?direct=true&db=f5h&AN =65454532&lang=pl&site=eds-live). Elias Berner also noted the diversified portrayal of the Jews: 'The Jews are actively, and in a self-organized way, hiding in the sewer; they do not passively await their extermination (or rescue). They are not shown as a collective either, but as a group of – often conflicting – individuals. The film neither focuses on one of them by means of a certain musical theme, nor does it bind them together through a specifically "Jewish" style of music, as in *Schindler's List*' (Berner 2021, 163).
20. In her recent book on the Holocaust, Matilda Mroz qualifies *In Darkness* as one of the '[p]ost-millennial films that continue to draw on narratives of Polish rescue' while also admitting that it 'trouble[s] the idealised vision of Polish helpers' (Mroz 2020, 34, n. 49).
21. For an extensive analysis of *In Darkness*, see Anita Pluwak (2015). She examines the film as ambivalently employing melodramatic structures.
22. This casting decision was especially important in Poland as the Czech actor was a striking opposition to muscular and tall Marek Perepeczko, who played the titular role in Passendorfer's TV series and film.
23. One of the Polish reviewers, Janusz Wróblewski, finds the erotic scene between Zuzanna and Janosik gratuitous, while also complaining about the character of Janosik, whom he sees as a cross-over between the figures of Hamlet and Jesus Christ (Janusz Wróblewski, '*Janosik. Prawdziwa historia*', *Polityka*, no. 36, 2009, 42–3).
24. The reviewer of *Variety* mentions the erotic scenes, commenting on them as typical of Holland's work: 'Holland goes out of her way to include a number of sexual encounters in the film, as if to say that even in the direst circumstances, man finds time to make love. Far from gratuitous, the scenes reveal important connections between characters; still, it's odd for the helmer [sic] to spotlight these details and leave out nearly anything that describes the dull routine of life underground' (Peter Debruge, 'In Darkness', *Variety* 424, no. 5, 2011, 27).
25. On the occasion of *Mr Jones* being accepted to the main competition of the Berlinale, a Polish journalist of the right-wing periodical *Do Rzeczy* sarcastically commented on the festival's profile, deriding it as a bastion of liberal leftist ideology promoting Marxism-Leninism and LGBT (Remigiusz Włast-Matuszkiewicz, 'Zemsta niedźwiedzia', *Do Rzeczy*, no. 9, 2019, 52).
26. For a comprehensive discussion of the ideological and geopolitical frameworks of the concept of Eastern Europe, see Starosta 2016, 3–46.
27. Fredric Jameson applied the term of magic realism to Holland's work much earlier. In his 1986 essay, 'On Magic Realism in Film', he considered *Fever* as an example of magic realism that he understood as 'as a possible alternative to the narrative logic of contemporary postmodernism' (Jameson 1986, 302).
28. The Polish reviewer reported in his review that the viewers were laughing at the image of the Holy Mother walking on the water (Paweł T. Felis, 'Słowiańska gorączka Janosika', *Gazeta Wyborcza*, no. 206, 2009, 15).
29. See 'The True Story behind the "True Story" of *Mr Jones*' by Gareth Jones' great nephew, Philip Colley, published on Gareth Jones website: https://www.garethjones.org/mr_jones/ true_story.htm (accessed 25 April 2023).

30. The film's subversive work is confirmed by Amy Taubin, who reported that when *Spoor* premiered at the 2017 Berlin Film Festival, where it won a Silver Bear (the Alfred Bauer prize), a correspondent for Poland's state media outlet wrote that Holland 'had made a pagan film promoting ecoterrorism'. She and Tokarczuk had already been branded *targowiczanin*, the vernacular Polish term for traitor (Amy Taubin, 'Mother Earth: An Unclassifiable Eco-Mystery, Agnieszka Holland's *Spoor* Shows off the Pioneering Pole's Stylistic Verve-And Nerves of Steel', *Film Comment* 54, no. 2, March–April 2018, 52).

CHAPTER 7

Performing authorship: from celebrity director to celebrity activist

In early October 2022,[1] I attended the Alina Margolis-Edelman Award[2] ceremony at the Marek Edelman Dialogue Centre in Łódź, Poland. The award is given to people and institutions that help children, and Agnieszka Holland is the chairwoman of the jury. I saw her swiftly moving across the hall while greeting, hugging, and chatting with the people in attendance. At one point, two women approached her and said something to her with a sheepish smile. Responding with a nod, she stood next to one of them, while the other photographed them with her mobile phone. Then the women changed places for another shot. Holland left them instantly after the impromptu session to join other guests, whom she welcomed with a smile and a brief exchange. Meanwhile the women, happy and proud, gazed at the screens of their mobile phones.

The selfies I witnessed with the two women leave no doubt whatsoever that Agnieszka Holland is a celebrity. However, the event she participated in provides a special context for her celebrity status. The main recipients of the 2022 award were people engaged in helping children who are victims of the migration crisis on the Polish-Belarusian border. Holland has long criticised the Polish government's migration policies, taking part in protests and giving supportive speeches. Using every opportunity to publicly protest any form of discrimination, she is an activist celebrity. Yet first and foremost, she is the most internationally recognisable Polish filmmaker.

In this chapter, I discuss how Holland's public persona has evolved from politically engaged director working within socialist cinema, through celebrity director embedded within the system of neoliberal democracy, to activist celebrity director advocating for human rights.[3] While examining this development, I comment on how this transformation of her public persona exemplifies the evolution of film authorship from the romantic notion of the artist, through the authorial agency conceived as a brand name, to a cultural worker who uses her symbolic capital to call for changes in global and local politics. The concept of the public persona, extensively used in sociology and cultural studies, implies 'construction, constitution, and production of the self through identity play and performance by the individual in social settings' (Marshall and Barbour, 2015, 2).[4] The process of self-construction has been subjected to analysis from various perspectives, for example Erving Goffman's concept of multiple life-roles (1973), Judith Butler's notion of performativity (1990) and Michel Foucault's self-fashioning (1988), which can all be employed in studies of authorship.[5]

Throughout her career, Holland has employed various methods and strategies to control her public persona, thereby implementing Foucauldian 'technologies of the self which permit individuals to effect by their own means or with the help of others a certain number of operations on their own bodies and souls, thoughts, conduct, and way of being' (Foucault 1988, 18). Self-fashioning can be related to authorship in that the filmmaker is self-fashioning herself into an *auteur* (see Van Belle 2019, 6–7; Staiger 2003, 50), which may be either acknowledged and reinforced or diminished and erased by other participants of the authorial discourse. In the first stage of her cinematic career, Holland self-fashioned herself into a politically engaged *auteur* working as a part of the creative collective of the film unit 'X' and contributing to the Cinema of Moral Concern (see Chapter Two). In the 1980s, when she decided to live in exile in France, she capitalised on her persona of dissident film *auteur*, while gradually shifting it towards the figure of celebrity director due to the two Oscar nominations (for *Angry Harvest* and *Europa, Europa*) and her later work in Hollywood. Systematically, her persona was gaining more visibility, which made her more recognisable in the transnational mediascape. In the last decade, she has self-fashioned herself into an activist celebrity director, thereby returning to a certain extent to her initial public persona of a politically engaged *auteur*.

While self-fashioning her persona, Holland has consistently gendered it in a more or less direct fashion. To address the issue, I take inspiration from Yvonne Tasker, who advocated for examining the visibility of women filmmakers and the contexts of their public appearances. As she claims, 'the female filmmaker remains a potent figure whose iconic presence has to do with the very possibility of a distinct women's cinema. She is significant in terms of her visibility within a field that remains male dominated' (Tasker 2010, 215). Therefore, according to Tasker, the category of women's cinema is established not only through the textualities of the films made by female filmmakers but also with their visibility in a mediascape that testifies to their presence and position in the film industry. Their visibility that, as Tasker argues, claims the position of the film *auteur* traditionally marked as male, results not only from feminist interventions in screen cultures but is also connected to the transformation of film *auteur* into celebrity: 'The image of the director as industry celebrity is distributed fairly widely and is increasingly tied into the marketing of individual films' (Tasker 2010, 215). The visibility of the female celebrity director that is disseminated and enhanced through interviews, public appearances at film festivals and award ceremonies, may significantly contribute to their successes or failures, determining their chances to make new films. As Tasker notes, 'it is apparent that criticism – including feminist criticism – has a role to play in this process' (Tasker 2010, 217–18). Along with various auxiliary discourses, feminist criticism describes some of female filmmakers, especially those included in the canon of women's cinema as celebrity female/feminist directors. But Holland has been rarely granted this status. Notwithstanding her films' problematic relationship with the feminist agendas, I contend that her absence in the critically established corpus of women's cinema is also due to her initial refusal to self-fashion herself into such a figure, while simultaneously on various occasions she would recognise the impact of her gender on her professional career.

In the last two decades or so, Holland's persona as a female filmmaker has evolved significantly. She eventually embraced a feminist agenda, while she has also changed from celebrity director into activist celebrity director. The two roles have been overlapping and emerging with various intensity in different circumstances and contexts. Holland uses her cultural capital acquired as celebrity director for her political activity, which is due to the 'convertibility of celebrity into other resources, such as economic or political capital' (Driessens 2013, 544). Among many ideological agendas, she vehemently supports women's issues and the LGBTQ movement, while protesting the migration policies in Poland and Russian aggression in Ukraine. Although she cannot be identified with celebrity feminism, she uses her celebrity status to support a feminist agenda responding to the needs of the post-feminist era:

> Feminism – especially in a context routinely celebrated as postfeminist, with its work thought to have been done – continues to need its celebrities; those women who receive the type of cultural legitimation that enables feminism to continue its vital work. And, of course, indicative of their symbiosis, the mainstream media continues to need feminism, including the high profile women it has authorised to publicly speak on its behalf. [. . .] celebrity feminism represents a specific mode of public subjectivity which needs to be seen not only in the context of broader debates about the mediatisation of feminism but in terms of the new media spaces that are being opened up for the public performance of feminist identities. (Taylor 2014, 771)

While examining how Holland uses various 'technologies of the self', I will be looking at her interviews and appearances in various media, at journalistic portrayals of her persona, and at instances of official recognition she has been given throughout her long-lasting career, in order to reconstruct her 'as a discursive figure who continually mediates and is mediated by her film, her publicity, and her own public articulations' (Lane 2000, 47). From these mediations, the *auteur*/celebrity nexus emerges with Holland making every possible effort to regulate it as possible in various social, political and cultural contexts.

'A LONELY WOMAN' IN POLISH CINEMA

Soon after returning to Poland from Prague, on 28 December 1972, Agnieszka Holland gave birth to her daughter, Kasia. The event was indirectly reported in the papers entitled 'Kasia's Birth' ('Narodziny Kasi') published in the women's magazine *You and Me* (*Ty i Ja*), where her mother, Irena Rybczyńska-Holland, worked as a journalist (see Chapter One). They included six 'Letters of Kasia's mother sent from the maternity hospital' and an article describing the multigenerational family living in a three-bedroom apartment prepared for Kasia's arrival. The letters reported on Holland's experience of giving birth and early maternity experiences, while also commenting on larger problems of health care and the social services available to young mothers and their spouses in socialist Poland. The letters were published anonymously, while the article was signed by Holland's mother with her penname, Ewa Borecka.[6] Keeping their authors anonymous was most likely done to protect the private lives of Holland and her family because they were still subjected to surveillance, and rumours surrounding her father's death were circulating, but it also helped to make an individual case of motherhood exemplary for various problems with which young couples had to struggle. Both the letters and the article address the insufficient healthcare available to pregnant women in Poland and highlight the insensitive medical personnel, shortage of apartments for young families, and the ineffective system of social care. Although not signed with their names, for many readers Holland and her mother's authorship would be easily recognisable due to many specific details and information. As insignificant as it may seem, the publication can be seen as a preliminary form of the collective (family) and self-effacing authorship, while also indicating Holland's concern with women's issues that she presented as individual and unique experiences but also as a more general example of the deficiency of social policy in socialist Poland.

Soon after giving birth, Holland resumed her professional career, and, as discussed in Chapter Two, relatively quickly achieved a strong position in the Polish cinema of the 1970s. A member of Andrzej Wajda's film unit 'X', in a short time she became its informal leader and one of the most important proponents

Figure 7.1 Agnieszka Holland with her daughter, Kasia Adamik, Warsaw 1972; photo by Pista Adamik, from Agnieszka Holland's family archive

of the Cinema of Moral Concern. She achieved her dominant position in the team by consistent self-fashioning of her persona into a masculine mode of behaviour, which she admitted only years later, after spending some time abroad. Simultaneously, in her interviews from the 1970s, she would comment on the difficulties she faced as a female filmmaker. The most burdensome issue was to combine professional and family life. In one of the interviews, she said, 'her family life always suffer[ed]', admitting that it was her daughter who was most affected, while her mother had to take over most of the domestic duties.[7] As is easy to predict, her male colleagues from the film unit 'X' did not comment on how their family life suffered as a result of their professional engagements.[8] One of the journalists asked Holland why she chose such an 'unfeminine' profession as film directing. In response, she said that she considered herself as equal to men.[9] However, in another interview, she admitted that women's situation in the 'masculine' profession of filmmaking was more difficult as they had to manage the 'double burden' of domestic and professional duties. While discussing it, she was very specific; for example, she said she needed to find a way to get meat for dinner (here she refers to the shortage of food in grocery shops in the Poland of late socialism) or time to make medical appointments for her child and then to remember to keep them and so on. In the interview entitled 'A strong feeling of injustice', she confessed, 'my Kasia is seven years old, and I would not manage without my mum's help'.[10] Importantly, she also mentions her mother's influence on her work; when asked about realism in her films, she said she owed it to her mother, a journalist. She recollected how, in the past, she would visit her at work and read the readers' letters to the editors which gave her insight into problems of real people.[11] In the 1981 interview, she reiterated her points concerning the difficulties of working in the masculinised film industry, while also disparagingly commenting on 'women's cinema' that she divided into feminist sectarian works and women's transgressive cinema, as represented, for example, by Liliana Cavani, that offered a cruel and uncompromising representation of sexuality. In response, the journalist assured Holland that she made 'male' films.[12]

In her interviews from the 1970s, Holland made her gender 'visible' and indicated how it affected her professional career, however she refused to locate it within a (Western) feminist framework. The simultaneous denouncing and denial of gender oppression is reflected in her films from the 1970s as many of them address the conflict between traditional and progressive models of femininity, often presenting these as a choice between family, professional life and individual self-fulfilment. These conflicts are rarely resolved, and the female characters remain trapped in opposing socio-cultural expectations, as was Holland at that time, as expressed in the interviews mentioned. The photos that accompanied these interviews were usually taken during conversations, and as such they are unadorned images of a young woman in thick glasses, whose facial expression and gestures express self-confidence and determination. From the early years in her career on, occasional photos of Holland on the set or behind the camera were also published, and these are of special importance as they imply her authorial agency. As noted by Deborah Jermyn: 'The commanding image of the director positioned authoritatively next to their camera is an iconic one in film histories' (Jermyn 2021, 378). It is worth mentioning that Holland decided to include a 'commanding image' of herself as a director in the collective project *Screen Tests*; as previously mentioned, she makes a cameo appearance in the third part of the movie as a director coordinating the process of casting for a film. She is the only woman in the fictious crew, yet also the most visible and active on the set (Fig. 7.2; see also Chapter Two). However, her 'commanding image' fades out when Andrzej Wajda – the young film personnel's mentor – enters the set and instantly occupies the central position that had been 'usurped' by Holland.

Holland used every opportunity to make herself visible in the 'X' unit. She would frequently accept episodic roles in the films of her male colleagues such as Krzysztof Kieślowski's *Scar* (*Blizna*, 1976),[13] Andrzej Zajączkowski's *A Shattered Mirror* (*Okruch lustra*, 1978) and the (in)famous *Interrogation* (*Przesłuchanie*, Ryszard Bugajski, 1982, prem. 1989)[14] that was notorious for its anti-communist message and was banned for several years. In the latter film, Holland played a role of a zealous communist who, convinced of the infallibility of the Party, accepted the false accusation of espionage and imprisonment (see Fig. 7.3). As her character absurdly explained, 'subjectively' she was innocent,

232 REFOCUS: THE FILMS OF AGNIESZKA HOLLAND

Figure 7.2 *Screen Tests* (1976)

Figure 7.3 Agnieszka Holland in *Interrogation* (Ryszard Bugajski, 1982/1989)

yet 'objectively' she committed an act of treason. Years later, she admitted that, during the Solidarity carnival, no one wanted to play a communist and so she decided to help her colleague and friend Ryszard Bugajski. On the set of this film, she met Krystyna Janda, who played the iconic role of Agnieszka in Wajda's *Man of Marble*, a role that allegedly was modelled on Holland's persona. As Janda recollects, 'No one knew what this girl was supposed to be like. Wajda took me to the set where Agnieszka Holland was making her *Sunday Children*, and told me to watch her' (quoted in Wajda 2000, 130). Although, as Janda later admitted, the visit on the set did not inspire her enough, for Wajda, Holland was the epitome of modern femininity that was 'visible' enough to serve as a point of reference for the actress to create a female character that was supposed to embody the 'new' womanhood. Although entering the Polish film industry as an 'outsider' due to her film education in Czechoslovakia, soon Holland became a recognisable figure in film circles.

Holland's reputation in Polish cinema in the 1980s was mostly due to her participation in the Cinema of Moral Concern that at that time was the epitome of dissident cinema. During this period, she accumulated solid symbolic capital, which Pierre Bourdieu defined as 'the *recognition*, institutionalized or not' that an individual can receive from a group (Bourdieu 1991, 72). Holland was recognised because of her cultural productions (scriptwriting, directing films and theatre productions for television), her strong position in the film community, her 'biographical legend' created around her father and her own political activity (even if it was circulated in a small circle of filmmakers and intellectual elites), her cameo or episode appearances in the films made by her friends, and her interviews in various types of magazines and periodicals. In the latter, Holland consistently emphasised the difficulties of combining her family and professional life, however, as gender discourse was significantly suppressed or subjugated to the national narrative, she did not make it a focal point of her personal narrative. Instead, she self-fashioned herself into a politically engaged film *auteur* opposing the political doctrine of communism, which secured her a prominent position within the local film community and, by extension, in Polish national cinema. From this reputation originated her symbolic capital which facilitated her entrance into transnational cinema.

When Holland decided to stay in exile in 1981, she solidified her reputation as a dissident *auteur*. In her interviews given in Sweden directly after the imposition of martial law in Poland she expressed harsh criticism of the Soviet-dependent regime. Although at first out of a job and separated from her family, she gradually found possibilities to continue her professional career, albeit initially with very limited scope (as discussed in Chapter Three). In the few interviews she gave at that time, her persona was mainly identified with political cinema. In one of them, she is introduced as Poland's leading woman film director and one of the most prominent representatives of the Polish 'New

Wave' (Holland and Pobóg-Malinowski 1982, 16). Her collaboration with Wajda and Krzysztof Zanussi is mentioned, as are various film festival prizes and professional accomplishments. There is also information on a censor ban on her last film made in Poland, *A Woman Alone*. Importantly, her Jewish father's death in suspicious circumstances is mentioned, on which she commented 'My father's death was probably the first open political provocation after 1956' (Holland and Pobóg-Malinowski 1982, 17).

In the same interview, Holland explained how Polish filmmakers were subjected to political control and censorship in the 1970s, while still making dissident cinema. The Polish Film Festival in Gdańsk in 1979 was, she claimed, a manifestation of political cinema that was camouflaged with the label 'moral concern'. While recollecting the Solidarity period, she said, 'we suddenly saw that we had a social authority. Not all of us, of course, but mainly Wajda. He became a symbol for the workers [. . .] it was a very nice feeling, this feeling of togetherness' (Holland and Pobóg-Malinowski 1982, 18). She presented herself as a member of the team of filmmakers working in Wajda's film unit 'X' that was tightly connected to the larger national community. While speaking on behalf of the collective of dissident filmmakers, Holland explained how martial law had affected her own situation:

> After December 13, a hysterical attack was made on my person [. . .]. I was immediately thrown out of work, so I am afraid that my situation after returning to Poland would be very bleak, I would not be able to do anything – and that would be the better of the possibilities. (Holland and Pobóg-Malinowski 1982, 19)

As she further admitted, the worst scenario for her would be imprisonment. She presented herself as a victim of the political regime and an artist in exile who is pessimistic about the future of vernacular cinema: 'I am afraid that Polish cinema was stopped at the most dynamic moment of its development and that the damage is irrevocable. I fear that we shall remain a lost generation' (Holland and Pobóg-Malinowski 1982, 19).

While being openly critical towards the political regime in Poland during the martial law period, Holland would also acknowledge the creative freedom she had in the 1970s. In the 1986 interview, after *Angry Harvest* was screened at the film festival in Montreal, while still waiting for its Oscar nomination, she recollected her Polish years as a time when, compared to her German experience, she had more agency as a director:

> The situation for making films is actually better in Poland than in Germany. I had lots of problems in Poland too, but they were very clearly political problems [. . .] But in Germany, and in America, too, you are allowed to

solve problems artistically only if you are well-known. (Holland and Brunette 1986, 17)

Indirectly, she acknowledged not having sufficient symbolic capital compared to her position in Poland before 1981.

The Oscar nomination for *Angry Harvest* was a turning point in Holland's career as it made her famous, while also solidifying her position in *auteur* cinema. The success was soon to be followed by the critical and box-office success of *Europa, Europa* that was expected to win the Oscar for the best foreign film (see Chapter Three). Paradoxically, the commotion around *Europa, Europa* buttressed her position within European cinema. As mentioned, many well-known German filmmakers such as Werner Herzog and Wim Wenders signed a protest letter against the official decision, while many filmmakers from other countries expressed their indignation individually. Holland had become an oppressed artist again, this time being a victim, not of the communist Polish regime but of biased German cultural politics. Years later, she ironically commented: 'Not submitting my film for Oscar was hara-kiri on the German part. [. . .] I have received enough awards for it and the Oscar would force me to spend several years in Hollywood that would be very tiresome'.[15] However, she soon left Europe for Hollywood, which, in her native Poland quickly assured her the status of celebrity director.

CELEBRITY DIRECTOR: BETWEEN ART AND COMMERCE

When, in 1988, after seven years abroad, Holland was finally allowed re-entry into Poland, her friends and colleagues waited for her at the airport and gave her a welcome worthy of a star or celebrity. She came in order to promote her film *To Kill a Priest* (1988), which was presented outside of the official system of distribution (see Chapter Three). Soon, Polish distributors and critics were working to establish Holland as a celebrity director. After her seven-year-long absence from the Polish mediascape, she had become visible again.

Deborah M. Sims explains that celebrity directors are usually *auteurs* who establish 'an elite community of auteur filmmaking that is coded as masculine and upholds admission standards predicated on maleness'. She also claims that 'fame itself is gendered', while '[t]he masculinization of fame [is] particularly apt in the case of filmmaking' (Sims 2014, 193). The photo of Polish filmmakers participating in the 43rd Cannes Film Festival testifies to Sims's observations. It shows five renowned male Polish directors (Andrzej Żuławski, Andrzej Wajda, Roman Polanski, Ryszard Bugajski and Krzysztof Kieślowski), with Holland as the only woman. All stand in a row holding a huge Polish flag that serves as the backdrop for the picture (see Fig. 7.4). The photo has acquired iconic status

Figure 7.4 Andrzej Żuławski, Andrzej Wajda, Agnieszka Holland, Roman Polanski, Ryszard Bugajski, Krzysztof Kieślowski at the 43rd Cannes Film Festival. Photo by Micheline Pelletier © Getty Images

in the history of Polish cinema, as evidenced by its use as a cover photo for the magisterial volume on the history of Polish cinema by the renowned scholar and film critic Tadeusz Lubelski (2009). Taken at the most prestigious European film festival, the photo symbolically confirmed Holland's 'membership' in this 'elitist masculine club' (Sims 2014, 193).[16] In 2022, she returned to Cannes as a juror of the documentary section, which was a sign that her symbolic capital had grown. She used it (as I explain in due course) as an arena for political activism. In the intervening years she enjoyed the status of celebrity director mostly in her native Poland, despite, or perhaps because of, not making films there until 2007.

To a significant extent, Holland owes her status as celebrity director to the promotional campaigns for her foreign films organised in Poland (see

Chapter Four) and the critical discourse which developed around her work and her persona. The 1995 book *Reżyseria: Agnieszka Holland* (*Directed by: Agnieszka Holland*), edited by Stanisław Zawiśliński (1995) included interviews with Holland and her collaborators as well as excerpts from reviews of her films. Compared to regular interviews published in newspapers and magazines, she shared biographical details more generously in this book. Once she had changed from renowned filmmaker to celebrity director, which coincided with the collapse of communism and the change in the public narration about the past relationship between Poles and Jews, Holland began talking about her father in a more open way. She spoke about his mysterious death and his Jewishness. She also admitted she was not emotionally connected with him, yet that he was important for her cultural education as it was he who took her to theatres, to the cinema, and to concerts (Zawiśliński 1995, 16–22). In another book-length interview first published in 2002, she called him a *bon vivant* who socialised with artistic and intellectual elites, while also commenting on how his persona had affected her life (Holland and Kornatowska 2012, 83–90). Tasker noted that personal narratives are important as manifestations of artists' subjectivity, yet in the case of female filmmakers, these are frequently embedded in patriarchal structures:

> The incorporation of biography, whether in criticism or promotion, involves the production of a version of events in which patterns of influence, early interests, and so on acquire a new significance. For women filmmakers – by virtue of their relative rarity – such an interest can often end up centering on the question of how they managed to get to the position they are in at all. Predictably, there seems to be a particular interest in the part played by men in their careers. (Tasker 2010, 222)

The best example of this tendency is John Tibbet's introduction to his interview with Holland published in 2008, in which he wrote:

> she came of age as a screenwriter under the mentorship of Krzysztof Zanussi and Andrzej Wajda, for whom she served as First Assistant Director on his *Man of Marble* (1977).[17] Films like this provided her examples of how to explore issues of political and moral dissent within the limitations imposed by the communist regime. [. . .] Encouraged by Wajda in her ambition to direct, she made *Provincial Actors* (1980). (Tibbets and Holland 2008, 133–4)

Tibbets perpetuates the myth of male mentorship as a necessary condition for a woman to enter the world of cinema. Although Holland has often emphasised the help she received from the two masters of Polish cinema,

Krzysztof Zanussi and Andrzej Wajda, she does not admit that they had any artistic influence on her films. Furthermore, she stressed that she did not need any encouragement to make a movie but simply help to make it possible in unfavourable circumstances. Furthermore, the recognition in world cinema she gained in the 1980s has allowed her to act as a protector of her erstwhile master and mentor, Andrzej Wajda. In various interviews, she defended Wajda against accusations of anti-Semitism in France after the screening of *Korczak* there (see Chapter Three). For example, in the interview with Gordana Crnković, she said, 'But Wajda is certainly not anti-Semitic, I know it, I am Jewish myself and I can judge it. He was strongly attacked for this movie in France and in the US. But he keeps doing movies about that, it's his own obsession, the guilt' (Crnković and Holland 1998–9, 6). In the 1990s and early 2000s, Holland frequently talked critically about Holocaust memory in Europe. In France, she argued, a common sense of guilt about collaboration with the Nazis has been displaced onto other European nations, with Poles being presented as the main perpetrators. Although Holland has firmly and frequently acknowledged Polish anti-Semitism, she vehemently protests ignoring it in other European societies and nations (Crnković and Holland 1998–9, 6).

The theme of the Holocaust and Polish anti-Semitism returned in a book-length collection of interviews with Holland by Maria Kornatowska (1935–2011), *Magic and Money* (*Magia i pieniądze*) published in 2002.[18] It contains the director's commentaries about her colleagues, friends, family and films, and her personal struggles with various obstacles she encountered as a (woman) filmmaker. Upon closer scrutiny of the interviews, it is difficult to find the main thread or issue that would serve as a key to Holland's persona. In another interview, she addressed this dispersion of herself when she ponders: 'Is it more important to be Polish or to be a woman or to be Agnieszka or to be a mother or anything else?' (Crnković and Holland 1998–9, 9). Kornatowska, who conducted the interviews for the book, did not push Holland to declare herself as any one of these personas or to say which one is the most important. Instead, the renowned film critic and professor at the Łódź Film School discusses with the filmmaker her life experiences, her films and contemporary culture and cinema in general. Kornatowska participates in the conversation not only by asking questions, but she also shares her thoughts or opinions on the issues they explore.

Magic and Money offers a conversation between two cultivated and successful women who share a passion for cinema. Their life experience is also somehow similar as Kornatowska was also of Jewish origins[19] and would regularly travel to the States, spending some time in New York. In 1986, she published a book, *Eros and Cinema* (*Eros i kino*), that examined the cinematic representation of the female body and sexuality, often from a feminist perspective. It is no wonder that she touched upon these subjects in her conversation with Holland, who retreated from her erstwhile critical attitude to feminism. Kornatowska recognised the factor of gender in Holland's persona as a celebrity director, which is demonstrated by the selection of visuals for the book: these include sixteen photos from her films, twelve of her on the film set or with actors, and fourteen of her with her family and friends (some of them doubling as her collaborators). The persona who emerges from these photos engages equally in professional and private life. Most importantly, she looks much the same in all these photos (except for the age difference between her childhood and adult life), which testifies to her authenticity and, possibly, integrity.

Deborah Jermyn usefully notes that the way a woman director looks informs 'the meaning/s she contains' (Jermyn 2021, 369). Holland's look and body language visible on the photos taken on the film sets suggest individualism and strength. Furthermore, she visibly distances herself from recent fashion trends – which does not mean that she neglects her attire – as most often she opts for a boho style that sends a subtle counterculture message. Equally eloquent, her professional photos testify to her director status as she is frequently shown behind the camera or on a film set in rather commanding postures, whereas the private photos reveal her intimate self. The professional photos are complemented with pictures taken at cinematic events such as the Cannes Film Festival. Overall, the photos in the book contribute to her celebrity persona. The reputation was strengthened by the two scholarly monographs that were published around the same time as the Kornatowska's interview, by Mariola Jankun-Dopartowa (2000) and Sławomir Bobowski (2001). They include some biographical information, yet the main focus is on Holland's films, examined as addressing universal human issues. Arguably, the three books sanctioned her work as internationally recognised *auteur* cinema, thereby establishing her as a celebrity director.

Although Holland's recognisability outside of Poland was significantly less, her persona in the 1990s and early 2000s attracted considerable attention. Her films were reviewed by the most prominent newspapers, such as *The New York Times*, *Variety*, *The Washington Post* and many others (see Chapter Four). She was also interviewed by the journalists of these newspapers, which increased her visibility and reputation. Her persona was presented as being as interesting as her films. In her interview with Holland, Crnković introduces her as 'as much of an outsider as they come – a woman and a foreigner, her life and career could easily be a subject of a movie of its own' (Crnković and Holland 1998–9, 2). To the question whether being a woman director made her work in the States more difficult or just different, she answered:

> when I did my first movie here, I was already an established director, so a lot of people in the industry were respectful of my work and were glad to

work with me. I don't know what happens if someone comes from nowhere and is a woman, it's certainly not so easy. (Crnković and Holland 1998–9, 2)

When, in an interview for *The Washington Post*, Rita Kempley asked provocative questions, Holland answered them just as provocatively. The item was published as 'Agnieszka Holland: A War on Stupidity – Polish-Born Director of "Washington Square" Faces Off against the Mindless Moviemaking Machine', and the journalist introduced Holland through both her films and her biography:

> Her critically acclaimed films have been banned in her homeland, snubbed by Germany's Oscar nominating committee and ignored in her adopted France. Additionally, she's been exiled from Poland, jailed by the Czechs and condemned as an antisemite even though she is half-Jewish and faced virulent racism herself.[20]

Kempley's brief description of *Washington Square* (1997) calls it a 'hardly typical Hollywood' film, which implies that it sooner belongs to European art cinema. While commenting on the story and the characters, Holland recollected her father, who was similar to Dr Sloper in that he also was incapable of unconditional love for his daughter. When Kempley mentioned Todd McCarthy's review, claiming that the film is 'imbued with something of a feminist twist', Holland spontaneously responded,

> This guy is completely stupid [. . .]. He reviewed a couple of my movies and those were the most stupid reviews I have ever had. I don't think it's feminist. I think it's told from a more female point of view than other adaptations.[21]

After a while, she admitted that, from a certain viewpoint, 'it is a feminist story'.[22] While describing Holland's relationship with her native Poland, Kempley stated: 'She's a celebrity now and can chide the Polish people as she pleases'. Holland caustically responded (in imperfect English): 'If I live there, they will eat me, you know. But because I am coming as a beloved visitor, it goes well'.[23] Holland reserved her most provocative statement for living in Los Angeles:

> I kind of like living in L.A., which surprises myself. There are only three things to do: go to movies, drive and shop. That's why I am not wearing black, you see. Suddenly in my forties I am the beeg [sic] shopper.[24]

Kempley commented ironically on this confession: 'Next thing you know she'll be popping Prozac'.[25]

Kempley recognised Holland's position in contemporary cinema that is presented as achieved with her European films, yet she also foregrounded her provocative statements that make her an exotic figure in the Hollywood world of filmmaking. One may assume that Holland's provocative and even offensive behaviour was an excessive way to fulfil the expectations of American critics who expected Otherness from a female filmmaker coming from Eastern Europe. The 'things to do' in LA that she mentioned are signs of her alienation in the town as these are mostly solitary activities to be performed in transitory spaces (such as a freeway), or the non-places, to use Marc Augé's concept, of the shopping mall or cineplexes (Augé 1995). These non-places will shelter one for as long as needed, yet without the prospect of settlement and inhabitation. Likewise, Holland's harsh words on the American critics do not necessarily express rudeness or arrogance but are symptoms of her alienation from American critical discourse, and occasionally from feminist discourse as well. In her interviews, she tried to personalise her films as much as possible through relating all of them to her life experience, yet the critics were not eager to embrace this, which is understandable, taking into account the generic, thematic and stylistic versatility of her American work. In her native Poland, she was able to retain her status of celebrity director for some time, yet it subsided significantly during her prolonged collaboration with television streaming platforms, which reduced her visibility. She regained it with the Oscar nomination for her 2011 film *In Darkness*, an international co-production made in Poland. Simultaneously, in the second decade of the twenty-first century she systematically increased her public activity in political and social life, which ultimately added to her persona as celebrity activist.

CINEMA, POLITICS AND CELEBRITY CULTURE

The promotional campaign organised around *In Darkness* and its Oscar nomination boosted Holland's visibility. Currently, her presence is prominent in contemporary (mostly European) film culture, Polish political life, and popular media culture, while her celebrity capital is accumulated and transferred among these three areas. Today, Holland is one of the most recognisable public figures in Poland. Suffice it to say that her name in a Google search yields 12,680,000 results, while Jarosław Kaczyński, the leader of the party Law and Justice (Prawo i Sprawiedliwość, PiS) gets 13,200,000 results. Moreover, her search results are also much higher compared to the stars and celebrities of Polish cinema such as Andrzej Wajda (3,040,000 results), Krystyna Janda (about 1,070,000 results) and Daniel Olbrychski (636,000 results). Compared to Anglophone directors in world cinema, Holland's score is much lower than Quentin Tarantino's (27,500,000 results), yet higher than that of Jane Campion, who apparently is the most recognisable female filmmaker in contemporary cinema (4,520,000 results), and Kathryn Bigelow's (3,540,000 results).[26] Holland's popularity originates mostly from her prolific participation in film cultures and as such will be discussed first.

CINEMA

Holland is a recipient of many awards and distinctions (see Chapter Six). At the local level, one of the most spectacular ceremonies honouring her was the occasion of implanting a star with her name on it on the main street of Łódź – the town where the Polish film industry was located during the period of state socialism, hence its nickname Hollyłódź, with the series of stars' names paralleling the famous Walk of Fame in Los Angeles (see Fig. 7.5). All her films made in the twenty-first century have been distinguished with various film festival prizes (see Chapter Six). In 2021, at the Polish Film Festival, she was awarded with the Platinum Lions for lifetime achievement in filmmaking. Holland is also active in European film culture; in 2014 she was elected the chair of the European Film Academy board and in 2021, its president.

Figure 7.5 Agnieszka Holland at the ceremony of implanting a star with her name on the main street of Łódź. Photo by Tomasz Komorowski © Tomasz Komorowski for the Museum of Cinematography in Łódź

Like other celebrities, Holland has received recognition from universities, and these are of special importance. They include honorary degrees from FAMU (Fig. 7.6) and Brandeis University, as well as the Viadrina University Award (in Frankfurt at Oder).[27] Although these distinctions granted by higher educational institutions are commonly seen as symbolic acknowledgement of the recipients' contribution to culture and science, they also serve to boost the prestige of these institutions. In other words, the higher educational institutions use the cultural capital of the people they honour. As P. David Marshall and Sean Redmond explain,

> On a basic level, universities have always been in an industry obsessed with impact: they want their individual location to be noticed, their impact and prestige to be recognised and their 'work' valued, and thus they have consistently wanted to be attached to those who were most visible in many domains of public activity. Thus, for centuries they have been the place for the provocative lecture and the site of invitation to the most famous literary or performing arts star. [. . .] In a much more systematic way, the relationship between celebrities and universities was built through the system of honorary degrees and doctorates where the individual university reached out beyond its borders to connect to some prominent individual. (Marshall and Redmond 2016, 3)

Figure 7.6 Agnieszka Holland receives honorary degree from FAMU in Prague. Photo by Petr Jan Juračka, © Archiv Akademie múzických umění v Praze, Udělení titulu 23.3

Thus, universities and artists-intellectuals-celebrities are 'friends with benefits' who participate in a mutual exchange of cultural capital that enhances the visibility of both parties. The ceremonies are always organised as spectacular events, with traditional academic gowns, mortarboards and imponderabilia, and as such they appeal enough to the media to be widely promoted and disseminated. Ultimately, these events increase the cultural capital of the academic institution, which can be transposed into economic capital through attracting more affluent patrons. In turn, the artists/intellectuals increase their chances to get their projects funded, while also enjoying increased demand for their cultural products.

The marketing of Holland's recent film and television projects relies on her brand name, which was initially established within the realm of politically engaged art cinema. For example, the English-language poster of one of her most recent films, *Charlatan* (2021), includes a logo of the Berlin Film Festival and the inscription 'Berlinale Special Gala', which stamps the film as art cinema, and by extension its director as a film *auteur*. In his review of the film published in *Variety*, Guy Lodge locates *Charlatan* within the context of Holland's participation in the Berlinale, while also commenting on the differences between its worldwide and Czech distribution:

> 'Charlatan' is the Polish director's third Berlinale premiere in four years, following the striking prize-winning mystery 'Spoor' and last year's 'Mr. Jones', a sturdy English-language biopic set against the backdrop of the Holodomor. Unspooling out of competition at the fest, the principally Czech-produced 'Charlatan' has dimmer international distribution prospects than those two titles, given its studious, few-fireworks approach and a niche subject largely unknown beyond home turf: In the Czech Republic, where it bows theatrical on March 26, it will have an easier time finding an audience, thanks in largely [sic] part to the forceful presence of local star Ivan Trojan in the lead.[28]

A different advertising strategy has been used to attract Polish diaspora audiences in the UK. The announcement for the special screening of *Charlatan* organised in London by the Polish Social and Cultural Association reads, 'Agnieszka Holland's Oscar-shortlisted film', and it quotes an excerpt from the review published in *The Guardian*: 'Holland once again proves she is the real deal'.[29] Holland herself actively constructs her authorship, frequently in a self-ironic and witty way, as in her presentation in 'The Playlist' podcast: 'I did one movie, *Europa Europa*, about the importance of a man's penis, and this one [*Charlatan*] is about the importance of human's urine. So, I am fateful [sic] to myself'[30]. She proves capable of adjusting her authorial voice to the profile of the platform from which she speaks.

POLITICS

Aside from various film awards, Holland's native Poland has recognised her with many honorary distinctions for her public activity and advocacy for democratic and inclusive societies. To name just a few: in 2013 she received the Saint George Medal from *Tygodnik Powszechny*, a progressive Catholic weekly – a prestigious award that honours those who campaign against any form of oppression or inequality (among its recipients are Adam Michnik, Václav Havel and Marek Edelman). In 2015, the Kościuszko Foundation granted her the Pioneer Award; in the same year she received the award Creator of Culture from the popular weekly *Polityka* for engaging with difficult historical and political issues in the accessible form of popular cinema. Among the distinctions she has garnered abroad, two deserve special mention: in 2014 she received the 'Gratias Agit' Award from the Czech Ministry of Foreign Matters, as well as the Order of Princess Olga that the president of Ukraine gives to women for their achievements in various areas of public and private life. Such international recognition increases Holland's symbolic capital, which she uses in socio-political life.

Holland's participation in political debates within Poland has intensified since the right-wing conservative party Law and Justice, which Monika Bartoszewicz describes as 'a highly centralised and micro-managed Führerpartei with its unquestionable supreme leader, Jarosław Kaczyński' (Bartoszewicz 2019, 481), came to power, first in 2005 until 2007, and then in 2015 until 2023. Since 2015, Polish society has been deeply divided between supporters of the ruling party and its opponents. PiS demonises women's right for abortion, same-sex marriage and sex education; it led restrictive migration politics during the 2015 refugee crisis in Europe and the 2021 crisis on the Polish-Belorussian border.[31] Large sectors of Polish society have frequently manifested their discontent with such governmental politics, which the media have either applauded or deplored. Their coverage significantly buttressed political dissent. Public television, TVP, channeled governmental propaganda, while the commercial station, TVN, a subsidiary of Warner Bros, vehemently criticised the government. Whereas TVN frequently invited Holland to comment on various political and social issues (see Fig. 7.7), TVP presented her persona as an example of social and political irresponsibility. Whether positive or negative, the prolific images of her in the media increase her visibility and her symbolic capital. A few years ago, Kaczyński made his contribution to her image when, in the Polish parliament, he commented critically on her political attitude by falsely claiming that she was calling for a return to communism.[32] Aside from the appropriateness or legitimacy of the comment, when the political leader of the country during his parliamentary speech expresses an opinion about a filmmaker, his doing so may be seen to revitalise Lenin's reported

Figure 7.7 Agnieszka Holland comments on current political situation in TVN news on 7 September 2022. Screenshot

statement: 'Cinema is the most important of arts'. Paradoxically, in depreciating her, Kaczyński's criticism made Holland more recognisable than ever.

Utterly devoid of any nostalgia for communism, Holland openly disapproves of PiS's blatant nationalistic historical narration, which has resulted, inter alia, in a revival of the idea of 'żydokomuna' (Judeo communism), the anti-Semitic concept that linked Polish Jews with Stalinist oppression. Her rejection of the nationalistic historical politics is motivated ideologically as well as personally, for it is linked to the tragic story of her father (see Chapter One). In a symbolic gesture of dissent from PiS's nationalistic historical narration, Holland accepted Krystyna Naszkowska's invitation to participate in the book *We're the Children of Communists* (*My, dzieci komunistów*). Published in 2019, the collection includes interviews with children of Polish communists who were involved in implementing the new political order in Poland and explores the communist heritage in contemporary life. As the interviewees are relatively recognisable public personas who are active in contemporary social, political or artistic life, the volume indirectly yet persistently calls for a nuanced approach to the communist heritage. In her interview, Holland emphasises her father's sincere and idealistic engagement with communism before the Second World War, followed by his bitter disillusionment with its implementation after 1945. She also admits that over the years she has developed sympathy and tenderness for him (Naszkowska 2019, 381). Like all the other entries in the volume, her story goes beyond the binary opposition of communism and anticommunism exploited by PiS.³³ It is worth mentioning that Naszkowska's invitation to participate in the project was rejected by many people who were either unwilling or afraid to talk about their communist and often Jewish heritage. Holland did not hesitate to accept it, and the symbolic capital she has accumulated as a celebrity director has solidified her position within the public discourse on memory.

POPULAR CULTURE

Although Holland has been interviewed in many books, periodicals and magazines, her celebrity status is mostly boosted by her frequent appearances on television, radio and the internet. Her participation in diverse actions protesting the restrictive abortion law (Women's Strike, 2020–22), the refugee crisis in 2021, and Russia's attack on Ukraine, is always documented on TVN news and on the internet platforms belonging to the consortium (see Fig. 7.8). In the complex nexus of politics, celebrity culture and infotainment, 'celebrity is a mechanism of power through which certain speakers are granted not only the ability to speak but to have such speech legitimated' (Taylor 2008, 105).

Figure 7.8 Agnieszka Holland at the rally against Russian aggression on Ukraine, 6 March 2022. Photo by Tomasz Molina. CC

Holland traverses the areas of politics and entertainment swiftly and efficiently. During the 2021 Polish Film Festival in Gdynia, when she received the honorary award of the Platinum Lions for lifetime achievement, she delivered a speech that was devoted as much to politics as to cinema. She commented on the immigrant crisis on the Polish-Belarusian border that was occurring at that time, while comparing the immigrants to the Holocaust victims depicted in her films. As she said, refugees also need to hide, and they also suffer from cold and hunger. Helping these people, she claimed, would be the only chance for Poles to save their humanity. In her speech, she performed the role of a politically engaged artist who dares to criticise the political powers if the situation demands it. Like many Polish national artists in the past, Holland here acted as the nation's conscience. She seemed to repeat Stefan Żeromski's often quoted call: 'Polish wounds must be torn open so that they do not heal with a membrane of meanness' (Żeromski 1956, 114).[34] In her speech, the suffering immigrants are a wound on the Polish body, thus, they must not be subjected to political reasoning but, instead, treated with compassion and respect. Only then will the wound be healed.

Rather unexpectedly, Holland, who in her work and public appearances has frequently tended to embrace transnational identities, performed in her Gdynia speech the role of the national artist as guardian of the moral order and the national spirit. Enthusiastic applause greeted her speech, to which other prize-winners often referred during the ceremony. Arguably, the event elevated Holland to the position of the master (or, better, mistress) of Polish national cinema. It could be claimed that she has returned from her transnational adventure to perform the role of the national artist previously played by Andrzej Wajda. And one may ponder whether the assumption of that part may evidence her acceptance, once again, of the masculinised role of the national film *auteur* or whether that role has evolved into a female form that privileges affect and emotion as central to cultural production.

Holland does not limit her public celebrity performance solely to the role of national artist. If needed, she enacts the role of the European artist deeply concerned with the larger community of the 'old continent'. For example, on the completion of Brexit, she reprimanded the UK for leaving the EU:

> Aren't you ashamed to be the first to back away from hope? Can you see an alternative? Do you really think that once we've broken our voluntary ties things will be just as they were before? No, they will not. So I cannot wish you all the best. I won't say 'Good bye and good luck.' Because I'm furious with you. [. . .] I'm sure you're making a mistake for which we'll all pay – you're sure to, but so are we. I'm afraid everyone's going to pay equally for the lies, cowardice, and arrogance of the few.[35]

Her voice was the harshest among the twenty-seven farewells expressed by renowned figures from the EU countries.[36] Similarly harsh was her comment delivered at the 77th Cannes Film Festival in 2022, where she was invited to serve as the president of the L'Œil d'or, Le Prix du documentaire jury. She reprimanded the organisers for screening the film of a Russian director in the main competition: 'If it were up to me, I would not include Russian films in the official programme of the festival – even if Kirill Serebrennikov is such a talented artist'. She added:

> Unfortunately, my bad feelings were confirmed by his words. He used [the film's festival press conference] to praise a Russian oligarch [the film's funder, sanctioned billionaire Roman Abramovich] and to compare the tragedy of Russian soldiers to Ukrainian defenders. I would not give him such a chance at this very moment.[37]

On this occasion, as on many others, Holland demonstrated that 'celebrities [. . .] sometimes [. . .] operate as what could be described as contemporary moral compasses' (Marshall 2016a, 156). However, Holland's pedagogical attitude cannot be explained solely by her personality, for it more generally relates to some aspects of European culture.

In her analysis of European literary celebrities, Rebecca Braun succinctly explains that the nineteenth- and twentieth-century American writers strove to fit within national narratives privileging 'the common man', while 'their European counterparts have [. . .] found themselves bound into a tradition that expects and correspondingly rewards intellectual and moral instruction'. Consequently, the former are manufacturing their personas (and their works, for that matter) for 'mass consumption', while the latter are 'liable to be received by a public that overplays the social and intellectual capacities of fallible individuals' and ultimately become 'intellectually fetishised' (Braun 2011, 323). Although Holland works in cinema and television, which might be seen as representing respectively high and popular culture, she speaks from the position Braun ascribed to European writers and hence she feels entitled and obliged to provide moral instruction whenever she thinks (or feels) it is needed.

Holland tirelessly calls for an inclusive society that will provide every citizen with equal rights. In interviews, she supports the LGBTQ+ movement and participates in related community events. Her engagement with the issue also has a personal dimension, for her daughter and regular collaborator, Kasia Adamik, came out as gay in 2012. In 2014, Holland consented to have her photo used for a cover of the fiftieth anniversary issue of *Replica* (*Replika*), the only Polish LGBTQIA+ magazine (see Fig. 7.9). Presumably, the editorial board believed that her face is recognisable enough to leverage the issue of non-heteronormative gender and sexual identities in the public debate. In

Figure 7.9 Agnieszka Holland on the cover of the Polish LGBTQIA magazine

her interview published in the same issue of *Replica*, she speaks as a celebrity director/activist and at the same time as the mother of a gay daughter. In the title of the interview, she addresses the parents of gay children with the words, 'Parents, be cool!' As much as she affirms the LGBTQIA+ community, she was ruthless in her criticism of the government's conservative gender politics. For instance, in a 2020 interview for *Gazeta Wyborcza*, she compared the government-run hate campaign directed at the LGBTQIA+ community to the twentieth-century persecution of the Jews, while expressing admiration for Polish youth's resistance to these attacks and support of their targets.[38] In 2021, the *Replica* interview was reprinted in a book format along with other conversations published in the magazine. The volume was titled *People, not Ideology* (*Ludzie nie ideologia*; Żurawiecki 2021), which boldly denounced a statement made by President Andrzej Duda during his election campaign in 2020 in the city of Brzeg: 'Attempts have been made to persuade us that they [LGBT] are people, but this is merely ideology'.[39] In this context, Holland's presence in the volume is an act of political dissent even stronger than the earlier loan of her face for the cover of *Replica*.

Holland's manifestations of political dissent develop what Liza Tsaliki calls 'the celebrity-in-the-public-service narrative', through which

> celebrities render the *consumption* of politics and activism – not just that of an extravagant lifestyle – an attractive imperative. They can be seen to instigate activist engagement and motivate public endorsement of their cause, while reinforcing their image as 'doers' of good deeds. (Tsaliki 2016, 235)

A celebrity 'lends credibility to political agendas' (Tsaliki 2016, 240) and may be called a 'celebvocate', the term Tsaliki uses for the merger of celebrity and advocacy of a cause. Since Holland's media presence is prolific and extends across various platforms, she also acts 'as an agent of dispersal, a driver of the extension of the TV medium as it reaches feelers out across ever more screens' (Kavka 2016, 297). Accordingly, the authorship of celebrity directors becomes dispersed, for it emerges not only from their texts, but also from the aesthetic and ideological frameworks constituted by the various screens on which they appear. In contemporary Poland, Holland's numerous media images as well as her films have unquestionably familiarised the country's audience with her and her cultural status.

Within contemporary screen cultures, Holland's political activism is by any measure unusual. As Deborah Sims notes, 'The influence of famous directors reaches well beyond the parameters of their own fields, into the scope of philanthropy and politics, or a synthesis between the two', while 'star power enables celebrity directors to bring national attention to the projects they choose, support the philanthropies dearest to them, and promote the political ideology that they value' (Sims 2014, 202, 203). This evolution is indebted to the development of celebrity culture. As Lilie Chouliaraki observed, in the two last decades or so celebrity has changed from a '"powerless" to a "powerful" elite'. While occupying this elevated position, a celebrity functions as 'a communicative figure that articulates aspirational performances of solidarity' (Chouliaraki 2013, 229). Holland eagerly engages in various non-governmental humanitarian actions while also providing material support for Polish institutions of social and health aid. The most famous is the annual action of the Great Orchestra of Christmas Charity, an NGO that raises money for paediatric and elderly health care and entails one of the seasonal events most publicised by the independent media, especially TVN. In 2020, Holland participated in the event and put on a silent auction a visit to the set of her next film project,[40] while in 2017 she offered a dinner with her in one of Warsaw's restaurants.[41] Her cultural capital is significant enough to be monetised.

Although in her public performances Holland behaves as a rational and nononsense person, she balances these characteristics with emotional warmth. For example, she gave a couple of interviews for women's magazines together

Figure 7.10 Agnieszka Holland with her daughter, Kasia Adamik. Photo by Weronika Ławniczak/ Papaya Films for *Zwierciadło*, © Weronika Ławniczak.

with her daughter, Kasia, in which she performed both the role of a professional filmmaker in possession of agency and power as well as the role of a caring mother who supports her daughter.[42] Importantly, the photos that supplemented one of these interviews present both women in a private space rather than on a set or during film production (see Fig. 7.10). The visuals foreground the familial rather than professional narration, and the emphasis on the personal may be attributed to Holland's preferences but equally may be seen within the context of an 'emotive turn' occurring in contemporary, especially celebrity culture. As Sean Redmond contends, 'celebrity is an emotive apparatus that engages with common modes of feelings and delirious forms of affect. Celebrities situate themselves within broad economies of intimacy, creating para-social relationships' (Redmond 2016, 351). It is safe to say that recently Holland has invested extensively in these structures of affective exchange.

(AUTO)BIOGRAPHY?

Karolina Pasternak's 2022 biography of Holland, *Holland: Biography Anew* (*Holland. Biografia od nowa*), instantiates the director's participation in the emotive turn. Along with two book-length interviews and three scholarly monographs devoted to her work, it testifies to her reputation as celebrity director. However, compared to the two previous books of interviews (Zawiśliński 1995; Holland and Kornatowska 2012), Pasternak's volume pays more attention to Holland's personal life. I propose to see the biography within a larger context of self-fashioning strategies employed by the director throughout her life. Pasternak begins her book with a description of the garage in Holland's house in Brittany, France, which indicates that she had access to the director's private space. She also explains that they met when a friend recommended that she run the question-and-answer sessions during Holland's retrospective in Berkeley, California. The sessions extended well beyond cinema theatres and continued at shared breakfasts, dinners and walks. Pasternak introduces herself as a close acquaintance, a friend, who is allowed to see what is closeted in the house and garage, and, by the same token, what is hidden behind Holland's public persona. When she enters the garage where the director keeps numerous boxes and folders containing documents and memorabilia, Pasternak randomly selects a box and opens it, to find a poem by the director written during the first years of her exile. When the journalist later asks Holland whether anybody knew about her poetic creations, she gets a negative answer. Yet in a letter to Wajda written on 23 January 1984, Holland mentioned that she had started writing poetry to distance herself from reality.[43]

The introductory chapter of the biography establishes Holland as a person who hides her gentle side even from her family and friends – with the poems locked in the box serving as proof of that fact – which instantly softens her familiar persona of a strong and authoritative woman. Accordingly, Pasternak emerges as a person who is close to Holland and enjoys her trust. After all, the filmmaker lets her rummage through her personal belongings and, as it later transpires, shares with her the most intimate experiences of her life. Since the private part of Holland's persona has seemingly remained hidden from the public for a long time, her story, Pasternak claims, needs to be retold, and she proceeds to retell it via Holland's own comments.

The first chapter, 'Prague', concerns Holland's studies at FAMU. It presents mostly the material already publicised by Holland in her previous interviews (see Zawiśliński 1995 and Holland and Kornatowska 2012), yet it also includes her ex-husband's (Laco) and a friend's (Andrzej Koszyk) recollections of their time spent together in the capital. Unlike in the earlier publications, Holland comments on her own and her fellow students' sex lifes,[44] mentioning her then illegal co-habitation with Laco. Later in the book, she tells Pasternak that her husband cheated on her with her best friend, which ruined their marriage. Holland reveals to Pasternak her vulnerable side.

The whole book expands on Holland's private life, her family and her friends from the perspective of the director herself. For example, Chapter Two, titled 'Mum' (Mama), depicts the history of Holland's family from the maternal side. Pasternak's decision to include this material fits Holland's narrative about the importance of her mother – a theme iterated for decades in her public statements about her family. Another chapter treats her father's family, most of whom perished in the Holocaust, leaving him and his sister as the only survivors. A special place within the family constellation is allotted to Holland's daughter Kasia, whom Holland had incorporated relatively early into her public persona. As mentioned, in interviews during the 1970s, she would frequently mention Kasia, confessing that she lacked adequate time to take proper care of her when she was growing up. In a 1989 interview, she hinted that her daughter's enrolment in a school in Paris limited her professional mobility while also mentioning that Kasia loved her school in Paris, which would not have been possible in Poland.[45] At a certain point, Holland expanded her family circle to include her sister, the film director Magdalena Łazarkiewicz, and other relatives. Currently, Holland's celebrity persona is firmly rooted in the family circle, within which, as Pasternak neatly concludes, she acts as a matriarchal protective figure of a predominantly female group.[46]

However, behind Holland's strong figure – whether performing the role of matriarch, authoritative director, or angry activist – Pasternak's book reveals a hidden memory of trauma. As mentioned, Holland divulged to the journalist that she had been sexually molested as a teenager, and Pasternak describes the whole process of the director's decision to allow her to include the incident in the book. As the journalist explains: 'Then in Prague we had a long conversation. She told me that she was sexually molested. The nightmare began when she was twelve and lasted up to the time when she left for Prague'. Pasternak recollects how Holland interrogated her on her intended use of the material. Initially, '[Holland] categorically forbade me to write about the story in the book. And I understood that. In my opinion, her censorship was not a constraint on the journalist's freedom of speech, but the sacred right of a victim' (Pasternak 2022, 153). Eventually, Holland gave her consent under one condition: that the name of the perpetrator not be revealed. Presumably, she did not want it to be marketed as a scandalous item but, rather, to offer a glimpse into her traumatic past.

Importantly, in a different section of the volume, Holland admits her own implication in the male molestation of women. She acknowledges that she acted as a passive observer to her male colleagues/friends' seduction of young women from the provincial towns in which they made films: 'I did not display a solidarity of sisterhood because this notion did not exist then' (Pasternak 2022, 161). One may also add that, at that time, the director was performing a male masquerade that precluded acting as a 'sister' to other women. Pasternak assumes that the #MeToo movement and the 2020 Women's Strike affected

Holland's attitude towards various forms of patriarchal oppression and prompted her confession of being sexually abused. On the one hand, sharing intimate and often traumatising details from her life can be attributed to the celebrity culture that fuses the personal with the public; on the other, it also testifies to Holland's changing attitude to feminism and eventual embrace of its agenda.

Pasternak explains Holland's initial rejection of feminism by her lack of familiarity with the movement: 'Feminism was an abstract slogan for her for a long time, as it was practically absent from the public debate in PRL [the Polish People's Republic]' (Pasternak 2022, 123). Holland herself explains that she had distanced herself from feminism in the 1970s because communism was the main enemy for both men and women, whereas patriarchy was so firmly ingrained in social life that nobody thought about changing it. While referring to her gradual embrace of feminism, she mentions the American feminist Shana Penn, whose book documented how many active female members of the Solidarity movement were erased from its history after 1989.[47] Pasternak records the director's eventual declaration of her commitment to feminism in the 1998 interview published in the women's magazine *Zwierciadło* (*Mirror*), in which she said to the journalist, 'I'm a feminist' if it means equality of women and men in professional, social and family life (Pasternak 2022, 125). Pasternak presents this evolution as a self-explanatory process, a volitional act, while not recognising the importance of the public gender discourse to which Holland was exposed while living and working abroad.

At no stage does Pasternak provide the reader with her own interpretation and analysis of Holland's biography and persona. Rather, she assumes the position of an understanding and empathetic friend, listening attentively to Holland and then sharing the latter's words with readers. The objectivity traditionally expected of a journalist rarely surfaces in her approach, which favours Holland's own self-presentation. Such a stance is all the more remarkable because at one point Pasternak acknowledges her potential control of the book's content:

> I know that in her work she is a perfectionist and that she has to control the process of filmmaking and sometimes this tendency to control things transfers to her private life [. . .]. But this book is mine. Not Agnieszka's. She gave her life into someone else's hands and took the position of an observer that is there, participates, yet cannot influence the flow of events but only look at it. (Pasternak 2022, 151)

Granted, Pasternak selected the material to be included in the book and structured it around the nodal points of Holland's life instead of simply following her lifeline. However, she rarely distances herself from the director's opinions or confronts them with the voices of those who might be unfavourable to her. For example, it is symptomatic that she selected Feliks Falk from the members of the film unit 'X' to talk about Holland's position in the collective, while not approaching Jerzy Domaradzki, who elsewhere expressed his criticism of the director's usurped leadership in 'X', which reportedly antagonised the collective (Wertenstein 1991, 62).

Pasternak's overreliance on Holland as a source of information also affects the sections of the book reporting on the director's surveillance by secret service agents. The author's exclusive use of the materials in the director's private archive makes one wonder whether she conducted any independent research in the archive of the Ministry of Internal Affairs (MSW) or the Institute of National Memory (IPN). That Pasternak developed Holland's life narrative within the space allocated to her by Holland herself may be deduced from the volume's blurb: 'In this book, Agnieszka Holland reveals the truth about her life for the first time' – a claim for veracity that establishes Holland as the ultimate agency standing behind the portrayal, not only the subject but also the covert author or co-author. Not unlike a celebrity writer, as discussed by Braun, Holland constructs herself 'as literary material that has been moulded into fruitful biographical and semi-biographical narratives by the on-going questions of personal proximity and social distance that characterise our experience of the modern media-led world' (Braun 2011, 321). Indeed, the book efficiently balances this blend of proximity and distance to Holland in that it softens her image yet is cautious not to abandon her carefully self-fashioned persona of a reputable director who is engaged in the current political and social debates advocating for a democratic and inclusive society.

The cover photo chosen for Pasternak's book deserves special attention. It shows a black-and-white frontal close-up of Holland's face, marked by many deep wrinkles (see Fig. 7.11). Given its raw aesthetic, the photo is almost a manifesto against beautification in the contemporary mediascape and a sign of courage in an old woman who does not care how she looks or perhaps is even proud of her age. The unadorned image of Holland resists the pressure of contemporary media to look young, beautiful and attractive. Above all, she looks authentic, as if testifying to the blurb's statement that 'in this book, Agnieszka Holland reveals the truth about her life for the first time'. Yet upon closer scrutiny the photo reveals traces of having been staged – a standard practice nowadays. From under heavy eyelids she looks directly, even confrontationally, at us, the readers. In this photo, Holland is anything but the 'object-to-look-at' as conceived by Laura Mulvey in her seminal essay. Rather, the opposite occurs here; it is Holland's interrogating and challenging gaze that is directed at us, the readers and consumers of her public image.

Figure 7.11 The cover of Agnieszka Holland's biography by Karolina Pasternak

PERFORMING AGNIESZKA HOLLAND

All representations of Holland that appear in contemporary media demonstrate her careful control of her public image and awareness of the semiotics of clothes, make-up (or the lack thereof), hairstyle, body posture and so on. While self-fashioning herself for the public, she carefully designs the mise-en-scène aspects of her persona, even if it is to make it look random. She does not offer a consistent style in that she often wears gender-neutral casual clothes, but also boho-style garments or evening attire if called for by the given occasion. For example, in the photos accompanying her and Kasia's interview for *Mirror* (*Zwierciadło*) magazine, the mise-en-scène connotes ordinariness, which was appropriate for a woman's magazine published since 1957 by the Polish Women's League. Although in the twenty-first century it had to undergo refashioning to meet the expectations of modern women functioning in a consumerist society, *Mirror* still differs from other glossies. It tries to balance traditional journalism concerned with important social issues with promotional materials required by the press market. In the interview entitled 'Agnieszka Holland and Kasia Adamik – close but separate',[48] Holland talks about how she brought up her daughter as a single mother whose profession required constant travel. She also admits that she knew about Kasia's gay identity long before her daughter came out. As she adds, 'Fortunately, we lived in the States then, where things were changing in terms of tolerance for homosexual people'. In the photos that accompany the material they both wear casual outfits, and the background is neutral. In one shot, they stand in a doorframe that marks the private space of home; the colours are darkish and unsaturated, their clothes are plain, and there are no special visual effects to enhance the image. The orchestration epitomises ordinariness and authenticity, and as such it serves as a potential point of identification for many ordinary parents of (non-normative) children. Likewise, Holland's outfits at the various protests are deliberately casual, even nondescript, and they de-celebrate and de-glamourise her, in accordance with the discourse promoting her authenticity. As Chouliaraki claims, for celebrities, 'humanization' strategies are necessary in order 'to domesticate their extraordinariness', while '[a]uthenticity emerges in the performance of the celebrity persona as a moral self' (Chouliaraki 2013, 196). Not unlike in her films belonging to the Cinema of Moral Concern that offered a harsh judgement of late-socialist Polish reality, now as a celebrity activist Holland berates Polish authorities for their immoral political decisions concerning the vulnerable and marginalised.

Although Holland has a tenuous connection to social media, she frequently appears on the internet and on television – specifically, TVN. Thus, her presence in contemporary screen cultures is significant, while the boldness of her public statements makes her one of the most recognisable as well as controversial public personas in contemporary Polish and, to a lesser extent, European media. She has accumulated a substantial symbolic capital in performing the roles of both celebrity director and celebrity activist, which testifies to Marshall's claim that

> the condition of celebrity status is convertible to a wide variety of domains and conditions within contemporary culture. Thus, the power of celebrity status appears in business, politics, and artistic communities and operates as a way of providing distinctions and definitions of success within those domains. (Marshall 2014, xlviii)

While moving swiftly between the roles of celebrity director and celebrity activist, Holland is invariably concerned with the realm of politics. She speaks against the powerful (mostly Polish) centre and for the powerless margins. Thus, I would argue, she performs the role of an intellectual who, as Michel Foucault noted, 'spoke the truth to those who had yet to see it, in the name of those who were forbidden to speak the truth; he [sic] was conscience, consciousness, and eloquence' (Foucault and Deleuze 1977, 207). However, as the French philosopher contends, with time, the intellectual became somehow obsolete as the masses began to possess knowledge and could express themselves. Yet, the mass audiences that seemed to replace erstwhile masses is still longing for moral instruction and hope, and activist celebrities fulfil this need with passion and persuasive authenticity. Agnieszka Holland perfectly performs this role, for she knows how to direct these spectacles of her celebrity persona.

NOTES

1. The chapter is an expanded and revised version of the chapter 'Agnieszka Holland's Starburst Career: From Persona non Grata to International Celebrity on Multiple Fronts', published in the volume *Stardust and Starlight: Slavic Screen Celebrities*, edited by Helena Goscilo, Academic Studies Press, 2024.
2. Alina Margolis-Edelman was a Polish-Jewish physician who survived the Holocaust. With her would-be husband, Marek Edelman, she participated in the Warsaw Ghetto Uprising. In 1968, she left Poland for France due to the anti-Semitic campaign. She joined Doctors Without Borders and later she participated in establishing the organisation Doctors of the World. She was especially engaged in helping children who were victims of violence.
3. David P. Marshall acknowledges this shift occurring in contemporary culture and discusses how 'establishing reputation and significance [changed], to its celebrity iconicity and the development of the visible presentation of different boundaries of public and private' (Marshall 2016b, 497). Jono Van Belle applied this approach to Ingmar Bergman's persona that in his native Sweden always functioned as 'both a popular celebrity and a high-art auteur, in part due to his own myth-making' (Van Belle 2019, 4).
4. Van Belle explains 'the difference between *celebrity* and *persona* [is] in the fame-aspect: a celebrity always has a persona, but a persona – as a collection of onstage and offstage roles – is not always a celebrity' (Van Belle 2019, 7).
5. For discussion of authorship as self-fashioning, see Staiger 2003, 49–50; Foucault's concept is used, for example, by Jono Van Belle in her examination of public persona of Ingmar Bergman (Van Belle 2019).
6. Anon., 'Narodziny Kasi', *Ty i Ja*, no. 4, 1973, 12–15.
7. Agnieszka Holland, 'Tępić łokcie', interview by Danuta Nowicka, *Opole*, no. 11, 1979, 4–5; see also: Agnieszka Holland, 'Mamy wspaniałą publiczność', interview by Alina Budzińska, *Panorama*, no. 13, 1979, 24.
8. I have conducted an extensive survey of published interviews with Polish filmmakers professionally active in the 1970s and only Barbara Sass, another female director whose position was comparable to Holland, mentioned her family life. She confessed: 'My professional path was long and difficult, and it was not only because I bore two kids'. She also claimed that film directing was not suitable for women as it was not possible to successfully combine professional and family life (Barbara Sass, 'Procenty dla mnie korzystniejsze', interview by Janina Pałęcka, *Zwierciadło*, no. 52, 1980, 8). In the same interview, she reported how feminists protested awarding her film *Without Love* (*Bez miłości*, 1980) at the film festival in Mannheim for not being feminist enough. As Sass recollected, she told these women that 'we Polish women, despite difficult circumstances, went further on the path towards emancipation'. As for male filmmakers, in one of his interviews, Krzysztof Kieślowski mentioned that he was married and his child was born, yet he did not comment on how it affected his professional life (Krzysztof Kieślowski,

'Chwila namysłu', interview by Zuzanna Jastrzębska, *Filipinka*, no. 21, 1979, 7). Janusz Zaorski, another representative of the Cinema of Moral Concern, said that 'If he had free time, he would have spent it with his family (wife plus daughter) and playing tennis'. Apparently, spending time with his family was for him a 'leisure time' (Janusz Zaorski, 'Zrobiłbym cyrk albo operę', interview by Agnieszka Baranowska, *Kobieta i Życie*, no. 25, 1985, 9).
9. Holland, 'Mamy wspaniałą publiczność'.
10. Agnieszka Holland, 'Poczucie silnej niesprawiedliwości. . .', interview by Barbara Bobecka, *Tygodnik Demokratyczny*, no. 10, 1979, 4, 13.
11. Agnieszka Holland, 'Rozmowy kuluarowe. Do filmu weszła nowa generacja', interview by Teresa Zwierzchowska, *Wieczór Wybrzeża*, no. 206, 1979, 2.
12. Agnieszka Holland, 'Minimalnie redukować', interview by Zofia Jaremko, *Walka Młodych*, no. 42, 1981, 17. Barbara Sass expressed similar disdain for the concept of women's cinema: 'In my opinion, there is nothing like this and it was invented for critics and journalists', while at the same time admitting the difficult situation of women in the film industry (see Barbara Sass, 'Przeciętność nie zainteresuje nikogo', interview by Janusz Kołodziej, *Sztandar Młodych* 123, 8 August 1982, 2). In another interview, she declared 'I do not have any feminist inclinations and I do not want to have them' (Barbara Sass 'Szukać prawdy w losach jednostki', interview by Małgorzata Dipont, *Życie Warszawy*, 15 August 1982, 4).
13. Kieślowski was not a member of the film unit 'X', however, his films from the 1970s belong to the Cinema of Moral Concern that was mostly associated with Wajda's cohort.
14. At the meeting of the Approval Commission for *Interrogation*, Czesław Petelski, the director who vehemently supported the political authorities of socialist Poland, claimed that the film is a piece of ugly and brazen anti-communist propaganda that shows the most despicable atrocities of Stalinism to have been committed by Jewish communists such as Holland's father (see Biełous 1994, 166).
15. Agnieszka Holland, 'Mówi Agnieszka Holland', *Tygodnik Powszechny*, no. 6, 1992, 5.
16. In her essay on the extratextual contexts of Kathryn Bigelow's authorship, Rona Murray notes that she established 'representation of herself as strong in masculine terms' (Murray 2011, 5), which Holland did in the 1970s in the Polish film industry. While admitting the gender essentialism informing such a claim, Deborah Jermyn agrees with Murray's observation (Jermyn 2021, 371).
17. This is a factual error (see Chapter Two).
18. In 2012, the second and expanded edition of the book was published, which testifies to its popularity and Holland's status as celebrity director.
19. In the conversations with Holland, Kornatowska does not mention it, although they talk about Jewishness several times, while discussing Holland's father and the critical attack of the French critics on Wajda's *Korczak*.
20. Rita Kempley, 'Agnieszka Holland: A War on Stupidity – Polish-Born Director of "Washington Square" Faces Off against the Mindless Moviemaking Machine', *The Washington Post*, 12 October 1997, G7.
21. Kempley, 'Agnieszka Holland'.
22. Kempley, 'Agnieszka Holland'.
23. Kempley, 'Agnieszka Holland'.
24. Kempley, 'Agnieszka Holland'.
25. Kempley, 'Agnieszka Holland'.
26. Accessed 3 October 2023.
27. Among other recipients of the award are Krzysztof Penderecki, Karol Dedecius, Volker Schlöndorff, Tadeusz Mazowiecki, Günter Grass and Adam Michnik.
28. Guy Lodge, '"Charlatan", film review', *Variety* 27, February 2020.

29. https://www.facebook.com/events/polish-social-cultural-association/posk-cinema-21-charlatan-oscars-2021-preview-thursday-2204-730pm/1106511953165356/ (accessed 12 May 2023).
30. Gregory Elwood, 'Agnieszka Holland on her "Urine" Oscar movie "Charlatan," "The Wire" & more' [podcast], 'The Playlist', 5 March 2020; https://theplaylist.net/agnieszka-holland-charlatan-podcast-20210305/ (accessed 12 May 2023).
31. This radically changed in the case of Ukrainian refuges escaping to Poland after Russia's invasion of the country. In 2022, Poland opened its borders to the Ukrainians without any restrictions and provided them with basic health care and work permission, in addition to education of children.
32. 'Fałszywy cytat w manipulacyjnym kontekście. Reżyserzy piszą o kłamstwie Kaczyńskiego', TVN24, 25 February 2019. https://tvn24.pl/polska/kaczynski-zacytowal-holland-polscy-rezyserzy-oskarzaja-go-o-manipulacje-ra912933-2304411 (accessed 4 November 2022).
33. Zygmunt Bauman's biography is the most conspicuous example of the complex relationship between an intellectual and communist doctrine to which he vehemently adhered during the Second World War and the period of Stalinism. An exhaustive and succinct examination of the issue is presented in a recently published biography of Bauman by Artur Domosławski, *Exile* (*Wygnaniec*, 2021).
34. In one of her recent interviews, while discussing her approach to cinema, Holland used Żeromski's quote ('Agnieszka Holland dla Interii: Nigdy nie jest moim celem, żeby szkodzić Polsce', interview by Krystian Zając, *InteriaFilm*, 5 May 2023), https://film.interia.pl/raport-off-camera-2023/news-agnieszka-holland-dla-interii-nigdy-nie-jest-moim-celem-zeby,nId,6759208#utm_source=paste&utm_medium=paste&utm_campaign=safari (accessed 31 July 2023).
35. Agnieszka Holland, 'Do widzenia', https://www.theguardian.com/politics/ng-interactive/2020/jan/31/27-europeans-say-farewell-to-britain-brexit-bjorn-ulvaeus-nicola-coughlan-wolfgang-tillmans (accessed 28 April 2023).
36. While reporting on Holland's farewell to Brexit, Polish journalists skipped the fact that she was one of twenty-seven people invited by *The Guardian* to share their reflections on Brexit. As a result, some Polish readers might have misperceived Holland's criticism as an individual voice coming from Central Europe.
37. Quoted in: Nick Holdsworth, 'European Academy President Agnieszka Holland Slams Cannes for Welcoming a Russian Movie', *Variety*, 21 May 2022, https://variety.com/2022/film/global/european-film-academy-agnieszka-holland-cannes-russia-1235274070/ (accessed 27 September 2022).
38. Agnieszka Holland, 'Agnieszka Holland: Mechanizm dzisiejszej nagonki na LGBT jest podobny do tej na Żydów w XX w.', interview by Magda Podsiadło, *Gazeta Wyborcza*, online version, 23 August 2020. https://wroclaw.wyborcza.pl/wroclaw/7,35771,26228592,agnieszka-holland-mechanizm-dzisiejszej-nagonki-na-lgbt-jest.html?disableRedirects=true#commentsAnchor (accessed 30 August 2022).
39. 'Andrzej Duda znów o LGBT', https://www.tokfm.pl/Tokfm/7,103087,26028952,andrzej-duda-znow-o-lgbt-probuje-sie-nam-wmowic-ze-to-ludzie.html (accessed 31 July 2023).
40. In the same year, Olga Tokarczuk put up for auction the replica of her Nobel medal. https://dzieckoifigura.pl/to-przekazaly-na-wosp-gwiazdy-niektore-byly-naprawde-hojne/ (accessed 1 May 2023).
41. The internet portal 'wpolityce.pl' announced it under the heading: 'It is a super attraction, dinner with Agnieszka Holland' https://wpolityce.pl/kultura/321946-to-ma-byc-super-atrakcja-kolacja-z-agnieszka-holland-wsrod-filmowych-aukcji-na-rzecz-wosp (accessed 1 May 2023).

42. Agnieszka Holland, 'Agnieszka Holland i Kasia Adamik – blisko, ale oddzielnie', interview by Alina Gutek. *Zwierciadło*, online edition, 25 September 2019. https://zwierciadlo.pl/zwierciadlo-poleca/318612,1,agnieszka-holland-i-kasia-adamik--blisko-ale-oddzielnie.read (accessed 30 August 2022).
43. Andrzej Wajda Archive. Apparently, Pasternak has not researched the Wajda Archive, which stores numerous documents concerning their professional and private relationship.
44. Holland also talks about this topic in the 2013 documentary *Return of Agnieszka H.*, directed by Krystyna Krauze and Jacek Petrycki, which presents Holland's recollections of her stay in Prague.
45. Agnieszka Holland, 'Robić filmy. Rozmowa "Przekroju" z Agnieszką Holland', interview by Wilhelmina Skulska, *Przekrój*, no. 2305, 1989, 8–9.
46. She also mentions relatively often her nephew, Antoni Komasa-Łazarkiewicz who has composed music for several of her films.
47. See Shana Penn, *Solidarity's Secret: The Women Who Defeated Communism in Poland* (Ann Arbor: University of Michigan Press, 2003).
48. Holland, 'Agnieszka Holland i Kasia Adamik – blisko, ale oddzielnie'.

Conclusion

Not long before I was finishing the book, I discovered that a meeting of Agnieszka Holland's 'clan' would be a key event of the 2023 edition of the annual Polish-Czech-Slovak film festival Cinema on the Border (Kino na granicy/Kino na hranicyi). The festival takes place in Cieszyn (Těšín), a Polish-Czech border town. The event's venue symbolically signals the transnationality of Holland's work, while also marking her connection with the Czech Republic and Slovakia where her cinematic journey began. I cannot think of a better phrase than 'cinema on the border' to encapsulate Holland's work and her life, and I separate these two for rhetorical reasons only. As demonstrated throughout this volume, the phrase aptly captures her whole oeuvre, which occupies borderline positions within theoretical and critical categories. Her works also inhabit an interstitial space between various modes of production, genres, and styles. Manoeuvring between art and popular cinema, the realistic and the supranatural, she explores contemporary and historical topics in big-budget dramas and independent arthouse productions. Although her authorship is not always manifestly present in the textualities of her work, it is efficiently exercised in the area of screen cultures. While often forced by various circumstances to work as 'a lonely woman', she has always been surrounded by many people she worked with.

On 1 May 2023, the Cinema on the Border festival attendees had a rare opportunity to meet and to listen to Agnieszka Holland, her sister Magdalena Łazarkiewicz, her daughter Kasia Adamik, her nephew and his wife, Antoni Komasa-Łazarkiewicz and Mary Komasa, her nephew Michał Bielawski, her niece Gabriela Łazarkiewicz-Sieczko, her long-term collaborator and friend Jacek Petrycki, and Krzysztof Zanussi, with whom she did her first assistantship and who later produced several of her films. I have mentioned all of them in the volume as Holland's collaborators, who happened to be also her relatives and friends. Łukasz Maciejewski, the Polish film critic and organiser of the event, labelled it a 'Meeting with the Holland clan'. The appearance of the group at the festival can be seen as a symbolic confirmation of her collaborative authorship as examined throughout the book. Importantly, the organisers decided to present not only Holland's works but also films made by her friends and relatives. Thus, Holland was not presented as a solitary *auteur* but as a central figure in a network of various people she has worked with. As always in her career, the personal has merged with the professional, while she occupied a position of matriarch of this multigenerational kinship company.[1] Her central position is twofold: in the professional field, she usually works as a director who possesses the highest control among the team (though in the case of TV series, the control is significantly limited), while in the family – a structure based on a loose concept of kinship – her position is due to her age and efforts to consolidate it on various fronts. As often commented on by her relatives, she inherited the role of matriarch from her mother, Irena Rybczyńska-Holland, a journalist. The relatively high number of Holland's female relatives working in the media industry may suggest that there is a matrilinear creative energy passed between generations.

The event celebrating Holland's clan can also be seen as symbolically marking the director's journey, from her beginnings in the film unit 'X', where to succeed she had to perform a masculinist masquerade, to her strong position in an informal, matriarchal creative team. In this, hers can be seen as akin to the professional trajectory of Alice Guy, who, as Kimberly Tomadjoglou convincingly demonstrated, started by conforming to the patriarchal structures of the French film industry, only to implement matriarchal rules and principles in her own studio in America (Tomadjoglou 2015). Holland has also developed her career within the patriarchal systems of Polish, Western European and Hollywood production cultures, while gradually strengthening her position within these industries and working towards what I call 'an affective filmmaking network'.

Family collaboration in cinema is nothing unusual, as exemplified by brother duos such as the Tavianis, Dardennes or Coens, not to mention marital couples such as Federico Fellini and Giulietta Masina, Jean-Luc Godard and Anna Karina, or Jerzy Kawalerowicz and Lucyna Winnicka, yet these usually consisted of a male director and an actress as his spousal muse. There is also the Makhmalbaf Film House founded by the renowned Iranian director Mohsen Makhmalbaf, who was joined by his wife and three children. However, this is not so much a collaborative network as a production company that facilitates the individual careers of the family members. Holland's 'clan' is an informal network replicating the structure of the extended family, or a modern modification of the kinship relationship –

including close friends, spouses and partners – who often work together on the same projects. Moreover, Holland frequently takes up the task of mentoring over the projects of younger filmmakers, with *Lure* (*Córki dancingu*, 2015) by Agnieszka Smoczyńska being the most remarkable example. Her current creative collective can be seen as an affective network that radically differs from collaborative or collective authorship as practised today in the global film industry. The team's work is regulated not only by the principles of production efficiency and professionalism but also by emotional exchanges between the members.

Although Holland's team consists mostly of female filmmakers, it does not correspond to Claire Johnston's concept of female creative collectives as the Polish filmmaker's works made together with her peers are anything but 'counter cinema' as conceived by the pioneering feminist film critic. Instead, Holland's clan can be linked with the ideological meanings ascribed to: Polish family, which in the nineteenth and twentieth centuries served as a site of resistance in national struggles; a pre-war tradition of emancipation that urged for women's cooperation; and communist advocacy for collective actions as efficient means of implementing social and cultural changes. Although each of these ideological formations has been often misused or abused – as in the case of the idea of collective work, which served during the period of Stalinism as a tool of totalitarian oppression and economic exploitation – in their revisionist variant they have also proved efficient in struggling with socialist authoritarianism. The film unit 'X' was a stellar example of such a creative collective that worked towards political change. Holland matured as a filmmaker in such an environment and has implemented the idea of collaborative authorship in her subsequent transnational work. Over the years, she gained a reputation that provided her with authority to decide who to work with, and on what terms. Although her collaborative authorship fits the neoliberal agenda of corporate work, it has a different genealogy to national and communist emancipatory collectives. Holland's team has also instigated a sort of continuity in her works that have been made within various production cultures. Having at her side a small number of people she knew and trusted may have made crossing borders between various geopolitical locations and professional environments easier and smoother. While entering these vast and diversified spaces of screen industries, she had to adjust to their rules but was also making some efforts to familiarise these through the people she had worked with before.

Apart from the support Holland has received from her collaborators, for most of her professional career she has had to struggle to penetrate the 'glass ceiling' limiting women's access to financial sources and means of production in film industries. Her determination to work emerges as instrumental in the development of her career since its very beginning as it required adapting to various media and genres. Her impressive productivity, as examined throughout the book, has resulted from both creative work and hard labour, which she has frequently acknowledged through commenting on the conditions on a film set, technical personnel and production organisation. Her sensitivity to the labour aspect of filmmaking originates no doubt from working in different production cultures such as the state-funded national cinema of socialist Poland, independent Western European cinema, global Hollywood, and post-communist transnational European cinemas. Within each of these systems, the variety in labour conditions affected her creative work as director. Over the years, she frequently foregrounded the material and laborious aspect of filmmaking regardless of genres and modes of cinema. Neither *auteur* cinema, nor industrial authorship, Holland's work represents post-auteurism, yet in its specific variant of affective laborious collaboration.

In a similar vein, Holland's work can be addressed as post-women's cinema. As the title of one of the volume's sections indicates, she has been navigating between being 'in' and 'out' of women's cinema. While at the beginning of her career, she distanced herself from both feminism and women's cinema her works privileged female characters and adopted their perspectives or resisted reproducing patriarchal structures. Holland's masculinist masquerades and performances in the Polish cinema of the 1970s were the only available option to work within the system of patriarchal socialist cultural production. Yet her strategy proved efficient in terms of achieved position and visibility within the public spaces of that time. Therefore, while approaching her work from the perspective of women's cinema, it is worth citing Christine Gledhill and Julia Knight's succinct observation, 'Like ourselves, the women we research are formed by their times – while they may push against the grain, they are nevertheless caught within what their times allow to their imaginations and roles' (Gledhill and Knight 2015, 5). The gap between the researcher and her object of study is not only of a temporal but also of a geopolitical nature. In authoritarian Poland of the 1970s, patriarchy was firmly embedded in nationalism, yet there was also a strong emancipatory tradition that dates back to the nineteenth century and merged with the communist concept of gender equality and state feminism after the Second World War. None of these traditions can be unproblematically embedded within the framework of Western-style feminism that, with a significant delay, has finally reached Polish society. Holland's strong position in Polish cinema of the 1970s originates from the vernacular model of emancipation that in both national and communist variants emphasised the liberating aspect of paid work as a condition for female subjectivity to emerge.

Since leaving Poland, Holland has been gradually detaching herself from the patriarchal scripts of Polish national culture, while exploring other individual and collective identities, something noted by the American film scholar

Barbara Quart. As Quart admitted, the Polish film director adapted well to the Western world, while 'reaccenting her work to stress its feminist rather than Polish strain, something perhaps partly facilitated by the way the ethos of traditional "Polishness" is tinged with a masculinist military virtue her gender made her question' (Quart 1988, 204). Indeed, *Angry Harvest* legitimises the claim, as does *Europa, Europa*, which American critics placed, as Paul Coates observed, in 'a largely feminist light on a work in which, for a change, a woman director shows a male naked and charts with black humour the dangers of betrayal by one's penis' (Coates 2005, 172). However, as Dina Iordanova noted, in the course of her international career, Holland has not made women's issues the central concern of her work (Iordanova 2003, 123). Recently, she occasionally engages with explorations of female subjectivity, while exercising her female agency in the field of film practice and socio-political activities. In her work and in her public appearances, she takes a position of the woman shaped by specific socio-political-cultural circumstances. Therefore, I see her as representing post-women's cinema, in order to shift the emphasis from the textualities of her work to her subjective agency. I contend that her gendered public persona contextualises her whole output, including also works that do not directly explore women's subjectivity yet were made from the perspective of a female filmmaker even if occasionally hidden in a masculine cultural attire.

Finally, her complex and multidirectional professional life trajectories give insight into developments in post-communist East Central European cinemas in terms of newly emerging modes of production and artistic scripts. Specifically, she epitomises East Central European transnationalism, which cannot be contained within either 'accented' migrant cinema or global Hollywood. While benefitting from various European schemes of funding, her recent films work towards incorporating East Central European historical experience into a larger body of European collective memory. For example, one of her recent films, *Mr Jones* (2019), telling the story of the Welsh journalist who attempted to inform the Western world about the Ukrainian Holodomor, demonstrates the intrinsic interconnection between various regions of the continent. Finally, the textually marked position of 'double occupancy' in these films epitomises the region's borderline location within European community.

Critical discourse around versatile Holland's work – as discussed throughout the book – is equally diversified, and as such it exemplifies the concept of 'situated knowledges' as proposed by Donna Haraway in her seminal essay published in 1988 (Haraway 1988). As she astutely explains, knowledge as a result of research or critical enquiry is undertaken and conducted within a specific context, 'a situation' that needs to be recognised: '[s]ituated knowledges require that the object of knowledge be pictured as an actor and agent, not as a screen or a ground or a resource, never finally as slave to the master that closes off the dialectic in his unique agency and his authorship of "objective" knowledge' (Haraway 1988, 592). Jane Feuer builds on this argument and relates it to the issue of aesthetic judgements: 'The judgement of quality is always situated. That is to say that somebody makes the judgement from some aesthetic or political or moral position' (2007, 145). These positions, as she further explains, are consolidated within what Stanley Fish calls an '*interpretive community*, that is, a professional community whose norms, ideals, and methods determine an interpretation's validity' (2005). Polish film critics and scholars' insistence on Holland's work representing *auteur* cinema with an emphasis on stylistic and aesthetic continuities are thus not to be either legitimised or falsified but rather approached as situated knowledge produced within a specific interpretive community. Likewise, the critical reception of her works abroad needs to be examined as expressing cultural formation rather than ultimate critical judgement.

Therefore, Holland's work and the corresponding ancillary discourses reveal that the concepts of authorship, women's cinema and (trans)national cinema need to be subjected to ongoing revisions and adjustments. While working on this book and subjecting Holland's work to analysis within specific theoretical frameworks, I have been gradually disclosing the situatedness of the existing critical discourse, as well as the employed critical categories themselves. Rather unexpectedly, Holland's work has emerged as a complex nexus of conflicting ideologies and aesthetics that resists embedding within customary categories of art cinema, popular cinema, women's cinema, national and transnational cinema. She represents embodied and situated, to borrow from Haraway, authorship in making visible her female experience of a (travelling) filmmaker who has moved across various geopolitical and economic locations adapting to their dominant discourses, while also subverting these whenever possible.

Finally, the book itself produces a 'situated knowledge' on Holland's work in that I have been writing it from a position of an academic woman who was brought up and educated in socialist Poland and then relocated to other geopolitical locations. Unavoidably, I have been employing simultaneously the inside and outside perspective on her oeuvre, while trying to foreground the situatedness of the produced knowledge. Yet, as mentioned in the preface, Holland is still active and productive, thus her work remains open for other differently 'situated' critical and theoretical interventions.

NOTE

1. Holland's 'clan' can be seen in the context of recent research on kinship. As Janet Carston noted 'kinship has undergone a rebirth. [. . .] It has become standard, in works on kinship published since the 1980s, for gender, the body, and personhood to
feature prominently in the analysis' (Carsten 2000, 3).

Filmography

FILM AND TELEVISION WORKS DIRECTED BY AGNIESZKA HOLLAND

The Debtors (*Dłużnicy*) (1974) Poland; Polish Television Theatre; 70 mins.
Girl and 'Aquarius' (*Dziewczyna i 'Aquarius'*) novella in an omnibus film *Pictures from Life* (*Obrazki z życia*) (1975) Poland; Film Unit 'X' for Polish Television; 15 mins.
An Evening at Abdon (*Wieczór u Abdona*) (1975) Poland; Film Unit 'X' for Polish Television; 38 mins.
Homemade Wine (*Wino domowej roboty*) (1975) Poland; Polish Television Theatre; 65 mins.
Sunday Children (*Niedzielne dzieci*) (1976) Poland; Film Unit 'X' for Polish Television; 73 mins.
Screen Tests (*Zdjęcia próbne*) (1976) Poland; Film Unit 'X'; 99 mins.
Something for Something (*Coś za coś*) (1977) Poland; Film Unit 'X' for Polish Television; 61 mins.
Provincial Actors (*Aktorzy prowincjonalni*) (1978) Poland; Film Unit 'X'; 104 mins.
Lorenzaccio (1978) Poland; Polish Television Theatre; 123 mins (co-directed with Laco Adamik).
Wheel Breaking (*Łamanie kolem*) (1979) Poland; Polish Television Theatre.
Fever (*Gorączka*) (1980) Poland; Film Unit 'X'; 116 mins.
The Trial (*Proces*) (1980) Poland; Polish Television Theatre; 119 mins.
A Woman Alone (*Kobieta samotna*) (1981) Poland; Film Unit 'X' for Polish Television; 92 mins.
Czapski (1985) France; Video Kontakt (Paris); 73 mins (co-directed with Andrzej Wolski).
Culture (*Kultura*) (1985) France; Video Kontakt (Paris) (co-directed with Andrzej Wolski).
Angry Harvest (*Bittere Ernte*) (1985) West Germany; West Germany – CCC, Admiral in association with ZDF; 101 mins.
KOR (1988), France: Video Kontakt (Paris); 53 mins (co-directed with Andrzej Wolski).
To Kill a Priest (1988) United States-France; Columbia Pictures, France 3 Cinéma, J. P. Productions, Sofica Valor; 117 mins.
Europa, Europa (1990) Germany-France-Poland; Les Films du Losagne, CCC-Filmkunst GmbH (West Berlin); 112 mins.
Largo Desolato (1991) France; France 3 Cinéma, France 3, La Sept Cinéma; 90 mins.
Olivier, Olivier (1991); France; Oliane Productions, Films A2 (in association with Canal+, Soficas Inverstimages, Centre National du Cinéma et de L'image Animée); 110 mins.
The Secret Garden (1993) United States; Warner Bros., American Zoetrope; 101 mins.

Total Eclipse (1995) France-United Kingdom-Belgium; FIT Productions, Portman Productions, Société Française de Production (SFP), K2 SA (in association with Capitol Films, European Co-production Fund, Canal+); 111 mins.

Red Wind (1995) an episode of the TV series *Fallen Angels* (1993–6, Showtime).

Washington Square (1997) United States; Hollywood Pictures, Roger Birnbaum Productions (in association with Alchemy Filmworks), Caravan Pictures; 115 mins.

The Dybbuk (Dybuk) (1999) Poland; Polish Television Theatre; 91 mins.

The Third Miracle (1999) United States; American Zoetrope, Franchise Pictures, Haft Entertainment; 119 mins.

Golden Dreams (2001) United States; Walt Disney Pictures, Golden Dreams Pictures; 22 mins.

Shot in the Heart (2001) United States; HBO, The Levinson/Fontana Company; 98 mins.

Julie Walking Home (2002); Germany-Canada-Poland-United States; Studio Filmowe Tor (in association with Polish Television, Canal+ Poland, The Cinematography Committee (Poland), Art Oko Film GmbH & Co. Filmproduktions KG, Das Werk Digitale Bildbearbeitungs GmbH, Hidden Films Inc., IMX Communications Inc., Telefilm Canada); 118 mins.

Cold Case (2004, 2007, 2009) TV Series; United States; Jerry Bruckheimer Television, CBS, Warner Bros. Television; 4 × 44 mins: 'Hubris' (S1 E11); 'The Plan' (S1 E22); 'Justice' (S5 E10); 'Lotto Fever' (S6 E12).

The Wire (2004, 2006, 2008); TV Series; United States; HBO Entertainment, Blown Deadline Productions; 3 × 58 mins: 'Moral Midgetry' (S3 E8); 'Corner Boys' (S4 E8); 'React Quotes' (S5 E5).

Copying Beethoven (2005) Germany-United Kingdom-Hungary; VIP Medienfonds 2 (in association with Copying Beethoven, Eurofilm Stúdió); 104 mins.

A Girl Like Me: The Gwen Araujo Story (2006) United States; Braun Entertainment Group; 88 mins.

The Crew (Ekipa) (2007); TV Series; Poland; ATM Grupa for Polsat; 6 × 50 mins.

Janosik – A True Story (Janosik. Prawdziwa historia) (Polish), *Jánošík – Pravdivá história* (Slovak), *Jánošík – Pravdivá historie* (Czech), *Janosik – Egy igaz történet* (Hungarian). (2009) Poland-Hungary-Czech Republic-Slovakia; Apple Film Productions (in association with In Film, Polish Television, Charlie's, HBO Europe, Eurofilm Studio); 137 mins (co-directed with Kasia Adamik).

Janosik – A True Story (Janosik. Prawdziwa historia) (Polish), *Jánošík – Pravdivá história* (Slovak), *Jánošík – Pravdivá historie* (Czech), *Janosik – Egy igaz történet* (Hungarian). (2009) TV Series; Poland-Czech Republic-Hungary-Slovakia; Apple Film Productions (in association with In Film, Polish Television, Charlie's, HBO Europe, Eurofilm Studio); 4 × 45 mins (co-directed with Kasia Adamik).

Treme (2010–1, 2013); TV Series; United States; Blown Deadline Productions, HBO Entertainment; 2 × 80 mins + 1 × 58 mins + 1 × 75 mins: 'Do You Know What It Means' (S1 E1); 'I'll Fly Away' (S1 E10); 'That's What Lovers Do' (S2 E10); 'To Miss New Orleans' (S4 E5).

The Killing (2011) TV Series; United States; Fox Television Studios, Fuse Entertainment, KMF Films, Fabrik Entertainment; 3 × 45 mins: 'What You Have Left' (S1 E6); 'Undertow' (S1 E9); 'Reflections' (S2 E1).

In Darkness (2011) Poland-Canada-Germany; Schmidtz Katze Filmkollektiv GmbH, Studio Filmowe Zebra, The Film Works; 138 mins.

Without Secrets (Bez tajemnic) (2013) TV Series; Poland; TV Series; Telemark, HBO Poland; 4 × 25 mins.

Burning Bush (Hořící keř) (2013) TV Series; Czech Republic; TV Series; HBO, Etamp Film Production, Nutprodukce; 3 × 75 mins.

Rosemary's Baby (2015) TV Series; United States-France-Canada; City Entertainment, KippSter Entertainment, Lionsgate Television for NBC; 2 × 120 mins.

House of Cards (2015) TV Series; United States; MRC, Trigger Street Productions, Wade/Thomas Productions, Knight Takes King Productions for Netflix; 4 × 55 mins.

Spoor (*Pokot*) (2017) Poland-Czech Republic-Germany-Sweden; Studio Filmowe Tor (in association with Heimatfilm GmbH, Nutprodukce, Chimney Group, National Audiovisual Institute, Odra Film, HBO Poland, Agora); 128 mins.

1983 (2018) TV Series; Poland-United States; The Kennedy/Marshall Company, House Media Company for Netflix; 2 × 55 mins.

The First (2018) TV Series; United States; Westward Endeavor Content, Channel 4 Television for Hulu and Channel 4; 2 × 45 mins.

Mr Jones (2019) Poland-United Kingdom-Ukraine; Parkhurst (in association with Kinorob, Jones Boy Film, Studio Produkcyjne Orka, Kino Świat, Kraków Festival Office, Silesia Film); 119 mins.

Charlatan (*Šarlatán*) (2020) Czech Republic-Poland-Ireland; Marlene Film Production (in association with Film and Music Entertainment Ireland, Madants, Studio Metrage, Moderator Inwestycje, Furia Film); 113 mins.

The Green Border (2023) Poland-France-Belgium-Czech Republic; Metro Films, Blick Productions, Marlene Film Production, Beluga Tree; 147 mins.

FILMSCRIPT WORK BY AGNIESZKA HOLLAND

The Debtors (*Dłużnicy*) (1974) Poland; based on a play by Leonid Zhukhovitsky.
An Evening at Abdon (*Wieczór u Abdona*) (1975) Poland; based on a novel by Jarosław Iwaszkiewicz.
Sunday Children (*Niedzielne dzieci*) (1976) Poland.
Screen Tests (*Zdjęcia próbne*) (1976) Poland; co-authored with Paweł Kędzierski, Jerzy Domaradzki, Feliks Falk.
Something for Something (*Coś za coś*) (1977) Poland; based on a play by Andrzej Szypulski.
Provinicial Actors (*Aktorzy prowincjonalni*) (1978) Poland, co-authored with Witold Zatorski.
A Shattered Mirror (*Okruch lustra*) (1978) Poland; Poltel; 65 mins; directed by Andrzej Zajączkowski.
Without Anesthesia (*Bez znieczulenia*) (1978) Poland; Film Unit 'X'; 125 mins; directed by Andrzej Wajda.
The Victors (*Zwycięzcy*) (1978) Poland; Documentary Film Studio; 13 mins; directed by Andrzej Zajączkowski.
The Trial (*Proces*) (1980) Poland; based on a novel by Franz Kafka; co-authored with Laco Adamik.
A Woman Alone (*Kobieta samotna*) (1981) Poland; co-authored with Maciej Karpiński.
Unwanted Man (*Mężczyzna niepotrzebny!*) (1981) Poland; Film Unit' X'; 95 mins; directed by Laco Adamik.
Danton (1982) Poland-France; Les Films du Losagne (in association with Film Unit 'X' and Les Films Moliere); 130 mins; directed by Andrzej Wajda; written by Jean-Claude Carriere; screenplay collaboration with Andrzej Wajda, Bolesław Michałek, Jacek Gąsiorowski.
Love in Germany (*Eine Liebe in Deutschland*) (1983) West Germany-France; CCC-Filmkunst GmbH, Gaumont, TF1; 102 mins; directed by Andrzej Wajda.
Czapski (1985) France; co-authored with Andrzej Wolski.
Angry Harvest (*Bittere Ernte*) (1985) West Germany; based on a novel by Hermann H. Field and Stanisław Mierzeński; co-authored with Paul Hengge.
Culture (*Kultura*) (1985) France; co-authored with Andrzej Wolski.
Anna (1987) United States; Vestron Pictures, Magnus Films; 100 mins; directed by Yurek Bogayewicz.
La Amiga (1988) Argentina-West Germany; Alma Film, Jorge Estrada Mora Producciones, Journal-Film Klaus Volkenborn, Sender Freies Berlin; 110 mins; directed by Jeanine Meerapftel.

Les Possédés (1988) France; Gaumont Production, Films A2, Les Films du Losagne (in participation with Centre National du Cinéma et de l'image Animée); 116 mins; directed by Andrzej Wajda; written by Jean-Claude Carriere; screenplay collaboration with Andrzej Wajda and Edward Żebrowski.

To Kill a Priest (1988) United States-France; co-authored with Jean-Yves Pitoun.

Europa, Europa (1990) Germany-France-Poland, based on a memoir by Salomon Perel.

Korczak (1990) Poland-Germany; Film Unit 'Perspektywa', Regina Ziegler Filmproduktion, Telmar Film International Ltd., Erato Films, ZDF, BBC Films; 113 mins; directed by Andrzej Wajda.

Largo Desolato (1991) France; based on a play by Václav Havel.

Olivier, Olivier (1991); France.

Trois Couleurs. Blanc (1993) Poland-France-Switzerland; MK2 Productions SA, France 3, CAB Production (Losanne), 'Tor' Film Studio; 88 mins; directed by Krzysztof Kieślowski; written by Krzysztof Kieślowski and Krzysztof Piesiewicz; screenplay consultant.

Trois Couleurs. Bleu (1993) Poland-France-Switzerland; MK2 Productions SA, CED Productions, France 3, CAB Production (Losanne), 'Tor' Film Studio; 94 mins; directed by Krzysztof Kieślowski; written by Krzysztof Kieślowski, Krzysztof Piesiewicz; screenplay collaboration with Edward Żebrowski and Sławomir Idziak.

Trois Couleurs. Rouge (1993) Poland-France-Switzerland MK2 Productions SA, France 3, CAB Production (Losanne), 'Tor' Film Studio; 95 mins; directed by Krzysztof Kieślowski; written by Krzysztof Kieślowski and Krzysztof Piesiewicz; screenplay consultant.

The Dybbuk (*Dybuk*) (1999) Poland; based on a play by S. Ansky translated by Michał Friedman.

Julie Walking Home (2002) Germany-Canada-Poland-United States; co-authored with Arlene Sarner, Roman Gren.

Enen (2009) Poland; Documentary and Feature Film Studios; 95 mins; directed by Feliks Falk; written by Feliks Falk; screenplay collaboration.

Spoor (*Pokot*) (2017) Poland-Czech Republic-Germany-Sweden; based on a novel by Olga Tokarczuk; co-authored with Olga Tokarczuk.

Marek Edelman . . . And There Was Love in the Ghetto (*Marek Edelman . . . I była miłość w getcie*) (2019) Poland-Germany; Otter Films; 80 mins; directed and written by Jolanta Dylewska; screenplay collaboration.

The Green Border (*Zielona granica*) (2023) Poland-France-Belgium-Czech Republic; co-authored with Gabriela Łazarkiewicz-Sieczko, Maciej Pisuk.

FILMS PRODUCED BY AGNIESZKA HOLLAND

The Offsiders (*Boisko bezdomnych*) (2008) Poland; 'Tor' Film Studio (in co-production with Polish Television, Documentary and Feature Film Studios, Non Stop Film Service); 119 mins, directed by Kasia Adamik.

1983 (2018) TV Series; Poland-United States; directed by Agnieszka Holland, Kasia Adamik, Olga Chajdas, Agnieszka Smoczyńska. Executive Producer.

AGNIESZKA HOLLAND AS AN ACTRESS

Illumination (*Iluminacja*) (1972) Poland; Film Unit 'Tor'; 87 mins; directed by Krzysztof Zanussi. Member of the Board of Examiners; uncredited.

Lasst uns frei fliegen über den garten (1974) Poland-West Germany; ZDF; 40 mins; directed by Stanisław Latałło. Writer on a congress; uncredited.

Scar (*Blizna*) (1976) Poland; Film Unit 'Tor'; 102 mins; directed by Krzysztof Kieślowski. Bednarz's secretary.

Man of Marble (*Człowiek z marmuru*) (1976) Poland; Film Unit 'X'; 153 mins; directed by Andrzej Wajda. Woman interviewing Mateusz Birkut for the Polish Film Chronicle; uncredited.

Screen Tests (*Zdjęcia próbne*) (1976) Poland; directed by Agnieszka Holland, Paweł Kędzierski and Jerzy Domaradzki. Agnieszka, the director; uncredited.

Interrogation (*Przesłuchanie*) (1982) Poland; Film Unit 'X'; 111 mins; directed by Ryszard Bugajski. Communist Witkowska.

The Crew (*Ekipa*) (2007) TV Series; Poland; TV Series; episode 14; directed by Agnieszka Holland. Participant in Szczęsny's funeral; uncredited.

The Offsiders (*Boisko bezdomnych*) (2008) Poland; directed by Kasia Adamik. Woman on the Warsaw Central Station; uncredited.

Amateurs (*Amatorzy*) (2020) Poland; Autograf (in co-production with Polish Television, Studio Fonograf, Studio Produkcyjne Orka, MX35, Gdynia City Hall); 95 mins; directed by Iwona Siekierzyńska. Self; uncredited.

DOCUMENTARIES ABOUT AGNIESZKA HOLLAND

Profession: Director. Agnieszka Holland (*Zawód: reżyser. Agnieszka Holland*) (2008) Poland; Polish Television; 19 mins; directed and written by Piotr Stasik.

I Was an Object of Surveillance: Agnieszka Holland (*Byłem figurantem SB. Agnieszka Holland*) (2008) Poland; TVN; 22 mins; directed and written by Marcin Więcław.

Agnieszka Holland (2008) Poland; Agencja Artystyczna Partus (for Polish Television); 57 mins; directed and written by Wiesław Dąbrowski.

In Lightness (*W świetle*) (2012) Poland; Buksfilm; 27 mins; directed by Jolanta Dylewska.

The Return of Agnieszka H. (*Powrót Agnieszki H.*) (2013) Poland-Czech Republic; Maur Film, Centrala; Česká Televize, Polish Television; 77 mins; directed by Krystyna Krauze and Jacek Petrycki; written by Krystyna Krauze.

Road to Mastery (*Droga do mistrzostwa*) (2016) Poland; BMW Group Poland; 53 mins; directed and written by Bartosz Konopka.

References

Adamczak, Marcin. 'Film Units in the People's Republic of Poland.' In *Restart Zespołów Filmowych/Film Units: Restart*, edited by Marcin Adamczak, Piotr Marecki and Marcin Malatyński, 231–70. Kraków: Ha!art, 2012.
Altman, Rick. 'General Introduction: Cinema as Event.' In *Sound Theory, Sound Practice*, edited by Rick Altman, 1–14. London: Routledge, 1992.
Andělová, Kristina. 'Czechoslovak Generational Experience of 1968: The Intellectual History Perspective.' *East European Politics and Societies and Cultures* 33, no. 4 (2019): 881–98. https://doi.org/10.1177/0888325419864418
Anderson, Benedict. *Imagined Communities: Reflections on the Origin and Spread of Nationalism*, revised ed. London: Verso, 2006.
Augé, Marc. *Non-places: Introduction to an Anthropology of Supermodernity*. Translated by John Howe. London: Verso, 1995.
Aymar, Jean Christian. *Open TV: Innovation beyond Hollywood and the Rise of Web Television*. New York: NYU Press, 2018.
Baker, Jayson. 'There's No Space Like Home: Anglo American Displacement in *Washington Square*.' *Adaptation* 7, no. 1 (2013): 1–13. https://doi.org/10.1093/adaptation/apt020
Ballesteros, Isolina. *Immigration Cinema in the New Europe*. Bristol: Intellect, 2015.
Baranowski, Henryk. *Spowiedź bez konfesjonału. Wędrówki pomiędzy sztuką, magią i medycyną*. Warsaw: Wydawnictwo Skorpion, 2013.
Barr, Charles. 'Introduction: Amnesia and Schizophrenia.' In *All Our Yesterdays: 90 Years of British Cinema*, edited by Charles Barr, 1–29. London: British Film Institute, 1986.
Barthes, Roland. 'The Death of the Author.' Translated by Stephen Heath. In *Theories of Authorship: A Reader*, edited by John Caughie, 208–13. London: Routledge in association with the BFI, 1981.
Bartoszewicz, Monika Gabriela. 'Celebrity Populism: A Look at Poland and the Czech Republic.' *European Politics and Society* 20, no. 4 (2019): 470–85. https://doi.org/10.1080/23745118.2019.1569342
Bastién, Angelica Jade. 'On Being Black in Film Noir.' *Sight and Sound* 26, no. 12 (2016): 42–5.
Bauman, Janina. *A Dream of Belonging: My Years in Postwar Poland*. London: Virago Press, 1988.
Bauman, Zygmunt. *Liquid Modernity*. Cambridge: Polity Press, 2000.

Berezhnaya Liliya, and Christian Schmitt, eds. *Iconic Turns: Nation and Religion in Eastern European Cinema Since 1989*. Leiden: Brill, 2013.

Berghahn, Daniela, and Claudia Sternberg, eds. *European Cinema in Motion. Migrant and Diasporic Film in Contemporary Europe*. Basingstoke: Palgrave Macmillan, 2010.

Berner, Elias. '"Remember Me, but Forget My Fate": The Use of Music in *Schindler's List* and *In Darkness*.' *Holocaust Studies* 27, no. 2 (2021): 156–70. https://doi.org/10.1080/17504902.2019.1637490

Bersani, Leo. 'Is the Rectum a Grave?' *October* 43 (1987): 197–222. https://doi.org/10.2307/3397574

Bersani, Leo, and Ulysse Dutoit. 'Sadism and Film: Freud and Resnais.' *Qui Parle* 6, no. 1 (Fall/Winter 1992): 1–34.

Betz, Mark. *Beyond the Subtitle: Remapping European Art Cinema*. Minneapolis: University of Minnesota Press, 2009.

Biełous, Urszula. *Wielcy Skromni: Rzecz o wybitnych artystach filmu i teatru którzy naprawdę są skromni*. Warsaw: Editions Spotkania, 1994.

Bittencourt, Ela. 'Animal Killers: Ecology, Feminism and Horror in Agnieszka Holland's *Spoor*.' *Lyssaria*, 6 January 2018. https://lyssaria.com/2018/06/01/animal-killers-ecology-and-horror-in-agnieszka-hollands-spoor/ (accessed on 22 March 2022)

Bittencourt, Ela, and Agnieszka Holland. 'A Woman Alone: An Interview with Agnieszka Holland.' *Cinéaste* 39, no. 3 (2014): 45–9.

Błoński, Jan. 'The Poor Poles Look at the Ghetto.' In *My Brother's Keeper? Recent Polish Debates on the Holocaust*, edited by Antony Polonsky, 59–68. London: Routledge, 1990.

Bobowski, Sławomir. *W poszukiwaniu siebie. Twórczość filmowa Agnieszki Holland*. Wrocław: Wydawnictwo Uniwersytetu Wrocławskiego, 2001.

Bock, Hans-Michael, and Tim Bergfelder, eds. *The Concise Cinegraph: Encyclopaedia of German Cinema*. New York: Berghahn Books, 2009.

Bolecki, Włodzimierz. '*Kultura* 1946–2000.' In *The Exile and Return of Writers From East-Central Europe: A Compendium*, edited by John Neubauer and Borbála Zsuzsanna Török, 144–88. Berlin: De Gruyter, 2009.

Bolton, Lucy. *Film and Female Consciousness: Irigaray, Cinema and Thinking Women*. Houndmills: Palgrave Macmillan, 2011.

Bordwell, David. *Ozu and the Poetics of Cinema*. London: BFI; Princeton: Princeton University Press, 1988.

Borowski, Krzysztof E. 'Poland under Martial Law in Netflix's *1983* as a Critique of Contemporary Polish Socio-Politics: An Intertextual Analysis.' *Studies in Eastern European Cinema*, published online: 3 February 2023. https://doi.org/10.1080/2040350X.2023.2170735

Bos, Pascale Rachel. 'Women and the Holocaust: Analyzing Gender Difference.' In *The Holocaust: Theoretical Readings*, edited by Neil Levi and Michael Rothberg, 178–86. New Brunswick, NJ: Rutger University Press, 2003.

Bourdieu, Pierre. 'The Forms of Capital.' Translated by Richard Nice. In *Handbook of Theory and Research for the Sociology of Education*, edited by John G. Richardson, 241–58. Westport, CN: Greenwood Press, 1986.

Bourdieu, Pierre. *Language and symbolic power*. Translated by Gino Raymond and Matthew Adamson. Cambridge: Polity Press, 1991.

Braun, Rebecca. 'Fetishising Intellectual Achievement: The Nobel Prize and European Literary Celebrity.' *Celebrity Studies* 2, no. 3 (2011): 320–34, https://doi.org/10.1080/19392397.2011.609340

Brown, William. 'Michael Winterbottom: A Self-effacing Auteur?' In *The Global Auteur: The Politics of Authorship in 21st Century Cinema*, edited by Seung-hoon Jeong and Jeremi Szaniawski, 79–94. London: Bloomsbury Academic, 2016.

Burszta Józef. *Kultura Ludowa – Kultura Narodowa. Szkice i Rozprawy*. Warsaw: Ludowa Spółdzielnia Wydawnicza, 1974.
Butler, Alison. *Women's Cinema: The Contested Screen*. London: Wallflower Press, 2002.
Butler, Alison. 'Feminist Perspectives in Film Studies.' In *The SAGE Handbook of Film Studies*, edited by James Donald and Michael Renov, 391–407. Los Angeles: SAGE Publications, 2008.
Butler, Judith. *Gender Trouble: Feminism and the Subversion of Identity*. New York: Routledge, 1999.
Bystydzienski, Jill. M. 'The Feminist Movement in Poland: Why So Slow?' *Women's Studies International Forum* 24, no. 5 (2001): 501–11.
Caldwell, John Thornton. *Production Culture: Industrial Reflexivity and Critical Practice in Film and Television*. Durham, NC: Duke University Press, 2008.
Carringer, Robert L. 'Collaboration and Concepts of Authorship.' *PMLA* 116, no. 2 (2001): 370–9.
Cartmell Deborah, and Ashley D. Polasek. 'Introduction.' In *A Companion to the Biopic*, edited by Deborah Cartmell and Ashley D. Polasek, 1–10. Chichester: John Wiley & Sons, 2019.
Caughie, John. *Theories of Authorship: A Reader*. London: Routledge & Kegan Paul, in association with the BFI, 1981.
Caughie, John. 'Authors and Auteurs: The Uses of Theory.' In *The SAGE Handbook of Film Studies*, edited by James Donald and Michael Renov, 408–23. Los Angeles: SAGE Publications, 2008.
Chałupnik, Agata. 'Pigułka.' In *Obyczaje polskie. Wiek XX w krótkich hasłach*, edited by Małgorzata Szpakowska. Warsaw: W. A. B., 2008. Kindle.
Chandler, Karen Michele. '"Her Ancient Faculty of Silence": Catherine Sloper's Ways of Being in James's *Washington Square* and Two Film Adaptations.' In *Henry James Goes to the Movies*, edited by Susan M Griffin, 170–90. Lexington: The University Press of Kentucky, 2015.
Chatzidakis, Andreas et al. *The Care Manifesto. The Politics of Interdependence*. London: Verso, 2020.
Chollet, Derek, and James Goldgeiger. *America Between the Wars: From 11/9 to 9/11*. New York: Public Affairs, 2008.
Chouliaraki, Lilie. *The Ironic Spectator*. Cambridge: Polity Press, 2013.
Christensen, Jerome. *America's Corporate Art: The Studio Authorship of Hollywood Motion Pictures*. Stanford, CA: Stanford University Press, 2011.
Coates, Paul. 'Exile and Identity. Kieślowski and His Contemporaries.' In *Before the Wall Came Down: Soviet and East European Filmmakers Working in the West*, edited by Graham Petrie and Ruth Dwyer, 103–14. Lanham, MD: University Press of America, 1990.
Coates, Paul. *Cinema, Religion and the Romantic Legacy*. London: Routledge, 2003.
Coates, Paul. *The Red and the White: The Cinema of People's Poland*. London: Wallflower, 2005.
Cobb, Shelley. *Adaptation, Authorship, and Contemporary Women Filmmakers*. Basingstoke: Palgrave Macmillan, 2015.
Corrigan, Timothy. 'The Commerce of Auteurism.' In *Critical Visions in Film Theory. Classic and Contemporary Readings*, edited by Timothy Corrigan, Patricia White and Meta Mazaj, 416–29. Boston: Bedford/St. Martin's, 2011.
Crnković, Gordana P. 'Inscribed Bodies, Invited Dialogues and Cosmopolitan Cinema: Some Brief Notes on Agnieszka Holland.' *Kinoeye* 4, no. 5, (29 November 2004). https://www.kinoeye.org/04/05/crnkovic05_no2.php (accessed 23 October 2021)
Crnković, Gordana P., and Agnieszka Holland. 'Interview with Agnieszka Holland.' *Film Quarterly* 52, no. 2 (Winter, 1998–9): 2–9.
Czerkawski, Piotr. *Drżące kadry. Rozmowy o życiu filmowym w PRL-u*. Wołowiec: Wydawnictwo Czarne, 2019.

Dabert, Dobrochna. *Kino moralnego niepokoju. Wokół wybranych problemów poetyki i etyki.* Poznań: Wydawnictwo UAM, 2003.
Davies, Norman. *Heart of Europe: The Past in Poland's Present.* Oxford: Oxford University Press, 2001.
Davis, Máire Messenger. '"A Bit of Earth": Sexuality and Representation of Childhood in Text and Screen Versions of *The Secret Garden*.' *The Velvet Light Trap*, no. 48 (2001): 48–58.
Deleuze, Gilles, and Félix Guattari. *Kafka: Toward a Minor Literature.* Translated by Dana Polan. Minneapolis: University of Minnesota Press, 1986.
Deleuze, Gilles, and Félix Guattari. *A Thousand Plateaus: Capitalism and Schizophrenia.* Translated by Brian Massumi. London: Bloomsbury Academic, 2019.
Deleuze, Gilles, and Claire Parnet. *Dialogues II.* Translated by Hugh Tomlinson and Barbara Habberjam. New York: Columbia University Press, 2007.
Diffrient, David Scott. *Omnibus Films: Theorizing Transauthorial Cinema.* Edinburgh: Edinburgh University Press, 2014.
Dillmann-Kühn, Claudia. *Artur Brauner Und Die CCC: Filmgeschäft Produktionsalltag Studiogeschichte 1946–1990: Ausstellung.* Frankfurt am Main: Deutsches Filmmuseum, 1990.
Domosławski Artur. *Wygnaniec: 21 scen z życia Zygmunta Baumana.* Warsaw: Wielka Litera, 2021.
Donahue, William Collins. 'Pretty Boys and Nasty Girls: The Holocaust Figured in Two German Films of the 1990s.' *New England Review* 21, no. 4 (2000): 108–24.
Driessens, Olivier. 'Celebrity Capital: Redefining Celebrity Using Field Theory.' *Theory and Society* 42, no. 5 (2013): 543–60, https://doi.org/10.1007/s11186-013-9202-3
Ďurovičová, Nataša, and Kathleen Newman, eds. *World Cinemas: Transnational Perspectives.* London: Routledge, 2010.
Dvořáková, Tereza Czesany. 'The Limits of Political Influence – the Limits of Creativity: The First 25 Years of FAMU.' *Historical Journal of Film, Radio and Television* 41, no. 3 (2021): 511–26. https://doi.org/10.1080/01439685.2021.1936981
Dyer, Richard. 'Heritage Cinema in Europe.' In *Encyclopedia of European Cinema*, edited by Ginette Vincendeau, 204–5. London: Cassell and BFI, 1995.
Dyer, Richard, and Ginette Vincendeau. 'Introduction.' In *Popular European Cinema*, edited by Richard Dyer and Ginette Vincendeau, 1–14. London: Routledge, 1992.
Elsaesser, Thomas. *European Cinema: Face to Face with Hollywood.* Amsterdam: Amsterdam University Press, 2005.
Elsaesser, Thomas. 'The Global Author: Control, Creative Constraints, and Performative Self-contradiction.' In *The Global Auteur: The Politics of Authorship in 21st Century Cinema*, edited by Jeong Seung-hoon and Jeremi Szaniawski, 21–42. London: Bloomsbury Academic, 2016.
Elsaesser, Thomas. 'National, Transnational and Intermedial Perspectives in Post-2008 European Cinema.' In *Contemporary European Cinema: Crisis Narratives and Narratives in Crisis*, edited by Betty Kaklamanidou and Ana Corbalán, 20–36. Abingdon: Routledge, 2019.
Erhart, Julia. '"But Do I Care? No, I'm Too Old to Care": Authority, Unfuckability, and Creative Freedom in Jane Campion's Authorship after the Age of Sixty.' *Studies in Australasian Cinema* 13, no. 2/3 (2019): 67–82. https://doi.org/10.1080/17503175.2019.1700022
Ezra, Elizabeth, and Terry Rowden, eds. *Transnational Cinema: The Film Reader.* London: Routledge, 2006.
Fellmer, Claudia, and Jon Raundalen. 'From East Germany to the West Coast: Armin Mueller-Stahl.' In *The German Cinema Book*, 2nd ed., edited by Tim Bergfelder et al., 148–55. London: Bloomsbury on behalf of the British Film Institute, 2020.
Feuer, Jane. 'HBO and the Concept of Quality TV.' In *Quality TV: Contemporary American Television and Beyond*, edited by Janet McCabe and Kim Akas, 145–57. London: I. B. Taurus, 2007.

Fidelis, Małgorzata. *Women, Communism, and Industrialization in Postwar Poland*. Cambridge: Cambridge University Press, 2010.
Fischer, Lucy. *Body Double: The Author Incarnate in the Cinema*. New Brunswick, NJ: Rutgers University Press, 2013.
Fish, Stanley. *Is There a Text in This Class*. Cambridge, MA: Harvard University Press, 1980.
Forman, Miloš, and Jan Nowák. *Moje dwa światy. Wspomnienia*. Translated by Jacek Illg. Katowice: Videograf II, 1993.
Formis, Barbara. 'Dismantling Theatricality: Aesthetics of Bare Life.' In *The Work of Giorgio Agamben: Law, Literature, Life*, edited by Alex Murray, Justin Clemens and Nicholas Heron, 181–92. Edinburgh: Edinburgh University Press, 2008.
Foucault, Michel, and Gilles Deleuze. 'Intellectuals and Power: A Conversation between Michel Foucault and Gilles Deleuze.' In *Language, Counter-Memory, Practice: Selected Essays and Interviews*, edited by Donald F. Bouchard. Translated by the editor and Sherry Simon, 205–17. Ithaca, NY: Cornell University Press, 1977.
Foucault, Michel. 'Technologies of the Self.' In *Technologies of the Self: A Seminar with Michel Foucault*, edited by Luther H. Martin et al., 16–49. Amherst, MA: University of Massachusetts Press, 1988.
Franklin, Cynthia G., and Laura E. Lyons. '"I Have a Family": Relational Witnessing and the Evidentiary Power of Grief in the Gwen Araujo Case.' *GLQ: A Journal of Lesbian and Gay Studies* 22 (2016): 437–66.
Frobose, Paul. H. 'The Film Adaptations of Frances Hodgson Burnett's Stories.' In *In the Garden: Essays in Honor of Frances Hodgson Burnett*, edited by Angelica Shirley Carpenter, 131–46. Lanham, MD: The Scarecrow Press, 2006.
Fuchs, Esther. 'Images of Women in Holocaust Films.' *Shofar* 17, no. 2, Special Issue: Women in Jewish Life and Culture (Winter 1999): 49–56.
Fukuyama, Francis. *The End of History and the Last Man*. New York: Free Press, 2006.
Galarte, Francisco J. Brown. *Trans Figurations: Rethinking Race, Gender, and Sexuality in Chicanx/Latinx Studies*. Austin: University of Texas Press, 2021.
Gallagher, Mark. *Another Steven Soderbergh Experience: Authorship and Contemporary Hollywood*. Austin: University of Texas Press, 2013.
Galt, Rosalind, and Karl Schoonover. 'Introduction: The Impurity of Art Cinema.' In *Global Art Cinema: New Theories and Histories*, edited by Rosalind Galt and Karl Schoonover, 3–27. Oxford: Oxford University Press, 2010.
Gerstner, David A., and Janet Steiger, eds. *Authorship and Film*. New York: Routledge, 2003.
Gillispie, Julaine. 'American Film Adaptations of "The Secret Garden": Reflections of Sociological and Historical Change.' *Lion and the Unicorn* 20, no. 1 (1996): 132–52.
Gilmore, Mikal. *Shot in the Heart*. New York: Anchor Books, 1994.
Glajar, Valentina, and Domnica Radulescu. 'Introduction.' In *Vampirettes, Wretches, and Amazons: Western Representations of East European Women*, edited by Valentina Glajar and Domnica Radulescu, 1–11. New York: Columbia University Press, 2004.
Gledhill, Christine, and Julia Knight. 'Introduction.' In *Doing Women's Film History: Reframing Cinemas, Past and Future*, edited by Christine Gledhill and Julia Knight, 1–12. Urbana: University of Illinois Press, 2015.
Goffman, Erving. *The Presentation of Self in Everyday Life*. New York: Overlook Press, 1973.
Gorji, Yasaman, Michael Carney and Rajshree Prakash. 'Indirect Nepotism: Network Sponsorship, Social Capital and Career Performance in Show Business Families.' *Journal of Family Business Strategy* 11, no. 3 (2020). Science Direct. https://doi.org/10.1016/j.jfbs.2019.04.004
Goscilo, Helena, and Beth Holmgren. *Polish Cinema Today: A Bold New Era in Film*. Lanham, MD: Lexington Books, 2021.

Graff, Agnieszka. 'A Different Chronology: Reflections on Feminism in Contemporary Poland.' In *Third Wave Feminism: A Critical Exploration*, edited by Stacy Gillis, Gillian Howie and Rebecca Munford,142–55, expanded 2nd ed. Basingstoke: Palgrave Macmillan, 2007.
Graham, James, and Alessandro Gandini. 'Introduction: Collaborative Production in the Creative Industries.' In *Collaborative Production in the Creative Industries*, edited by James Graham and Alessandro Gandini, 1–14. London: University of Westminster Press, 2017.
Grant, Barry Keith, ed. *Auteurs and Authorship: A Film Reader*. Malden: Blackwell Publishing, 2008.
Grant, Catherine. 'www.auteur.com?' *Screen* 41, no. 10 (2000): 1–8.
Grant, Catherine. 'Secret Agents: Feminist Theories of Women's Film Authorship.' *Feminist Theory* 2, no. 1 (2001): 113–30.
Gray, Jonathan, and Derek Johnson. *Television Goes to the Movies*. New York: Routledge, 2021.
Grewal, Inderpal, and Caren Kaplan. 'Warrior Marks: Global Womanism's Neo-Colonial Discourse in a Multicultural Context.' In *Multiculturalism, Postcoloniality, and Transnational Media*, edited by Ella Shohat and Robert Stam, 256–78. New Brunswick, NJ: Rutgers University Press, 2003.
Griffin, Susan M., ed. *Henry James Goes to the Movies*. Lexington: University Press of Kentucky, 2003.
Grodal, Torben Kragh. 'Frozen Flows in von Trier's *Ouevre*.' In *Visual Authorship: Creativity and Intentionality in Media*, eds. Torben Grodal, Bente Larsen and Iben Thorving Laursen, Northern Lights Film and Media Studies Yearbook, 129–67. Copenhagen: Museum Tusculanum Press, University of Copenhagen, 2005.
Grodal, Torben Kragh, and Bente Larsen and Iben Thorving Laursen. 'Introduction.' In *Visual Authorship: Creativity and Intentionality in Media*, edited by Torben Kragh Grodal, Bente Larsen and Iben Thorving Laursen, 7–14. Copenhagen: Museum Tusculanum Press, University of Copenhagen, 2005.
Guzek, Mariusz. 'W cieniu Olgi Hepnarovéj – totalitaryzm XX wieku w optyce czesko-polskich koprodukcji filmowych.' *Kultura i Edukacja*, no. 3 (2019): 36–49. https://doi.org/10.15804/kie.2019.03.03
Gwóźdź, Andrzej. *Zaklinanie rzeczywistości. Filmy niemieckie i ich historie 1933–1949*. Wrocław: Oficyna Wydawnicza ATUT, 2018.
Hadas, Leora. *Authorship as Promotional Discourse in the Screen Industries: Selling Genius*. London: Routledge, 2020.
Hake, Sabine. *German National Cinema*, 2nd ed. London: Routledge, 2002.
Haltof, Marek. *Polish National Cinema*. New York: Berghahn Books, 2002.
Haltof, Marek. *Polish Film and the Holocaust. Politics and Memory*. New York: Berghahn Books, 2012.
Hames, Peter. *The Czechoslovak New Wave*, 2nd ed. London: Wallflower Press, 2005.
Hames, Peter. 'The Golden Sixties: The Czechoslovak New Wave Revisited.' *Studies in Eastern European Cinema* 4, no. 2 (2013): 215–30. https://doi.org/10.1386/seec.4.2.215-1
Hames, Peter. 'Jánošík: The Cross-Border Hero.' In *Postcolonial Approaches to Eastern European Cinema: Portraying Neighbours On-Screen*, edited by Ewa Mazierska, Lars Kristensen and Eva Näripea, 115–46. London: I. B.Tauris, 2014.
Haraway Donna. 'Situated Knowledges: The Science Question in Feminism and the Privilege of Partial Perspective.' *Feminist Studies* 14, no. 3 (Autumn 1988): 575–99.
Hendrykowska, Małgorzata. 'Rzecz o *Wyzwoleniu* (*Aktorzy prowincjonalni* Agnieszki Holland).' In *Widziane po latach. Analizy i interpretacje filmu polskiego*, edited by Małgorzata Hendrykowska, 181–93. Poznań: Wydawnictwo UAM, 2000.
Hicks, Alexander, and Velina Petrova. 'Auteur Discourse and the Cultural Consecration of American Films.' *Poetics* 34 (2006): 180–203.

Higson, Andrew. 'Re-presenting the National Past: Nostalgia and Pastiche in the Heritage Film.' In *Fires Were Started: British Cinema and Thatcherism*, edited by Lester Friedman, 109–29. Minneapolis: University of Minnesota Press, 1993.

Higson, Andrew. *Waving the Flag: Constructing a National Cinema in Britain*. Oxford: Oxford University Press, 1995.

Higson, Andrew. 'The Heritage Film and British Cinema.' In *Dissolving Views: Key Writings on British Cinema*, edited by Andrew Higson, 232–48. London: Cassell, 1996.

Higson, Andrew. *English Heritage, English Cinema: Costume Drama since 1980*. Oxford: Oxford University Press, 2003.

Hill, John. *British Cinema in the 1980s*. Oxford: Clarendon Press, 1999.

Himka, John-Paul, and Joanna Beata Michlic. 'Introduction.' In *Bringing the Dark Past to Light: The Reception of the Holocaust in Postcommunist Europe*, edited by John-Paul Himka and Joanna Beata Michlic, 1–24. Lincoln: University of Nebraska Press, 2013.

Hjort, Mette. 'On the Plurality of Cinematic Transnationalism.' In *World Cinemas, Transnational Perspectives*, edited by Nataša Ďurovičová and Kathleen Newman, 12–33. New York: Routledge, 2010.

Hjort, Mette. 'Introduction: More Than Film School – Why the Full Spectrum of Practice-Based Film Education Warrants Attention.' In *The Education of the Filmmaker in Europe, Australia, and Asia*, edited by Mette Hjort, 2–22. New York: Palgrave Macmillan, 2013.

Hodsdon, Barrett. *The Elusive Auteur: The Question of Film Authorship throughout the Age of Cinema*. Jefferson, NC: McFarland & Company, 2017.

Hofer, Stefanie. 'Out of the Box.' *American Imago* 74, no. 1 (Spring 2017): 41–73.

Hole, Kristin Lené et al. 'Introduction. Decentering Feminist Film Studies.' In *The Routledge Companion to Cinema and Gender*, edited by Kristin Lené Hole et al., 1–11. London: Routledge, 2017.

Holland, Agnieszka. 'Kilka uwag o młodym kinie polskim.' *Zeszyty literackie*, 1 (1982): 140–9.

Holland, Agnieszka. 'Inna płeć?' interview by Łukasz Maciejewski. *Kwartalnik Filmowy* 62/63 (2008): 154–65.

Holland, Agnieszka. '"Be Cool!" Interview by Mariusz Kurc and Bartosz Żurawiecki.' In *Ludzie nie ideologia. Wywiady*, edited by Bartosz Żurawiecki, 133–40. Warsaw: Wydawnictwo Krytyka Polityczna, Fundacja Replika, 2021.

Holland, Agnieszka, and Peter Brunette. 'Lessons from the Past: An Interview with Agnieszka Holland.' *Cinéaste* 15, no. 1 (1986): 15–17.

Holland, Agnieszka, and Marek Hendrykowski. 'Sztuka reżyserii. Interview.' In *Debiuty polskiego kina*, edited by Marek Hendrykowski, 240–53. Konin: Wydawnictwo 'Przegląd Koniński', 1998.

Holland, Agnieszka, and Maria Kornatowska. *Magia i pieniądze*, 2nd expanded ed. Kraków: Wydawnictwo Znak, 2012.

Holland, Agnieszka, and Tomasz Pobóg-Malinowski. 'Poland's Lost Generation.' *Index on Censorship* 11, no. 5 (1982): 15–19.

Holmlund, Chris. 'Introduction. Movies and the 1990s.' In *American Cinema of the 1990s: Themes and Variations*, edited by Chris Holmlund, 1–23. New Brunswick, NJ: Rutgers University Press, 2008.

hooks, bell. 'Marginality as Site of Resistance.' In *Out There: Marginalization and Contemporary Cultures*, edited by Russell Ferguson et al. 341–4. Cambridge, MA: MIT Press, 1990.

Huggan, Graham. *The Postcolonial Exotic: Marketing the Margins*. London: Routledge, 2001.

Hunter, Aaron. *Authoring Hal Ashby: The Myth of the New Hollywood Auteur*. New York: Bloomsbury Academic, 2016. Bloomsbury Collections. http://dx.doi.org/10.5040/9781501308468-006

Imre, Anikó. '"Affective Nationalism" and Transnational Postcommunist Lesbian Visual Activism.' In *Transnational Feminism in Film and Media*, edited by Katarzyna Marciniak, Anikó Imre and Áine O'Healy, 147–62. New York: Palgrave Macmillan, 2007.
Imre, Anikó. 'Adventures in Early Socialist Television Edutainment.' *Journal of Popular Film and Television* 40, no. 3 (2012): 119–30. https://doi.org/10.1080/01956051.2012.697790
Imre, Anikó. *TV Socialism*. Durham, NC: Duke University Press, 2016.
Imre, Anikó. 'Gender, Socialism, and European Film Cultures.' In *The Routledge Companion to Cinema and Gender*, edited by Kristin Lené Hole et al., 88–97. Abingdon: Routledge, 2017.
Imre, Anikó. 'HBO's e-Eutopia.' *Media Industries* 5, no. 2 (2018): 49–68.
Imre, Anikó. 'Streaming Freedom in Illiberal Eastern Europe.' *Critical Studies in Television: The International Journal of Television Studies* 14, no. 2 (2019): 170–86.
Imre, Anikó. 'Television and the Good Times of Socialism.' In *The Oxford Handbook of Communist Visual Culture*, edited by Aga Skrodzka et al., 611–28. Oxford: Oxford University Press, 2020.
Ince, Kate. *The Cinema of Mia Hansen-Løve: Candour and Vulnerability*. Edinburgh: Edinburgh University Press, 2021.
Insdorf, Annette. *Indelible Shadows: Film and the Holocaust*, 3rd ed. Cambridge: Cambridge University Press, 2003.
Iordanova, Dina. 'East Europe's Cinema Industries Since 1989: Financing Structure and Studios.' *Javnost – The Public* 6, no. 2 (1999): 45–60. https://doi.org/10.1080/13183222.1999.11008710
Iordanova, Dina. 'Feature Filmmaking within the New Europe: Moving Funds and Images across the East-West Divide.' *Media, Culture & Society* 24, no. 4 (2002): 517–36. https://doi.org/10.1177/016344370202400404
Iordanova, Dina. *Cinema of the Other Europe: The Industry and Artistry of East Central European Film*. London: Wallflower Press, 2003.
Iordanova, Dina. 'Mediating Diaspora: Film Festivals and "Imagined Communities."' In *Film Festival Yearbook 2: Film Festivals and Imagined Communities*, edited by Dina Iordanova and Ruby Cheung, 12–19. St. Andrews: St. Andrews Film Studies, 2010a.
Iordanova, Dina. 'Migration and Cinematic Process in Post-Cold War Europe.' In *European Cinema in Motion: Migrant and Diasporic Film in Contemporary Europe*, edited by Daniela Berghahn and Claudia Sternberg, 50–75. Basingstoke: Palgrave Macmillan, 2010b.
Jagielski, Sebastian. *Przerwane emancypacje. Polityka ekscesu w kinie polskim lat 1968–1982*. Kraków: Universitas, 2021.
Jameson, Fredric. 'On Magic Realism in Film.' *Critical Inquiry* 12, no. 2 (1986): 301–25.
Jameson, Fredric. 'Realism and Utopia in The Wire.' *Criticism* 52, nos. 3 & 4 (Summer & Fall 2010): 359–72.
Janion, Maria. *Kobiety i duch inności*. Warsaw: Sic!, 1996.
Jankun-Dopartowa, Mariola. *Gorzkie kino Agnieszki Holland*. Gdańsk: słowo/obraz/terytorium, 2000.
Jeong, Seung-hoon, and Jeremi Szaniawski. 'Introduction.' In *The Global Auteur: The Politics of Authorship in 21st Century Cinema*, edited by Seung-hoon Jeong and Jeremi Szaniawski, 1–20. London: Bloomsbury Academic, 2016.
Jermyn, Deborah. 'How Does She Look? Bigelow's Vision/visioning Bigelow.' *New Review of Film and Television Studies* 19, no. 3 (2021): 367–82, https://doi.org/10.1080/17400309.2021.1952036.
Johnston, Claire. 'Women's Cinema as Counter Cinema.' In *Notes on Women's Cinema*, edited by Claire Johnston. London: Society for Education in Film and Television, 1973; reprinted in *Movies and Methods*, edited by Bill Nichols, 209–17. Berkeley: University of California Press, 1985.
Johnston, Ruth. 'The Jewish Closet in Europa, Europa.' *Camera Obscura* 18, no. 1 (2003): 1–33.

Kalinowska, Izabela. 'Exile and Polish Cinema: From Mickiewicz to Slowacki and Kieslowski.' In *Realms of Exile: Nomadism, Diasporas, and Eastern European Voices*, edited by Domnica Radulescu, 107–21. Oxford: Lexington Books, 2002.

Kałużyński, Zygmunt. *Diabelskie zwierciadło*. Warsaw: Wydawnictwa Artystyczne i Filmowe, 1986.

Kane, Paula. '"Yes, We Have No Bernanos!" Catholics in Three Recent American Films.' *U.S. Catholic Historian* 19, no. 3 (Summer 2001), special issue: Popular Piety and Material Culture: Art, Film, and Liturgical Experience: 81–96.

Kapsis, Robert E. *Hitchcock: The Making of Reputation*. Chicago: University of Chicago Press, 1992.

Kavka, Misha. 'Celevision. Mobilizations of the Television Screen.' In *A Companion to Celebrity*, edited by P. David Marshall and Sean Redmond, 295–314. Chichester: Wiley Blackwell, 2016.

Keathley, Christian. *Cinephilia and History, or the Wind in the Trees*. Bloomington: Indiana University Press, 2006.

Kleinhans, Chuck. '1993 Movies and the New Economics of Blockbusters and Indies.' In *American Cinema of the 1990s: Themes and Variations*, edited by Chris Holmlund, 91–114. New Brunswick, NJ: Rutgers University Press, 2008.

Klejsa, Konrad. *Pamięć lat nazizmu w niemieckim filmie fabularnym lat 1946–1965*. Łódź: PWSFTiTv and Wydawnictwo Uniwersytetu Łódzkiego, 2015.

Koniczek, Ryszard. 'Kultura filmowa, polityka repertuarowa i produkcyjna.' In *Historia filmu polskiego 1968–1972, tom VI*, edited by Rafał Marszałek, 477–509. Warsaw: Wydawnictwa Artystyczne i Filmowe, 1994.

Kornatowska, Maria. *Wodzireje i amatorzy*. Warsaw: Wydawnictwa Artystyczne i Filmowe, 1990.

Kozloff, Sarah. *The Life of the Author*. Montreal: Caboose, 2014. Kindle.

Kristeva, Julia. *Powers of Horror: An Essay on Abjection*. Translated by Leon S. Roudiez. New York: Columbia University Press, 1982.

Królikowska-Avis, Elżbieta. *Prosto z Piccadilly. Kino brytyjskie lat 90*. Kraków: Rabid, 2001.

Kuhn, Annette, and Susannah Radstone. *The Women's Companion to International Film*, Berkeley: University of California Press, 1994.

Kumbier, William. 'Beethoven's Birdstrokes: Figuration, Subjectivity, and the Force of the Score in the *Pastoral Symphony* and *Copying Beethoven*.' *Literature Compass* 7/8 (2010): 639–50. https://doi.org/10.1111/j.1741-4113.2010.00724.x

Kurz, Iwona. 'Obiecanki-wycinanki, czyli "Ty i Ja" jako katalog rzeczy niespełnionych.' *Widok. Teorie i praktyki kultury wizualnej*, no. 1, (2013). https://www.pismowidok.org/pl/archiwum/2013/1-widzialnosc-rzeczy/obiecanki-wycinanki-czyli-ty-i-ja-jako-katalog-rzeczy-niespelnionych (accessed 24 July 2023)

Labov, Jessie. *Transatlantic Central Europe: Contesting Geography and Redefining Culture Beyond the Nation*. New York: CEU Press, 2019.

Lane, Christina. *Feminist Hollywood: From* Born in Flames *to* Point Break. Detroit, IL: Wayne State University Press, 2000.

Latour, Bruno. *Reassembling the Social: An Introduction to Actor-Network-Theory*, Oxford: Oxford University Press, 2005.

Lebeau, Vicky. *Childhood and Cinema*. London: Reaction Books, 2008.

Lev, Peter. *The Euro-American Cinema*. Austin: University of Texas Press, 1993.

Levitin, Jacqueline, Judith Plessis and Valerie Raoul, eds. *Women Filmmakers: Refocusing*. London: Routledge, 2003.

Lewis, Ingrid. *Women in European Holocaust Films: Perpetrators, Victims and Resisters*. Cham, Switzerland: Palgrave Macmillan, 2017.

Lewis, Jon. 'The End of Cinemaass We Know It and I Feel . . .: An Introduction to a Book on Nineties American Film.' In *The End of Cinema as We Know It: American Film in the Nineties*, edited by Jon Lewis, 1–8. New York: New York University Press, 2001.

Lewis, Simon. 'Border Trouble: Ethnopolitics and Cosmopolitan Memory in Recent Polish Cinema.' *East European Politics and Societies* 33, no. 2 (2019): 522–49. https://search-1ebscohost-1com-10a01bj6r1c8f.han3.lib.uni.lodz.pl/login.aspx?

Liehm, Mira, and Antonín J. Liehm. *The Most Important Art: Soviet and Eastern European Film After 1945.* Berkeley: University of California Press, 1977.

Linville, Susan E. 'Agnieszka Holland's *Europa, Europa:* Deconstructive Humor in a Holocaust Film.' *Film Criticism* 19, no. 3 (1995): 44–53.

Litman, Barry R. *The Motion Picture Mega-Industry.* Boston: Allyn and Bacon, 1998.

LoBrutto, Vincent, and Harriet R. Morrison. *The Coppolas: A Family Business.* Santa Barbara, CA: Praeger, 2012. Kindle.

Loewy, Ronny. '"The Past in the Present." The Films of Producer Artur Brauner and the Dominant Narratives on the Genocide of European Jews in German Cinema.' In *Cinema and the Shoah: An Art Confronts the Tragedy of the Twentieth Century*, edited by Jean-Michel Frodon, translated by Anna Harrison and Tom Mes, 173–80. Albany, NY: Suny Press, 2010.

Loist, Skadi, and Elizabeth Prommer. 'Gendered Production Culture in the German Film Industry.' *Media Industries* 6, no. 1 (2019): 95–115. https://doi.org/10.25969/mediarep/14849

Lopez, Ana M. 'Crossing Nations and Genres: Traveling Filmmakers.' In *Visible Nations: Latin American Cinema and Video*, edited by Chon A. Noriega, 33–50. Minneapolis: University of Minnesota Press, 2000.

Lott, Eric. 'The Whiteness of Film Noir Author.' *American Literary History* 9, no. 3 (Autumn, 1997): 542–66.

Lubelski, Tadeusz. *Wajda.* Wrocław: Wydawnictwo Dolnośląskie, 2006.

Lubelski, Tadeusz. *Historia kina polskiego. Twórcy, filmy, konteksty.* Katowice: Videograf II, 2009.

Lubelski, Tadeusz. 'Obrona przed bezdomnością? *Gorejący krzew* – czeski film polskiej reżyserki.' In *Kino polskie jako kino transnarodowe*, edited by Sebastian Jagielski and Magdalena Podsiadło, 287–99. Kraków: Universitas, 2017.

Ludzie Nowej 1977–2007. Warsaw: Niezależna Oficyna Wydawnicza NOWA, 2007.

Lugo de Fabritz, Brunilda Amarilis. 'Agnieszka Holland: Continuity, the Self, and Artistic Vision.' In *Women Filmmakers: Refocusing*, edited by Jacqueline Levitin, Judith Plessis and Valerie Raoul, 96–108. London: Routledge, 2003. VitalSource Bookshelf, Taylor & Francis, 2016.

Łysak, Tomasz. 'The Diary of Anne Frankenstein: Broadening of the Field of Studies on Popular Culture and the Holocaust.' *Teksty Drugie*, no. 3 (January 2020): 355–66. https://doi.org/10.18318/td.2020.3.22

Mackey, Margaret. 'Strip Mines in the Garden: Old Stories, New Formats, and the Challenge of Change.' *Children Literature in Education* 27, no. 1 (1996): 3–22.

Madej-Stang, Adriana. *Which Face of Witch: Self-Representations of Women as Witches in Works of Contemporary British Women Writers.* Newcastle upon Tyne: Cambridge Scholars Publishing, 2015.

Majer, Artur. 'Quality by Design: TV Series in Poland.' In *A European Television Fiction Renaissance: Premium Production Models and Transnational Circulation*, edited by Luca Barra and Massimo Scaglioni, 262–74. London: Routledge, 2021.

Majmurek, Jakub, ed. *Holland: Przewodnik Krytyki Politycznej.* Warsaw: Wydawnictwo Krytyki Politycznej, 2012.

Mąka-Malatyńska, Katarzyna. *Agnieszka Holland.* Warsaw: Biblioteka 'Więzi', 2009.

Marciniak, Katarzyna. 'Second World-Ness and Transnational Feminist Practices: Agnieszka Holland's *Kobieta samotna* (*A Woman Alone*).' In *East European Cinemas*, edited by Anikó Imre, 3–20. New York: Routledge, 2005.

Marciniak Katarzyna, Anikó Imre and Áine O'Healy. 'Introduction: Mapping Transnational Feminist Media Studies.' In *Transnational Feminism in Film and Media*, edited by Katarzyna Marciniak, Anikó Imre and Áine O'Healy, 1–18. New York: Palgrave Macmillan, 2007.

Margulies, Ivone, and Jeremi Szaniawski. 'Introduction: On Women's Films: Moving Thought across Worlds and Generations.' In *On Women's Films: Across Worlds and Generation*, edited by Ivone Margulies and Jeremi Szaniawski, 1–24. London: Bloomsbury Academic, 2019.

Marshall, P. David. *Celebrity and Power: Fame and Contemporary Culture*, 2nd ed. With a new introduction. Minneapolis: University of Minnesota Press, 2014.

Marshall, P. David. 'Celebrity Value. Introduction.' In *A Companion to Celebrity*, edited by P. David Marshall and Sean Redmond, 155–9. Chichester: Willey Blackwell, 2016a.

Marshall, P. David. 'Exposure: The Public Self Explored.' In *A Companion to Celebrity*, edited by P. David Marshall and Sean Redmond, 497–517. Chichester: Willey Blackwell, 2016b.

Marshall, P. David, and Kim Barbour. 'Making Intellectual Room for Persona Studies: A New Consciousness and a Shifted Perspective.' *Persona Studies* 1 (2015): 1–12. https://doi.org/10.21153/ps2015vol1no1art464

Marshall, P. David, and Sean Redmond. 'Introduction.' In *A Companion to Celebrity*, edited by P. David Marshall and Sean Redmond, 1–13. Chichester: Willey Blackwell, 2016c.

Maule, Rosanna. *Beyond Auteurism: New Directions in Authorial Film Practices in France, Italy and Spain Since the 1980s*. Bristol: Intellect, 2008.

Mayne, Judith. *The Woman at the Keyhole: Feminism and Women's Cinema*. Bloomington: Indiana University Press, 1990.

Mayne, Judith. *Directed by Dorothy Arzner*. Bloomington: Indiana University Press, 1994.

Mazierska, Ewa, Matilda Mroz and Elżbieta Ostrowska, eds. *The Cinematic Bodies of Eastern Europe and Russia: Between Pain and Pleasure*. Edinburgh: Edinburgh University Press, 2016.

Mazierska, Ewa, and Elżbieta Ostrowska. *Women in Polish Cinema*. Oxford: Berghahn Books, 2006.

McCabe, Janet, and Kim Akas, eds. *Quality TV: Contemporary American Television and Beyond*. New York: I. B. Taurus, 2007.

McGinn, Colin. *The Meaning of Disgust*. Oxford: Oxford University Press, 2011.

McHugh, Kathleen. 'The World and the Soup: Historicizing Media Feminisms in Transnational Contexts.' *Camera Obscura* 24, no. 3 (2009): 111–51. https://doi.org/10.1215/02705346-2009-011

McNeilly, Kevin. 'Dislocating America: Agnieszka Holland Directs "Moral Midgetry".' In *The Wire: Urban Decay and American Television*, edited by Tiffany Potter and C. W. Marshall, 203–16. New York: Continuum, 2009.

Michalak, Bartosz. *Wajda. Kronika wypadków filmowych*. Warsaw: Wydawnictwo mg, 2016.

Michałek, Bolesław, and Frank Turaj. *The Modern Cinema of Poland*. Bloomington: Indiana University Press, 1988.

Mierzeński, Stanisław, and Hermann Field. *Okiennice*. Warsaw: Państwowy Instytut Wydawniczy, 1958.

Mills, Jane. 'Sojourner Cinema: Seeking and Researching a New Cinematic Category.' *Framework* 55, no. 1 (2014): 140–64. muse.jhu.edu/article/556151

Monk, Claire. 'The British "heritage film" and its critics.' *Critical Survey* 7, no. 2 (1995): 116–24.

Monk, Claire. 'The British Heritage-film Debate Revisited.' In *British Historical Cinema: The History, Heritage and Costume Film*, edited by Claire Monk and Amy Sargeant, 176–98. London: Routledge, 2002. eBook Academic Collection (EBSCOhost)

Mroz, Matilda. *Framing the Holocaust in Polish Aftermath Cinema: Posthumous Materiality and Unwanted Knowledge*. London: Palgrave Macmillan, 2020.

Mrozik, Agnieszka. *Architektki PRL-u. Komunistki, literatura i emancypacja kobiet w powojennej Polsce*. Warsaw: Instytut Badań Literackich Wydawnictwo PAN, 2022.

Mulvey, Laura. 'Visual Pleasure and Narrative Cinema.' *Screen* 16, no. 3 (Autumn 1975): 6–18. https://doi.org/10.1093/screen/16.3.6

Murray, Rona. 'Tough Guy in Drag? How the External, Critical Discourses Surrounding Kathryn Bigelow Demonstrate the Wider Problems of the Gender Question.' *Networking Knowledge: Journal of the MeCCSA Postgraduate Network* 4, no. 1 (2011): 1–21.
Naficy, Hamid. *An Accented Cinema: Exilic and Diasporic Filmmaking*. Princeton: Princeton University Press, 2001.
Naremore, James. *More than Night: Film Noir in Its Contexts, Updated and Expanded Edition*. 2nd ed. Berkeley: University of California Press, 2008.
Naszkowska, Krystyna. *My, dzieci komunistów*, Warsaw: Czerwone i Czarne, 2019. Kindle.
Neale, Steve. 'Art Cinema as Institution.' *Screen* 22, no. 1 (1981): 11–39. https://doi.org/10.1093/screen/22.1.11
Newell, Kate. '*Washington Square*'s "Virus of Suggestion": Source Texts, Intertexts, and Adaptations.' *Literature-Film Quarterly* 34, no. 3 (July 2006): 204–11.
Nochimson, Martha P. *Television Rewired: The Rise of the Auteur Series*. Austin: University of Texas Press, 2019.
Nowakowski, Jacek. *W poszukiwaniu niezależności w filmie i kulturze okresu PRL. Szkice*. Poznań: Wydawnictwo Naukowe UAM, 2019.
O'Sickey, Ingeborg Majer, and Annette Van. '*Europa Europa*: On the Borders of *Vergangenheitsverdraengung* and *Vergangenheitsbewaeltigung*.' In *Perspectives on German Cinema*, edited by Terri Ginsberg and Kirsten Moana Thompson, 231–50. New York: G. K. Hall; Prentice Hall International, 1996.
Ostrowska, Dorota. 'An Alternative Model of Film Production: Film Units in Poland after World War Two.' In *A Companion to Eastern European Cinemas*, edited by Anikó Imre, 453–65. Chichester: Wiley-Blackwell, 2012. https://doi.org/10.1002/9781118294376.ch23.
Ostrowska, Dorota, Francesco Pitassio and Zsuzsanna Varga, eds. *Popular cinemas in East Central Europe: Film Cultures and Histories*. London: I. B. Tauris, 2017.
Ostrowska, Dorota, and Małgorzata Radkiewicz. 'Poland: Costume Dramas: Cine-televisual Alliances in the Socialist and Post-socialist Poland.' In *European Cinemas in the Television Age*, edited by Dorota Ostrowska and Graham Roberts, 107–24. Edinburgh: Edinburgh University Press, 2007.
Ostrowska, Elżbieta. 'Filmic Representations of the "Polish Mother" in Post-Second World War Polish Cinema.' *The European Journal of Women's Studies* 5 (1998): 419–35.
Ostrowska, Elżbieta. 'Agnieszka Holland's Transnational Nomadism.' In *Polish Cinema in the Transnational Context*, edited by Michael Goddard and Ewa Mazierska, 289–309. Rochester, NY: Rochester University Press, 2014.
Ostrowska, Elżbieta. 'Duma i uprzedzenie – krytyczne dyslokacje filmu "Zabić księdza" Agnieszki Holland.' *Kwartalnik Filmowy*, no. 116 (2021): 146–70. https://doi.org/10.36744/kf.918
Ostrowska-Chmura, Elżbieta. 'Kto polubi Mary Lennox? *Tajemniczy ogród* Agnieszki Holland i współczesne kino familijne.' *Kwartalnik Filmowy*, no. 81 (2013): 52–68.
Owen, Jonathan L. *Avant-garde to New Wave: Czechoslovak Cinema, Surrealism and the Sixties*. London: Berghahn Books, 2011.
Pakier, Małgorzata. *The Construction of European Holocaust Memory: German and Polish Cinema after 1989*. Frankfurt am Main: Peter Lang Academic Research, 2013.
Pasternak, Karolina. *Holland. Biografia od nowa*. Kraków: Wydawnictwo Znak, 2022.
Paszkiewicz, Katarzyna. *Genre, Authorship, and Contemporary Women Filmmakers*. Edinburgh: Edinburgh University Press, 2018.
Pehe, Veronika. 'The Colours of Socialism: Visual Nostalgia and Retro Aesthetics in Czech Film and Television.' *Canadian Slavonic Papers* 57, no. 3–4 (2015): 239–53. https://doi.org/10.1080/00085006.2015.1090758
Penn, Shana. *Solidarity's Secret: The Women Who Defeated Communism in Poland*. Ann Arbor: University of Michigan Press, 2005.

Persak. Krzysztof. *Sprawa Henryka Hollanda*. Warsaw: PAN & IPN, 2006.
Petrie, Duncan. 'Theory, Practice, and the Significance of Film Schools.' *SCANDIA* 76, no. 2 (2010): 31–46.
Pidduck, Julianne. *Contemporary Costume Film: Space, Place and the Past*. London: BFI, 2004.
Pisters, Patricia. *New Blood in Contemporary Cinema: Women Directors and the Poetics of Horror*. Edinburgh: Edinburgh University Press, 2020.
Plotz, Judith. 'Secret Garden II; or *Lady Chatterley's Lover* as Palimpsest.' *Children's Literature Association Quarterly* 19, no. 1 (1994): 15–19. https://doi.org/10.1353/chq.0.0891
Pluwak Anita. *Ambiguous Endeavours: The Evolution of the Melodramatic Mode in Polish Holocaust Narratives from Hanna Krall to the Aftermath*. Lund: Centre for Languages and Literature Lund University, 2015.
Podsiadło-Kwiecień, Magdalena. 'Między dawnymi i młodszymi laty – (neo)animistyczne i (neo)pogańskie tropy w kinie polskim.' *Kwartalnik Filmowy*, no. 114 (2021): 65–86.
Polan, Dana. 'Auteur Desire.' *Screening the Past* 12 (2001a). http://www.screeningthepast.com/issue-12-first-release/auteur-desire/.
Polan, Dana. *Jane Campion*. London: BFI, 2001b.
Preizner, Joanna. *Kamienie na macewie. Holokaust w polskim kinie*. Kraków: Austeria, 2012.
Prince, Stephen. *A New Pot of Gold: Hollywood Under the Electronic Rainbow, 1980–1989*. New York: C. Scribner's, 2000.
Quart, Barbara. *Women Directors: The Emergence of New Cinema*. New York: Praeger Publishers, 1988.
Quart, Barbara. 'Three Central European Women Directors Revisited.' *Cinéaste* 19, no. 4 (1993): 58–61.
Rakowski, Mieczysław F. *Dzienniki polityczne 1981–1983*. Warsaw: Iskry, 2004.
Raßloff, Ute. 'Ungar, Slawe, Gorale, Slowake: Jánošík als mythischer Volksheld.' *Osteuropa* 59, no. 12 (2009): 53–75.
Raw, Laurence. 'Rethinking the Costume Drama: Agnieszka Holland's *Washington Square* (1997).' *The Henry James Review* 24, no. 1 (Winter 2003): 69–81.
Raw, Laurence. *Adapting Henry James to the Screen*. Lanham, MD: The Scarecrow Press, 2006.
Redmond, Sean. 'Emotional Celebrity: Introduction.' In *A Companion to Celebrity*, edited by P. David Marshall and Sean Redmond, 351–4. Chichester: Wiley Blackwell, 2016.
Renders, Hans, Binne de Haan and Jonne Harmsma. *The Biographical Turn: Lives in History*. London: Routledge, 2017.
Ringelheim, Joan Miriam. 'The Unethical and the Unspeakable: Women and the Holocaust.' In *The Holocaust: Theoretical Readings*, edited by Neil Levi and Michael Rothberg, 169–77. New Brunswick, NJ: Rutger University Press, 2003.
Rivi, Luisa. *European Cinema after 1989: Cultural Identity and Transnational Production*. New York: Palgrave Macmillan, 2007.
Rothberg, Michael. *Multidirectional Memory: Remembering the Holocaust in the Age of Decolonization*. Stanford, CA: Stanford University Press, 2009.
Rothberg, Michael. *The Implicated Subject: Beyond Victims and Perpetrators*. Stanford, CA: Stanford University Press, 2019.
Rowe, John Carlos. 'Henry James and the United States.' *The Henry James Review* 27, no. 3 (Fall 2006): 228–36.
Rowe, John Carlos. *Our Henry James in Fiction Film and Popular Culture*. New York: Routledge, 2023.
Rybczyńska, Irena. *Jak kochać córkę?* Posłowie: Agnieszka Holland. Warsaw: Wydawnictwo 'Skorpion', 1995.
Sadoff, Dianne F. '"Intimate Disarray": The Henry James Movies.' *The Henry James Review* 19, no. 3 (1998): 286–95.

Sadoff, Dianne F. 'Appeals to Incalculability: Sex, Costume Drama, and *The Golden Bowl.*' *The Henry James Review* 23, no. 1 (Winter 2002): 38–52.

Sariusz-Skąpska, Izabella, ed. *Sztuka jako rozmowa o przeszłości.* Warsaw: Fundacja im. Stefana Batorego, 2009.

Scholz, Anne-Marie. *From Fidelity to History: Film Adaptations as Cultural Events in the Twentieth Century.* New York: Berghahn Books, 2013.

Shachar, Hila. *Screening the Author: The Literary Biopic.* Cham, Switzerland: Palgrave Macmillan, 2019.

Shohat, Ella. 'Post-Third-Worldist Culture: Gender, Nation, and the Cinema.' In *Feminist Genealogies, Colonial Legacies, Democratic Futures*, edited by M. Jacqui Alexander and Chandra Talpade Mohanty, 183–209. London: Routledge, 1997.

Shohat, Ella, and Robert Stam, eds. *Multiculturalism, Postcoloniality, and Transnational Media.* New Brunswick, NJ: Rutgers University Press, 2003.

Silverman, Kaja. *The Acoustic Mirror: The Female Voice in Psychoanalysis and Cinema.* Bloomington: Indiana University Press, 1988.

Sims, Deborah. M. 'Genre, Fame and Gender: The Middle-Aged Ex-Wife Heroine of Nancy Meyers's *Something's Gotta Give.*' In *Star Power: The Impact of Branded Celebrity*, edited by Aaron Barlow, 191–205. Westport, CT: Praeger, 2014.

Singer, Irving. *Cinematic Mythmaking: Philosophy in Film.* Cambridge, MA: MIT Press, 2008.

Sitarski, Piotr. 'Video in the Polish People's Republic: Technology and Its Users.' In Piotr Sitarski, Maria B. Garda and Krzysztof Jajko, *New Media behind the Iron Curtain: Cultural History of Video, Microcomputers and Satellite Television in Communist Poland*, 49–109. Łódź: Łódź University Press, 2020.

Skoczek, Tadeusz. *Motyw zbójnika Janosika w filmie i telewizji.* Bochnia, Poland: Mazowiecka Oficyna Wydawnicza, 2007.

Skrodzka, Aga. *Magic Realist Cinema in East Central Europe.* Edinburgh: Edinburgh University Press, 2012.

Skrodzka, Aga. '*Komunistki*: Visual Memory of Female Communist Agency.' In *The Oxford Handbook of Communist Visual Culture*, edited by Aga Skrodzka et al., 672–92. Oxford: Oxford University Press, 2020.

Skrodzka, Aga. 'Feminist Worlding and World Cinema: The Case of Małgorzata Szumowska.' *Studies in World Cinema* 1 (2021): 176–97.

Sloan, Jane. *Reel Women: An International Directory of Contemporary Feature Films about Women.* Lanham, MD: Scarecrow Press, 2007.

Smith, Susan. 'Opening up *The Secret Garden.*' In *Film Moments, Criticism, History, Theory*, edited by Tom Brown and James Walters, 49–52. London: BFI, Palgrave, 2010.

Snyder, Timothy. *Bloodlands: Europe between Hitler and Stalin.* New York: Basic Books, 2012.

Socha, Jakub. *Żebrowski. Hipnotyzer.* Wołowiec: Wydawnictwo Czarne, 2018.

Sordyl, Alina. *Teatr Telewizji – pomiędzy reprezentacją a symulacją teatru.* Katowice: Studio Noa, 2010.

Sroka, Stanisław. *Janosik. Prawdziwa historia karpackiego Janosika.* Kraków: Wydawnictwo Homini, 2004.

Staiger, Janet. 'Authorship Approaches.' In *Authorship and Film*, edited by David A. Gerstner and Janet Staiger, 27–57. New York: Routledge, 2003.

Stalnaker, Maria T. 'Agnieszka Holland Reads Hollywood.' *Living in Translation: Polish Writers in America*, edited by Halina Stephan, 313–30. Amsterdam: Rodopi, 2003.

Starosta, Anita. *Form and Instability: Eastern Europe, Literature, Postimperial Difference.* Evanston, IL: Northwestern University Press, 2016.

Stewart, Garrett. 'Film's Victorian Retrofit.' *Victorian Studies* 38, no. 2 (Winter, 1995): 153–98.

Stilwell, Robynn J. 'Scribal Error: *Copying Beethoven* and the Pitfalls of Perspective in Cinematic Portraiture.' *Beethoven Forum* 14, no. 2 (Fall 2007): 197–204.

Stimmel, Joanna K. 'Between Globalization and Particularization of Memories: Screen Images of the Holocaust in Germany and Poland.' *German Politics & Society* 23, Special Issue: Transformations of the Past in Contemporary German Politics and Culture, no. 3 (Fall 2005): 83–105.

Stubbs, Andrew. 'Packaging *House of Cards* and *The Knick*: How Talent Intermediaries Manage the Indie-auteur Brand to Sell Premium Television.' *Critical Studies in Television: The International Journal of Television Studies* 15, no. 2 (2020): 129–47.

Sweeney, Carl. 'Kathryn Bigelow as a Neo-star Director.' *New Review of Film and Television Studies* 19, no. 3 (2021): 348–66. https://doi.org/10.1080/17400309.2021.1949203

Szczawińska, Weronika. 'Dwuznaczność formy.' In *Agnieszka Holland. Przewodnik 'Krytyki Politycznej'*, edited by Jakub Majmurek, 138–47. Warsaw: Wydawnictwo 'Krytyki Politycznej', 2012.

Szczepanik, Petr. 'HBO Europe's original programming in the era of streaming wars.' In *A European Television Fiction Renaissance: Premium Production Models and Transnational Circulation*, edited by Luca Barra and Massimo Scaglioni, 243–61. London: Routledge, 2021a.

Szczepanik Petr. *Screen Industries in East-Central Europe*. London: British Film Institute, 2021b.

Szczepanik, Petr. 'Transnational Crews and Postsocialist Precarity Globalizing Screen Media Labor in Prague.' In *Precarious Creativity: Global Media, Local Labor*, edited by Michael Curtin and Kevin Sanson, 88–103. Berkeley: University of California Press, 2016. https://doi.org/10.1525/luminos.10

Szczepańska, Anna. *Do granic negocjacji. Historia Zespołu Filmowego 'X' Andrzeja Wajdy (1972–1983)*. Kraków: Universitas, 2017.

Talarczyk-Gubała, Monika. *Biały mazur. Kino kobiet w polskiej kinematografii*. Poznań: Galeria Miejska Arsenał, 2013.

Tasker, Yvonne. 'Vision and Visibility: Women Filmmakers, Contemporary Authorship, and Feminist Film Studies.' In *Reclaiming the Archive: Feminism and Film History*, edited by Vicki Callaghan, 213–30. Detroit, IL: Wayne State University Press, 2010.

Taylor, Anthea. *Mediating Australian Feminism: Rereading the First Stone Media Event*. Oxford: Peter Lang, 2008.

Taylor, Anthea. 'Germaine Greer's Adaptable Celebrity.' *Feminist Media Studies* 14, no. 5 (2014): 759–74, https://doi.org/10.1080/14680777.2013.810165

Thornham, Sue. *Spaces of Women's Cinema: Space, Place and Genre in Contemporary Women's Filmmaking*. London: BFI Publishing, 2019.

Tibbetts, John C., and Agnieszka Holland. 'An Interview with Agnieszka Holland: The Politics of Ambiguity.' *Quarterly Review of Film and Video*, no. 25 (2008): 132–43.

Tincknell, Estella, and Ian Conrich. 'Introduction.' In *Film's Musical Moments: Music and the Moving Image*, edited by Ian Conrich and Estella Tincknell, 1–12. Edinburgh: Edinburgh University Press, 2006.

Tomadjoglou, Kimberly. 'Alice Guy's Great Cinematic Adventure.' In *Doing Women's Film History: Reframing Cinemas, Past and Future*, edited by Christine Gledhill and Julia Knight, 95–109. Urbana: University of Illinois Press, 2015.

Toniak, Ewa. 'Histeria historii. Wokół *Gorączki* Agnieszki Holland.' *Kwartalnik Filmowy*, no. 57/58 (2007): 278–86.

Tsaliki, Liza. 'Tweeting the Good Causes: Social Networking and Celebrity Activism.' In *A Companion to Celebrity*, edited by P. David Marshall and Sean Redmond, 235–57. Chichester: Willey Blackwell, 2016.

Turk, Edward Baron. 'Agnieszka Holland's *Total Eclipse*: A Contemporary "Film Maudit."' *The French Review* 72, no. 2 (1998): 260–72.

Tzioumakis, Yannis. 'Marketing David Mamet: Institutionally Assigned Film Authorship in Contemporary American Cinema.' *The Velvet Light Trap* 57 (2006): 60–75. https://doi.org/10.1353/vlt.2006.0023

Ungureanu, Camil. 'Uses and Abuses of Post-secularism: An introduction.' In *Democracy, Law and Religious Pluralism in Europe: Secularism and Post-Secularism*, edited by Ferran Requejo Coll and Camil Ungureanu, 1–18. London: Routledge, 2014.

Uricaru, Ioana. 'Follow the Money – Financing Contemporary Cinema in Romania.' In *A Companion to Eastern European Cinemas*, edited by Anikó Imre, 427–52. Chichester: Wiley-Blackwell, 2012.

Valck, Marijke de. *Film Festivals: From European Geopolitics to Global Cinephilia*. Amsterdam: Amsterdam University Press, 2007.

Valck, Marijke de, and Malte Hagener. 'Down with Cinephilia? Long Live Cinephilia? And Other Videosyncratic Pleasures.' In *Cinephilia: Movies, Love and Memory – Film Culture in Transition*, edited by Marijke de Valck and Malte Hagener, 11–24. Amsterdam: Amsterdam University Press, 2005.

Van Belle, Jono. 'Re-conceptualizing Ingmar Bergman's Status as Auteur du Cinema.' *European Journal of Cultural Studies* 22, no. 1 (2019): 3–17. https://doi.org/10.177/13675494171821

Verhoeven, Deb. *Jane Campion*. London: Routledge, 2009.

Vidal, Belén. *Period Film and the Mannerist Aesthetic Book*. Amsterdam: Amsterdam University Press, 2012.

Voigts-Virchow, Eckart. 'Heritage and Literature on Screen: Heimat and Heritage.' In *The Cambridge Companion to Literature on Screen*, edited by Deborah Cartmell and Imelda Whelehan, 119–37. Cambridge: Cambridge University Press, 2007.

Wajda, Andrzej. *Wajda mówi o sobie*, edited by Wanda Wertenstein. Kraków: Wydawnictwo Literackie, 2000.

Waterhouse-Watson, Deb, and Adam Brown. 'Mothers, Monsters, Heroes and Whores: Reinscribing Patriarchy in European Holocaust Films.' *Dapim: Studies on the Holocaust* 30, no. 2 (2016): 142–57. https://doi.org/10.1080/23256249.2016.1166592

Waxman, Zoë. *Women in the Holocaust: A Feminist History*. Oxford: Oxford University Press, 2017.

Wells, Karen. 'Embodying Englishness: Representations of Whiteness, Class and Empire in *The Secret Garden*.' In *Adaptations in Contemporary Culture. Textual Infidelities*, edited by Rachel Carroll, London, 123–33. New York: Continuum, 2009.

Wertenstein, Wanda. *Zespół filmowy 'X.'* Warsaw: Wydawnictwo 'Officina', 1991.

Wexman, Virginia Wright, ed. *Film and Authorship*. New Brunswick, NJ: Rutgers University Press, 2003.

White, Patricia. *Women's Cinema, World Cinema: Projecting Contemporary Feminism*. Durham, NC: Duke University Press, 2015.

Więch, Karol. 'Re-sentymenty wobec PRL-u. Niezależna twórczość filmowa Studia Video Kontakt w Paryżu.' In *1984: Literatura i kultura schyłkowego PRL-u*, edited by Kamila Budrowska, Wiktor Gardocki and Elżbieta Jurkowska, 353–69. Warsaw: Wydawnictwo Instytut Badań Literackich PAN, 2015.

Wilson, Emma. *Cinema's Missing Children*. London: Wallflower Press, 2003.

Wiśniewska, Agnieszka. 'Holland jako mężczyzna.' In *Agnieszka Holland. Przewodnik 'Krytyki Politycznej'*, edited by Jakub Majmurek, 20–35. Warsaw: Wydawnictwo 'Krytyki Politycznej', 2012.

Wojcik-Andrews, Ian. *Children Films: History, Ideology, Pedagogy, Theory*. New York: Garland Publishing, 2000.

Wojtczak, Mieczysław. *O kinie moralnego niepokoju . . . i nie tylko*. Warsaw: Wydawnictwo Studio Emka, 2009.

Wolff, Larry. *Inventing Eastern Europe: The Map of Civilization on the Mind of the Enlightenment*. Stanford, CA: Stanford University Press, 1994.
Wong, Cindy H. *Film Festivals: Culture, People, and Power on the Global Screen*. New Brunswick, NJ: Rutgers University Press, 2011.
Wyatt, Justin. 'Economic Constraints/Economic Opportunities: Robert Altman as Auteur.' *The Velvet Light Trap*, no. 38 (1996): 51–67.
Wyatt, Justin. 'Marketing Marginalized Cultures: *The Wedding Banquet*. Cultural Identities, and Independent Cinema of the 1990s.' In *The End of Cinema as We Know It: American Film in the Nineties*, edited by Jon Lewis, 61–71. New York: New York University Press, 2001.
Xavier, Subha. *Migrant Text: Making and Marketing a Global French Literature*. Montreal: McGill-Queen's University Press, 2016.
Zagzebski, Linda. *Exemplarist Moral Theory*. Oxford: Oxford University Press, 2017.
Zamysłowska, Krystyna, and Mieczysław Kuźmicki, eds. *Twarze Agnieszki Holland*. Łódź: Muzeum Kinematografii, 2013.
Zaremba, Marcin. '1968 in Poland: The Rebellion on the Other Side of the Looking Glass.' *The American Historical Review* 123, no. 3 (June 2018): 769–72. https://doi.org/10.1093/ahr/123.3.769
Zawiśliński, Stanisław. *Reżyseria: Agnieszka Holland*. Warsaw: Wydawnictwo 'Skorpion', 1995.
Żeromski, Stefan. *Dramaty. Tom drugi. Sułkowski, Turoń*. Warsaw: Czytelnik, 1956.
Żukowski, Tomasz. 'Fantazmat "Sprawiedliwych" i film "W ciemności" Agnieszki Holland.' *Studia Litteraria et Historica* 1 (2012): 1–10. https://doi.org/10.11649/slh.2012.005
Żurawiecki, Bartosz, ed. *Ludzie nie ideologia*. Warsaw: Wydawnictwo Krytyki Politycznej, 2021.
Zwierzchowski, Piotr, and Daria Mazur, eds. *Polskie kino popularne*. Bydgoszcz: Wydawnictwo Uniwersytetu Kazimierza Wielkiego, 2011.

Index

Adamczak, Marcin, 46
Adamik, Kasia, xi, 77n, 125, 139, 147, 171, 177, 178, 179, 181, 191, 194, 198, 223n, 229–30, 249, 252, 257–8, 259n, 263
Adamik, Laco, 34, 35, 37, 49, 61–2, 63, 77n, 83, 99, 253
Adams, Patrick J., 173
Aftermath (*Pokłosie*), 201
Agamben, Giorgio, 206, 218
Akerman, Chantal, 33
Alessandri, Jean-Pierre, 93
Allred, Gloria, 166
Altman, Rick, 145–6
Andělová, Kristina, 36, 43n
Anderson, Benedict, 61
Andrejevic, Mark, 182
Angry Harvest (*Bittere Ernte*), 15, 17, 21n, 23n, 82, 85, 86, 87–93, 98, 99, 106, 127, 141, 145, 174, 200, 211, 227, 234, 267
Angry Harvest (*Okiennice*), novel, 87
Ansen, David, 152n
Ansky, S., 177
Araujo, Gwen Amber Rose, 165, 166
Atai, Behi Djanati, xi
Augé, Marc, 241

Babel, Isaac, 38, 43n
Bach, Leon, 81
Bachman, Larry, 81
Baez, Joan, 94
Baker, Jayson, 150n, 151n

Baranowski, Henryk, 83–4, 109n
Barbour, Kim, 227
Barr, Charles, 150n
Barthes, Roland, 2, 7, 20n, 25, 40n
Bartoszewicz, Monika, 245
Bastién, Angelica Jade, 160–1
Bauman, Janina, 42n
Bauman, Zygmunt, 172, 261n
Be' Tipul, 181
Beckmann, Gerhard, 113n
Bergman, Ingmar, 259n
Berner, Elias, 224n
Bersani, Leo, 127, 134
Betz, Mark, 96
Biedrzycka-Shepard, Anna, 75n, 94, 125, 139
Bielawska-Adamik, Hanna, 35
Bielawski, Michał, 59, 263
Biermann, Rudolf, 191, 193
Bigelow, Kathryn, 21n, 242, 260n
Bittencourt, Ela, 44
Błoński, Jan, 92, 97, 201
Bobowski, Sławomir, 20n., 51, 77n, 92, 97, 239
Bogart, Humphrey, 159, 160
Bolton, Lucy, 22n, 23n
Bołtuć, Irena, 49
Bordwell, David, 25, 26
Borowski, Krzysztof E., 187
Borušovičova, Eva, 194, 198
Bos, Pascale Rachel, 206
Bourdieu, Pierre, 21n, 233
Bradshaw, Peter, xiii

Braun, Rebecca, 249, 256
Brauner, Artur, 85–8, 91, 93, 98–9, 108, 110n, 112–13n
Brodzki, Stanisław, 31, 41n
Brown, Adam, 206
Brown, William, 5
Bugajski, Ryszard, 75n, 77n, 109n, 231, 233, 235
Bukowiecki, Andrzej, 154n
Burnett, Frances Hodgson, 116, 119, 121, 151n
Burning Bush (*Hořící keř*), 181, 182–6, 190n
Burszta, Józef, 223n
Bush, George W., 118
Butler, Alison, 7, 8, 12
Butler, Judith, 227

Caldwell, John, 23n
Camouflage (*Barwy ochronne*), 60
Campion, Jane, 6, 9, 121, 129, 148, 156n, 189n, 241–2
Carney, Michael, 179–80
Carringer, Robert L., 5, 21n, 181
Carston, Janet, 268n
Caughie, John, 2, 7, 20n, 21n, 172
Cavani, Liliana, 231
Chałupnik, Agata, 77n
Chajdas, Olga, 179
Chandler, Karen Michele, 128
Chandler, Raymond, 159, 160, 161, 187n
Charlatan (*Šarlatán*), 18, 192, 197, 198, 205, 210–11, 212, 213, 214, 221, 244
Chekhov, Anton, 49
Chojecki, Mirosław, 84, 110n
Chollet, Derek, 118
Chopin, Frédéric, 83
Chouliaraki, Lilie, 251, 258
Chytilová, Věra, 34, 43n
Coates, Paul, 21n, 88, 94, 109n, 115n, 140, 142, 267
Cobb, Shelley, 153n
Cold Case, 18, 158, 168, 169, 174, 176
Conrich, Ian, 128
Coppola, Francis Ford, 117–18, 139, 140, 149, 150n
Copying Beethoven, 13, 17, 116, 117, 120, 130, 135–9, 144, 147, 149, 153–4n, 198, 211
Corrigan, Timothy, 6
Craig, Stuart, 119
Crew, The (*Ekipa*), 177–8, 191
Crnković, Gordana, 24n, 238, 239
Cuarón, Alfonso, 121, 159

Čulík, Jan, 190n
Culture (*Kultura*), 84
Czapski, 84

Dabert, Dobrochna, 61, 72, 77n
Danton, 83, 98
Davies, Norman, 35
Davis Máire, Messenger, 122–3, 160
Deakins, Roger, 119
Debtors, The (*Dłużnicy*), 49–50
Debruge, Peter, 224n
Deep Cover, 160
de Havilland, Olivia, 126, 128
Delerue, Georges, 94
Deleuze, Gilles, 12, 16, 26–7, 30, 32, 35, 40, 82, 85, 116, 149, 191, 211
de Valck, Marijke, 212
Devil in a Blue Dress, 160
Dichant, Mark-Daniel, 195
DiCaprio, Leonardo, 131, 135, 146, 153n, 199
Domaradzki, Jerzy, 51, 53, 57, 58, 59, 256
Domosławski, Artur, 261n
Donahue, William Collins, 100, 102
Doyle, Carol, 126
Driessens, Olivier, 228
Drive Your Plough over the Bones of the Dead (*Prowadź swój plug przez kości umarłych*), 196
Duda, Andrzej, 251
Duke, Bill, 160
Dutoit, Ulysse, 127
Dvořáková, Tereza Czesany, 34
Dybbuk, The, 141, 177
Dyer, Richard, 120, 151n

Ebert, Roger, 92–3, 95–6, 112n, 125, 151n, 155n
Edelman, Marek, 104, 245, 259n
Elsaesser, Thomas, 5–6, 18, 21n, 33, 103, 114n, 192, 215–16, 220
Erhart, Julia, 25, 41n, 107, 138
Eros and Cinema (*Eros i kino*), 239
Europa, Europa, 13, 15, 17, 21n, 76n, 82, 86, 98–103, 104, 106, 108, 113n, 117, 118, 119, 127, 143, 149, 167, 170, 178, 200, 211, 227, 235, 244, 267
Evening at Abdon, An (*Wieczór u Abdona*), 50–1, 62, 68, 77n, 157
Everything for Sale (*Wszystko na sprzedaż*), 58
Ezra, Elizabeth, 14

INDEX 293

Falk, Feliks, 50, 51, 61
Fallen Angels, 158, 162
Family Situation (*Sytuacje rodzinne*), 52
Family Situations of the Unit 'X' (*Sytuacje rodzinne Zespołu 'X'*), 59
Fassbinder Rainer, Werner, 88, 111n
Felis, Paweł T., 224n
Fellmer, Claudia, 111n
Felperin, Leslie, xiii
Feuer, Jane, 75n, 187n, 268
Fever (*Gorączka*), 62, 68–71, 76n, 99, 106, 127, 163
Fidelis, Małgorzata, 42n, 66, 73, 77n
Field, Hermann, 87
Fincher, David, 157, 187n
Finkielkraut, Alan, 104
First, The, 176, 177
Fischer, Lucy, 138
Fish, Stanley, 103, 149, 268
Fontana, Tom, 163
Forman, Miloš, 43n, 53, 57, 145
Formis, Barbara, 206
Foucault, Michel, 4, 7, 19, 227, 258–9
Franklin, Carl, 160
Frobose, Paul H., 149n
Fuchs, Cynthia, 113n
Fukuyama, Francis, 118

Galarte, Francisco J., 164–5
Gallagher, Mark, 4, 7, 24n
Giedroyć, Jerzy, 84, 110n
Gilbert, Martin, 194
Gillispie, Julaine, 151n
Gilmore, Gary, 162
Gilmore, Mikal, 162, 163, 164
Girl and 'Aquarius' (*Dziewczyna i 'Aquarius'*), 52, 62, 76n
Girl Like Me: The Gwen Araujo Story, A, 18, 158, 162, 164–8, 169, 176
Glajar, Valentina, 204
Gledhill, Christine, 10, 265
Gliński, Piotr, xii
Glover, Danny, 159–61, 188n
Goetz, Ruth and Augustus, 126
Goffman, Erving, 227
Goldgeiger, James, 118
Gombrowicz, Witold, 152n
Goodman, Tim, 163–4
Gorij, Yasaman, 179–80
Goscilo, Helena, 207

Graff, Agnieszka, 11
Grant, Catherine, 21n, 24n, 26, 41n
Grąziewicz, Zofia, 50, 53
Green Border, The (*Zielona granica*), xi–xiii, 24n, 179
Gregor, Jan, 186
Grewal, Inderpal, 23n
Grodal, Torben, 41n
Gross, Jan Tomasz, 200–1
Guattari, Felix, 12, 30, 40, 82
Gutek, Roman, 96
Guthmann, Edward, 151n
Guzek, Mariusz, 186
Guy, Alice, 9–10, 264
Gwóźdź, Andrzej, 110n

Hake, Sabine, 86, 102
Haltof, Marek, 32–3
Hames, Peter, 198
Hampton, Christopher, 130
Hanauerová, Angelika, 34
Haraway, Donna, 267–8
Harris, Ed, 94, 135, 140
Havel, Václav, 36, 104, 245
Haynes, Todd, 157, 159
Heiress, The, 126, 128, 152n
Hendrykowska, Małgorzata, 66
Hengge, Paul, 87, 98, 113n
Herling-Grudziński, Gustaw, 84
Hertz, Zofia, 84
Heymann, Danièle, 103–4
Higson, Andrew, 120, 151n
Hill, John, 133, 153n
History of One Bullet (*Dzieje jednego pocisku*), 68
Hjort, Mette, 13, 24n, 43n
Hofer, Stefanie, 173
Hoffman, Jerzy, 42n, 110n
Holender, Adam, 94
Holland: Biography Anew (*Holland. Biografia od nowa*), 252–7
Holland, Henryk, 28, 29–30, 41n
Holloway, Dorothea, 58–9
Holmgren, Beth, 207
Holmlund, Chris, 118
Homemade Wine (*Wino domowej roboty*), 76n
hooks, bell, 221
House of Cards, 157, 177
How He Looks from a Close Distance? (*Jaki jest z bliska?*), 138

Hrubý, Tomáš, 182
Huggan, Graham, 192, 220
Hulík, Štěpán, 182

Idziak, Sławomir, 68
Illumination (*Iluminacja*), 46–7
Imre, Anikó, 10, 12, 48, 66, 75n, 182, 190n, 223n
Ince, Kate, 22–3n
In Darkness (*W ciemności*), 18, 76n, 192, 194, 198, 200–2, 205–8, 211–12, 213, 214, 241
Insdorf, Annette, 88–9, 90–1
Interrogation (*Przesłuchanie*), 75, 231, 260n
In the Sewers of Lvov, 195
In Treatment, 181
Iordanova, Dina, 11, 14–15, 195, 196–7, 215, 267
Iwaszkiewicz, Jarosław, 50

Jabłoński, Dariusz, 193, 194
Jaehne, Karen, 91, 111n
Jagielski, Sebastian, 62, 66
James, Henry, 21n, 121, 125, 126, 127, 135, 150n, 152n, 153n
Jameson, Frederic, 69, 188n, 224n
Janda, Krystyna, 77n, 138, 233, 241
Janion, Maria, 74
Jankun-Dopartowa, Mariola, 20n, 72, 78n, 79n, 92, 114n, 239
Janosik – A True Story, 18, 184, 191, 192, 193–4, 197, 198–9, 203–4, 210, 214, 216–18, 221
Janosik (1973), 198, 223n
Jánošík, Juraj, 198
Jeong, Seung-hoon, 7, 20n
Jermyn, Deborah, 231, 239, 260n
Jesus Christ's Sin (*Hřích boha*), 16, 37–40, 62, 68, 75n, 141, 175
Jiráček, Václav, 194, 203
Johnston, Claire, 21–2n, 180, 265
Johnston, Ruth, 101, 113n
Jones, Gareth, 198
Jopkiewicz, Tomasz, 149
Julie Walking Home, 116, 139, 141, 141, 142–4, 147, 148–9, 154n, 177, 194, 195

Kaczmarek, Jan A. P., 125, 139, 146, 179
Kaczyńska, Elżbieta, 65
Kaczyński, Jarosław, 241, 245–6
Kafka, Franz, 61
Kalinowska, Izabela, 109n
Kałużyński, Zygmunt, 155n

Kamiński, Zbigniew, 75n
Kane, Paula, 154n
Kaplan, Caren, 23n
Kapsis, Robert E., 155n
Karpiński, Maciej, 58, 76n
Kavka, Misha, 251
Kempley, Rita, 96, 240–1
Kędzierski, Paweł, 53, 57, 75n
Kieślowski, Krzysztof, 45, 49, 50, 76n, 83, 94, 99, 114n, 115n, 117, 146, 164, 231, 235, 259n, 260n
Kijowski, Janusz, 50, 68, 85, 110n
Killing, The, 157, 176
Klaczyński, Zbigniew, 85, 110n
Klaus, Václav, 36
Kleinhans, Chuck, 118
Klos, Elmar, 34
Kluge, Alexander, 88, 111n
Knight, Julia, 10, 266
Kołodyński, Andrzej, 154n
Komasa-Łazarkiewicz, Antoni, 179, 194, 262n, 263
Koniczek, Ryszard, 33, 42n
Konwicki, Tadeusz, 47, 75n,
Korczak, 103–4, 108, 238, 260n
Kornatowska, Maria, 64, 114n, 238–9, 253, 260n
Koszyk, Andrzej, 253
Kotkowski, Andrzej, 51
Kozloff, Sarah, 26
Kozłowski, Maciej, 37
Krauze, Krystyna, 186, 262n
Kristeva, Julia, 127
Królikowska-Avis, Elżbieta, 119
Kumbier, William, 135–6
Kundera, Milan, 34
Kuroń, Jacek, 96
Kusturica, Emir, 14, 115n

Labov, Jessie, 197
Labuda, Barbara, 147
Lady Chatterley's Lover, 151n
Lambert, Christopher, 94, 96
Lane, Christine, 19, 118–19, 132, 144–5, 152n, 153n, 229
Lanzmann, Claude, 104
Largo desolato, 104
Latałło, Marcin, 99
Latałło, Stanisław, 45, 47, 99
Latour, Bruno, 47, 98, 117, 139

Lebeau, Vicky, 123–4
Lee, Spike, 171
Leigh, Jennifer Jason, 126, 128
Lenarciński, Michał, 148–9
Lev, Peter, 94
Levi, Primo, 111n
Levin, Ira, 174
Levy, Emanuel, 155n
Lewis, Ingrid, 89–90
Lewis, Jon, 150n
Lewis, Simon, 195, 200, 202, 219
Liehm, Mira, 20n
Liehm, Antonín, 20n
Linville, Susan, 102, 103
Lipták, František, 194
Litman, Barry R., 119
LoBrutto, Vincent, 117
Lodge, Guy, 243
Loewy, Ronny, 86
Loist, Skadi, 212
Lopez, Ana M., 14
Lorber, Marc, 181
Lorenzaccio, 61–2
Love in Germany (*Eine Liebe in Deutschland*), 83, 85, 86, 88, 99, 110n
Loves of a Blonde (*Lásky jedné plavovlásky*), 53, 57
Lubelski, Tadeusz, 97, 114n, 182, 184, 186, 236
Lugo de Fabritz, Brunilda Amarsllss, 66–7
Lure (*Córki dancingu*), 179, 265
Łazarkiewicz, Magdalena, 28, 41n, 99, 177, 178, 254, 263
Łazarkiewicz-Sieczko, Gabriela (Gabrysia), xi, 31, 179, 263
Łysak, Tomasz, 201

Macdonald, Moira, 154n
Maciejewski, Łukasz, 264
Maciejko-Kowalczyk, Katarzyna, 138
Mackey, Margaret, 116
Madej-Stang, Adriana, 204
Magic and Money (*Magia i pieniądze*), 238
Majer, Artur, 178
Man of Marble (*Człowiek z marmuru*), 52–3, 60, 61, 76n, 77n, 138, 185, 233, 237
Marciniak, Katarzyna, 21n, 23–4n, 71, 73
Margolis-Edelman, Alina, 104, 259n
Margulies, Ivone, 22n
Marshall, Robert, 195
Marshall, P. David, 227, 243, 249, 258, 259n

Maule, Rosanna, 42n
Mazierska, Ewa, 113n
Mayne, Judith, 22n, 41n
Mąka-Malatyńska, Katarzyna, 20–1n, 44, 77n, 79n, 92, 139
McCarthy, Todd, 132, 240
McGinn, Colin, 133
McHugh, Kathleen, 8–9, 43n
McNeilly, Kevin, 170–1
Ménégoz, Margaret, 98, 108, 112n
Michałek, Bolesław, 20n, 48, 59, 76n, 79n
Michnik, Adam, 96, 178, 245
Mickiewicz, Adam, 36, 49, 82–3
Mierzeński, Stanisław, 87
Mikolášek, Jan, 198
Mitchum, Robert, 159, 160
Mitek, Tadeusz, 112n
Moczar, Mieczysław, 35
Monk, Claire, 120, 124–5, 129, 150n
Morituri, 85–6
Morrison, Jim, 135, 199
Morrison, Harriet R., 117
Mr Jones, 18, 192, 197, 198, 205, 208, 212, 213, 214, 218–19, 267
Mroz, Matilda, 224n
Mueller-Stahl, Armin, 88, 111n, 142
Mulvey, Laura, 100, 256
Murray, Rona, 260n

Naficy, Hamid, 13, 81–2
Naked, 132
Naremore, James, 187n
Naszkowska, Krystyna, 246–7
Naumiuk, Tomasz, xi, 179
Neale, Steven, 3
Neighbors, 200–1
Newell, Kate, 153n
Nina, 179
1983, 186–7
Nochimson, Martha P., 172, 173, 189n
Norwid Cyprian, Kamil, 83
Nowakowski, Jacek, 110n
Nurczyńska, Ewa, 76n, 79n

Obłamski, Jerzy, 51
Offsiders, The (*Boisko bezdomnych*), 179
Olbrychski, Daniel, 58, 241
Olivier, Olivier, 13, 17, 21n, 82, 104–8, 119, 141, 146, 168, 170, 211
Ontiveros, Lupe, 166

Ostrowska, Elżbieta, 72–3, 111n, 112n, 185
Ostrowska, Dorota, 20n, 46, 50, 76n
Other Lamb, The, 23n
Overmyer, Eric, 172
Oxman, Steven, 188n

Paciarelli, Dorota, 87
Palach, Jan, 183
Parnet, Claire, 16, 26–7, 191
Pasikowski, Władysław, 201
Paskaljević, Goran, 14
Paskin, Sylvia, 95
Passendorfer, Jerzy, 198, 223n
Pasternak, Karolina, 41n, 67, 107, 252–7, 262n
Pauhofová, Tatiana, 183, 203
Pawlikowski, Paweł, 60, 175, 189n
Pec-Ślesicka, Barbara, 48, 59, 81, 99
Pehe, Veronika, 184
Penderecka, Elżbieta, 147
Penn, Shana, 70–1
Perel, Salomon, 98, 101
Persak, Krzysztof, 30, 41n
Petelski, Czesław, 260n
Peters, Clarke, 173
Petrie, Duncan, 34
Petrycki, Jacek, 45, 99, 139, 162–3, 164, 179, 186, 262n, 263
Piano, The, 121
Pictures from Life (*Obrazki z życia*), 51–2, 85
Pilichowski, Czesław, 113–14n
Pisters, Patricia, 208
Pisuk, Maciej, xi
Pitassio, Francesco, 20n
Piwowarski, Radosław, 75n
Plotz, Judith, 151n
Podsiadło-Kwiecień, Magdalena, 208
Pokorná, Jaroslava, 38, 183, 205
Polan, Dana, 3, 4, 108
Polanski, Roman, 42n, 43n, 145, 174, 175, 189n, 235
Popiełuszko, Jerzy, 93, 94
Portrait of a Lady, The, 121, 129
Prakash, Rajshree, 179–80
Preisner, Zbigniew, 94, 99, 114n, 139, 179
Preizner, Joanna, 113–14n
Pretty Woman, 122
Prince, Stephen, 93
Provincial Actors (*Aktorzy prowincjonalni*), 4, 50, 62, 63–8, 77n, 79n, 81, 99, 106, 121, 137, 138, 163, 167, 211, 237

Prowse, Heydon, 121
Pugliese, Frank, 162
Puttnam, David, 93, 108, 120

Quart, Barbara, 267

Radkiewicz, Małgorzata, 50, 76n
Radulescu, Dominica, 204
Radziwiłowicz, Jerzy, 52, 61, 181
Rakowski, Mieczysław, 108n
Raundalen, Jon, 111n
Raw, Laurence, 125, 151n
Red Wind, 18, 158–61, 162, 176
Redmond, Sean, 243, 252
Return of Agnieszka H., The (*Powrót Agnieszki H.*), 186
Rich, Frank, 118
Rimbaud, Arthur, 130, 135, 146
Ringelheim, Joan Miriam, 206
Rivele, Stephen J., 135
Rivi, Luisa, 196, 222n
Romney, Jonathan, 114n
Root, Anthony, 182
Rosemary's Baby, 174–5, 176
Rosenbaum, Jonathan, 113
Rothberg, Michael, 17, 86, 91, 110n, 111n, 200, 201, 207
Rowden, Terry, 14
Rowe, John Carlos, 129
Różewicz, Tadeusz, 32, 49
Ruehl, Mercedes, 166
Rybczyńska-Holland, Irena, 28, 31, 41n, 81, 229, 254, 264

Sadoff, Dianne F., 129, 152n
Saldaña, Zoe, 173
Sarris, Andrew, 2
Sass, Barbara, 51, 259n, 260n
Scar (*Blizna*), 231
Scholz, Anne-Marie, 126–7, 150n, 151n
Schulz, Bruno, 76n
Screen Tests (*Zdjęcia próbne*), 53, 57–9, 63, 64, 67, 68, 106, 127, 137, 138, 167, 231
Secret Garden, The (film), xi, 117–25, 126, 129, 130, 139, 141, 144, 145, 146, 147, 148, 150–1n, 160, 178, 211
Secret Garden, The (novel), 116, 119, 121
Shachar, Hila, 130
Shakespeare, William, 49

Shamoon, David F., 194–5
Shattered Mirror, A (Okruch lustra), 83, 231
Shohat, Ella, 23n
Short Film about Killing, A, 164
Shot in the Heart, 18, 139, 158, 162–4, 167, 168, 176, 177
Silverman, Kaja, 22n
Simon, David, 170, 171, 189n
Simon, John, 152n
Sims, Deborah M., 235, 236, 251
Singer, Irving, 153n
Sitarski, Piotr, 96–7
Skoczowska, Ewa, 142–3
Skolimowski, Jerzy, 42n
Skonieczny, Krzysztof, 200
Skrodzka, Aga, 23n, 217–18
Sloan, Jane, 154n
Smith, Susan, 124
Smoczyńska, Agnieszka, 179, 265
Snyder, Timothy, 218
Sobolewski, Tadeusz, 140–1, 151n, 164
Socha, Leon, 198, 200, 201
Soderbergh, Steven, 157, 159, 187n
Something for Something (Coś za coś), 52, 55–6, 63, 67, 68, 76n, 77n, 99, 106, 163
Spáčilová, Mirka, 186
Spielberg, Steven, 119, 148
Spoor (Pokot), 18, 76n, 192, 196, 197, 202, 208–10, 211, 212, 213, 214, 219–21
Stalnaker, Maria, 114n
Starski, Allan, 99, 125
Steinkühler, Manfred, 102
Stewart, Garret, 151n
Stilwell, Robynn J., 153n
Stimmel, Joanna, 111–12n
Štrba, Martin, 184, 194
Strug, Andrzej, 68
Stubbs, Andrew, 187n
Sunday Children (Niedzielne dzieci), 52, 53–5, 62–3, 67, 68, 71, 76n, 77n, 78n, 106, 127, 233
Svaton, Pavel, xi
Szabó, István, 14, 111n
Szaniawski, Jeremi, 7, 20n, 22n
Szczepanik, Petr, 181–2, 186, 190n, 222n
Szczepańska, Anna, 48, 51–2
Szczepański, Tadeusz, 77–8n
Szumlas, Jacek, 146, 147
Szumowska, Małgorzata, 23n, 213

Tagliabue, John, 96
Talarczyk-Gubała, Monika, 11, 56, 77n, 78n
Talent Competition (Konkurs), 57
Tasker, Yvonne, 135, 153n, 227–8, 237
Taubin, Amy, 225n
Taylor, Anthea, 228
Thewlis, David, 131, 132
Third Miracle, The, 21n, 116, 139–43, 144, 147, 148, 154n, 177, 211
Thornham, Sue, 22n
Tibbetts, John, 63, 75n, 237
Tincknell, Estella, 128
Tokarczuk, Olga, 196, 197, 225n, 261n
To Kill a Priest, 17, 21n, 75n, 76n, 82, 93–8, 103, 106, 127, 139, 141, 167, 178, 235
Tołłoczko, Zbigniew, 59
Tomadjoglou, Kimberly, 9–10, 264
Tomashevsky, Boris, 25
Toniak, Ewa, 69–70
Total Eclipse, 116, 120, 127, 130–5, 136, 137–8, 139, 144–9, 151n, 153n, 167, 198, 199, 211
Treme, 18, 157, 158, 171–4, 176
Trial, The, 61, 62
Tsaliki, Liza, 251
Turaj, Frank, 20, 79n
Turk, Edward Baron, 134, 135, 153n
Turner, Tyrin, 161
Tworkowska, Maria, 37
Tzioumakis, Yannis, 6

Ungureanu, Camil, 141–2
Unwanted Man (Mężczyzna niepotrzebny), 77n, 83
Urban, Jerzy, 51, 52, 85
Uricaru, Ioana, 223n

Van Belle, Jono, 259
Varda, Agnès, 33
Varga, Zsuzsanna, 20n.
Vávra, Otakar, 34
Verhoeven, Deb, 4, 6
Verlaine, Paul, 131
Vidal, Belén, 128–9
Volčič, Zala, 182

Wachelko-Zaleska, Krystyna, 53, 77n
Wajda, Andrzej, 46, 48, 49, 50, 51, 52–3, 58, 59, 61, 75n, 77n, 81, 83, 85, 98, 99, 103, 110n, 113n, 138, 139, 147, 172, 185, 194, 229, 231, 233, 234, 235, 237–8, 241, 248, 260n, 262n

Warlikowski, Krzysztof, 201
Washington, Denzel, 160
Washington Square (novel), 121, 135
Washington Square (film), xi, 13, 17, 21n, 75n, 76n, 116, 117, 120, 125–30, 134, 139, 144, 145, 147, 148, 150–2n, 155n, 170, 240
Waterhouse-Watson, Deb, 206
Weil, Simone, 104
Weinstein, Henry, 152n
Wells, Karen, 119, 121–2
We're the Children of Communists (*My, dzieci komunistów*), 246
Wertenstein, Wanda, 256
Wetz, Jean, 29
Wheel Breaking (*Łamanie kołem*), 79n
White, Patricia, 20n, 22n
Wieroński, Marek, 76n
Wilkinson, Christopher, 135
Wilms, André, 100
Wilson, Emma, 21n, 105–6, 107–8
Winiarczyk, Mirosław, 146, 150n, 152n, 154n
Winners (*Zwycięzcy*), 83
Wire, The, 18, 157, 158, 168, 169–71, 172, 176, 177
Without Anesthesia (*Bez znieczulenia*), 60, 79n, 83
Without Love (*Bez miłości*), 259n
Without Secrets (*Bez tajemnic*), 181
Witkacy, 49
Włast-Matuszkiewicz, Remigiusz, 224n
Wojciechowski, Piotr, 152n, 155n
Wojcik-Andrews, Ian, 119
Wojtyszko, Maciej, 78n
Wolff, Larry, 216

Wolski, Andrzej, 84
Woman Alone, A, x, 21n, 44, 62, 67, 68, 71–3, 82, 99, 106, 121, 127, 141, 234
Woman in the Fifth, The, 175, 189
Wong, Cindy, 213
Workers '71: Nothing about Us without Us (*Robotnicy '71: nic o nas bez nas*), 45
Wróblewski, Janusz, 224n
Wróblewski, Stefan, 200
Wyatt, Justin, 4, 153n
Wyler, William, 126, 128
Wyspiański, Stanisław, 63

Xavier, Subha, 221

Zach, Ondřej, 181
Zachwatowicz, Krystyna, 83, 138
Zagzebski, Linda, 201
Zajączkowski, Andrzej, 83, 231
Zanussi, Krzysztof, 46–7, 52, 60, 76n, 85, 143, 149, 234, 237–8, 263
Zaorski, Janusz, 78n
Zaremba, Marcin, 36
Zatorski, Witold, 49, 50, 63
Zawierucha, Marek, 194
Zawiśliński, Stanisław, 145, 237, 253
Zhukhovitsky, Leonid, 49
Zieliński, Jerzy, 125, 139
Ziobro, Zbigniew, xiii
Zygadło, Tomasz, 45
Żebrowski, Michał, 194
Żeromski, Stefan, 248, 261n
Żukowski, Tomasz, 201–2
Żygulski, Kazimierz, 113n